I0083882

Ideas and Frameworks of Governing India

Ideas and Frameworks of Governing India and its companion volume *Neo-Liberal Strategies of Governing India* tell the story of governance in independent India and address the critical question: how is a post-colonial democracy governed? Further, they attempt to understand why the process of governing a post-colonial democracy, particularly in the neo-liberal age, should be studied as the central question within the history of post-colonial democracy. The volumes offer hitherto unexplored analyses of governance – political and ideological aspects along with technological characteristics – in a historical framework.

This volume discusses:

* ideas and issues at the core of governance in post-colonial India
* constitution, state-making and government formation
* the asymmetrical nature of the anti-colonial foundations of governance.

In breaking new ground in the study of what constitutes the political subject, these volumes will be indispensable to scholars, researchers and students of politics, public administration, development studies, South Asian studies and modern India.

Ranabir Samaddar is the Distinguished Chair in Migration and Forced Migration Studies at Calcutta Research Group, India. Among foremost critical theorists, he has worked extensively on issues of forced migration, dialogue, nationalism and post-colonial statehood in South Asia, and new regimes of technological restructuring and labour control. His significant interventions on justice, rights, peace, nation-state and critical post-colonial thought include *The Politics of Dialogue* (2004), *The Materiality of Politics* (2007), and *The Emergence of the Political Subject* (2009). His co-authored work *Beyond Kolkata: Rajarhat and the Dystopia of Urban Imagination* (2013) examines new town and accumulation in the context of urban post-colonial capitalism. His co-edited volumes include *Political Transition and Development Imperatives in India* (2012), *New Subjects and New Governance in India* (2012) and *Conflict, Power, and the Landscape of Constitutionalism* (2008).

Ideas and Frameworks of Governing India

Ranabir Samaddar

Routledge
Taylor & Francis Group

LONDON AND NEW YORK

First published 2016 by Routledge

2 Park Square, Milton Park, Abingdon, Oxfordshire OX14 4RN
52 Vanderbilt Avenue, New York, NY 10017

Routledge is an imprint of the Taylor & Francis Group, an informa business

First issued in paperback 2019

Copyright © 2016 Ranabir Samaddar

The right of Ranabir Samaddar to be identified as author of this work has been asserted by him in accordance with sections 77 and 78 of the Copyright, Designs and Patents Act 1988.

All rights reserved. No part of this book may be reprinted or reproduced or utilised in any form or by any electronic, mechanical, or other means, now known or hereafter invented, including photocopying and recording, or in any information storage or retrieval system, without permission in writing from the publishers.

Notice:
Product or corporate names may be trademarks or registered trademarks, and are used only for identification and explanation without intent to infringe.

British Library Cataloguing in Publication Data
A catalogue record for this book is available from the British Library

Library of Congress Cataloging-in-Publication Data
A catalog record has been requested for this book.

ISBN: 978-1-138-67023-5 (hbk)
ISBN: 978-0-367-17722-5 (pbk)

Typeset in Sabon
by Apex CoVantage, LLC

Contents

Preface

In this book the founding history of India's post-colonial governance is seen as constituted by two principal elements: (a) contesting ideas of self-government that have shaped the nature of governance and (b) an overarching framework made of constitutionalism, police and legality.

In the companion volume the history of post-colonial governance is followed up through discussion of two more elements: (c) the mutually constitutive relationship between rulers and the ruled based on popular claims, rights and the governmental process; and finally, (d) governance as a strategy of protecting private property, securing conditions of accumulation and rule.

Together these two volumes on governing India aim not only to tell the story of post-colonial governance, but also present an answer to the vexing but significant question, namely, how is a post-colonial democracy governed? Or, to put it differently, why should we study the process of governing a post-colonial democracy as the central question in the history of the post-colonial democracy itself? In trying to answer, these two volumes take forward the ideas and analyses of governance proposed first in the two books on governance (*Political Transition and Development Imperatives in India* and *New Subjects and New Governance in India*, 2012) brought out by the Calcutta Research Group (CRG). The characteristics of those two volumes lay in combining analysis of the political and ideological aspects with that of the technological aspects of governance. This was important because the conventional books on governance had hitherto ignored the said dual nature of governance and had thus practically banished history from the study of governance itself. CRG's massive collective research on autonomy, social justice, governance, developmental democracy and citizenship enabled it to make the breakthrough. This book develops the insights of the two volumes and aims to present them in a historical frame.

In order to do so, this volume proposes to go back to some of the foundational issues of governance. Readers will not fail to notice the importance given in this book to the decade of the forties of the past century as the symbol of our contentious time. It was in that decade that various ideas, actions and institutions in their combustible mixture foreshadowed the relations between nation, governance and democracy in the impending post-independent time. We have to admit that a fuller history of the significance of those ten years still waits to be written. The anti-colonial foundations of our politics are deep, and while some aspects of our anti-colonial consciousness and practices have faded with time, others have passed the test of the neo-liberal assaults of the past twenty odd years. The building blocks of anti-colonial foundations were not symmetrical. Their asymmetry became more evident as post-colonial governance developed. Part I is written on the basis of such an understanding. Part II follows this up through examining the process of transformation of the subjects into citizens. The book argues that it was not a simple story of enabling the people into rights-bearing subjects, but a complex story of the constitution of the political subject, which had within it, from the beginning, the possibility of governmental domination over a democracy, and thus citizens becoming mere objects of governance. It is in that intertwined narrative that we shall find the mutually conditioning account of the formation of a state and the making of rules on which post-colonial governance would be based. This is the reason as to why this book does not proceed much beyond the initial decades, except for one chapter where the foundational story of the religious nature of our governance had to be told in the form of narrating certain events from the recent past. But the question remains foundational.

The place of the decade of the forties in the evolution of post-colonial governance, however, is significant in a deeper way. If the forties showed new trends to be repeatedly observable in later years of our post-colonial life and how the nationalist ideas of autonomy would be caught in the vortex of the contentious events of the decade, they also showed how rules of governance assiduously built over a century could crumble within just ten years. The collapse of the colonial mode of governance (some of the elements of which would be rule of law, limited representation, administration geared to surplus extraction, rule based on difference, combining violent and suppressive mode with civilian mode of rule, centralization, iron conduct of bureaucracy and administration based on management of group relations) through war, Quit India Movement, Bengal Famine, Calcutta Killings, Partition, a chaotic transfer of power, widespread agrarian unrest, mutiny in the Royal Indian Navy and the institution of constituent assembly demonstrated the wide disconnect between the actually existing social and political life of the people and the rules of governance. The manuals of administration and governance, one may say, were the displaced site of the political life of the people. In time these manuals along with other reports (particularly the reports of the Administrative Reform Commissions) and manuals added later, would aim at creating a science of governance, once autonomous and self-sufficient, in whose mirror the actual political life of the people would always appear as unruly and chaotic. That is the part to be described in detail in the companion volume. Issues of rights, entitlements, regulations, accumulation would feature prominently there.

To arrive at such an understanding what was required was a clearer understanding of various ideas of governance in the form of self-governance, popular attitude to legality, the emergence of the city as the most dense site of claim-makings, the dual nature of the founding exercise of constitution-making, namely state building through elaborating the rules of governance, and the phenomenon of popular constitutionalism as distinct from governmental ideas of constitutional rule. Only on that account the later story could be meaningfully told. Also on that dual understanding one would be able to make sense of the materiality of our political practices, and the contradictory nature of our political subjectivity.

There is one last comment as a preface to the arguments of this book. The underlying contention of this book is that there is no possibility of breaking out of the bind in which the governmental question is locked in India today, unless we think in terms of radical democracy. The chapter on the religious nature of our governance shows how governance as a secular field of rule makes little sense till caste and religion operate as the masks of racism in the country. Our discussions on secularism had hitherto ignored the interplay of caste, race and religion. Similarly the chapter on other ideas of democracy and self-governance, for instance reflected in Jayaprakash Narayan's writings, discusses how the early post-colonial decades suggested such possibilities of radical democracy. However, most of the chapters are self-explanatory in the context of these introductory remarks. Given the remorseless nature of the capitalist accumulation process in India, these chapters are meant to prepare the ground in the companion volume for an intense discussion on rights, claims and justice.

Acknowledgements

The book along with the companion volume was written over a period of the past seven years. Some of the material was published earlier in the form of articles in journals or delivered as public lectures or papers written as invitations to edited volumes. However, they have been substantially revised, in some cases merged, broken up or amalgamated with other material to become parts of this book. My acknowledgement is to various journals, institutions and editors whose invitations occasioned these writings. These occasions helped me to see the evolution of post-colonial governance in the context of the founding questions of a post-colonial democracy.

While writing this book I have incurred debts to several colleagues and friends. Bishnu Mahapatra, a rigorous analyst of ideas, has always provoked new lines of inquiry whenever I broached with him some of the themes of this book. I recall my discussions with him through years on possible angles to study governance afresh. Likewise I remain indebted to Kalpana Kannabiran. I have always returned enriched after rounds of discussion with her on the interface of law and the politics of justice. This work also draws from the decade-long study of post-colonial democracy and governance by the Calcutta Research Group (CRG) conducted with the help of the Ford Foundation and the Indian Council of Social Science Research (ICSSR). My debt to the work of CRG is there for all to see. Several colleagues at CRG read and commented on the draft chapters. My thanks go all of them. My debt to them has only accumulated over the years. I desist from writing their names, the list would have been long.

Sibaji Pratim Basu, Subhas Chakrabarty, Avijit Majumder, Arun Patnaik, V. Ramaswamy, Anita Sengupta, Sucharita Sengupta, Rajat Sur and Uttam K. Ray helped me access some of the research material used in this book. I thank them.

The editors at the Routledge, Shoma Choudhury and Aakash Chakrabarty, have been patient with me and persuasive with their ideas about how to improve the two companion volumes on governance. I have deferred to their advice. My sincere thanks go to both Shoma and Aakash.

Finally, my unforgettable debt is to the caregivers in my household who not only kept my ailing wife happy but also enabled me to continue with my research. But of course Krishna by retaining her smile when she was alive was the best inspiration. She would have been the happiest to know that I am still working. This book is dedicated to her memory.

27 October 2015
Kolkata

Part I
Ideals of governance

1 Radicalism, violence and the task of governing

War, violence and creating a new society

We shall begin with *Hind Swaraj* (1909), because that is where we shall find the first systematic effort in modern India to conceptualize the main task of government as controlling radicalism and violence in society.[1] Gandhi in *Hind Swaraj* saw the way out in the form of self-governance. Even after more than hundred years have passed after the first exposition of that idea, the main task of government remains so. Governments still ask the people to exercise self-restraint in moments of violence and radical fury.

In the late nineteenth- and early twentieth-century colonial India it was an anxiety about war and violence – and a need to take a stance about war and violence – that determined principally if not wholly, the attitude towards the emerging nation form. The concern about violence had its origin in concern about war, and not so much in the concern for the ubiquitous violence in society. Violence and war became the crucial gradient in determining relations in colonial India between various emerging national groups, classes, communities and increasingly individuals; and this was not surprising considering that almost one hundred and fifty years of wars had dominated the immediate history of the land. It is not that there had not been wars earlier, all kinds of wars – dynastic, war of succession, local mutiny, battle over emergence of a new kingdom, invasion from abroad, trade-war, we can include all these in the earlier wars – had preceded British rule in India. But this was a matter of kings and princes. Occasionally it concerned local advices of the ministers, advisers and the knowledge class, but it was not a matter of concern to general social thinking. But colonial wars including the Mutiny of 1857 and other revolts and consequent pacification campaigns throughout the nineteenth century changed all that. Political thinking that emerged in the shadow of this more than century long violence was around the question: if war had marked the decline of an empire and had brought in a new power, and indeed was now producing the nation, what should be the attitude towards war, and by implication the colonial power that was unleashing the all-consuming wars?

A discourse of war as distinct from a discourse of right made the incipient nationalist thinking in late nineteenth- and earlier twentieth-century India characteristic of what it was. It certainly articulated the idea of nationalist right, but it had little of the contractarian thinking that had marked nationalist thought elsewhere. Therefore whatever variety we may think of – the ideas in the Wahabi movement, proclamations of the mutineers in 1857, Syed Ahmed Khan, Bankim Chandra or the pamphlets and journals of militant revolutionary groups such as *Jugantar* – these had no trace of the idea of contract and rights derived from and guaranteed by the new rule. This historical intelligibility of that time tried to make sense of events such as the collapse of the earlier empire and the advent of new rule, in short the fact of British conquest of the country legitimized by the Queen's proclamation of 1858. Therefore war more than rights constituted the principal pillar around which the historical intelligibility of that period developed. It was later that right that is to say national right which meant rights not under the rule but against the rule, right to evict the rule, took concrete shape. Gandhi's *Hind Swaraj* (1909) appears in that period of overwhelming concern about war and what to do with war and violence – a concern that conjured up the great fear that the nation would be caught up in a war without end, and therefore human relations, also national relations, would be of the order of violence and domination. This had twofold implications: how could the emerging nation become sovereign without dominating or being dominated? And, second, in what way could the nation be governed so that it could claim that it was governing itself – that is to say a government without domination? In this inquiry a peculiar kind of historical discourse emerged, of which the *Hind Swaraj* was a major text, in which the past and the imagination of the future of the nation were irrevocably linked with the issue of war and peace. To be truthful the past was suspended in *Hind Swaraj*. The idea of what the country should be had sprung as if from a void – no past of self-rule, no past of power and domination, but a deep void created in the wake of colonial conquest. The moderates and the extremists in the Indian National Congress may have had various differences; but violence and disobedience were the principal issues at stake. Not that the discourses of these two camps were clearly articulated in that manner, Gandhi and others in fact combined disobedience with non-violence thus blunting the strategy of Aurobindo and others of combining disobedience with violence; but war remained right up to the great Partition wars of 1946–48 the principal issue of contention and anxiety, with camps and persons at times switching sides.

As we know, the problem of war was not destined to fade away as an issue in anti-colonial thinking, precisely because the anti-colonial struggle was never simply violent or only non-violent; the violent phases and modes were effective because the anti-colonial movements at times took on sustained and massive nature – marked with low key violence and often using old and new forms of mobilization. Hence violent phases appeared sudden and effective with streams mixing with one another. Along with that appeared persistently before the nation other massive wars – the two World Wars in particular, sucking the nation within the vortex of wars. Nationalist thinkers from Aurobindo to Subhas Chandra Bose and even Nehru tried to achieve a good and true equilibrium through tactics, but also through formulating what can be called appropriate 'political lines'. Through all these exercises a peculiar kind of historical discourse emerged, best illustrated by Nehru's *Discovery of India* (1946). Yet in *Hind Swaraj* unlike in all these texts there is no attempt to find this equilibrium, no tactical politics, no anti-strategic thinking. We have there the most determined attempt to expunge violence and war from nationalist thinking, and are presented with a solution to the problem of war whose nature can be understood today only in the light of the historical discourses of that time. At this stage it is enough to mention that war as a problem for mankind, in particular for India, is inverted in that book through posing morals to war, which was contradictory to various strands of earlier Indian thinking that had traditionally combined the two (right from the writings of the *Mahabharata*), so much so that in *Hind Swaraj* a particular kind of attitude to morals and governance takes the place of war, and tries to achieve a state or condition where that equilibrium would not be needed. That state, Gandhi thought, could be achieved by a scrupulous 'government of the self', to borrow a phrase from Michel Foucault.

I do not think, however, that this inversion of the problem of war within the discourse of history in any way solved the problem – I have just mentioned that the Partition wars marking the birth of the Indian nation-state are the best examples of the persistence of the problem – but it served the purpose of shifting the focus from the ubiquitous physicality of war to the ubiquitous needs of the soul of the nation. This dream of governance without violence was if one likes the ultimate recipe for the social body which would hereafter call forth only for care and not power, government but not rule (though this was a tract for home rule), constitutionalism but not the violence of law. Gandhi tried to erase the ghosts of Shyamji Krishnavarma and Bhikaji Cama – active nationalist revolutionary figures in the first decade of the twentieth century – in this way, though through these texts such as the *Hind Swaraj* neither the abolition of war as a problem for the nation nor the aim of achieving equilibrium was achieved in the historical thought of that time. As I argue in the next chapter, in the last decade of his life he possibly realized that the inversion he had effected thirty years ago had not made war disappear from social and political relations. The polemics in *Hind Swaraj* through which he had defined contemporariness had only interpolated issues putting the contemporary time in a strange position in relation to the actual powers in society. In that sense his investigations had served only rhetorical purpose. On this – the style and form of his interrogation – dialogic but argumentative and law-like interrogation of issues – we shall come back later in some detail. The unnamed figures in the text continued to haunt Indian politics all through, thus remaining equally contemporary, and therefore the debate remains surprisingly contemporary, and unresolved.

From 2009 onwards beginning with the book's publication centenary there has been a spectacular resurgence of interest in Gandhi's *Hind Swaraj*. Yet in the discussions in the wake of the publication centenary of the book there is little attention to the historical factors that had shaped the tract and that made it a text of governance contingent on certain conditions of the time.

The urge for truth and self-government

Because the ideas of *Hind Swaraj* came in Gandhi's life and mind amid his experiences and interactions abroad, and it was composed on a sea voyage, the nation, the *Hind*, which emerges through his early political life and travels, has very little to do with the actual nation-form India was taking. Gandhi refused to have the nation marked with violence and war. Therefore, *Hind* invoked a particular kind of sensibility about people getting caught in war, violence and rule, and this sensibility was more a product of transnational thinking than one of the universalism of classical Indian thought. The anxiety of war and violence in *Hind* is not related to a determinate nation-state, or a particular territory, but an indeterminate people down with modern civilization, whose chief markers would be violence, war, competition, speed and professionalization of human activities. *Swaraj* similarly evokes a principle of autonomy in the form of a de-territorialized freedom marked by the ethical practice of the individual, with self-mastery and self-discipline as the two most important anchors. For self-mastery and self-discipline, not right but duty became important. Hence on one hand he defined 'Home rule' as opposition to alien rule and an alien presence that wanted to force war and domination on people, and therefore he wrote referring to Macaulay's *Minutes of Education* (1835), 'The foundation that Macaulay laid of education has enslaved us. . . . Is it not a sad commentary that we should have to speak of Home Rule in a foreign tongue?' But on the other hand he had to remind his reader in *HS*, 'Civilization is that mode of conduct which points out to man the path of duty' (*HS*, Ch 13). 'The English have not taken India; we have given it to them. They are not in India because of their strength: but because we keep them' (*HS*, Ch 7). *Swaraj*, more like the Kantian principle of autonomy, would mean a categorical imperative of self towards mastery over itself and self-control, and thus a duty to clean the inside of the presence of evils that colonialism presented.

Therefore *swaraj* would mean the duty to do welfare of the people with a sense of self-respect. 'By patriotism I mean the welfare of the whole people, and, if I could secure it at the hands of the English, I should bow down my head to them' (*HS*, Ch 15). Since *swaraj* was not something to be given by the leaders or by the British, but had to be taken by the people for themselves by ensuring self-dignity and the duty for service, the nation did not require war. War and violence was the mode of the shortsighted, who neither saw within nor realized the duty of the self. In this metaphysics that Gandhi set up as answer to the physicality of war the *Hind* became the land of the autonomous.

For this the rural had to be privileged over the urban, a minimal state had to be privileged over collective governance and the most important, the destiny of the individual had to be linked with the hypothetically combined fates of the oppressor, oppressed and the path of emancipation. This was what he called *satyagraha* or 'urge for truth' (or firmness for truth, also for the good, *sadagraha*) a word he used frequently in *Hind Swaraj*. Clearly the mode of war that calls for a resolution of the same entanglement in a different way could not be a mode that the nation could adopt ('methods of violence to drive out the English' would be a 'suicidal policy' (*HS*, Ch 15) – because the nation was to be built on the urge for truth, duty, welfare and the inter-linked emancipation of the dominant and the dominated. Of course, this called for appropriate politics. He adopted methods of mass disobedience and innovated some new strategies, but the moment this political strategy came into contact with actual physicality of politics (Chauri Chaura, Poona Pact, August upsurge, communal riots, Partition wars, etc.), it would break down after covering some distance. Therefore contrary to Bhikhu Parekh's assertion that *satyagraha* was an indigenous strategy,[2] war remained indigenous to society, and the constant din of social wars all around would not allow the individual seeker of truth to emerge. The soul could not be re-made and reinterpreted from within. The village could not become a 'set of values', but a place that symbolized a set of relations, of which caste oppression and degradation was one, and against which Ambedkar reacted so much because he could never reconcile with the metaphysics of *Hind Swaraj*. *Hind Swaraj* has to be seen thus in the light of the different and rival historical intelligibilities of that time.

Gandhi was aware of these rival intelligibilities and the passions they created or were marked with. One challenge to him therefore was: if he abjured the path of war, considered to be the highest form of passion, and asked everyone to be a *satyagrahi*, where would he locate the passion needed for search for truth? This was a huge dilemma characterizing his texts including the *Hind Swaraj*. Gandhi's answer was of course self-control and dialogues with others as constructed in that tract, and thus a conversation between the mind and the soul. The mind is blind reason, soul is empathy and introspection. It is through self-control that the passion for truth can be led towards non-violent resistance and can conquer fear. Passion also leads to restlessness, and restlessness or unrest leads to decisive actions and reforms. Therefore he said,

> Unrest is, in reality, discontent. This discontent is a very useful thing. As long as a man is contented with his present lot, so long is it difficult to persuade him to come out of it. Therefore it is that every reform must be preceded by discontent. We throw away things we have, only when we cease to like them.
>
> (*HS*, Chapter 3)

Or, 'Strength lies in absence of fear, not in the quantity of flesh and muscle we have on our bodies' (*HS*, Chapter 7). Here is the point to note: in setting up the nationalist metaphysics he had to make a credible effort. Therefore we find Gandhi defining and distinguishing civilization and *swaraj*. Civilization is interpreted in *Hind Swaraj* as bodily happiness and comforts such as the Roman baths, cosmetics, or, varieties of wine, perfumes and others. In moden context it would mean better housing, clothing, weaponry or shoes. Manual labour in agriculture is replaced by machines and tractors. He said,

> "Formerly, men travelled in wagons. Now, they fly through the air in trains at the rate of four hundred and more miles per day. In future men may not need hand and feet. This is considered the height of civilization. . . . They will press a button and they will have their clothing by their side. . . . Formerly men were made slaves under physical compulsion. Now they are enslaved by temptation of money and luxuries that money can buy. There are now diseases of which people never dreamt before. This is a test of civilization. . . . Civilization seeks to increase bodily comforts and it fails miserably even in doing so. . . . Women, who should be the queens of households, wander in the streets or they slave away in factories. . . . This civilization is such that one has only to be patient and it will be self-destroyed."
>
> (*HS*, Chapter 6)

On the other hand *swaraj* would mean self-control, self-regulation and thus self-government and government of the nation. War is physical, *swaraj is spiritual.*

Nation is thus a spiritual entity; in his words, India was a nation in religious and cultural sense long ago, prior to the British conquest. The British had conquered the nation, and not created it. It is through this metaphysics that Gandhi arrived at his attraction and devotion to *Gita*. We know that he first read the English version by Sir Edwin Arnold as recommended by his English friends, and was captivated for the rest of his life by Gita's message. He felt his concept of dharma was summarized in those verses. He took to reading Gita daily. During his prison years he undertook a careful study of the book. While there were earlier commentaries on the *Gita* in the framework of monism or dualism, or in terms of action (*karmayoga*), Gandhi interpreted action as one without expectation of fruit (*anasaktiyoga*); and selfless action was the essence of work. Therefore while in the case of many other thinkers (for instance Bankimchandra) the *Mahabharata* was the great text – the drama which was being re-enacted through the struggles, deaths, defeats and victories in the nationalist age, to Gandhi the *Mahabharata* (in the light of *Gita*) was only a pretext; he felt it was an allegory. It served as the occasion for reminding the individual the fact that even victory in war may not bring happiness. Along with losses, it could bring regret and remorse to all. It proved that mere material gains never brought peace within. Krishna of *Bhagavad-Gita* was thus not the figure of action, but wisdom personified. The lessons of the Gita were important because they taught that religion and politics were inseparable just as inseparable were thought (likened to religion) and practice (likened to politics). They legitimized the concept of *satyagraha* (relentless search for truth), which involved purifying vow and action towards truth. These two combined ensured control of self and detachment. We have to remember in this context however that there were other discourses on *Gita* at that time, as the prison reminiscences of the Bengal revolutionaries tell us, which dealt with themes of action, desire and the role of self, and which attempted to bridge the gap between an action-oriented interpretation of the *Gita* and the theory of *anasaktiyoga*.

These rival intelligibilities (expressed in other writings of the time, for instance in Bankimchandra, *Yugantar,* and Bal Gangadhar Tilak) help us to understand why *Hind Swaraj* makes sense as an important text only in the context of the great battle of the nationalist discourses.

Social violence in contemporary India and historical resurgence of interest in *Hind Swaraj*

This question also helps us to understand why suddenly in the late eighties of the past century *Hind Swaraj* became to many Indian thinkers the text of the century. Bhikhu Parekh, Ashis Nandy, Thomas Pantham and several others appraised *Hind Swaraj* as the great text of anti-colonialism and indigenousness, cultural protest against alien rule, the expose of the scandal called modernity and a call to purge the native self of the enemy within, whose boundary with the enemy without was blurred. Post-colonialists re-discovered the text, jumped over the re-discovery, interpreted and re-interpreted it in the closest manner so much so that, ascribed intentions, interpretations and the supposed great results were seldom checked against the grain of the historical development of the thoughts of the time. We have already indicated that the second half of the nineteenth century and early twentieth century produced in India the discourses of violent anti-colonialism, militant nationalism, pro-labour thinking, socialist ideas, religious nationalism, race and counter-race discourses, parliamentary nationalism, anarchist thinking and millenarian nationalism. In all these two questions were paramount: the question of war, which is to say the issue of the method of evicting alien rule and the possible philosophical basis of how the nation was to be governed once freedom came – in other words the nation form. These two questions were linked; nationalist thinking therefore called for a programme, which combined in it the two great questions of *how* and *why*. Gandhi was quick to see the connection; hence what he produced became, in no time, a manifesto. If there was to be least government, and only government of the self by the self was to be the reason of the programme of replacing foreign rule, then war was to be banished from nationalist thinking. This was because war occasioned social conflicts that would then engulf and eventually destroy the self and along with the self the nation. This was Gandhi's response to the question of *why* while he responded to the question of how by his idea of *satyagraha*.

This was precisely the same impulse and anxiety in the aftermath of the national emergency in 1975–77, and in the wake of the violent caste wars (1977–85), agrarian insurgency, urban revolts and ruthless suppression of them by the state armed forces (generally known as the Naxalite violence, that led these thinkers to bring *Hind Swaraj* back in the centre of reformist thought in India.[3] The materiality of the social war was to be met with the metaphysics of *swaraj*. Indian thought was to be reformed in this way. It is interesting to read the way in which Ashis Nandy interprets in *The Intimate Enemy* (1983) the epistemic revolution that Gandhi sought to create in nationalist thinking. As we have argued, Gandhi wanted to achieve this change by way of banishing war as a mode of anti-colonialism and installing a moral and evangelical orientation to the nationalist project through linking nationalism with the responsibility of changing the heart of the colonizer. *Hind Swaraj* is replete with instances of that strategy. Gandhi of course did it first by underplaying the role of colonial violence and wars of conquest and annexation. Nandy approvingly writes,

> Colonialism is first of all a matter of consciousness and needs to be defeated ultimately in the minds of men. . . . As Gandhi was to so clearly formulate through his own life, freedom is indivisible, not only in the popular sense that the oppressed of the world are one but also in the unpopular sense that the oppressor too is caught in the culture of oppression. . . . Did Gandhi really construct human nature and society. . . . Perhaps the question is irrelevant. As Gandhi so effortlessly demonstrated, for those seeking liberation, history can sometimes be made to follow from myths.[4]

But we know history did not follow from myth. The heart of the colonizer did not change. The British rulers left India without showing any symptom of change of heart, and exactly within a decade of leaving India they embarked on one of the most brutal suppressions in the history of twentieth-century colonialism – in Kenya, another

British colony.[5] In *The Intimate Enemy* we have also this explanation that Gandhi used with effect the weaknesses of the colonized to change the terms of the contest between the colonizer and the colonized, which explains why he took the said positions in *Hind Swaraj*. Therefore, 'Gandhi's non-violence was not a one sided morality play',[6] Nandy argues, there was design. The design was to use cunningly West's dictum of non-violence against the violence of the West. *The Intimate Enemy* is an engrossing text. It suspends as Gandhi did history. Erecting the colonial world at the edge of psychology, the text takes interpretation to a new height. But what it cannot is erasing the historical problematic that Gandhi had wrestled with, namely the problematic of war, the problematic of other competing anti-colonial discourses and the problem that grows out of the strategy of wishing away war by wishing away the historical anti-colonial discourse of war.

There is a remarkable similarity between the two situations – the situation between 1860 and 1910, and that between 1977 and 2000. The first period marked the clash of the various nationalist thoughts and the second period marks the clash between various ideas about the reconstruction of India in the wake of the constitutional and political disaster brought in by the Emergency, brutal suppression of the Naxalite revolutionaries and the anti-Muslim riots. Both periods are characterized by the consequences of ruthless suppression and pacification of revolts, strategies for constitutional re-making of the country, and desperate efforts to find out a blueprint for a resurgent India. This background helps us to appreciate the legends that have periodically marked the nationalist discourse – then and now.

The sparse historical facts mentioned in the *Hind Swaraj* help to create the legend of a peaceful India. In a similar way in the writings of the later period (in the eighties and early nineties) on *Hind Swaraj* that in attempt some sense 'to rediscover' history is suspended. In the later bunch of writings therefore, there is not much effort at engaging with the other voices in *Hind Swaraj* with which Gandhi battles through the apparent conversation between the editor and the reader.[7] These battles of the nationalist ideas reflected the wars that characterized the life of the colony, and the traces of these battles were sought to be swept away by an accompanying mythology of an unchallenged reception of *Hind Swaraj*. The entire nationalist epoch was marked in this way by a sort of 'national duality' that reflected the ideas of the two different and at times hostile groups that constituted the permanent sub-stratum of the anti-colonial world. So when Gandhi was laying down his ideas, he was arguing neither for freedom of speech, nor for the possibility of religious choice, nor even for the freedom of choice between alien rule and Indian rule, he was telling a story which attempted to lay down a different model of government. Not sovereignty, but the style and ethics of governance – indeed what constitutes self-governance was the theme. The theme of government provided the definite link between his critique of colonialism, princely absolutism and the project of national reconstruction on the basis of a quasi-historical, quasi-mythological model of a past that was crucial for reviving the forgotten soul of the country. Hence the book is full with the theories and references relating to what can be alluded to as power of the soul.

Shifting in this way the plank of discussion from issues relating to an intense physicality of colonial existence to the question of self and power of the soul through insistence on truth, Gandhi effected a critical displacement in the terms of discussion among the nationalist intelligentsia and political thinkers. Up to this point history had been the history of political power, also royal and imperial power, as told by power itself. That history was suspended. *Hind Swaraj* destroyed the very working of that historical knowledge, possibly not intentionally, but through the very process of setting up a different knowledge, whose intelligibility was in recounting a mythological account of the subordination of the soul and prescribing an alternative route of the revival of the self. This new type of discourse started playing an important political role, and acted as the hinge between the moderate and the extremist segments of nationalist political thinking. It succeeded in strengthening the moderate segment by co-opting the extremist strategy of mass civil disobedience. With the advantage of hindsight we may say that this combination of a moderate type of political ethos, faith in British constitutionalism, abhorrence of strategies for war and putting pressure on the state through civic actions including peaceful disobedience has proved to be the main gradient of Indian democracy. The knowledge produced out of this combination and built up through one hundred years since this book was written characterizes the Indian political discourse of democracy. It also characterizes the official notion of justice, which allows civic actions and appeals, but there has to be trust on the rule and the rulers, and therefore social violence must not be permitted. This trust will build up the collective but will not permit collective action beyond a certain point. At the centre of trust will be the individual seeker of truth, ready to face the consequences of his or her action of disobedience. After *Hind Swaraj* appeared with its peculiar ethos, content and appeal, and succeeded in being the dominant discourse for nationalist thinking, violence and social war were banished from official nationalist politics. Henceforth governance-centric and government-centric thinking would form the core of nationalist politics and strategy. Violence became the other scene of politics. This is how a new type of political discourse and historical knowledge of democracy emerged on the Indian scene.

The appreciative, interpretive and endorsing literature on *Hind Swaraj* that appeared in the last two decades of the preceding century reflects that historical knowledge. In this background, chapters 3 and 4 of *Hind Swaraj* ('Discontent and unrest' and 'What is Swaraj') seem to provide the key to the development of a new type of discourse and historical knowledge of democracy.

The aim of the dialogic style in *Hind Swaraj*

To understand the success of *Hind Swaraj* in producing a particular kind of nationalist discourse we must also look into its style. The style is dialogic, conversational, yet we must not lose sight of the legalistic way in which the 'Editor' tries to pin down the 'Reader'. We can again look up to chapter 4. The issue is 'What is Swaraj?' The editor chooses not to reply to the question of the reader and his or her statement that British rule is like associating with a tiger. A tiger does not change its nature; therefore the reader asserts there is no point in thinking whether Indians should be ready to live under a gentle British rule. When the editor again asks the reader if Indians should have self-government similar to the Canadian or the South African form and if that would be 'good enough', again the reader says that this question is useless. Gandhi in fact uses the dialogic style to press home the point that violence and war have nothing to do with expulsion of the conqueror and attainment of freedom and *swaraj*. Until the mind is freed and the basis of *swaraj* is laid down, expulsion of the alien rulers will prove to be of no worth. The word *swaraj*, at once political and mystical, in this way proves crucial to the dialogic strategy of Gandhi. By using that word, *swaraj*, new to Indian political vocabulary, and making it central to his argument, he manages to sideline many other contemporary ideas.

So what is *swaraj*? Is it home-rule – that reviled word to the nationalist revolutionaries? Is it freedom? Is it independence? Is it autonomy? Rule of the self? Government of the villages, or the locals and localities, or is it rule of the Indians as a collective self? Does it abjure altogether British parliamentary-constitutional system? Does it mean infidelity to British rule? One can re-read *Hind Swaraj* to see how Gandhi re-constitutes the nationalist thinking by marginalizing other contemporary discourses through a web of juristic arguments, thwarting all objections to his way of thinking, and grounds for other thoughts, and re-creates a world of nationalism in which anti-colonialism has been sanitized off its fury, venom, physicality and clarity of goal, and has been sublimated by mysticism, at whose core lies the phrase 'urge for truth', 'passive resistance' – the will to resist and meet death (chapter 17). *Swaraj* is not only *swadeshi* and *swadesh* – the words around which militant revolutionaries and all other nationalists had united. *Swaraj* substituted these two words with itself, because these two words were not enough to deny the war-like model of politics of its legitimacy. What was needed was the idea of *swaraj*, which needed no violence and war, but called for and depended on if we like a redemption of the self. Hence, the emphasis is on ethical reform (chapter 6).

Significant in this respect is the way the *Hind Swaraj* ends (chapter 20). The Reader makes his or her last comment, 'For our purposes, it is the nation you and I have been thinking of, that is those of us who are affected by European civilization, and who are eager to have Home Rule.' The reader thinks that he or she has been able to bridge the two perceptions: on one hand the sceptic, interrogating and the more materially minded, and on the other the reassuring, spiritual and the redemptive. But Gandhi does not yield an inch. In reply therefore, he sidesteps the question of the 'nation', and avoids defining it. He instead lists out nineteen (19) criteria for self-rule, which may form anything but not a nation. They reflect all that is there in the earlier elucidations by the Editor, including the demands that a new India must eschew professionalization, speed and others and must be ready for 'suffering' in passive resistance more than suffering in war. Indeed that is the way to win war. To this long reply, the Reader makes his or her last observation before leaving the scene, 'This is a large order. When will all carry it out?' (p. 118). The Editor replies, 'You make a mistake. You and I have nothing to do with the others. Let each do his duty' (p. 118). And then he comments, 'Real home-rule is self-rule or self-control', and the 'way to do it is passive resistance that is soul force or love force' The Editor in fact makes the last comment by way of saying that how we govern ourselves will justify our goal, which is *swaraj* or home rule.

The Gandhian dialogue thus does not aim at reaching some new ground of understanding through conversations. It aims at converting the interlocutor by always spinning new arguments, a process in which other ideas, at the beginning looking supplementary to the main point, succeed in overwhelming the objections, yet avoiding any definition of the main point in contestation. This is the reason why the dialogues in *Hind Swaraj* remind us of legal language. They reflect his professional training; they succeed in suspending history, and are able to build up a new world of subjectivity and ethics refusing at the same time to acknowledge the materiality of all kinds of contradictions (caste, class, national, etc.).

This is the way he defines and explains what he means by civilization (pp. 38, 72, 116). In this way he is also able to avoid the natural war/peace binary. He avoids the question, if war is not a virtue, is peace so? He counterposes the issue of war with power of the soul, and hence he says that peace is not mental strength, mental strength is absence of fear (p. 44). In short, in *Hind Swaraj* Gandhi does not act as an insider to the anti-colonial ethos. He is outside the world of killings, frenzy, schisms, polemics and others. In this sense Judith Brown is right that Gandhi was a 'critical outsider'.[8] By not appearing as an insider Gandhi was thus able to dispute the efficacy of the actions and discourses of Madan lal Dhingra, Veer Savarkar, Shyamji Krishnavarma, Bhikaji Rustom Cama, Tarak Nath Das, Virendra Chattopadhyay and others. Disputing them was important for Gandhi because these figures were crucial in the international life of the early nationalists, who got support from these figures, in particular from Madan lal Dhingra's spectacular assassination of William Curzon-Wyllie in the heart of the empire in 1909. Through his polemics with them Gandhi was also engaging with Tilak and Aurobindo, and at a greater level with the entire tradition of early nationalism still untouched with constitutional-parliamentarian ideas, and still carrying the smell of the firing guns of the colonial forces and the anti-colonial musketeers. Through all these dialogic strategies Gandhi was thus able to pose against the 'fanatic' nationalist the *satyagrahi*, and against the war-like life of the revolutionary a Socratic way of life, in his word, the life of the truth seeker.

The dialogues of Gandhi in this way succeed in removing any trace of the spectacle in anti-colonial epic. The language is mostly thus self-referential; it avoids narratives, and removes history and temporality altogether through the self-referential technique, which is common to all mystic and quasi-mystic discourses. The voice is the voice of death, the repeated message is that the *satyagrahi* must die – not in war, he or she dies in self-sacrifice. The questioning 'reader', who seeks clarification and wants to understand the politics of nationalism in an analytical way, is defeated before this voice of dying. In *Hind Swaraj* this is the function of the editor's voice. In this post-historical enunciation of the nationalist life the collective is replaced by the individual, who must now inculcate asceticism through vegetarianism, ethico-political practices of the self and spiritual involvement in making this new nation of truth seekers.

Although this is no more than a crude sketch, it provides a starting point to reconstruct and characterize what was specific about this new form of discourse, different from other anti-colonial and early nationalist discourses, for instance, on Wahabi revolts and the terrorist revolutionaries of Bengal.[9] Until *Hind Swaraj*, the historical discourse of anti-colonialism was deeply involved with the question of sovereignty. Thus the questions thrown up by *Jugantar*, *Sandhya* and other early nationalist journals were: Who is the ruler? Who has to be driven out? How can the Indians rule? What can be the methods of ending British rule? Why should these new rulers be considered as oppressors? Why do they kill us? And, therefore why should they be killed? Which are therefore the parties in war? As a corollary we find also in this early nationalist discourse the first signs of republicanism, essential for nationalist thought. Classic instance of this war-nationalism-republicanism copula was the publication by Savarkar of *The Indian War of Independence of 1857* (1909), which Anthony Parel dubs as 'militaristic'.[10] The new form of discourse was no longer the discourse of sovereignty or even race and races, but about the moral aims of governance. Therefore the new questions raised in *Hind Swaraj* were: What do we mean by self-government? What is the power of the self and force of the soul? These questions as we can see were in complete antithesis of the discourse of war, and aimed at raising questions pertaining to the *within* of the nation and *within laws* – but in a way where war and the din of social battles are absent, all we find is a new identification of people with the individual search for truth.

The replacement of the issue of sovereignty with that of governance had enormous consequence. First, it divided the anti-colonial politics in a hitherto unforeseen way. It led to the peculiar stance that the Indian National Congress adopted towards the Act of 1935, the elections held under it and its participation in the ministries. Second, it delinked governance from the ongoing ideas of rule. This had both positive and negative results. But most important, it delinked governance from the question of sovereignty; the Indian National Congress took another twenty years after 1909 to resolve for *purna swaraj*. The question of how do we govern became anchorless. Before the force of the soul all other forms of power were supposed to vanish away. In this new type of discourse, sovereignty no longer held everything in unity, because the implication of this new type of idea was that sovereignty no longer held everything together in unity, it enslaved. From *Hind Swaraj* onwards, we may say and here we may include all the relevant comments made later by Gandhi on this book and its material, the question of race (so central to colonialism) in the nationalist discourse was dissolved in the question of the individual. Anti-colonialism which was the weapon of the poor and the insur-rectionists was now replaced by nationalism which took on the great religious form of prophecy and promise, the latter being based on a mix of the promised rise of the individual and the merits of constitu-tional and moderate rule.

Though successful in creating the individual *satyagrahi* as the subject of nationalism and the promised new India, these dialogues and the specific dialogic mode could not stop from exposing the intense dislike of the ascetic for the dirt and blood of the world of anti-colonialism. In some cases this dislike almost bordered on hatred against the sub-jects of war and the war-minded nationalists. There was no middle ground in *Hind Swaraj*, although as we argue in the next chapter in the last decade of his life Gandhi was not sure of the method and its universal efficacy. Where did this intense dislike come from? There is ground to argue that his centrist position in great many aspects of life (in South Africa or in India or in his personal life) was a cause. But I think the ineluctable historical necessity felt by the new Indian politi-cal class of breaking the chord between war and anti-colonialism in order to chart out a new path of nationalism was responsible for this dislike. This dislike is expressed by Jawaharlal Nehru also in his *Auto-biography* where he uses the word 'terrorist' again and again with regard to the militant nationalists, and shows almost a surreal attitude towards persons like Chandrasekhar Azad the militant revolutionary of the United Provinces. Reading the laconic lines in the couple of pages on Chandrasekhar Azad it is difficult to make out if Nehru con-sidered nationalists like Azad as belonging to his own country.[11] The same attitude is shown by Gandhi towards Bhagat Singh. This dislike is akin to the dislike of the shepherd who does not like the members of his flock going astray because of his absence. Politics cannot afford to be the 'lost shepherd'. If the shepherd is lost, then ethics must bring it back.

This then is a strange arrival at modernity. This arrival has much resemblance to the way, for instance, charted out by Michel Foucault who argued in the first volume of his *History of Sexuality* series that modern power was characterized by a fundamentally different ration-ality than that of sovereign power. Whereas sovereign power was char-acterized by a right over life and death, summarized by Foucault in the dictum of 'killing or letting live', modern power was now character-ized by a productive relation to life, encapsulated in the dictum of 'fos-tering life or disallowing it'. The threshold of modernity was reached with the transition from sovereign power to bio-power, in which the 'new political subject' of the population became the target of a regime of power that operated through governance of the uncertainties of biological life itself. In the strange arrival at modernity in *Hind Swaraj*, war as the mode of sovereign power is disowned; in place we have the life of the individual truth seeker who dissociating from various aspects of modern power becomes the centre of a new universe which protects and elevates life through a series of ethico-political practices. The result is the same, namely war as the sovereign mode is replaced in the centre of politics by (self-) controlled and (self-) regulated life. The unconditional power over life, represented by colonial rule, is replaced with incessant conditioning of life through the search for truth, one of whose forms would be passive resistance. What war cannot communicate, *satyagraha* can. At stake is the communicability of truth, which can be ensured only by the ethical life of the individual.

This was the modern route taken by Gandhi. Its arrival was not without conflict. Colonial life with its violence and intense physicality of resistance did not allow the Gandhian discourse first set out in *Hind Swaraj* an un-problematic and un-challenged life. And no one was more aware of this reality than the author himself as the problem of war again engulfed India and threatened to consume the country in the last year and months of his life – the Partition wars, the Indo-Pakistan war and the pacification war to quell the agrarian revolutionary movement in one part of the south of the country.

Notes

1 Citations from *Hind Swaraj* here are in the style of *Hind Swaraj* scholarship, thus referring only to the chapters; page numbers wherever given are from Anthony Parel (ed.), *Hind Swaraj and Other Writings* (Cambridge: Cambridge University Press, 1997).

2 Bhikhu Parekh writes of 'a vernacular model of action'; See his *Gandhi's Political Philosophy: A Critical Appreciation* (Delhi: Ajanta, 1995), p. 211.

3 Ashis Nandy refers to the context of the eighties in the emergence of postcolonial thinking in his "*The Intimate Enemy* after 25 Years – A Postscript," in Ashis Nandy, *The Intimate Enemy – Loss and Recovery of Self under Colonialism*, 2nd Edition (New Delhi: Oxford University Press, 2009), pp. 114–125; though his analysis of that perspective differs from mine.

4 Nandy, *The Intimate Enemy*, p. 63.

5 On this, Caroline Elkins, *Britain's Gulag – The Brutal End of Empire in Kenya* (London: Junathan Cape, 2006).

6 Nandy, *The Intimate Enemy*, p. 51; Thomas Pantham, another commentator writing in the mid-eighties of the last century, however found the Gandhian strategy of *satyagraha* as having strong link with 'communitarian

ethics'. See his article, "Beyond Liberal Democracy – Thinking with Mahatma Gandhi" in Thomas Pantham and Kenneth L. Deutsch (eds.), *Political Thought in Modern India* (New Delhi: Sage Publications, 1986), pp. 339–342; see also in this context, Dennis Dalton, "The Ideology of Sarvodaya – Concepts of Politics and Power in Indian Political Thought," in *Political Thought in Modern India*, pp. 275–296. In all these discussions war as a problem for politics is by and large absent.

7 On these other voices, Anthony Parel's editorial introduction to his edited *Hind Swaraj and Other Writings* is instructive; see pp. xiii–lxii.

8 On Judith Brown's views, see her *Gandhi's Rise to Power – Indian Politics 1915–1922* (Cambridge: Cambridge University Press, 1972); and *Gandhi and Civil Disobedience – The Mahatma in Indian Politics 1928–34* (Cambridge: Cambridge University Press, 1977). Brown's studies are significant in the sense these historical works appeared in the 1970s; and then from the eighties interpretive works started appearing, while historical studies waned.

9 Ranabir Samaddar, *The Materiality of Politics*, Volume 1, *The Technologies of Rule* (London: Anthem Press, 2007), Chapter 2, "Law, Terror, and The Colonial State", pp. 59–106; more details on the various militant discourses, R. Samaddar, *The Emergence of the Political Subject* (New Delhi: Sage, 2010).

10 Anthony Parel, *op. cit.*, p. xxvii.

11 Jawaharlal Nehru, *An Autobiography* (1936, New Delhi: Penguin Books, 2004), pp. 274–275.

2 Crisis in the nationalist ideal of self-governance

Governance as a test of the ability to emerge as supreme power

Communal riots and recurrent events of civil strife marked the Congress rule in several of the eight Indian provinces in which it came to power in the elections of 1937. In almost all these cases, the ministers had to call in police and other security forces to quell riots, control strife and pacify the dissenters, as in Allahabad and Varanasi (Benaras) in 1939.[1] Gandhi wrote in the *Harijan*,

> The communal riots in Allahabad – the headquarters of the Congress, and the necessity of summoning the assistance of the police and even the military show that the Congress has not yet become fit to substitute the British authority. It is best to face the naked truth, however unpleasant it may be.

He then went on to say,

> The Congress claims to represent the whole of India, not merely those few who are on the Congress register. It should represent even those who are hostile to it and even want to crush it, if they can. Not until we make good that claim shall we be in a position to displace the British Government and function as an independent nation.

Gandhi was of course referring here to the issue of dual power – colonial rule and the anti-colonial power growing within the colonial rule, and asking the Congressmen on the occasion of the Allahabad riot and the demonstrated incapacity of the nationalist power to prevent and stop it, namely, if they were ready to fill in the vacuum in the event of the country's independence. He was asking: had they become capable of replacing alien rule? [2]

This was an important question. It basically revolved around, and such question still revolves around, the question of transition. Yet, clearly Gandhi did not sense in this problem purely a question of transition, he sensed also a closure. In this small entry in the *Harijan* to which we are referring here, he further said that the Congress understandably felt confident of its growth and strength to replace the British; he too had earlier felt similarly confident. Yet now he had doubt. Because, he said that while he was sure that the adoption by the Congress of the policy of non-violence was the main reason of its success, he was not sure as to whether this policy was being adopted as the weapon of the weak, or of the strong. What was the difference? If it was in fear of the repressive measures of the administration to be used in the event of violent protest, that is if non-violence was practised in fear of reprisal, that is as a weapon of the weak, then people's strength will be found wanting in preventing riots, controlling the rioters and other mischief-makers. Nobody would be prepared to court death to stop a rioter from arson, killing and looting. In his words, 'A few hundred, may be a few thousand, such *spotless deaths* [italics mine] will once for all put an end to the riots.' This was non-violence of the strong, any day better than deploying the police and the army. The Congress needed an army based on the non-violence of the brave, and the strong. It was not there; and the Congress had used the means of the adversary (that is police method), and in his words, 'we have failed'.

Of course, we have to remember that when Muhammad Ali Jinnah repeatedly sought a permanent solution to the 'communal question' and durable guarantees for Muslims, Gandhi had shifted his ground, and would repeatedly say, that let independence first come to the country, a free country would be able to solve the seemingly intractable issues, free citizens would freely decide among themselves the ways of resolving fratricidal conflicts. To this Jinnah invoked a completely separate argument, which denied Gandhi any exit from that closed situation, and if anything it reinforced the closure. Jinnah as we know invoked the principle of self-determination and claiming for the Muslims of the subcontinent the right to self-determine, commented in his presidential address to the Muslim League in Lahore in 1940,

> Babu Rajendra Prasad . . . only a few days ago said, 'Oh, what more do the Musalmans want?' I will read you his words. Referring to the minority question, he says: 'If the British would concede

our right of self-determination surely all these differences should disappear.' How will our differences disappear? . . .

The word 'nationalist has now become the play of conjurers in politics . . .

The problem of India is not of an inter-communal but manifestly of an international character, and must be treated as such. So long as this basic and fundamental truth is not realized, any constitution that may be built will result in disaster and will prove harmful not only to the Musalmans, but also to the British and Hindus . . .

Musalmans are not a minority . . . Musalmans are a nation according to any definition of a nation, and they must have their homelands, their territory and their State.[3]

One can see here not only the reappearance of the transition problematic, but also a reappearance of a closure – hence Gandhi's own subsequent haphazard responses all through the forties, changes in stance, considerable straining of efforts to convince the interlocutors of the consistence of his approach, in one phrase, the situation of an impossible exit.

To break out of that kind of situation, Gandhi asked for *spotless deaths*, but what sort of events and sacrifices would make death spotless? If we are startled by the deployment of such words, we must also notice here the extreme effort by Gandhi to find the right expression of what he had in mind and wanted to convey, also therefore the extreme economy of words to describe the aporia. Of course, in politics the idea of the power of sacrifice plays a significant role, and has attracted enormous attention of political movements and thinkers. Revolutionists throughout the entire anti-colonial era again and again spoke of the power of death, spotless death, death not contaminated by cowardice, betrayal, hesitation, self-interest, revenge, or lure of reward and glory.[4] Such spotless deaths were there, though Gandhi and others could have differed among themselves as to which deaths to crown with the honour of spotlessness. Gandhi himself was always in two minds in passing judgements on the deaths of militant revolutionists – at times he would honour them. He refused to criticize Jatindranath Mukherjee, the leader of the Bengal revolutionaries, who before dying in a gun battle on the shores of the River Buribalam had inspired and planned the killings of colonial officials. But at times he would blame the revolutionists for their violent policies and refused to honour their sacrifice and death. He disagreed for instance with Bhagat Singh and did not honour his death at the gallows, and had no word of appreciation for Sachindranath Sanyal, another famous revolutionary, who had sent him a letter requesting him to explain his norms in honouring the ethical standards of an anti-colonial movement.[5] This ambivalence only increased as the nationalist movement gained momentum and fury with the onset of the forties, marked not only by the August upsurge of 1942 that began as the Quit India Movement, but also the communal disturbances in Noalkhali in Bengal. Gandhi used all kinds of arguments, pleaded in every possible way with agitated masses, to defend non-violence while refraining on several occasions from condemning violence. Increasingly it was difficult to find 'spotless death'. In short, as conflicts increased, deaths became common, and the smell of burning and rotting flesh marked cities, town and villages, he had to increasingly judge case by case the ethicality and efficacy of violent/non-violent method as an exit from a closed situation.[6] As we know, this encounter with the reality of an all-enveloping social war finally drained his energy, and consumed him at the end.

Yet, this is not the point here. The point is that in thinking that death could bring about an exit from an impossible situation, he could only less and less rely on a theory of non-violence, and more and more he had to adjust his attitude and stance to the particularities of the situation, or of the event, to formulate what courage, strength and power of the nation would mean in such circumstances. Politics, less and less remained a strategy, it became more and more a matter of tactical adjustment – and this was perhaps for him the saddest part of an already-ironical situation. Not that he was unaware of this new reality, or of the ineluctable of nature of reality itself – he in fact showed enough signs of being a realist, some say that he was all through a supreme realist – but the great point of this conundrum was that the events were now forcing his hands. He was no longer the agenda-setter; he had to now constantly find exits from impossible situations that presented themselves to him in form of events.

That of course makes us ask, what is an event? An event is a privileged instant, often viewed as a decisive moment, a congealed expression of a relationship of forces embroiled now in a conflictive moment, scarcely seen at its hour of emergence as arising from an already-existing virtual existence, that is from a possibility thriving for realization. Yet *event* as a phenomenon shows that the category of the possible never existed, that the virtual existences of various social practices take their leave as the event takes place in the real, emptying all meanings from the possible, redefining the real in the process. As Gandhi faced questions about the universal efficacy of non-violence – when asked if he justified violent method to prevent a woman about to be raped as in a village in Tamluk by a police officer in 1942 or by a communal fanatic and rioter as in 1946–47 in Noakhali – the event was deciding for him the meaning of the possible.[7] As more and more Gandhi searched for answers to such events, it was clear from his answers that his policy was being subjected increasingly to the simultaneous crisis of historical thought and historical reality. Events (in this case we are referring to the war and riots) were overthrowing the structure of his thoughts in as much as they were overthrowing the structures of reality. The result was ambiguous: exit in the established sense was ruled out, in the ambiguous and complex set of situations exit in the frame of given meanings was impossible. Just as, if a thousand men and women ready for spotless deaths had been available to stop the riot in Allahabad, the riot in all probability would not have taken place, or if the power to stop the mass rape and arson had been present in Tamluk, there would have been little of the actual dishonour and death. Gandhi was clearly looking for an impossible exit in a situation where politics as strategy was failing, where events were overwhelming the given solutions and lines of thinking. Possibly he knew also the impossibility (of exit) I am referring to here. He said as war gathered momentum in Europe threatening to engulf the world,

> One more question (of the writer) remains to be answered. If war is a wrong act, how can it be worthy of moral support or blessings? I believe all war to be wholly wrong. But if we scrutinize the motives of two warring parties, we may find one to be in the right and the other in the wrong. For instance, if A wishes to seize B's country, B is obviously the wronged one. Both fight with arms. I do not believe in violent warfare, but all the same, B, whose cause is just, deserves my moral help and support.[8]

But of course this realization was not related to Gandhi's rationale in those days alone, it continues to have validity beyond that specific. We can speak here of the relation between politics, war and peace – as a set of shifting scenarios marked by impossible exits – transforming only through the emergence of *new dimension, the third dimension, the other face.* Therefore there is no exit from war to peace or peace to politics, or for that matter from politics to war, or vice versa. We have to keep in mind that the shifts allow the traces to remain.

Limits of the political principle in the time of war

The Second World War presented the anti-colonial politics with one of the most difficult moments in relation to the question of war and peace. It had to redefine its position *vis-à-vis* the war in Europe, in the making or conclusion of which it had no role. It could not be the victor or the vanquished, yet had to now become a party to it, and was being asked to contribute to it, allow its people to perish in it, without any clear prospect that war would lead to freedom of the colony. Gandhi typically wrote in *Young India* (7 February 1929) on this, 'What I feel is that I am looking at peace through a medium to which my European friends are strangers. I belong to a country, which is compulsorily disarmed and has been held under subjection for centuries. My way of looking at peace may be necessarily different from theirs.' In this situation of closure, where an exit was impossible, Gandhi had to define what the policy of truth and non-violence would be.

Here we arrive at the heart of the question we are discussing here. Of course, we must remember that two other anti-colonial leaders – Mao and Ho Chi Minh – negotiated the transition problematic, and they did so not by trying for an exit from the war/peace copula, that is either from a particular war to peace or from a particular politics to war and then vice versa, but by managing to bring in another dimension, which we can name as *the third dimension*, as the *other scene of politics*, always lurking in the horizon, rarely appearing as a possibility, yet brought to the centre of the vortex by the event. But this is not occasion to generalize those specific lessons, and also we are not discussing Mao or Ho Chi Minh. We are discussing India, India at the war time, the closure of the nationalist politics the war brought about, and the exit Gandhi wanted to make.

Indeed, it became clear quite early as the war started that the old straightforward conflict between the colonial power and the nation was yielding place to a complicated scenario, to a process which later on came to be known as *decolonization*, and therefore the nationalist leadership was at its tether's end in finding a suitable response to the developing situation marked by new elements making their unanticipated appearance. The nationalist leadership was used to thinking of a world made up of colonial power and nationalist challenge; in short what is described as the colonial world had little sense of the world beyond – a world inhabited by other existences and formations towards which the nation could not have a *policy*. But the truth is that the *international* was always in the *national* for a long time. Jawaharlal Nehru, open to the West since childhood with the connection being

reinforced by scores of visits to the West (particularly after his participation in the Brussels Conference against Imperialism, 10–15 February 1927), had always advocated the need for a policy. Gandhi was
aware of the transnational nature of colonialism since his South Africa
days. He had supported the British in the First World War and had
been duly rewarded for his loyalty. In the critical years of the decade of
the thirties Subhas Chandra Bose had argued for tactical decisions in
place of adopting a policy in the area of the *international*. Vithalbhai
Patel too was aware of British colonialism elsewhere – particularly in
Ireland. He had met the Irish president Eamon de Valera in 1933 in
search of support to the nationalist cause before he died at Geneva
same year. Yet, all these played only marginal role in the encounter of
the nationalist world with the extra-nation forces. Therefore when the
reality of the Second World War finally sank in the minds of the nationalist leadership, the leaders searched for a consistent policy *vis-à-vis* the
war, only to repeatedly flounder.

But if the nationalist world had no resource to cope with the new
reality – a worldwide war that would affect its own destiny – and
had to rely on an unconditional pacifism in the hope that in this way
the *international* marked by the presence of Great Powers would take
notice of the national, the *international* too was equally baffled at the
nationalist response, and was driven to despair to make sense of the
latter. Needless to say, these were two distinct social texts at work,
competing with each other for legitimacy and attention in a situation of two different logics of sovereignty and government. Gandhi's
exhortations of pacifism to quell both internal conflicts such as riots
and international conflicts such as the war not only constituted a distinct social text, but it became a contentious text. And herein is the
irony, namely that a seemingly neutral text appeared as adversarial. If
Gandhi's colleagues found his views hard to follow, his enemies were
also hard put to make sense of them, as some of the war-time British
commentaries on India show. To a Great Power like Britain Gandhi's
position seemed as a challenge to established reality, as the affirmation
of a banality characteristic of a small creature.

One British commentator Alfred Watson described him in a pamphlet as 'extremist', bull headed and lacking in common sense.[9] Divided
in four sections and dealing with three related themes of Congress attitude to war, the Governor-General's offer of 1940 and the failure of
the Cripps Mission, the thrust of this pamphlet was to emphasize Gandhi's role in the hardening of Congress attitude, the subsequent withdrawal of the Congress from the ministry in the provinces it was in
power, its rejection of the 1940 offer of the Governor-General, also the

subsequent proposal of the Cripps Mission. What is interesting in this pamphlet is the bewilderment of the writer, namely that someone in India was unable to understand the worldwide significance of British democracy and the lack of willingness and eagerness to come forward in the defence of British democracy, and further that such a person was being allowed to lead the Congress and sabotage the war effort. If such was the extent of the obduracy of the person and if the country was willing to be a hostage to his stubbornness then it was only in the propriety of things that the British administration had crushed the August unrest with ruthlessness. He also examined the record of Gandhi's intractable nature in this context. He reviewed Gandhi's moves from 1935 to 1940, and the latter's direction to Congress to oppose the bill (that became an act subsequently), which intended to punish any discouragement of enlisting in the army, and instigation to that effect. He noted one of Gandhi's draft notes among the Congress papers seized by the police in a raid in 1942, which said, 'that India bears no enmity either towards Japan or towards any other nation . . . If India were freed her first step would probably be to negotiate with Japan'. Watson also noted Gandhi's famous war-time statement, 'Britain cannot make India independent by saying that's he is so; India can become independent only if she can hold her own when the British goes out.'

But Watson was wrong on one count. He had correctly noted Gandhi's reluctance to come to the help of the British. But he should have noted Gandhi's reluctance to launch any mass campaign at all during the war. August uprising took place not because of Gandhi, but in spite of Gandhi's doctrine and policies. No one was clearer than Gandhi in admitting this when he said in a visit to Medinipur after the war that violence had caused more hardship to people than what would have been otherwise, and that the movement had not helped the cause of independence.[10] In a similar way when communal conflicts and violence seemed unending, and the colonial power was using this as the pretext or the cause for not leaving India outright and immediately, Gandhi said with despair, and this Watson noted, 'Let them entrust India to God, or, in modern parlance, to anarchy. Then all parties will fight one another like dogs, or will, when real responsibility faces them, come to a reasonable agreement.'[11]

The complaints and fulminations spoke not only of the presence of two outlooks and responses, but more importantly the way in which politics of truth functioned in a milieu of war, violence, mass uprising and the determination of the colonial power to maintain ways of occupation and control, all of which marked the *international*. When Watson was describing Gandhi as an extremist, he was not only echoing one of the old rules of war, namely *Inter Arma Silent Ledges* (in times of war laws are silent), and therefore Gandhi had no right to remain neutral, but also suggesting that laws of neutrality could not apply to subjugated peoples, and the age-old friend-enemy distinction in politics applied to war situation drastically and without qualification. Gandhi in that sense reflected the vanishing middle position, which marked many other nationalist leaders of Southeast Asia in the war time. Yet this charge of extremism and other appellations tell us more of an important aspect of nationalist politics, and this concerns the way the truth question functioned in nationalist politics particularly before and during the war.

The Congress won the elections in eight provinces in the elections of 1937, a fact that belied the Congress claim that it represented the entire nation. Therefore Gandhi's statements started reflecting this reduced stature of Congress and the caution that the nation was bigger than the Congress. Within Congress this was not the accepted position, and hence C. Rajagopalachari and others soon found themselves taking different positions than the ones taken by Gandhi. But more importantly, Congress did not know how to govern; it thought that it was learning the art by the ropes. But the fact is that the nationalist imagination, structured as it was in a particular way, had no place for imagining new ways of governing *relations*, new techniques, and it had to fall back repeatedly on the colonial ways of rule. Therefore communal relations, industrial relations, land relations and general politico-economic relations worsened further damaging the legitimacy of the Congress. In the absence of a dialogic framework, only competitive politics could flourish – the framework in which modern governmentality functions. The Congress thought that resignation from the ministry was the best way out.

But two factors spoilt such an exit strategy. First was Gandhi's own insistence on non-violent method and the implication of that insistence that Congress must carry everyone else, every part of the nation in its journey, and only then Congress would be able to prove that it was ready to govern the country. Implicit in this instance was a different idea of government – less government yes, but not in the sense of laissez faire, but from the point of autonomy and dialogue. Second was the fact that this was the time of war. With it decolonization took a different character. It established new relations between the national and the international. Both these factors prevented the strategy of withdrawal from the administration from being a success for the Congress in terms of exiting from a situation that was fast closing in on the party, indeed on nationalist politics.

The moment of deadlock appeared in this way. Constituted by factors mentioned just now, the event of 1942 arrived – neither as a programme of the party nor as a programme of the radical nationalists – and when the event left, India was not what it was before 1942 and the war. The moment of truth for the nationalist politics appeared as an extremely disconcerting moment, marked as I have mentioned by the other scene of politics. It is tempting to view the closure as a consequence of a series of binaries, such as (a) anarchy/the emphasis on order, (b) war-time necessities/old politics of democratic agitation, (c) policy of non-violence/all around atmosphere of social war, (d) the intransigence of Gandhi/a flexible party called the Congress, (e) the old nationalist goal of achieving independence/dictates of governmentality and finally (f) the dream of anti-colonialism and freedom/the reality of the international producing the process of decolonization.

Yet we must understand the links between these, which made clear choices difficult, and made the reality of the nationalist journey a complex one. In this sense the complexity of the war-time situation forced the nationalist politics and its principal exponent Gandhi to face the moment of truth. It was particularly ironic for Gandhi because he had all along said that non-violence was linked to the pursuit of truth. We began this book with *Hind Swaraj or the Indian Home Rule* (1909), called by some as 'that incendiary book of the nation'. We can refer to it again in this context. *Hind Swaraj* was perched from the beginning on the following dilemma, namely that the three ways to realize the self (which also implied self-rule), namely, achieving self-respect, self-realization, and finally achieving self-reliance, depended on a successful mode of self-government. He could not elaborate the idea of self-government except in course of his sundry comments on concrete historical situations. And, there was no way Gandhi could have bypassed the question of the state and the related issue of sovereignty in his quest for self-government. Within self-rule therefore lay two related but different things – *state* of the nation and *government* of the self, which presumably would be the way to governing the nation. Gandhi was of course aware of this irreducible dilemma, and he therefore said on the occasion of a later edition of *Hind Swaraj,*

> I would like to say to the diligent reader of my writings and to others who are interested in them that I am not at all concerned with appearing to be consistent. In my search after Truth I have discarded many ideas and learnt many new things. Old as I am in age, I have no feeling that I have ceased to grow inwardly or that

my growth will stop at the dissolution of the flesh. What I am concerned, with is my readiness to obey the call of Truth, my God, from moment to moment, and, therefore, when anybody finds any inconsistency between any two writings of mine, if he has still faith in my sanity, lie would do well to choose the later of the two on the same subject.[12]

The burden of governing

Yet, notwithstanding the fact that Gandhi knew that his views evolved with the evolution of the situation, he as we have seen had positioned himself within the nationalist order of reasoning as a figure of the absolute – absolute value, absolute non-violence, absolute discipline of life – a non-historic position that not only turned a concrete historical situation in the life of the nation into a problem, but it also turned its own position into a problem for the historic nation, for his own party, even for his rival party. As a result, even though the situation was new after the war, in fact, the new situation began with the war, the old politics of sovereignty represented above all by Gandhi failed to realize that with this new situation a new set of relations had appeared. In fact it is impossible not to be struck by the non-correspondence of an idea of sovereignty and the complex reality of a nation caught in all round war – civil, social and international.[13]

In some way, one can say, this situation reminds us of two earlier times of great transition – the transition to East India Company rule in the early part of the second half of the eighteenth century, and then roughly one hundred years later the passage to direct colonial rule after 1857.

On the first instance, we have the two-volume account, *Sier Mutaqherin*, in which the author Syed Ghulam Hussain Khan (Tabatabaite) tells us in detail of the ways in which the old rule was crumbling down, treachery was all around, greed ate into the levels of society and administration and the political oligarchy along with the financial-military clique survived on intrigue and self-serving measures. He tells of the communal riots during the reign of the later Mughal emperor Farukh Siyer (Feroh-syur), repeatedly mentions 'the surrender of common sense', 'vanity' of the aristocracy, the uncertainties of peace, war, and truce in that age, and asks rhetorically who is a 'high sovereign', what are the marks of princely character, princely qualities, and ends his account of the murder of Siraj, the Bengal prince, and the 'display of the mutilated body on the back of an elephant' by saying that the prince was 'slaughtered by way of notifying the accession of new sovereign', and how Mir Zafar began his reign by placing himself 'in the abode of sovereignty'. In fact, Syed Ghulam Hussain tells us, Mir Zafar began his reign in a state of intoxication and then sleep; meanwhile Siraj was murdered, and in an incomparably economic description of the event of transition, Syed Ghulam Hussain quotes the murderer of Siraj, Miran the son of Mir Zafar, as addressing a curious crowd in front of the palace, 'the abode of sovereignty', on receiving the instruction of his father to take care of the custody of Siraj, '"Pray Gentlemen, is not my father a curious man with this message? And indeed as a son to Aaly-verdy-Qhan's sister, how could I prove dilatory in so important a matter?" Such was the end of Seradj-ed-doulah'.[14] Revenge brought in 'revolution'. *Sier Mutaqherin* is not a simple chronicle, massive in size, but an advice to rulers on how to conduct public affairs, and restrict private greed and self-service. Syed Ghulam Hussain tells us that sovereignty passed from the Sultans to the Company because government failed; anarchy ensued because the princes lost the art of governing. Thus though the transfer of sovereignty from one emperor or prince to another was marked regularly by public acts such as ceremonial entry of the new sovereign in the capital, public prayers, display of the standard, coining of money in the new sovereign's name and above all by the murder of the old sovereign and display of the dead body (Tabatabaite of course does not list these like this, but mentions them at several places in his account), rule could not be stable, as besides the confusing presence of so many 'nations' and 'races' (as in Azimabad),[15] mercenary administration, and 'dissensions, ruins and desolation crept under the columns of the Timurian throne',[16] and there was now a 'tremendous sign in the air by which Heaven signified its wrath'.[17] Syed Ghulam Hussain was clear in his advice in this hour of transition, and he put the lines of advice in verse,

'See and take warning / It was in the manner the wind shifted and the face of the thing changed / O World, fickle and fragile! O World, incapable of stability / Like a dancer, that goes everyday from house to house /. . . You shall carry no more with you than what you have enjoyed or bestowed / Do good today, since the field is yours, and have the power of it / Make haste, for the next year the field will pass on to another hand.'[18]

If lines in verse were not enough, he made clear his suggestion that the new methods (of the Company) had become 'natural' in view of their merits, and therefore he ended his massive two-volume account with these words,

> At present our intention is to restrain ourselves to such events only as concern more particularly to the English government in those parts; and we shall attempt to give an idea of the revenue regulations, and of the institutions, which they have established themselves; or which having been introduced by the Viceroys or rulers of their own appointing, have since *passed into a custom and become a law* (italics mine).[19]

Law, the author pointed out, discretely evolved after regulations proved successful in receiving acceptance and became custom before they became laws. Another Ghulam Hussain, Ghulam Hussain Saleem, also wrote in the same vein in *Riaz us Salatin* (1788) in accounting for the way Sultan rule in Bengal ended and gave way to the Company rule. In fact *Riaz us Salatin* ends with these words of lesson comparing the British way of life with the anarchy of the Sultans:

> But the English-Christians are knowledgeable and able to determine their duties and obligations. They are courteous and wise. They are alert and economical in war and eating. No one is equal to them in imposing justice in order to maintain security of the subjects, protection of the weak, and preventing exploitation of the poor. They risk lives to keep pledges, and do not allow liars in their midst. They are broad-minded, reliable, tolerant, and honest. They have not learnt deceit or read the book of treachery. Though there is difference in faith, they do not interfere in the faith, laws, and religion of the Muslims.[20]

We of course know that in less than one hundred years of these words being written, everything mentioned here as the virtue of the new race was belied. But interesting is the way in which Ghulam Hussain Saleem saw certain virtues as the root of politico-military success, virtues that prevented anarchy and made government possible. Nearly one hundred and fifty years later almost, around the time when Gandhi was writing those lines we mentioned earlier in this chapter, the *Sier* again surfaced in discussions on sovereignty. The famous essayist of Bengal Qazi Abdul Wadud referred repeatedly to *Sier Mutaqherin* as one of most graphic chronicles of the 'closed destiny of Bengal' when light simply went out of Bengal's life.[21]

In the first instance then we find the early symptoms of a state trying to grow within the rubric of an empire – a process cut short by colonial intervention. But the more interesting part of that time is the fact that not only the legitimacy of the government depended on power, power in this case denoting actual military authority, but the presence of government depended on the existence of a strong ruler. In this closed situation where state could grow only if there were an effective government, and effective government could be a reality only if there was a strong ruler, and a ruler could be strong only if he had the backing of actual military power and actual military power could materialize only if the revenue extracting authority could link up with avenues and institutions of trade, wealth and prosperity – as the *Sier* tells us, murders and anarchy indicated a complete void. The crisis of governing had enveloped the entire society.

Now we can briefly have a look at the second instance I have in mind. We find a similar strain in Mirza Ghalib's writings in the wake of Delhi's downfall in 1857 – again the same idea that with imperial governance being reduced to zero, and the aristocracy not having the knowledge, skill and determination to govern while problems of unruly relations mounted, Delhi the seat of sovereignty would have fallen.[22] Ghalib spoke of the fleeting nature of sovereignty in those days, 'a cup of wine, which constantly changes hands', not like the one reserved exclusively for Jamshed, the Persian king who could look into his chalice and find out what was happening to the world. 'Now every English soldier that bears arms / Is sovereign, and free to work his will . . . / The city is thirsty for Muslim blood / And every grain of dust must drink its fill.'[23] 'The Muslim never became a true ruler at any time'. The West had science and technology and other means to govern. Yet, unlike Syed Ghulam Hussain, who saw merits in new regulations being issued by the new power and gradually becoming custom and then law, Ghalib was sceptical of the new ways of governing, and wondered what was this administration, when 'Everyday in this city a new law is proclaimed / One just cannot understand what happens here'.[24] Again the same lesson on transition, namely that sovereignty is not the only key issue; modes of governing become important as changes gather steam. This is not to suggest that the times of 1757, 1857 and 1939 were same, or the reason of governing had the same character. Yet, it is remarkable how the question of governmentality arose repeatedly and remained a mark of a closed situation in modern time.

Ayesha Jalal in her magisterial work on *Self and Sovereignty* (2001) shows in great detail how in a period of transition sovereignty becomes a complicated contest, when the question becomes: sovereignty of the self, of the community or of the political power, or at times dual sovereignty? This was exactly the idea that Gandhi was expressing in his own way; yet as I show, inbuilt in this problematic of sovereignty during transition is the issue of governing. Ayesha Jalal's own account also lends such a reading, though she thinks it is still a problem of the cultural nation, not primarily a question of power in the time of transition configured in terms of governing. Her account that begins with Ghalib and ends with Iqbal, therefore, still consigns the nation in that void I have referred to earlier, and shows no exit route. She can only cite Iqbal's poignant lines (a comment of 1924 addressed towards the Muslims of the subcontinent) to end her book:

> Don't compare your nation with the nations of the West / Distinctive is the nation of the Prophet of Islam / Their solidarity depends on territorial nationality / Your solidarity rests on the strength of your religion / When faith slips away, where is the solidarity of the community? / And, when the community is no more, neither is the nation.[25]

Perhaps we are stressing all this too much, perhaps all these analyses are products of hindsight, but clearly at least in our own nationalist time we have here the politics of truth at play – the truth of the nation, the truth of competing ideas of the nation, the truth of transition, the truth of Gandhi, the truth of war, the truth of the relations between communities requiring to be governed, the truth of mass uprising, the truth that Congress could govern the nation only by copying colonial methods and finally the truth of colonialism and decolonization. The politics of truth was thus constituted by several discourses besides being bolstered by the rhetorical quality of the old nationalist discourse. In this situation as I have indicated Gandhi tried to repeat an old ploy: once again suggesting reconstruction activities besides the vocation of politics. But this time, the techniques of self (as means to strengthen nationalism, such as spinning, cattle rearing, farming or fasting,) failed in face of the techniques of domination. Governing people, he found, was not the same thing as governing the self. Recurrent fast, as a technique, had its value diminishing. In the all-round atmosphere of wars, slaughters and despotism, his techniques appeared as geared towards producing individual subject of an ethical world – the classic individual *satyagrahi*, the lonely individual seeker of truth. He wanted to do away with history (of war, violence and sovereignty) and the modern ways of governing and power – in short the two ways in which political reason of our time functions, and replace them with the truth seeking subject, who must learn how to govern his or her soul in place of modern governmental ways in order to persevere on the path of truth. But this was the moment when the centrality of the subject was being substituted by the centrality of the question of position and action based on that position. Truth seemed to elude any objective criterion.

The lessons of the nationalist closure are not to be dismissed lightly. We cannot think that a socialist orientation (that is revolution, class struggle, violent means, etc.) would have been able to create the subject of freedom, and was therefore the way out. A similar deadly closure affected socialist politics in mid and late eighties of the past century; socialism has not fared better, and the enigma of transition has not still cleared up. Maybe the lesson is that politics of sovereignty as the core of a politics of freedom will not work anymore, or at least not in the way in which it worked earlier. Maybe that to escape the tribulations of transition, we have to learn new ways of governing, which will transcend the iron rules of modern governmentality, and will combine the daily flexibility of dialogic autonomies. Maybe we shall have to learn new mode of combining the national and the international. In short, perhaps we shall have to learn new techniques of the national-popular.

Notes

1 On the riots and the summoning of the police see Nandini Gooptu, *The Politics of the Urban Poor in Early Twentieth Century India* (Cambridge: University of Cambridge, 2005), pp. 129–132.

2 Gandhi, "Our Failure," in M. K. Gandhi, *Non-Violence in Peace and War* (hereafter *NVPW*), 2 volumes (Volume 1, Ahmedabad: Navajiban Publishing House, 1942 and Volume 2, Ahmedabad: Navajiban Publishing House, 1949), Volume 1, pp. 142–144.

3 Reprinted in Mushirul Hasan (ed.), *India's Partition – Process, Strategy and Mobilization* (New Delhi: Oxford University Press, 1993), pp. 44–45.

4 I have already written on the role of death in the lives and tracts authored by militant nationalists. See, R. Samaddar, *The Materiality of Politics*, 2 Volumes (London: Anthem Press, 2007), Chapter 2, "Terror, Law, and the Colonial State", Volume 1.

5 On the instances involving Mukherjee and Sanyal we can read with interest a hitherto unpublished note on a meeting between Gandhi and Charles Teggart, the Calcutta Police Commissioner, on 25 June 1925. The record of the meeting was left in the form of a note by Teggart in his papers. We owe this information to Amiya Samanta, who has summarized the note for our benefit in a two-part published article, "Strange Meeting", *The Statesman*, 30–31 January 2009.

6 For instance, "The Purpose of the Tour", *Harijan*, 26 January 1947, *NVPW*, Volume 2, p. 197; in it he appreciated Subhas Chandra Bose's success in maintaining communal harmony in the Indian national Army; also, "The New Experiment" in *NVPW*, Volume 2, p. 200; more significantly his writings in 1946 on the INA and the prisoners, *NVPW*, Volume 2, pp. 33–41.

7 For Gandhi's comments on Tamluk, "Non-Violence and Molestation of Women", *Harijan*, 10 February 1946, and "Non-Violent Technique and Parallel Government", *Harijan*, 17 February 1946 – *NVPW*, Volume 2, pp. 6–10; for his short notes and prayer speeches on Noakhali, *NVPW*, Volume 2, pp. 188–199.

8 *Harijan*, 18 August 1949, *NVPW*, Volume 1, p. 334.

9 Alfred Watson, *India's Extremists and the Axis – Would the Indian Congress Party Aid the War? Facts Sweeping Away Much of the Nonsense Talked about India* (London: Great Britain and the East Limited, 1943/ National Archives, Delhi, embargoed till 1972).

10 Gandhi, "Non-Violent Technique and Parallel Government", *Harijan*, 17 February 1946, *NVPW*, Volume 2, pp. 8–11.

11 Watson cited Viceroy Linlithgo, who said, 'It is because agreement cannot be reached between the conflicting interests in this country as to who is to take over the responsibilities which Britain is only too ready to transfer to Indian hands that the deadlock has arisen. It is from no reluctance on our part to transfer them.' Watson concluded the tract with the comment, 'But Great Britain cannot contemplate anarchy in India with, the calm indifference to the fate of its people that Mr. Gandhi professes.' *India's Extremists and the Axis*, p. 26.

12 "Preface to the New Edition", *Harijan*, 29 April, 1933, p. 2.

13 After the war, Gandhi expressed similar feelings, when he wrote a note, "The Real Danger", *Harijan*, 14 July 1946, *NVPW*, Volume 2, pp. 100–102.

14 Syed Ghulam Hussain Khan (Tabatabaite), *Sier Mutaqherin Being the History of India from the Year 1118 to the Year 1194 (This Year Answer to the Christian Year of 1781–82) of the Hadjirah Containing in General the Reigns of the Seven Last Emperors of Hindostan and in Particular an Account of Bengal with Circumstantial Detail of the Rise and Fall of the Families of Seradj-ed-Dowlah and Shujah-ed-Dowlah, the Last Sovereigns of Bengal and Oud to Which the Author Has Added a Critical Examination of the English Government and Policy in Those Countries Down to the Year 1783, the Whole Written in Persian By Seid Ghulam Hossain Khan, an Indian Nobleman of High Rank Who Wrote Both as an Actor and as Spectator*, trans. Nota Manas, or Hajee Mustapha, or M. Raymond, 2 Volumes (London and Kolkata: R. Cambray and Co., 1789; reprint, Kolkata: Royal Asiatic Society of Bengal, 1902), Volume 2, p. 244.

15 Khan, *Sier Mutaqherin*, Volume 1, p. 97 (Azimabad is known as Patna today).

16 Ibid., p. 101.

17 Ibid., p. 201.

18 Khan, *Sier Mutaqherin*, Volume 2, p. 243.

19 Ibid., p. 587.

20 Ghulam Hussain Saleem, *Riaz us Salatin*, translated in Bengali by Akbaruddin as *Bangler Itihas* from the English version prepared by Abdus Salam Riaz from original Persian in 1904 (Dhaka: Bangla Academy, 1974), p. 205.
21 Qazi Abdul Wadud, *Saswata Banga* (1959, Dhaka: BRAC, 1983); see for instance, pp. 163–166, 209.
22 On this I have taken recourse to Ralph Russell and Khurshid Islam (eds.), *Ghalib 1797–1869 – Life and Letters* (New Delhi: Oxford University Press, 1994).
23 Ibid., p. 149.
24 Cited by Ayesha Jalal in Ayesha Jalal, *Self and Sovereignty – Individual and Community in South Asian Islam since 1850* (Lahore: Sang-e-Meel Publications, 2001), p. 32.
25 Ibid., p. 578.

3 The power of the aesthetic and a different style of governing the self

We are still in that time when governing meant inculcating a distinct way of life – practising the art of living in a distinct way. In that context if Gandhi's vision indicated a particular way of emphasizing government of the self, Tagore's vision stressed the aesthetic mode in which the country could practice self-government.

Rabindranath Tagore lived a long life and his life spanned a period beginning with the robust growth of anti-colonialism to almost the end of the nationalist time. He also, almost (with some exaggeration we can say) single-handedly, transformed a language (Bengali language) beyond recognition from its mid-nineteenth-century form to the versatile shape in which he left in order for the language to become a language of many universes that we live in and traverse, namely, poetry, essay writing, philosophical speculation, political essays and analysis, drama, commentary, satire, letter writing, journal keeping, grammar composition, music and songs, child literature, travelogues and not to say the least, state running.

It is futile to search for the source of this creativity, and try to arbitrarily make it contemporary, because such creativity has defied our sense of time and epoch, and will therefore remain contemporary as well as classic, that is to say, present yet marking the time of its origin and subsequent history. Out of the confluence of many trends over centuries and emerging from within a (felt) void such aesthetic subject emerges with a burst of creativity that we wait for centuries to re-emerge. Yet what is often ignored amid the deluge of praise, commemoration and admiration is the question: What made possible for a language to attain such leap? Or, to be more precise, what made possible what we may call the 'aesthetic turn' and made it relevant to the entire range of sensibilities in the life of the colonized? In an attempt to find that answer we shall not only become alert to an important contemporary question, but also find out the locus of classicality in the nation's mind and life.

But before we begin that inquiry, we must also calmly consider the necessity of this inquiry. Consider the madness about Tagore in Bengal fifty three years ago on the occasion of the celebration of the birth centenary of the poet, reminding us of the way songs were sung, meetings were held and publications blossomed – the ecstasy of a massive devotional public spread all through the land. The government participated both at central and state levels, Satyajit Ray made the famous documentary on the poet and the centenary edition of Tagore's works came out making for the first time his entire works accessible to readers. In Bangladesh, then East Pakistan, the centenary occasioned a surge of linguistic creativity and study of Tagore amid all obstacles and prejudices. China, Japan, Europe, Soviet Union – cultural delegations from India went far and wide to these countries on that occasion. Delegations from abroad visited India. It seemed, even with the failure and breakdown of hope of the fifties, nation's ideals were still alive and the desire to bring back the creativity of the bygone years, besmirched by famine, bloodshed and Partition, was still strong. But now that fervour is absent, the energy has withered and the misery of life ravaged by various fault lines seems to have exhausted our love for the aesthetic. So, the big question: Have we passed that stage? Has the post-colonial misery consumed us? What has happened to the aesthetic subject that helped our nationalism grow?

Foundations of a new way of thinking

In recent years there have been some writings on Rabindranath which seek to examine the applicability of his thoughts, ideas and outlook in discussing affairs of the nation. By and large they have concluded that either his ideas are too contradictory or nebulous (perhaps befitting a poet) to be of any practical value or antiquated to be of interest in this globalized time. People have noted in his lectures in Japan, China and England his resistance to nationalism, and have asked if he was creating a new path of cosmopolitanism. Much of this is unexceptionable, save that all these he did as a *Bengali*, most of the time working his way through while being situated in Bengal, that too often in rural Bengal, to the extent that someone like Ramchandra Guha while appreciating Tagore's cosmopolitanism has complained that people in Bengal want to see him as a Bengali, and that Tagore could not have been satisfied with provincial adulation and devotion.[1] In short, the complaint is that the cosmopolitan in Tagore was often hindered and minimized by his provincial roots and milieu. Shakespeare and Goethe – the two with whom Rabindranath has been most compared – did not have to face this complaint in their lives or after-life careers. But this only shows that Tagore could not escape the post-colonial destiny.

Clearly Rabindranath had made a choice or several choices: he chose to be open to external influences, and he travelled extensively, interacted widely and developed an idea of what he called 'humanity' again and again in his poems, essays, lectures, stories and novels. Yet he wrote almost solely in Bengali, Bengal was his nation, in as much as India was the nation. Benedict Anderson in *Under the Three Flags* writing of the life and death of Filipino revolutionary nationalist Jose Rizal writes of the confluence of anti-colonial imagination with cosmopolitan ideas, and says how imperial subjection created openings into the broader universe beyond the nation, as the early nationalists tried to make connections with other nationalists within the same imperial universe.[2] Rizal who was a novelist and a revolutionary and died facing a firing squad wrote in Spanish. Tagore went beyond the British imperial universe in his aesthetic search for truth, beauty and humanity. Of course, his knowledge of English helped him. Yet all these found expression in his working in Bengali language. Aesthetics and language – these two choices of his life were remarkable in his negotiation with nation and nationalism. Probably while theoreticians of nationalism have pointed out many elements of a nationalist universe – maps, media, culture, memory, history, kinship, sense of economic subordination and so on – they have paid inadequate attention to the role aesthetics (within which language has its part) plays in the making of the anti-colonial mind – national yet cosmopolitan.

This was, however, not unique in Tagore's case. In the nineteenth- and early twentieth-century Europe, likewise in Latin America, such a combination was visible. These regions have their distinct histories. What was unique in Rabindranath's case was that unlike in the case of Europe or Latin America he did not inherit a vast linguistic zone (Spanish in Latin America) or a zone of multiple contacts and fluidity (Europe and Eastern Europe in particular with three multinational empires present – Russian, Ottoman and Austro-Hungarian). He had to rely on travels, imagination, ideas of nature (both Nature and human nature), reading, literary sense, his own philosophical sense (as opposed to common sense) and religiosity (again distinct from the usual sense of the term) to build up the *spirit of the unbound*. We have to note here the power of inspiration. In this sense, choice meant a resurrection of agency, of subjectivity – an escape from the trap of identity. But this resurrection of agency would not mean aggressive nationalism and imperial violence he found in Japan and the West. He condemned such nationalisms, because they went against his idea of humanity. He could arrive at such an idea of the human through his overwhelming engagement with the aesthetic aspects of life and existence. In all these, summarized as choice, Rabindranath was working for the recognition of the aesthetic subject.[3]

Therefore, commentators are only partially correct when they say that they can make sense of the political ideas of Tagore without referring to his poems or his life as a poet, but one can also say, his life as a painter, dramatist, playwright, educationist, pedagogue, story writer, singer, composer, and not the least, linguist. It does not mean that we cannot discuss him in a specific sense, but that we cannot forget that the aesthetic loomed large over his views, deeds and the entire range of creation. Aesthetic inquiries developed in him the *spirit of the unbound.*

In arriving at an understanding of truth and beauty that would brook no interference of pragmatism, empiricism and realism, many things must have played parts. Commentators on Rabindranath have routinely mentioned and then ignored the fact that he was born and grew up in the colonial world of the nineteenth century. We have to see what it concretely means.

Briefly speaking it means, first, that he had a chance to distinguish between anti-colonialism and nationalism. In the twentieth century particularly after the advent of Gandhi this became impossible in India. Nationalism became the only possible ideology of the colonized world. In the nineteenth century this was not the case. Tagore grew up in a more discerning milieu – still not overwhelmed by ideas of constitutionalism, nationalism and the Congress Party, the three symbols of political modernity in India.

Second, the nineteenth century could still afford him the time to play with different philosophical thoughts and form his own philosophy from different thoughts. Thus the *Upanashads, Sankhya* ideas, some elements of Buddhism, devotional philosophy including the Vaishnava thought, mysticism (which attracted him to the *Bauls*), mendicant traditions along with many other notions formed in Rabindranath a chiaroscuro of ideas. He was a poet. Therefore, he did not care to systematize them. If he were a nineteenth-century philosopher, he would have gone further than Ram Mohan in presenting systematic tracts on Vedanta and Brahmo Dharma, particularly when the cult was in crisis in the wake of the split between *adi* and the followers of Keshab Chandra Sen (1865), and the reconstitution of the *sadharan samaj* (1880). Here too he made a choice. It was double. After making peace with the quarrels within the Brahmo Sabha and later Samaj and choosing his side, he went ahead to mingle his broad understanding with engagements with other possible aspects of life. He was not a doctrinaire. He would say doctrinal truth was not Truth. We must use here a phrase dear to Marxists of classical age, namely, *worldview*. That is where aesthetics kept on working as if secretly to produce the eclectic Rabindranath. Like Picasso, he lived long, passed through many ages, took up and left by the wayside many styles. His enormous respect for Ram Mohan was possible because of the open-ended universe of the nineteenth century. On this sense of openness he built his ideas of modernity. He could become a critical modernist because the more nationalism grew the more he developed an outlook of non-correspondence with his time (recall the debates with Gandhi and with terrorist revolutionaries) – almost a situation where aesthetics dictated his ethics, and certainly nationalist ethics.

Third, nineteenth century was still the time when grammarians held the rein of language. Rabindranath mastered grammar and drove the chariot of language built on that mastery. In several ways this would have been difficult later. Nineteenth century was the time when several regional languages came into their own present forms. In case of Bengali it meant de-linking from Sanskrit, and linking up with other traditions of the language from the sixteenth century. That required innovation, a certain kind of fluidity to be able to travel back through centuries, and capacity to traverse back and forth the worlds of poetry and prose. This is important. It is of course not difficult to see that he was fortunate in his time. He had great prose writers and great poets before him. Michael Madhusudan Dutta and Bankim Chandra preceded him. And this allowed him to develop the capability to traverse both the worlds in his aesthetic pursuits. Others later took advantage of the openings he made. But it was in nineteenth century that Bengali language attained its famous plasticity. Language allowed him to see things in a different way. In this, possibly, we can remember Iqbal when we speak of Rabindranath.[4]

All these three aspects – ability to make a distinction between anti-colonialism and nationalism, eclecticism in philosophical outlook and capacity to play with language – which I have said were nineteenth-century legacies enabled Rabindranath to constitute a new meaning of freedom. When 1905 (the first Partition of Bengal) arrived Rabindranath was ready to meet the crisis in his unique way.

The aesthetic interrogations

In many ways the first decade of the twentieth century found Tagore at the height of his inspiration, power and creativity. He was still not a savant. The global recognition was still quite some years away. He still had not started philosophising. He put his huge energy in social commentaries besides writing poems and building his dream institution of the new human in Santiniketan. His direct experiences of the nationalist movement of that decade were invaluable, and he was to draw upon them again and again. Hence is the importance of 1905 in our discussion.

He produced around this time an unbelievable number of poems, stories and novels, with his poems and songs in particular celebrating nature. Bengal became nature to him around this time – the romantic land now to be cut into two. And, it was precisely this celebration of Bengal as an idea – emblem of beauty and nature – that dissuaded him from thinking of Bengal as a clearly defined dominant group of people. He therefore could not equate the land with any particular population group, howsoever dominant that group may have been. So as soon as he understood that Muslims and low-caste groups were suspicious of the hegemonic ambitions of upper-caste Hindus who were opposing the Partition, he started reasoning that the Swadeshi movement with such divide could not effectively articulate the objective of nationhood. The movement according to him had the duty to recognize that the Muslims and low castes saw in the Swadeshi and the boycott campaign an insidious attempt to take away the limited opportunities that they had gained under colonial rule. If nationhood contained truth, then it must widen the concept of humanity. If it encouraged divisions and monopolization of power, then it was not representative of human truth, and therefore that path had to be discarded. In his inimitable style based on moral-aesthetic-political elements that made something uniquely social yet ethical, he wrote in 'Bangabibhag' referring to the division, if divisions remained within the society, why blame the outsiders that they had utilized the same for the partition or division of the society? Therefore he urged the countrymen and women to begin work for unity leaving behind the effort to appease or appeal the colonial rulers to be kind to the ruled and abrogate the act of Partition of Bengal. The people must realize what had caused in the first place the weakness that allowed the rulers to make use of that weakness, what the roots were, and whither the path of remedy lay. He said,

> Who can divide us if the roots of relations are spread deep between the west and the east (of Bengal, now to stand divided)? If power from outside wants to break us, the force of love will protect.[5]

Invoking in this way the theme of desire against power – the power/ desire opposition and dichotomy – a theme the philosopher Deleuze was to play on in his own writings many decades later, the poet went on to say,

> Where we are strong, we shall remain resolute. Where it is our duty, we shall remain aware and be responsible for it. Where we have our soul mates (in Bengali *atmiya*), we shall place our faith and reliance. We shall be never unhappy or dejected. We shall never say that with one act of the government our all round doom is scripted. If that were to be so, then we shall never be saved with an act of cleverness or an opportunity got through providence or government mercy . . . [6]

He further wrote, 'We have demanded closeness and brotherhood from them without ever trying to be close to them. . . . We imagine that the Mother has become real for the whole country through songs and emotional ecstasy alone.'[7] How could the nation allow this we / they division (caste-educated Hindus on one hand and Muslims and Namasudras on the other), when truth disallowed such split? There are countless instances to show that this type of reasoning did not grow from only *bhakti* or devotion, or even what in banal language is called romanticism, but an eclectic combination of rationality, devotion, mysticism and romanticism that made it possible for him to develop an attitude uniquely social at the same time aesthetic. It is this power of the aesthetic that enabled him to search throughout his life for singularities within Nature – a sense of Deleuzian *fold*.

The truth of Rabindranath's larger criticism is not to be missed. This is about the dialogic virtue the nation form seemed to lack. He said, we had never conversed, we had never attempted to understand other experiences, and our power was fragmented because we were non-dialogic. What for then is a language if we cannot converse? In asking his fellow Bengalis to be dialogic, he was refusing the indulgence we allow the artists and men of letters who devote their energy in building a monolithic nation at the cost of marginalizing and at times expelling several groups, while paradoxically he was suggesting at the same time that the nation may not be the only legitimate category of analysis even though it remained an important locus of power in the modern world. This is how we must make sense of Rabindranath composing the songs *Banglar mati, Banglar jal* or *Bidhir bandhan katbe tumi emon saktiman*, to be followed by *Ghare Baire*. If in one the land is Nature, in the other nation has betrayed our inner self, our *nature*, and the woman (Bimala) – all that is to be loved and adored. This is the power of the aesthetic that can prise open the aporia of politics.

We can even say that his responses to the Partition of 1905 and the Swadeshi movement showed the double play of convergence and non-convergence – the two elements involved in any excess. What his poems could not conceive was conceived in his letters, stories, novels, essays and addresses. What his addresses, essays, novels, stories and letters did not tell was there in his poems. These 'acts of literature', to borrow a phrase from Jacques Derrida,[8] were constantly producing excesses only to find expression in other forms and acts. Excesses are finally the products of the joint operation of correspondence and non-correspondence. There were also other phases in Tagore's life that expressed the same dual play of correspondence and non-correspondence. The last decade of his life – the decade of thirties in the past century – was one such phase. As inter-nation rivalry grew, threats of inter-imperialist war became real, devastation within the country and communal split became irrevocable and the Indian National Congress seemed clueless as to how to face the world and unite the nation, the future in this time of drift seemed bleak to him. The poems composed in this decade appear to address the future (*Aji hote shotobor-sho porey*); he seems to have lost interest in the contemporary except the contemporary life on the margins (*Cheleta, Camelia*). Destiny and a sense of impending death combined to make him face the fundamentals of life, his paintings become what his poems (at least most of his poems) never could be, and except faith in humanity and a hope that East will replace the declining West (possibly an influence of Spengler and others) there was nothing left for him.[9] Again, what is critical here is his idea of an aesthetic life, and not just aesthetics in life, propelling him forward. I do not intend to say that he had before him a fundamental text of aesthetics on the basis of which he acted as the aesthetic subject. But notions of art, beauty, truth, literature, ethics and spirit, while changing in their import or relative significance over the years, remained constant in order to make the human. With this sense of the self and the practices of self, Rabindranath faced 1905, 1919, and in particular 1941, the greatest crisis of his faith, and eventual death.

Therefore politics of the nation journeyed back to him again and again even though he criticized nationalist politics. Leaders listened to him. Revolutionaries read him. Martyrs sang him before they died. He was the voice of the nation because he had exceeded the nation; belonging to it, he had surpassed it. The nation could become a nation only in accepting him. The power of aesthetic subjectivity allowed him the transcendence.

Rabindranath came closest to an open acknowledgement of the power of the aesthetic in his novel *Gora* (1909).[10] At once a novel and a manifesto, a political critique and a philosophical statement, a fictive work but immensely historical – *Gora* was an authentic act of literature. Aesthetic power allowed Rabindranath to turn the novel into a literary *act*. By *literary act* I mean acting through literary mode on society, history and the contemporary time. How did Rabindranath achieve it? Tanika Sarkar in her study of the novel points out the multiple displacements the novelist makes us experience through the novel.[11] Gora is Indian but fair skinned like the European or like Sri Chaitanya. Gora is caste Hindu, but he realizes towards the end that his birth is linked to the Mutiny of 1857 and European parentage. Gora adores the motherland and wants to empathize with the conditions of the low caste, Muslims and other marginal groups, but values the customs and rituals of caste Hindus. Gora's past, one may say, is Bankim Chandra's hero in *Anandamath*, who discovers the mother goddess instructing him to slay the Muslims to make the nation an organic whole capable of making it free of alien rule. Gora's future is in a nation that must accept all singularities to be genuinely free. Gora loves a woman who is rational and will not agree to caste ascriptions, arrogance and domination. This love is in conflict with Gora's love for his imagined motherland redolent with past cultural glory of an ancient Hindu civilization. Love of all kinds in intense conflict with each other – love for the past/present, nature/people, chosen people/ the marginal groups, territory/inhabitants, race/cosmopolitanism, and most significantly, man/woman.

Nation to be worthy of humanity and thus capable of serving truth must effect all these displacements. Politics cannot do it. The swadeshi movement had proved it. Economic nationalism cannot achieve this. Mere emotion cannot ensure it as his own experiences had brought this truth home to him. He realized: songs had been sung, poems had been written as odes to motherland; bombs had been thrown. Muslim peasants' huts had been torched. Foreign goods had been burnt and boycotted. Yet the agitators had not been able to win over different sections of the nation. Even the ethical call to self-sacrifice in the form of a monk's service to the nation (Vivekananda's call, perhaps symbolized by Gora; also the story of Brahmabandhab Upadhyay) was not adequate.

This then forms the background of Rabindranath's search for an aesthetic life, which encompasses all aspects of the nation, yet transcends its form. This search continued from *Gora* (1909) to *Ghare Baire* (1916). It was a search in which various forms of love engaged in mutual attrition; and the theme of love – always contingently defined – finally resolved the dilemma. Or, as Tanika Sarkar seems to suggest, love showed that the conflict remained unresolvable, and we could only pass from one form to another. In any case the theme of love allowed Rabindranath to interrogate each specific milieu with greater rigour, face the 'grounded patriots' with the possibility that there could be other legitimate though unstable locations from which to construct one's land – the nation – and thereby face politics with the power of the aesthetic.

Local and the cosmopolitan – the aesthetic link

Not only contradictions of life but contradictions of location and virtues were to be negotiated by the power of the aesthetic. Observers have noted two different meanings, resonances and intonations, in his two distinct appearances[12] – as Rabindranath and as Tagore. Rabindranath the local, the vernacular, poet, romantic, singer, composer, the celebrator of leisure and the idle vagabond, who loved above all the freedom of life, the freedom with life; and, Tagore who was the philosopher, the seer who addressed the world and humanity at large, the responsible, the symbol of cosmopolitan virtues, the famous, the polemicist, the wise and the rational voice of India. If this is true, and that there is some valuable insight in this, then one can say this had two implications – one, the fluidity of the space in between the two virtues and locations; second, the truth of subjectivity that made this fluidity possible. Rabindranath said of this subject within him, 'Spark got its wings' rhythm for a moment / It flew, then spent itself / but this was its pleasure, its moment of joy.' Or, in different words, the same expression of fleeting autonomy, 'How easy it is / to mock the sun: / the light by which / it is caught / is its own.'[13]

He, of course, increasingly disliked the world role that modernity had thrust on him. That became his terrible burden. Yet as he realized the power of aesthetics and started welding it, he could at best self-mock, resort to occasional irony, but could no longer be the 'natural poet' – better expressed in the Bengali phrase *swabhab kabi*. Virtue proved to be too much a burden for him. Aesthetics as power could then become a fetter for creative pursuits. Radice reminds us of what the poet wrote to his friend C. F. Andrews from New York in 1921, 'When the touch of spring is in the air, I suddenly wake up from my nightmare of giving "messages" and remember that I belong to the eternal band of good-for-nothings; I hasten to join in the vagabond chorus. But I hear the whisper around me: "This man has crossed the sea" and my voice is choked.' His prose became even more witty, sharp and imaginative at the same time. Today it is difficult for those who read him in translation to imagine its power and spell on the readers. As indicated at the outset, by mastery of language and his position as almost the ultimate craftsman of the medium, he could invoke a power capable of facing the political and other intellectual forces of his time. As he himself would say,

> Tumultuous days
> Rush towards night.
> Seas are the goal
> Of streams in full spate.
> Impatient spring-flowers
> Long to be fruit.
> Restlessness strives
> To be calm and complete.

Language should allow one the sovereignty in own world as he would say often, and he would wonder as to why this recognition would have to wait for recognition from afar, across the shores, from imperial land as to the merits of one's work, precisely because that aesthetic world created by language was untranslatable, and any outside recognition was therefore accidental, and almost superfluous. Yet, it was this aesthetic power which took away to some extent from what was Rabindranath in order to create the person we know as Tagore, but also enabled him to bridge a connection between the two. His life as the founder of Visva Bharati, the educational institution, was one instance of this bridge. There were others. The debates with Gandhi were another occasion when he could unite his two selves – intellectual argument and aesthetic vision of freedom. Equally significantly in the novels *Chaturanga* and *Char Adhyaya*, where he was continuing his polemics with revolutionary nationalists, he carried the structuralist method introduced some time back in Bengali literature (besides others by him also) to deploy various artistic and literary tools with devastating effect. We may or may not like their political content, but these come back to us again and again forcing us to engage with the arguments and ideas suggested there. This power which he acquired through practice of decades was too much for him to leave aside and become the rural bard of Bengal. He could combine his two selves in poems also, as we read one of his most famous poems, *Prashna* (translated by Radice),

> My voice is choked today;
> I have no music in my flute:
> Black moonless night has imprisoned my

world, plunged it into nightmare.
And this is why, with tears in my eyes,
I ask: Those who have poisoned
your air, those who have extinguished your light,
Can it be that you forgave them?
Can it be that you love them?

We have to wait here. We can see this is not a complaint, but high-lighting through the technique of rhetoric a state of injury. It is at one level a complaint against God, against the colonial and imperial powers, industrial monsters and moneybags, but at a more powerful level it is expressing one's helplessness, a sustained *state of injury*. In the poem *Dui Bigha Jami* again what is brought out is wound, a state of injury. In this state of injury, which cannot by definition be entirely political, but markedly spiritual, Tagore could suggest that no political doctrine could have an invariable, fixed meaning. Therefore with his usual irony he would say,

> When I get the news that somebody has tried to extract my politi-cal, social, or religious views from my writings, then I know for sure that his own opinion on the subject will be mixed up with my opinion. When the lawyer's explanation uses documents as wit-nesses then the end result cannot be counted as evidence. Because the opposition lawyer too will use the same documents to say the opposite thing; that is why, the particular meaning of extracts from writings depends entirely upon the selection made.[14]

Therefore, he was not only asserting that no amount of citation and interpretation could exhaust the meanings and implications of what the poet was saying, because he was not a political scientist but one situated in a state of injury engaged now in search of human truths, his denunciation of nationalism was also beyond the usual analysis. He therefore said,

> Even though from childhood I have been taught that idolatry of the nation is almost better than reverence to God and humanity, I believe I have outgrown that teaching, and it is my conviction that my countrymen will truly gain their India by fighting against the education which teaches them that a country is greater than the ideals of humanity.[15]

Finding the human in a state of injury allowed him to form a new idea of freedom, which would be able to address the injuries of indignity due to marginalization and subordination. Colonial legality, education, bureaucracy all these only served to perpetuate this state of injury. In such a world, only freedom to vote or to go to school or to participate in the affairs of the Indian National Congress could not address the condition. Freedom of nature with which Rabindranath began must now transform into freedom from injury, indignity, which is to say, freedom of life itself. This notion of sustainable freedom, able to cope with state of injury and indignity, kept him free of liberal trap and provided the bridge between Rabindranath and Tagore. Tagore may have been a person of the world, but he was not on a liberal voyage. His critical aesthetics sustained his inquiry into conditions of humanity – the human condition, the lasting state of injury. Contemporary reflections on him in the wake of new thinking in India in the past two three decades have moved away from the earlier literary and a biography-based understanding of him. But the intellectual debates on him in the process of moving away from earlier line of discussion have done away with Rabindranath altogether – the aesthetic visionary who wanted to introduce a new style of living. As a result these reflections while having many new things to say have ended up in closures of all kinds, some of which I have indicated earlier.

This idea of a new style of leading one's life – was it new? Throughout the nineteenth century, anti-colonial and extra-colonial thinking, which in many cases was also early modern thinking, had to contend with the question: how to make sense of life that was gone possibly forever after the British conquest? In this sense, contrary to what some commentators of Enlightenment have said, modernity's main quest was not simply who we are and what sense we make of our present history, but who we were, what changes have been brought upon us and a sense of a discerning judgement on our past. He had once said,

> Perhaps it is well for me to explain that the subject-matter of the papers published in this book has not been philosophically treated, nor has it been approached from the scholar's point of view. The writer has been brought up in a family where texts of the Upanishads are used in daily worship; and he has had before him the example of his father, who lived his long life in the closest communion with God, while not neglecting his duties to the world, or allowing his keen interest in all human affairs to suffer any abatement. So in these papers, it may be hoped, western readers will have an opportunity of coming into touch with the ancient spirit of India as revealed in our sacred texts and manifested in the life of to-day. . . .

For western scholars the great religious scriptures of India seem to possess merely a retrospective and archaeological interest; but to us they are of living importance, and we cannot help thinking that they lose their significance when exhibited in labelled cases – mummified (in original, 'mummied') specimens of human thought and aspiration, preserved for all time in the wrappings of erudition.[16]

Naturally in this quest from Ram Mohan Roy onwards, ethical, social, religious, literary, philosophical, economic and not the least political – all kinds of inquiry proceeded. Gradually from mid-nineteenth century we find less and less the idea of returning to the past, but of a new style of life based on a critical inheritance of the past – we can even precisely say whence, that is from Madhusudan onwards – and thus a selective, critical attitude in order to make one's modernity. Even the most nationalist journal in the first decade of the twentieth century, *Jugantar*, adopted a discerning outlook. More than inventing new forms, the emphasis was on mixing and experimenting with different forms – alien and indigenous both – in order to arrive at the *new*. This was why Tagore would caution the *Kollol* age littérateurs (1923–35) about modernity's tinsel nature, and to Nazrul, Premen Mitra, Achintya Kumar Sengupta, Buddhadev Basu and others towards whom he had great affection he would say, with sword you are only shaving beard (this to Nazrul who took it in stride). In other words, literature was a matter of life and not simply of playing with form. We have to only see how in this exercise he constantly reinterpreted the past – the past he had inherited. Gandhi in this sense was much more of a modernist with not much hermeneutic interest in the past. Gandhi was a man of the time, immersed in his time. But Tagore's interpretative quest as expressed in his addresses and essays on Ram Mohan, Vidyasagar, Ramakrishna, Vivekananda, Sister Nivedita and others shows that for him hermeneutic exercise was an important element of modernity that could serve the purpose of truth and beauty. Freedom is a style of leading life, and not merely liberty to exercise certain rights. The privations we face add to our injured condition. They are not trivial for they affect life, strain and impoverish it, and thus for the post-colonial existence to be fulsome and thus free, aesthetics had to lead. For Rabindranath then, to put the matter a bit simplistically, not politics but aesthetics was the road to transformation of style of life, and aesthetics gave the clue to an emancipatory style. Emancipation was not a state of existence; freedom was the state of existence, alternative to state of injury. Emancipation was a style, a way of doing things. *Upanishads* and the devotional literature and philosophy combined to give him the sense that the mode must be emancipatory. Aesthetics enabled him to achieve the union and arrive at such position. Not without reason even being well versed in the ancient philosophy including the *Upanishads*, he formulated principles of harmony. Possibly we have still not paid adequate attention to the principle of harmony, steeped as we are in the principle of conflict and disharmony as a way of organizing life. How does one return to classics but remain unorthodox?

That was the secret question he resolved and in the process he had to return to the principle of harmony again and again in order to face the assault of a variety of formalisms that to him appeared to be empty. With scepticism therefore, he could say like Kabir, whom he adored and had translated,

> Tell me, Brother, how can I renounce Maya?
> When I gave up the tying of ribbons, still I tied my garment about me:
> When I gave up tying my garment, still I covered my body in its folds.
> So, when I give up passion, I see that anger remains;
> And when I renounce anger, greed is with me still;
> And when greed is vanquished, pride and vainglory remain;
> When the mind is detached and casts Maya away, still it clings to the letter.
> Kabîr says, "Listen to me, dear Sadhu! The true path is rarely found."[17]

In *Sadhana* he wrote,

> Things in which we do not take joy are either a burden upon our minds to be got rid of at any cost; or they are useful, and therefore in temporary and partial relation to us, becoming burdensome when their utility is lost; or they are like wandering vagabonds, loitering for a moment on the outskirts of our recognition, and then passing on. A thing is only completely our own when it is a thing of joy to us.
>
> The greater part of this world is to us as if it were nothing. But we cannot allow it to remain so, for thus it belittles our own self. . . .
>
> But what is the function of our sense of beauty in this process of the extension of our consciousness? Is it there to separate

truth into strong lights and shadows, and bring it before us in its uncompromising distinction of beauty and ugliness? If that were so, then we would have had to admit that this sense of beauty creates a dissension in our universe and sets up a wall of hindrance across the highway of communication that leads from everything to all things.

But that cannot be true. As long as our realization is incomplete a division necessarily remains between things known and unknown, pleasant and unpleasant. But . . . man does not accept any arbitrary and absolute limit to his knowable world. Every day his science is penetrating into the region formerly marked in his map as unexplored or inexplorable. Our sense of beauty is similarly engaged in ever pushing on its conquests. Truth is everywhere; therefore everything is the object of our knowledge. Beauty is omnipresent; therefore everything is capable of giving us joy.

In the early days of his history man took everything as a phenomenon of life. His science of life began by creating a sharp distinction between life and non-life. But as it is proceeding farther and farther the line of demarcation between the animate and inanimate is growing more and more dim. In the beginning of our apprehension these sharp lines of contrast are helpful to us, but as our comprehension becomes clearer they gradually fade away.

The Upanishads have said that all things are created and sustained by an infinite joy. To realise this principle of creation we have to start with a division – the division into the beautiful and the non-beautiful . . . At first we detach beauty from its surroundings, we hold it apart from the rest, but at the end we realise its harmony with all. Then the music of beauty has no more need of exciting us with loud noise; it renounces violence, and appeals to our heart with the truth that it is meekness inherits the earth.

In some stage of our growth, in some period of our history, we try to set up a special cult of beauty, and pare it down to a narrow circuit, so as to make it a matter of pride for a chosen few. Then it breeds in its votaries affections and exaggerations . . .

In the history of aesthetics there also comes an age of emancipation when the recognition of beauty in things great and small become easy, and when we see it more in the unassuming harmony of common objects than in things startling in their singularity. . . . We are then tempted in defiance to exaggerate the commonness of commonplace things, thereby making them aggressively uncommon. To restore harmony we create the discords which are a feature of all reactions. We already see in the present age the sign of this aesthetic reaction, which proves that man has at last come to know that it is only the narrowness of perception which sharply divides the field of his aesthetic consciousness into ugliness and beauty. When he has the power to see things detached from self-interest and from the insistent claims of the lust of the senses then alone can he have the true vision of the beauty that is everywhere; then only can he see that what is unpleasant to us is not necessarily unbeautiful, but has its beauty in truth.[18]

Tagore here speaks of the Partition of the sensibilities. Thus even more significantly, like a classical dialectician, he wrote in the same *Sadhana* on the 'Problem of Evil',

Pain, which is the feeling of our finiteness, is not a fixture in our life. It is not an end in itself, as joy is. To meet with it is to know that it has no part in the true permanence of creation. It is what error is in our intellectual life. To go through the history of the development of science is to go through the maze of mistakes it made current at different times. Yet no one really believes that science is the one perfect mode of disseminating mistakes. . . .

As in intellectual error, so in evil of any other form, its essence is impermanence, for it cannot accord with the whole. Every moment it is being corrected by the totality of things and keeps changing its aspect. We exaggerate its importance by imagining it as a standstill. Could we collect the statistics of the immense amount of death and putrefaction happening every moment in this earth, they would appall us. But evil is ever moving; with all its incalculable immensity it does not effectually clog the current of our life; and we find that the earth, water, and air remain sweet and pure for living beings. All statistics consist of our attempts to represent statistically what is in motion; and in the process things assume a weight in our mind which they have not in reality. For this reason a man, who by his profession is concerned with any particular aspect of life, is apt to magnify its proportions; in laying undue stress upon facts he loses his hold upon truth. A detective may have the opportunity of studying crimes in detail, but he loses his sense of their relative places in the whole social economy. When science collects facts to illustrate the struggle for existence that is going on in the kingdom of life, it raises a picture in our minds of 'nature red in tooth and claw.' But in these mental pictures we give fixity to colours and forms which are really evanescent. It is like calculating the weight of the air on each square inch of our body to prove that it must be crushingly heavy for us. With every weight, however, there is an adjustment, and we lightly bear our burden. With the struggle for existence in nature there is reciprocity. There is the love for children and for comrades; there is the sacrifice of self, which springs from love; and this love is the positive element in life. [19]

A new style of life

Let us continue little more along the path that Tagore indicated in *Sadhana*, namely that Partition occur in our sensory activities, hence in sensibilities, and by implication these partitions between seen and unseen, heard and unheard, good and evil, beauty and ugliness, crooked and simple and so on are reproduced in our intellectual, particularly historical argumentations and even in artist's attitudes. This invariably drags in politics. But aesthetics, as distinct from art, takes these partitions as challenges, and becomes aesthetics by negotiating these partitions of sensibilities. Aesthetics or better put aesthetic sensibility enables one to emerge from the darkness, in which senses have plunged and taken leave of the individual, and say (Tagore says appealing to God and quoting from the *Vedas*), 'Let me arise into the world of light'. This is what he had said in his poem of passion in youth, *Nirjharer Swapnabhanga*, for instance: 'I shall rush from peak to peak / I shall sweep from mount to mount / With peals of laughter and songs of murmur / I shall clap to tune and rhythm.' Metaphorically though then aesthetics leads us to the power of the senses, Rabindranath is not speaking here of the 'night of the poet' from which the poet emerges. Rabindranath here in fact re-asks the question of the partition between aesthetics and life, senses and life, intellect and senses, and between senses and sensibilities, and provides a new answer. Throughout nineteenth century we find repeated invocations of the 'night', 'death', 'amnesia', 'paralysis', 'slumber' and so on from which the subject must awaken.[20] Tagore makes an advance from these invocations. He argues that the partition of senses deprives us from a full appreciation of beauty and truth. Aesthetics will allow us to cross the division between the visible, utterable and thinkable and their opposites.

Modern literary theory flourishing in the past few decades has stressed these distinctions. Rabindranath stressed the need to be sensitive to crossings-over and paradoxes in our historical experience of arts and aesthetics. As he said, limits, closures and exclusions are real, but asked, what about transgressions? The power to transgress makes the aesthetic subject autonomous and capable of acquiring new forms of life. Literature, as a system of ostensibly dispersed arts of writing, belongs to the aesthetic mode, which is a paradoxical combination of autonomy and subjection to certain rules. In one of his most famous poems, *Sonar Tori* (*The Golden Boat*) criticized for being vague, he wrote (Radice's translation),

Clouds rumbling in the sky; teeming rain.
I sit on the river-bank, sad and alone.
The sheaves lie gathered, harvest has ended,
The river is swollen and fierce in its flow.
As we cut the paddy it started to rain.

One small paddy-field, no one but me-
Flood-waters twisting and swirling everywhere.
Trees on the far bank smear shadows like ink
On a village painted on deep morning grey.
On this side a paddy-field, no one but me.

Who is this, steering close to the shore,
Singing? I feel that she is someone I know.
The sails are filled wide, she gazes ahead,
Waves break helplessly against the boat each side.
I watch and feel I have seen her face before.

Oh to what foreign land do you sail?
Come to the shore and moor your boat for a while.
Go where you want to, give where you care to,
But come to the bank a moment, show your smile-
Take away my golden paddy when you sail.

Take it, take as much as you can load.
Is there more? No, none, I have put it aboard.
My intense labour here by the river-
I have parted with it all, layer upon layer:
Now take me as well, be kind, take me aboard.

No room, no room, the boat is too small.
Loaded with my gold paddy, the boat is full.
Across the rain-sky clouds heave to and fro,
On the bare river-bank, I remain alone-
What I had has gone: the golden boat took it all.

In this play of autonomy and subjection Rabindranath reconfigured the aesthetic dimension of the relationships between doing, seeing and saying that mark the being-in-common, inherent to every subject. This reconfiguration of the perceptible attributes has a political dimension as well. I showed elsewhere how in Bengal the aesthetic often played the part of politics, though we cannot suggest for a moment that everything was political.[21] On the contrary it is important to realize that these forms such as books, theatre, music, drama, choirs, dance, paintings, murals are what Ranciere has called somewhere 'modes for framing a community'. The political may emerge as one dimension of this community frame, but its aesthetic specificity cannot be confused with the political. The life and time of Rabindranath offer us individual and collective experience of the relations between aesthetics, literature and politics. It will be important to remember that if today we have in India oppositional ethical voices that stand up whenever any fascistic idea of the nation asserts itself, it is because of the lasting impact of those community building efforts in the anti-colonial time through aesthetic modes. Those modes built a community not so much on the basis of a single political will, but on the broad ethico-spiritual ideas of freedom, which of course had the idea of political independence as one element but signified something more.

In short then we must raise the question, if Tagore reminds us of the issue of the aesthetic amid everything, in everything, what shall we mean by aesthetics here? Is aesthetics then a specifically determined general mode of visibility? Is it about the contending modes of perceiving, a matter of how to look into? If that is so, which I think it is, then it is opposite to the idea of representation which stresses the division between what can be represented and the unrepresented also un-representable, and disregards the distinction between voluntary and the involuntary? Months before he died, he had said in anger against what he perceived to be useless modernist interpretation of his work, referring to himself in third person, 'In his own field of creativity Rabindranath has been entirely alone and tied to no public by history. Where history was public, he was there merely as a British subject but not as Rabindranath himself.'[22] Western philosophy (for instance Hegel) had thought of aesthetics as 'art as thought outside of itself'. Beauty is externalized. It has objective forms. Hegel had said,

> Such we may take to be the articulated totality of the particular arts, viz., the external art of architecture, the objective art of sculpture, and the subjective art of painting, music and poetry. . . . Thus architecture is treated as crystallization; sculpture, as the organic modeling of the material in its sensuous and spatial totality; painting, as the coloured surface and line; while in music, space, as

such, passes into the point of time possessed of content within itself, until finally the external medium is in poetry depressed into complete insignificance . . .

This higher principle we have found in the types of art – symbolic, classical, and romantic – which are the universal stages or elements of the Idea of beauty itself. For symbolic art attains its most adequate reality and most complete application in architecture, in which it holds sway in the full import of its notion, and is not yet degraded to be, as it were, the inorganic nature dealt with by another art. The Classical type of art, on the other hand, finds adequate realization in sculpture, while it treats architecture only as furnishing an enclosure in which it is to operate, and has not acquired the power of developing painting and music as absolute form for its content. The romantic type of art, finally, takes possession of painting and music, and in like manner of poetic representation, as substantive and unconditionally adequate modes of utterance. Poetry, however, is conformable to all types of the beautiful, and extends over them all, because the artistic imagination is its proper medium, and imagination is essential to every product that belongs to the beautiful, whatever type it may be.

And, therefore, what the particular arts realize in individual works of art, are according to their abstract conception simply universal types which constitute the self-unfolding Idea of beauty. It is as the external realization of this Idea that the wide Pantheon of art is being erected, whose architect and builder is the spirit of beauty as it awakens to self-knowledge, and to complete which the history of the world will need its evolution of ages.[23]

Beauty was thus a principle externalized. In fact Hegel opened his lectures with this line, 'The idea of the beautiful as the absolute idea contains a totality of distinct elements, or of essential moments, which as such, must manifest themselves outwardly and become realized'.[24] In contrast Tagore avoided classification and emphasized the principle of harmony that made beauty a reality. We can see that in fact Tagore chose a different path – a path that transgressed the division of inside and outside, lyricism and realism and notably history and revelations of daily life, and prepared the way for every experience to be thinkable. Towards the end of the poem *Banshi* (penultimate stanza), the poet wails out in despair against realisms of all kind,

Suddenly one evening
The strain of the raga *Sindhu-baroan* is in the air,
The whole sky resonates

With the pain of separation of all times
And then in a moment
It becomes clear that this lane is a terrible lie
Like the insufferable delirium of a drunkard.
In a moment then it occurs to me
That there is no difference between
Emperor Akbar and clerk Haripada.
Sailing the sad strains of the flute
The imperial canopy and the broken umbrella have gone
together toward
The same heaven.[25]

To achieve this significance of aesthetics, also a transformation of poetics, it required an extraordinary life and an equally extraordinary series of attempts at recovering or registering experiences. It required rebuilding from ruins an extra-colonial universe of senses and sensibilities. It required re-connecting with an old and bygone world – not through history, for that was not possible, not even through politics, for that could only half achieve this re-connection, but through constructing a world of language always poised to transcend the limits of language to enter the fluid world of senses. In his social essays he had all along refused to recognize power as an argument for truth, as if 'the good is good, not because it is victorious, but because it resists victory'.

The belief in the union of ethicality and aesthetic truth enabled him to arrive at a theory of beauty, which was not an Idea, 'the externalised spirit', but was perfectly able to reconcile with the mundane – as mundane as the 'a dew drop on grass'. It was this special kind of aesthetic sensibility that would enable him to retain a critical edge to his ideas and writings. When Gandhi was emphasizing the ethic of duty (*kartavya*) as a nation building virtue, he was arguing, let us not kill joy (*ananda*) in life – the pleasure of work and of doing what we want to do, the joy in the discovery of our own pleasures and ecstasy.[26] Thus we get in *Raktakarabi*[27] Nandini telling us the value of joy in life.[28] Or we can note the sudden appearances of the messengers of joy in some of his other works. These techniques enabled him also to establish a kind of metaphysics of language within a negative utopian frame born out of a paradoxical combination of hope and pessimism. The interpretive struggle thus continued till the last moment of his life. Language from a pure medium of communication became a means of experiencing. One can say that such metaphysics of language helped him overcome the *facts* of reality. This again is the reason as to why we have to see the links between his prose works and poems, his essays and stories, satires and songs. There were particularities and specifics of genres. Yet there was always a supplement suggesting other ideas, other aspects of life and experiences.

It was this aesthetic abundance, whose genealogy I have tried to draw, that enabled Rabindranath to steer the course of language away from say that of Kaliprasanna and Michael Madhusudan, and later noticeably from the powerful prose of his contemporary Narendranath Dutta (famous as Swami Vivekananda) who had given Bengal an idea of what a robust Bengali language could be. In that sense aesthetics was instrumental for Tagore to gentrify the language. With this gentrification of language he was able to escape and at the same time steer Bengali literature from the morass of factional gossips and scandals, sex-talk, calumny and so on – a literary world in which say Kaliprasanna had found himself and from which he had tried to come out. Madhusudan demonstrated this was possible while retaining the vitality of the language. Rabindranath seized the chance presented to him by his own time, and gifted with other kinds of aesthetic feelings bequeathed by Vaishnava literature, other forms of spirituality, and the rationality he had learnt from the Upanishads and Brahmo outlook, he created a language capable of facing and negotiating greater purposes of the world. He had to invent different literary tools to produce that change. For instance, it is instructive to see the way the woman became the figure of transformation that he effected – the role that women played in the aesthetic transformation he wanted to achieve. Critics have not still taken adequate notice of this. He feminized the language in all possible senses so that love could take the place of quarrel, dialogue could take the place of war, and metaphor could take the place of logic. He did not need any Walter Raleigh to create this power of the aesthetic. In this sense, gentrified Bengali language gave him the power to address issues of life and spirit in a unique way. It generated a kind of power, intrinsically aesthetic in nature, owing its origin to an abundance of aesthetics, and capable of providing a distinct view of life.

It does not matter if this aesthetic abundance cannot be theorized. Indeed it cannot be theorized. In *Sesher Kavita*[29] Rabindranath made the distinction between style and fashion. Aesthetics provided him a style of leading life. On the abundance of aesthetics, on the aesthetic supplement of all actions and statements of life this style was to be built. To do so, he had to claim and assert the autonomy of the aesthetic subject. This was a lasting legacy. Possibly, the time has come to reclaim the legacy.

It is not irrelevant to think however if modern governance has ended forever the power of the aesthetic. I think that beyond the governmental politics and the remorseless effort to governmentalize our autonomy, the aesthetic presence still marks the subject. We shall have to study the ways in which this aesthetic subjectivity resurfaces as an autonomous presence and as defence to face the demeaning banalities of a government with which the subject cannot identify himself or herself – far less with the oppressions, humiliations and exclusions that mark the conditions of governance in India. It is not only in the return of awards by the Sahitya Academy laureates today that we suddenly become aware of this (a tradition that follows Tagore's return of the knighthood after the Jalianwallah massacre), but in thousand and one less celebrated ways in which people conduct their dialogic politics and try to rebuild their lives after each cataclysmic events of governance that we find traces of the aesthetic legacy of our anti-colonial imagination.

Notes

1 Ramchandra Guha, "Travelling with Tagore," in Anjan Ghosh, Tapati Guha-Thakurta and Janaki Nair (eds.), *Theorizing the Present – Essays for Partha Chatterjee* (New Delhi: Oxford University Press, 2011), pp. 152–153.
2 Benedict Anderson, *Under the Three Flags – Anarchism and Anti-Colonial Imagination* (London: Verso, 2005).
3 Amartya Sen also in his remarks on Tagore brings up the question of choice, though he does not discuss what influenced the choice making; Amartya Sen, "Is Nationalism a Boon or a Curse?", *Netaji Oration*, Kolkata, 27 December 2007, *Economic and Political Weekly*, 16 February 2008, pp. 39–44.
4 On a similar appreciation of Muhammad Iqbal, Javed Majeed, *Muhammad Iqbal – Islam, Aesthetics and Post-Colonialism* (New Delhi: Routledge, 2009).
5 "Bangabibhag", reprinted in Rathin Chakraborty (ed.), *Bangabhanga Pratirodh Andolan – Satabarsha Smarak Sangraha* (Kolkata: Natyachinta, 2006), p. 74.
6 Ibid., p. 75.
7 Ibid., p. 75.
8 Jacques Derrida, *Acts of Literature*, ed. Derek Attridge (New York: Routledge, 1991).
9 Rabindranath Tagore, *Sabhyatar Sankat* (Calcutta: Visva Bharati, 1348 B.S.), pp. 655–669; also published in English as *Crisis in Civilization* same year (1941) – also as *Crisis of Civilisation* (Bombay: International Book House, 1941). I have written on the seminal place of this tract in the evolution of anti-colonial consciousness in "Dreams of the Colonised", *Futures*, 36, 2004.

10 Rabindranath Tagore, *Gora, Rabindra Rachanabali,* Volume 9 (Centenary Edition, Calcutta: West Bengal Government, 1961).
11 Tanika Sarkar, "Rabindranath's *Gora* and the Intractable Problem of Indian Patriotism", *Economic and Political Weekly,* xliv (30), 25 July 2009, pp. 37–46.
12 Among others C. William Radice, "Lyrical Alchemist – Rabindranath Tagore" http://www.india-today.com/itoday/millennium/100people/tagore .html (accessed on 12 April 2011).
13 Of the two poems, the first translated by me, the second one is by Radice in "Lyrical Alchemist – Rabindranath Tagore".
14 Rabindranath Tagore, *Rabindranather Rashtranaitik Mat* (1936), *The Oxford India Tagore – Selected Writings on Education and Nationalism,* ed. Uma Dasgupta (New Delhi: Oxford University Press, 2008).
15 Rabindranath Tagore, *Nationalism* (1917, Kolkata: Rupa, 2002), p. 83.
16 Rabindranath Tagore, *Sadhana – The Realisation of Life* (New York: MacMillan, 1916), "Author's preface".
17 *Songs of Kabir,* trans. Rabindranath Tagore (New York: MacMillan, 1915), poem 5.
18 Tagore, *Sadhana,* Chapter 7, "The Realisation of Beauty" http://www. sacred-texts.com/hin/tagore/sadh/index.htm (accessed on 5 April 2011).
19 http://www.sacred-texts.com/hin/tagore/sadh/sadh05.htm (accessed on 5 April 2011).
20 Vivekananda's speeches are an instance of such exhortation.
21 R. Samaddar, "Eternal Bengal," in Mridula Nath Chakraborty (ed.), *Being Bengali – At Home and in the World* (London: Routledge, 2014); published earlier in the journal, *Scienza & Politica,* 45, 2011; also on the web http://scienzaepolitica.unibo.it/article/download/2715/2112
22 "Sahitye Aitihasikata", translated by Ranajit Guha at the end of Guha, *History at the Limits of World History* (New York: Columbia University Press, 2002), p. 97.
23 G.W.F. Hegel, *Selections from Hegel's Lectures on Aesthetics,* ed. Bernard Bosanquest and W. M. Bryant, *The Journal of Speculative Philosophy,* 1886; chapter, "The Idea of Beauty" – see http://www.marxists.org/reference/ archive/hegel/works/ae/ch03.htm#45 (accessed on 15 April 2011).
24 Ibid., http://www.marxists.org/reference/archive/hegel/works/ae/intro.htm#0 (accessed on 15 April 2011).
25 Based on Dipesh Chakrabarty's translation.
26 Recall the first line of the excerpt from *Sadhana,* cited on p. 13.
27 *Raktakarabi (Red Oleanders)* is one of most discussed among the more than sixty plays, dance dramas and dramatic sketches that Tagore wrote. It was written in Shillong in 1923–24 'inspired by the image of a red oleander plant crushed by pieces of discarded iron that Tagore had come across while walking. A short time later, an oleander branch with a single red flower protruded through the debris, as if, he noted, "created from the blood of its cruelly pierced breast."' Ananda Lal, *Rabindranath Tagore – Three Plays* (Kolkata: M.P. Birla Foundation, 1987), pp. 129–132.
28 Indeed *Raktakarabi* by itself demonstrates much of what I am arguing. In the play until Nandini appears on the scene, the king's workers cannot imagine that there is any other way of leading life than the one they know. They live and work like machines driven by the king and his entourage

among whom are the governor, the priest and the professor. Nandini has been ordered from her village home and forced away from her lover Ranjan in order to be made useful in adding to the king's wealth. But she defeats all plans by spreading everywhere an atmosphere of love and freedom – from the study room of the professor to the office of the file-grinding governor, the temple of the sinister priest and the guard's room where the attendance register was kept. Like the blossoming of the flower, red oleander, happiness too is a result of love, labour, sympathy and consideration. But this happiness will have marks of pain and blood. In *Sadhana* and elsewhere Tagore would say, this is the truth of life. This is how beauty and truth would connect.

29 Serialized in *Prabasi* in 1928 from Bhadra to Chaitra, it was published in 1929.

4 Another idea of democratic governance

Democracy and self-governance

In the context of the raging debates in our contemporary history on modes of self-governance the question was bound to emerge sooner rather than later: what kind of democracy was possible in a setting defined by the simultaneous, at times clashing, discourses of autonomy of the self, the nationalist politics of sovereignty, constitution-making and the remorseless governmentalization of rule? On one hand ideas and events of constituent assembly, elections, formation of independent legislature, press freedom, independent judiciary and others marked the emergence of representative democracy. On the other hand, the democratic discourse refused to be limited to this representative structure and satisfied with it. It periodically brought back the question of the autonomy of the self and meaning and the possible institutionalization of self-government. The way democratic discourse in India shaped governance was deeply marked with these two contradictory aspects that make popular politics in India. The question of autonomy never faded from Indian democratic thought and forced the nation to periodically face the question: what is government of the self? What is self-governance? It is in this context that we should visit the writings of Jayaprakash Narayan.

Two questions persisted with Jayaprakash Narayan as his life went through tumultuous experiences, programmes, organizations, initiatives and doctrinal quarrels, not the least because he was one of the most profound nationalist thinkers in the last century, and helped articulate resolutions of some of the political issues of our country, which we have now come to accept as normal. The two questions that persisted with him were nationalism and democracy. While clearly nationalism and the likely form of the nation occupied his attention before 1947, increasingly the question of democracy became his sole concern to the point where he was to raise in the last days of his life the issue he had raised much earlier in his youth, namely what kind of nation do we want? Is there a choice between democracy and the nation? What would a democratic nationhood mean? If it were not to be a monolithic, conservative republican nation, but one that must be open to and hospitable to newer and wider array of democratic yearnings, forces and institutions, would it not mean then an expansion of subjects of sovereignty? Did it signify recognition of the autonomy of those distinct, variegated, yearnings? At times he seemed to be raising the unutterable question for a nationalist, is the nation a true nation that cannot represent democracy? Democracy was, of course he was to say innumerable times before he died, a problematic of representing people, therefore was his surprise, how could one person (Indira), or one party (the Congress), represent the nation that had to represent democracy which symbolized variegated masses?

Yet the issue of a nation representing democracy was not only a matter for the nation to seek the proper ground of legitimacy. For him it was a deeper question involving the history and dynamics of representative democracy and the complexities of time in the process of representation. These questions were not issues of simple political temporalities, as if democratic thought would follow and succeed nationhood. It was a question of appreciating the plural temporalities of the political.

The temporalities of the political are usually considered a matter of simple technical constraints. For instance, democracies have thought that too short a term of the executive reduces its capacity to govern a democracy. Or, the longer the term is of the representative, the weaker becomes the bond between the representative and the represented. But the issue of the temporality of the political cannot be a simple one. The subject cannot remain indifferent to his or her time. If representation is a part of democracy, direct government as Jayaprakash Narayan (called JP) thought was also a simultaneous legacy. In his last texts in those tumultuous days preceding the imposition of the *Emergency*, he claimed repeatedly that direct rule meant *immediate* democracy that must cut, and only that can cut, Gordon's knot of representative democracy, which means that legislators must (be made to) resign if people turn against them, government of the day must leave if popular trust is lost, that *janata sarkars* must evolve to put in place alternative institutions of power, and only in these and other myriad ways immediate democracy could ensure direct democracy. Here we can see that while the then prime minister, Indira Gandhi, in accusing JP of undermining both nation and democracy through his stress on immediate democracy was placing herself in the solid tradition of representative democracy, JP was arguing for an understanding of the plural temporalities of the political on which, according to him, depended the relation of democracy to time.

Immediate democracy of course means democracy based on immediate actions, thus, a denial of mediacy, denial of what Marx had called long ago 'the insertion of the third' between 'an individual and his mode of action' as the feature of the capitalist age. In *The German Ideology* Marx had written that in the guise of interest the bourgeoisie had always inserted the third that is the mediating instrument. This was ruinous mediation, as it constructed the individual only at the cost of making him a stranger to himself.[1] Therefore the significance of the question JP raised in the last phase of his life: can we rescue democracy from the process of special interest formation growing out of the mediating mechanisms, such as representation, government, legislative councils, laws attuned to special purposes? How can the individual recover from the condemned life of repeated vote giving, and only vote giving, and be restored to his individuality as a political actor in democracy? To JP the importance of immediate democracy and therefore the advocacy for plural temporalities of the political were enormous. Historically democratic sovereignty was built around the electoral procedure as the central mechanism for legitimation and rule. But JP within twenty years of this proceduration in independent India broke away with this legacy. In the context of rising mass discontent of the late sixties and early seventies of the past century, he started arguing that the life of democracy could never be reducible to the electoral moment alone. He argued in his innumerable essays and lectures of that time (to which we shall turn to shortly) that the moment of loyalty to the Indian nation through participating in the electoral rite had passed. Besides loyalty there remained the two other elements of the social modality of expression, namely, voice, and exit. The people of India must access the various avenues of voicing protests and opinions by forming and participating in associations, embarking on direct actions, and conjuring up newer methods of mobilization in order to gain the identity of the collective subject of democracy. These ways of voicing also meant the exercise of the option of exit from the given institutional path of representative democracy. We all know how the government of the time reacted, and all governments of the time react. The official argument was and still remains that democracy would be diluted because of too many associations, too many ways of configuring democratic procedures and too much multiplication of the ways to relate to institutions and one another. At the end of the day, it was a deep dispute between the national form of democracy, and the possibility of a non-national democracy, unconcerned or unworried about the possible dilution of the nation form. Also in this dispute lay the issue of sovereignty and its possible form, and the open question as to whether democracy and sovereignty remain indefinitely compatible.

JP's speeches abound with these questions as he prepared his public to rise up against the dreary republic of universal suffrage. At the same time he was fashioning a new discourse of immediacy and the multiple temporalities of the political. Through launching civil disobedience and contesting the electoral outcomes JP was questioning the legal framework of representative democracy and drawing attention of this republic of universal suffrage to the juridication of politics, and its implications in terms of the decline of the political will. Not only was he disputed the old institutional and ethical framework of representative democracy, but he was also questioned with the particular experiences of post-colonial India the abstract generality of democracy, its necessity and received validity.

JP thereby did two things: first, he posed the problem of democracy in an age of distrust of the representatives, and second, he brought forward the issue of political will with which the power of the representative sovereign was to be confronted. By raising the question of social majority *vis-à-vis* the representative majority, and therefore the issue of mediation, double figures and double wills, he suggesting a re-politicization of democracy. This was significant, because in pursuing the two themes of nation and democracy he concentrated on the issue of *will* that predicated both the themes. Therefore in his quarrel with Indian communists too, he was not taking a liberal position, but he was taking a voluntarist stand and complaining that the communists in India had little patience with the question of the will of the political. That such an attitude would always produce quarrels and non-conformism, and thus JP was to be known by his intransigence and disputes throughout his life, should not therefore astonish us.

The way Jayaprakash Narayan theorized and articulated the problematic of representative democracy involved reorienting three issues of classical politics: (a) the interface of nation and democracy, (b) the issue of government and its legitimacy in popular democracy and (c) the immediacy of democracy and the issue of political will in forging its direct nature.

The interface of nation and democracy

It was an extraordinary asset of anti-colonial nationalism in a country particularly India where political thinking always zoomed on the possible and desirable character of the nation on gaining freedom. Therefore visions, directions and disputes raged throughout the anti-colonial period among thinkers and activists alike as to the social nature of anti-colonial nationalism. As we have indicated, Gandhi's idea of *swaraj* was not the only vision or direction. There were many other ideas and plans. These raging ideas moulded the fundamentals of Indian democracy. Many of these were neither purely anarchist nor classically liberal nor soviet-socialist. But whatever may be the form, unlike the historic bourgeois revolutions, the political was not a pure one in the anti-colonial revolutions. It was always marked by the social, which explains why democracy in India could never remain limited to issues of representation. And even when the republic of universal suffrage was held up as an independent dream, the issue always loomed from behind: why representation, what is the goal? Thus, it was in Jayaprakash Narayan's early enunciations of socialism, his dispute with Gandhi, his quarrel with liberal ideas of the propertied classes and his effort to strike a socialist path separate from the Indian communist thinking that his vision of democracy developed. He like other great anti-colonial thinkers sought to define the legitimacy of the nation in the social and not primarily in the political, and this in turn defined the emerging framework of democratic understanding in India.

In 1936 he opened his tract on the objectives of the Congress Socialist Party with these words,

> The objectives of the Congress Socialist Party, as laid down in its Constitution, are 'the achievements of complete independence, in the sense of separation of the British Empire, and the establishment of a socialist society'.
>
> This is direct and simple enough. The Party has two objects: the first is the same as that of the Indian National Congress, except that the Party wishes to make it clear that the complete independence of India must include separation from the British Empire.
>
> The second object of the Party simply means that independent India must reorganise its economic life on a socialist basis. Why?
>
> The question at bottom is one of values and ultimate objectives, which once determined, the rest becomes a matter of logical sequence.
>
> If the ultimate objective is to make the masses politically and economically free, to make them prosperous and happy, to free them from all manner of exploitation, to give them unfettered opportunity for development, then socialism becomes a goal to which one must irresistibly be drawn. If again, the objective is to

take hold of the chaotic and conflicting forces of society and to
fashion the latter according to the idea of utmost social good and
to harness all the conscious directives of human intelligence in the
service of the commonwealth, then again socialism becomes an
inescapable destination.[2]

What were the measures necessary to bring about this goal? 'What
must the Swaraj government do in addition to nationalising key industries . . .?' He proposed fifteen such measures, and pointed out the
more important ones. 'Transfer of all power to the producing masses'
was the most significant one. He said,

> The cornerstone of the whole scheme is the transference of all
> power, political as well as economic, to the producing masses, i.e.,
> to those engaged in producing goods or rendering service either by
> hand or by brain. If all power goes into the hands of those who
> work, it follows that those who do not work shall have no power.
> The principle involved here is a basic one. Hitherto, in all the
> known form of social organisation, sovereign power has always
> rested not with the labouring masses, who in every society pre-
> ponderated in numbers, but with the possessing classes. Before
> the rise of modern democracy, this was obvious in all the political
> systems that preceded it. The State was openly in the hands of the
> ruling class; it was an instrument of class oppression. It was so
> even in the so-called Greek democracies in which a small group of
> citizens ruled over and oppressed a much larger number of slaves
> who worked for them.
> It was with the appearance of the ballot box and the party sys-
> tem of government that the fiction of democracy came into being.
> These two institutions were supposed to have conferred power on
> the whole people, equally on the humblest and the highest. But the
> economic order which weighs the scales too heavily on the side of
> propertied interests makes of this democracy a mockery. The rich
> have their great resources, their huge election funds, their great
> newspapers, their schools and colleges . . .
> And even this sham democracy, this mockery, turns against the
> poor workers when in spite of all odds, they seem strong enough
> to disturb the scale of the economic order ever so little in their
> favour. The cry of revolution and 'reds' goes up, and what looked
> like democracy disappears like a mist. The ballot box is with-
> drawn from the reach of the workers; party government is thrown
> over on the scrap heap . . .

Against such background we inscribe the words: 'All power to the masses'.

But Jayaprakash did not stop here. He added these words to the section from which we are citing:

> We might be told that we are talking through our hats – the thing is just not possible. We firmly declare that it is. We do so, because we know the secret of power – economic domination. When those who toil become masters of the economic order, the thing is not only possible, but natural. If we were to content ourselves merely with this one item, without the proposals, which follow, we would no doubt have been guilty not only of talking through our hats but also of perpetrating a fraud.[3]

This was then the other scene of democracy, its secret, the secret of democratic power. The power is to run own schools and colleges, gather huge election funds, control social resources and to declare to the public the menace of insurgency or revolt at the first sign of unrest from below. This was the other scene, against which the anti-colonial cry had to be 'All power to the masses'. It can hardly fail to attract our attention that while these words were similar to the famous words of Lenin, Jayaprakash did not think of any representative organ to which power could be transferred. In his dream of national freedom maturing into socialism, he remained distrustful of representative mechanisms.[4] Like a true anarchist-socialist he was focusing on the immediacy of transfer of power. In his debate with the Indian communists of his time he was asking if the state could be held representative of the society of the producing masses. Surely the histories of the past two hundred years of socialist thoughts and practices tell us not to be sweeping in our judgements about paths, and look back at the great history of democracy as being enriched by various ideas and practices of socialism.

Years later in 1959, as if recalling these words, JP wrote in his 'A Plea for Reconstruction of Indian Polity',

> The old faith that State ownership of the means of production, distribution, and exchange plus planning will bring about socialism has been falsified. . . . But a new faith has not been created to take the place of the old. For this the socialists will have to go back to the pre-Marxian socialist idealists, the philosophical Anarchists: to Tolstoy, Ruskin, and Morris; to the post-Marxian

social idealists: to Gandhi and Vinoba. The 'communities of work' of France have a great deal to teach the socialists; and so have the *Kibbutzim* of Israel and some of the *gramdan* villages of India. The socialists must also take from Marx what is still valid and from science it has to the best to offer.[5]

Clearly, JP did not think that there was much to learn from the masters of the art of representative government, Locke, Jefferson or Mill, in forging a society of democratic relations, which to him meant reducing the mediation in relations to a minimum, and certainly in political relations. Was JP wrong? This is not the occasion to go into the history of the ideas and practices of representative government. But considering, for instance, what Mill (the younger one) thought, and re-reading his wisdom today, JP possibly was wise in cutting through all the white mythologies about representation in order to put his ideas directly as matter of political practice. Mill for instance did not think that representative government could ever in the name of the people curtail anyone's liberty to ensure social reconstruction, and wrote, 'I deny the right of the people to exercise (such) coercion, either by themselves or by their government. The power itself is illegitimate. The best government has no more title to it than the worst.'[6] And, if the people did not have such right, did the individual have? Again, he was concerned here with social stability. The main goal of representative government was not to defend liberty, but to govern people efficiently and adequately, to rule people in the name of people and popular interests. Mill wrote,

> Though society is not founded on a contract, and though no good purpose is answered by inventing a contract in order to deduce social obligations from it, everyone who receives the protection of society owes a return for the benefit, and the fact of living in society renders it indispensable that each should be bound to observe a certain line of conduct towards the rest. The conduct consists, first, in not injuring the interests of one another; or rather certain interests, which either by express legal provision or by tacit understanding, ought to be considered as rights; and secondly, in each person's bearing his share (to be fixed on some equitable principle) of the labours and sacrifices incurred for defending the society or its members from injury and molestation.[7]

The virtue of representative government rests thus on the idea of social stability. And, yet even this amount of representational facility was not to be universally available. Apart from whatever he wrote in the infamous tract on *The Subjection of Women*,[8] Mill further said, if the government was found to be lacking in power, 'adequate to preserve order and allow progress of the people', it was an incident 'rather to a wild and rude state of society generally'. And then the line, on which every dead anti-colonial political thinker would turn in his grave, comes: 'When the people are too much attached to savage independence, to be tolerant of the amount of power to which it is for their good that they should be subject, the state of society (as already observed) is not yet ripe for representative government'.[9] Therefore, Mill would go on to argue that representative government could perfectly accommodate 'government of dependencies' (an euphemism for colonial government), but interestingly, in a differential manner, that is white colonies could be allowed greater self-rule than coloured colonies.[10]

In short, representative government was little about democracy and popular welfare. It was about the science of ruling well. The nation of the toilers therefore under representative arrangements could not be represented in an adequate democratic form – adequacy here meaning sufficient degree of directness and immediacy. What were the other significant measures that Jayaprakash Narayan suggested to bring about the congruence of nation and democracy? These were among others, development of the economic life of the country to be planned and controlled by the state, socialization of key industries, organization of cooperatives for production, distribution and credit in the un-socialized sector of economic life, state encouragement of cooperatives and collective farming, recognition of the right to work or maintenance by the state and finally adult franchise on a functional basis. Here he wrote,

> This means that representation instead of being on a territorial basis would be on the basis of occupations. Representatives are supposed to represent interests, but interests within a given country are not distributed territorially but functionally, occupationally. Therefore functional representation means truer representation.[11]

The same thinking was evident as he closely examined in 1936 what he termed as the 'Gandhian Alternative' to the socialist path, and critiqued Gandhi's idea of trusteeship, because it called for 'change of hearts without changing relations', and once again this mode of representing the interests of the national majority did not ensure the union of democracy and the nation. In his polemic against other socialist parties he was of course insistent of the authenticity of the views of the Congress Socialist Party, which meant socialism aligned along the path of Congress that was to slowly transform in his admission into 'democratic socialism'; but noticeably here too he was objecting to the trend dominant among Indian communists, particularly among those who had returned from the Soviet Union, namely that 'it alone was the real Marxist party, and that every other party had therefore to be exploited, captured, or destroyed'. The 'Problems of Socialist Unity', as he saw in 1941, were the problem of democracy. He put tersely,

> A Marxist never tries to understand a social fact by itself. He understands it historically and in relation with other facts. We all wish that there were only one Marxist party. But, if we wish to understand how in a concrete situation two Marxist parties came to exist, we must look at the matter historically. During the national struggle of 1930–34 there was a considerable radicalisation of the younger cadres of the Congress. By 1934 a coherent socialist group crystallised. Between this group and the existing group, i.e., the Communist party, there was an impenetrable wall in the shape of the latter's attitude towards and isolation from the Congress. A new party was bound to be formed; the Congress Socialist Party thus came into being as a result of the mistaken policy of the Communist party and the Communist International.[12]

Reading these lines more closely, we can realize that for JP even in those days (1941) the problem of democracy was the problem of the nation also, because the traditional communists had a 'mistaken policy towards the Congress' – in other words, towards the national question. As the impending final round of the battle for independence approached, he spoke more and more of the need for an 'efficient organisation and a complete programme of National Revolution' ('To All Fighters for Freedom – 1', issued in February 1943 after escape from prison). In another three years, in 1946, in his third call ('To All Fighters for Freedom – 3', issued in 1946 shortly after release from prison), his idea of what this organization would mean had become clearer. 'I have come to the conclusion that the CSP should become the organisation of all fighters of freedom.' Clearly the national will demanded the democratic charter. He was to make this point clearer as the country gained independence. In his tract, 'The Structure of Socialist Party' (1948) he wrote,

> Some have the fear that while democratic conditions might exist today they may not be present tomorrow and if the Party is organised so as to function under today's conditions, it may not be able

to function properly in the conditions of tomorrow. This fear is unfounded. If democratic methods are not divorced from a revolutionary outlook, the Socialist Party, if it has functioned properly as a democratic party under conditions of democracy, would have the organisational strength, the popularity, the necessary mass contact, the resilience and the revolutionary will to function equally effectively in conditions of social breakdown . . .

What is a revolutionary will, I may be asked. It is (i) the will that allows no compromise with fundamentals or blurring of the final objectives; (ii) it is the will that does not flinch before danger and suffer and deviate from the right path on their account . . . [13]

The key to the solution of the problem of combining the national and the democratic was to be searched therefore not in the representative mechanisms drawn from liberal theory or received from the colonial practices of British rule, or in *etatism* of one variety or another, but in the realities of mass politics, popular unity, variety of popular initiatives and revolutionary will, which has the courage and the consistency to be democratic. We can say today on hindsight that besides re-orienting the nation towards the democratic question Jayaprakash Narayan in this search was actually presenting for us an agenda for re-politicizing democracy itself, because only in that re-politicised democracy the national could finally find its home. Giving meaning back to democracy, he was not only showing the way to re-vitalise the nation (which became clear in 1972–75), he was also suggesting a framework involving a whole range of practical works (for instance, bhoodan, building *gramswaraj*, cooperatives, struggling against the institution of caste, educational initiatives, preparing *sangharsh bahinis* and setting up *janata sarkars*) towards the production of a new generality. In all these and consequently the production of a new generality, the issue of will was significant. The sacralization of will, hitherto considered a problem in the conventional dynamics of representative democracy, which is always scared of an unruly will often appearing in form of street politics, and therefore requires trained and disciplined political behaviour, was now turned into an asset by anti-colonial political theory. In this respect few could match up to JP. He made political will a question of the general (because the nation must finally transform into direct democracy and socialism) thereby at one stroke pointing out that the nation and democracy could unite only by removing the obstacles in the form of sham representative institutions.

As we shall see, he was to become more focused on this problematic as years passed.

The issue of government and its legitimacy
in popular democracy

Jayaprakash Narayan, as every student of modern Indian political history knows, moved away not only from Marxism as the first decade after independence advanced, but he also moved away from socialism. Yet he did not go back to the liberal ghetto unlike the commentators of the *failing God*. Instead he delved deeper in the democratic problematic, the issue for him always being: how democratic is our democracy? Or, to say in different words, how much democratic can we make our democracy? His new critique of representative rule started to develop from his thoughts on popular democracy. Socialism did not have any answer to the dangers posed by the practices and the culture of a total government, which killed popular democracy. Socialist democracy, at least in India, could never be popular democracy, because it did not give importance to 'freedom' of the people, which had been 'one of the beacon lights of (his) life', the 'goodness of ends', the dynamics of 'cooperation in a community of direct producers', 'decentralisation' – all these signifying an emphasis on democracy. *Sarvodaya* would signify, 'means morally consistent with ends'. Thus if the end was the realization of democracy, the means must be democratic, that is going closest to the people, evolving schemes out of popular desire, making people their own teachers. In this noticeably, for instance in his self-explanatory pamphlet, 'From Socialism to Sarvodaya' (1957), he went at length to critique socialist theory and practices, but there was no praise for liberal democracy and liberal representative institutions. Indeed, he said repeatedly, 'The Indian freedom movement was a people's movement *par excellence* [italics mine]. It was not *rajniti* (politics of the State), but *lokniti* (politics of the people).'[14]

Thus not governmental politics, but popular politics – and that difference would remain even when governmental politics would try to legitimize itself by way of incorporating popular elements. JP said in 1959,

> Perhaps it would be well, at the outset, to keep in mind that the ideal [of democracy] can never be fully realised in India or anywhere else. All that is possible is to approach the ideal as nearly as possible.
>
> It is for this reason that many political writers narrow down the ideal considerably and advance a realisable definition of democracy. Consider the following from an internationally recognised political authority: 'Government of the people by the people',

'Government of the nation by its representatives', these are fine phrases for arousing enthusiasm and fashioning eloquent perorations. Fine phrases with an empty ring. No people have ever been known to govern itself and none ever will. All government is oligarchic; it necessarily implies the domination of the many by a few. . . . The formula 'Government of the people by the people' must be replaced by this formula 'Government of the people by an *elite* sprung from the people'. (JP was referring here to Maurice Duverger's *Political Parties*, London, 1954, pp. 424–25)[15]

He went on to say that the most authentic case of democracy would be where people governed them directly, making own laws, dispensing justice and carrying out and overseeing administrative functions. But he also realized that at least in large political units no such self-government existed, and thus at best there could be what he termed as 'democratic oligarchy'. Hence was his plea for a reconstruction of Indian polity along the lines of decentralization, autonomy of communities, village work and all those work that the political representatives and the representative government loathe. He wanted voluntary limits on wants, invention of egalitarian social institutions and re-imagining of the community (hence the issue of occupation or territorial orientation) essential for a democracy, which would be least burdened by the institution of the government. If the government failed to facilitate these political tasks, such a government was illegitimate.

It is clear then that JP was not faulting the institution of government on account of this omission or that commission. His main point was that it could not by its methods represent popular interest. Its legitimacy is suspect because governmental methods are not dialogic, and will always represent elite interest. Thus, when he was accused fifteen years later by Indira Gandhi of trying to cause the downfall of a legitimately elected government in Bihar, he replied in a letter to Indira Gandhi,

If all this adds up to an attempt to paralyse the Bihar government, well it was the same kind of attempt as was made during the freedom struggle through non-cooperation and satyagraha to paralyse the British government. But (you may say) that was a government established by force, whereas the Bihar government and legislature are both constitutionally established bodies. . . . The answer is that in a democracy the people do have the right to ask for the resignation of an elected Government if it has gone corrupt and misrules. And if there is a legislature that persists in supporting such a government it too must go, so that the people might choose better representatives.

But in that case how can it be determined what the people want? In the usual manner. In the case of Bihar, the mammoth rallies and processions held in Patna, the thousands of constituency meetings held all over the state, the three day Bihar *bandh*, the memorable happenings on the 4th of November and the 'largest ever' meeting held at the Gandhi maidan on 18 November 1974 were a convincing measure of the people's will. . . . If that was not conclusive enough proof, I had asked repeatedly for a plebiscite . . .

While I am on the Bihar movement, let me mention another important point that would illumine the politics of such a type of movement. The students of Bihar . . . met the Chief Minster and the Education Minster. . . . But unfortunately the inept and corrupt Bihar Government did not take the students seriously. . . . In Bihar, the government was given a chance to settle the issues across the table. None of the demands of the students was unreasonable or non-negotiable. But the Bihar Government preferred the method of . . . unparallel repression . . .

I have pondered over the riddle: why did not those Governments act wisely? The conclusion I have arrived is that the main hurdle has been corruption.[16]

Here we can locate an interesting turn in his argument. In this letter from prison JP was not speaking of ordinary corruption. He spoke of the way in which the act of governing destroys the ethics of friendship and community, government develops a self-serving attitude and mode and government develops vested interest in the act of governing, in perpetuating order. Corruption is thus intrinsic to representative organs of rule. Government promotes security at the cost of democracy. Thus it is always the government that first cries 'danger to the nation' whenever democracy tends to cross the limits of administration. Therefore he told the prime minster in that letter, 'You are reported to have said that democracy is not important than the nation. . . . It is a false choice.' Government in the name of representing the nation destroys or at least seriously jeopardizes popular democracy. The reason is that it inverts the pyramid; it recalls the motto of *swaraj from above*.

The striking point about the critique of representative democracy that Jayaprakash Narayan was developing through the years culminating in the fierce arguments in the last phase and decade of his life depended on rising above the traditional liberal/communist divide and creating the image of a possible strategy of going deep, *endlessly deep*, into the people – a strategy only partly grounded in historical experi-ences of anti-colonialism, but mainly in conjuring an ethical site of democracy. In this strategy, the act of *going endlessly deep into the people* had no other separate objective; its objective was sheer ethical-ity of the work of going itself. He was thus carrying a profound legacy of anti-colonialism, the legacy of setting up ethics against politics. Ethics represented the people. Politics represented elite mechanisms of rule. In his plea for reconstruction of the Indian polity, we find arguments for combining socialism with democracy, revolution with Gandhi's precepts, emphasis on land redistribution, non-violent con-frontational tactics and others. To the anti-colonialist the nation was ethical, it had an indestructible ethical core; likewise democracy was an ethical project, therefore the possibility that it would be never fully realized, yet as an ethical objective it had to be striven for.

The world of anti-colonialism was in this sense made up of images, regardless of whether this world was figurative, whether its inhab-itants recognized any identifiable character in it, whether some his-torical figure required to be re-created, or identifiable spectacles re-demonstrated. Noticeably the colonial power wanted to re-create the imagery of continuity of past spectacle, as Tagore remarked of the colonial attempt to re-create the *Darbar* in 1912. In contrast the anti-colonial world had the capacity to create new images, images of a possible new world. What emerged thus was, as we can see from the way JP's critique developed, a fascinating scenario where there was persistent effort to distinguish the genuine image from its simula-crum on the basis of a precise mode of reproduction of politics. Thus genuine democracy was to be distinguished from its make-up, self-management from government, socialism from state bureaucracy and ethics from its political mask – and all these could be done because there was the constant reproduction of anti-colonial politics even after colonialism had left the scene at least in its direct form. This is the imprint of anti-colonial politics, nation and democracy combining in eternal alterity, never imitating each other, yet never leaving each other forever. In this world of unbounded communication between nation and democracy, images of people and popular desires and interests formed the powerful intermediary that would not tolerate any compe-tition from any other institution aspiring for that role. Representative government thus could be tolerated, but never beyond a point. If nec-essary in the interest of immediacy, this institution had to be sent back to the depths of hell to which it belonged.

Representative government cannot behave like autocratic gov-ernment. Hence it has to always oscillate between consensus that it demands in the interest of legitimacy and schizophrenia it suffers from in the absence of the former. It is this strange link or disjunction in the institution of government that JP was targeting. No drama could be successfully built around this institution for long, because whatever the government represented would remorselessly try to come out on its own. Will, as he suggested repeatedly, could not be represented. Only actions like the ones he initiated in the sixties of the past century or other popular actions of that time spoke of the presence of will.

The immediacy of democracy

All these discussions were turned in JP's writings towards vindicating what he thought to be the only authentic way in which democracy could be practised, namely the direct way. Political will generates the determination to strive for direct democracy, which means least mediation by the so-called representatives (who actually form a political class), and therefore immediate democracy. Socialism, Gandhi's teachings, *Sarvodaya*, rural reconstruction, *sangharsh* (confrontation against autocracy), *janata sarkars* (people's organs for self-rule to be formed at the lowest level and then moving upwards as alternatives to governmental organs), total revolution – each of these signified for him direct actions by the producing masses. Here I think we have a broader historico-political lesson for us that will call for standing the conventional wisdom on its head.

We have been told that the national movement against alien rule took the form of demanding democratic representation of the people. People demanded free elections, universal voting rights, constituent assembly and own constitution and of course 'no taxation without representation'. This was the model of nationalism, of building the nation-state. But this is only one side of the story. I have already indicated that in the anti-colonial world there were persistent attempts to make distinction between the original imaginations and thus the genuine images (of freedom) and their simulacrum. Thus from 1857 onwards we find the anti-colonial political thinkers again and again coming up with models of direct action with, as I have argued elsewhere, the decade of the forties in the last century providing the most striking illustrations of direct thinking and actions.[17]

From the attempt to produce parallel institutions of society (schools, clubs, colleges, academies, civil guards, etc.) in the early part of the twentieth century to forming parallel army (Hindustan Republican Army) in the twenties, to the direct call for Quit India ending with the infamous direct action in 1946–47, we have countless instances of anti-colonial politics striving for immediate democracy. Immediate democracy involved similar countless instances towards social reconstruction in diverse fields including education, aesthetic and ethical reorientation and science. This was the developing area of popular power – a kind of alternative to juridical sovereignty that we see in situations of dual power. JP therefore least talked of sovereignty as if he hated this juridical concept, as if he saw in it the demise of *sarvodaya*, direct programme of the people, the demise of political will and the final triumph of colonialism. This line of thinking in our nationalist thought was not exceptional; indeed it had a strong presence. Let us only consider for a moment the fact that almost seventy years ago in the forties of the past century, people in Nandigram dug roads, cut all approaches and built barricades in defence of their rule; and decades later they did the same against Left Front government's attempt to dispossess them of land. Thus the question: when does the surge for immediate democracy happen? As JP said, when government acts foolhardy, refuses to dialogue, when the representational, that is governmental majority, and social majorities become acutely different from each other, direct democracy becomes the call of social majority at that moment.

Today as we look around at the debris of representative democracy throughout the post-colonial world, we can get a sense of the historical background against which the popular assault on representative democracy is taking place with both good and bad effects. The struggle against colonialism and neo-colonialism today has been for immediate democracy and not for some far-away goods to be realized some day through representative mechanisms.

Yet all these are not very difficult to understand. The difficult point to reflect in this context will be: was anti-colonial politics (which JP was carrying in the post-colonial period) anti-representation? Did not Congress and Gandhi quarrel for seats in the Roundtables, and did not they quarrel over representational right – a quarrel that led to the Partition of the country? True as these and perhaps many other such instances were, they reflect what we can call the passive side of the revolution – the eternal attempt to resolve the revolutionary problematic (the problem of direct democracy) in a passive, least conflictive way leading to the setting up of indirect organs of rule at the cost of autonomous spaces in society. However, equally true have been attempts to realize direct democracy bypassing the representational problematic. It is in this sense that the anti-colonial politics was anti-representational.

This was possible in two ways: (a) first, the anti-colonial world in terms of its general destiny was self-demonstrative. Even though there were elaborate arguments at the end of the nineteenth century and the beginning of the twentieth century to demonstrate why alien rule had to go, by and large anti-colonial politics needed no such brief. This is one more reason why I have argued that, unlike bourgeois democratic politics or liberal politics, anti-colonial politics needed no big theory; actions were self-demonstrative.[18] That is why JP in his letters and pamphlets would say in defence of his steps that the explanation was simple. They needed no big theory or big wisdom. We may say, actions being the critical element in this non-representational dynamics settled the tension between the speculative-effect and the passion-effect. Anti-colonial politics to sum up the point was exactly opposite of what our theoreticians of nationalism have claimed. It never sought resemblance or verisimilitude; there was no model; the non-representational character was because this politics did not depend on figures or models (of leaders, kings, parliamentarians, etc.). (b) Second, to the anti-colonial subject the representative regime owed its existence to colonial rule. Representation in the colonial framework meant spectacle, distance, centralization, authority and withdrawal from the autonomous aspects of life. The opposite was thus always immediate democracy. The disjunction between representation and immediacy of democracy was too much. JP's writings in the last phase remind us of this disjunction, and the periodic demonstration of this disjunction in the post-colonial life.

JP observed how the imported institutions of representative rule in some countries of Asia were proving non-functional, and therefore he commented,

> It is not the abstract virtues of democracy that so excite us, the democratic intelligentsia, but the concrete fruits of democracy in terms of welfare and the palpable stake they have or part they play in working it, that determine the attitude of the mass of the people anywhere to the institutions and processes of democracy.[19]

Further he observed that *panchayati raj* was becoming a governmentalized form of self-rule, and democracy needed moral force, collective feeling and service to the people to rescue it from the bureaucratic trap. Soon JP was speaking of 'revolution on the agenda' (1969), which would mean now not only reconstruction and 'voluntary action' but direct action. He argued,

> Take the case of sharecroppers. We hear about the Naxalites. I have sympathy for the Naxalbari people. They are violent people. But I have every sympathy with them because they are doing

something for the poor. There is some limit to the patience of the people. Why cannot the question of sharecroppers be settled. . . . Thousands of sharecroppers are being evicted because the land-owners have the right to resume the land . . . these things are happening today and the law is absolutely impotent to help these poor people.

If the law is unable to give to the people a modicum of social and economic justice, if even whatever is on papers not imple-mented, what do you think will happen if not violence erupting all over? Do you think that mere *mantras* of *Shanti, Shanti* are going to save the situation or the political parties which are responsible for this legislation? The very people who pass these laws have seen to it that the laws are not implemented.[20]

And so JP proceeded to highlight the issue of bonded labour, agri-cultural labour, poor peasants and sharecroppers. Here again he saw that legislations like the Minimum Wages Act were proving of no avail, the recommendations of local revenue and development offic-ers were being ignored and even one act (Privileged Persons Home-stead Tenancy Act passed in January 1948) had to wait for twenty-two years to be implemented in a serious manner. Recommendations of the Administrative Reforms Commissions were by and large ignored. Democracy thus had to meet 'face to face' the conditions of the people. And democrats had to decide 'first things first'. This was the clearest signal that JP was now interpreting direct democracy as immediate democracy. This was 1973. He spoke of the procrastination over the Lok Pal bills, the statutory powers of the Lok Ayukta, of the neglect of the Santharam Committee report, the ways in which parties collected funds, the massive corruption that lections stoked, and therefore in the background of all these the need for total revolution.

'There must be people's direct action.' These direct actions he stressed must be at all levels, because it was at all levels that popu-lar aspirations were being prevented from being realized. Primacy of the people meant not substituting one government with another, but 'going over the heads of organized parties and (people) asserting their will'. He wrote as the National Emergency was clamped on the coun-try in 1975,

> . . . There is no possibility in sight and in the near future of India having any other type of democracy than she has today. Hopefully, if the opposition wins the next parliamentary elections, the present constitution and the electoral laws, rules etc. might be improved.

But the 'type' of democracy will not change much. Therefore there seems to be no way for a people's movement (which term should include the students and youth) to carry forward its programmes of revolution except in the context of a party (or a coalition of parties) government.

In respect of 'improvement' in the present type of democracy, I have mentioned constitutional and statutory amendments under an Opposition government. But there may be extra-constitutional and legal ways of doing it also. This can be possible only in the context of an on-going people's movement. These Struggle Committees or People's Committees, or *Navanirman Samitis*, *Viplavi Samitis* (whatever be the name given to the organs of people's struggles) may perform, as we were aiming to do, the function of (a) being sounding boards or consultation media at the time of candidate selection, (b) and acting as 'watch-dogs' and accountability enforcers over their local representatives as well as over the whole working of the government.[21]

Clearly, we have here the rumblings of the thought that representative democracy will stymie constituent power as representative mechanisms emerge as the constituted power out of the void. Hence some ways must be found out to recover the constitutive power of the founding moment. JP suggested his ways; even if he had not thought of anything else, the fact that he could think along this line makes him one of most astute thinkers in post-independent India. He could see that the future political battle will be not between autocracy and democracy, but between representative democracy and the direct democratic demands of the people.

A different political history

Today it is difficult to believe or appreciate that these and similar other writings and the prescient points were made as part of political struggles and actions, and did not emerge out of a theoretical exercise. At the same time we can also note that these writings and actions had a specific idea of politics behind them whose history is irrevocably marked with the history of democracy. It is in this sense that we can say that in modern time the history of the political and the history of democracy are enmeshed with each other. To speak of the boundaries of political realm would be to speak of the boundaries of democracy.

Why is it so? We can locate two reasons. First, democracy evokes the issue of power related to the demos thereby demonstrating the principle of unity. Second, and this is a paradox, democracy besides meaning life in common also exhibits dissemblance, 'disembodied power splintered between diverse agencies of legitimacy, in particular agencies of the law and knowledge'.[22] JP hinted his frustration at this situation and pointed out on various occasions this situation in democracy, namely *disembodied power splintered between diverse agencies of legitimacy*, and said that one of the many factors responsible for this situation is the multiplication of the representative institutions. Both these reasons tell us why the modern history of the political is linked to the history of democracy, which is continuously challenging the political to renew itself in the form of participation or counter-power. As JP's life and themes dear to him showed, this continual renewal of the will through actions opens up the possibility of the emergence of the political subject.

We may wonder how easily he cast away the burden of law in his confrontation with the representative mechanisms of democracy; yet we should remember that this could happen because inspired with the virtue of directness and immediacy he could throw out the idea of legislator as a teacher. He concentrated his examination throughout his life on what we can call the crisis of governability, and as a scientist he threw light on the intermediary bodies that had made government possible, and had helped the democratic state become a network state full of seemingly autonomous institutions, organs and associations. As I have shown, he was not lured by the multiplicity of images of freedom, because he could say that after all these images contributed to a collective imagery of being together – a false imagery, an imagery that needed to be shown what worth it was.

But the fine point here is that, and this too we should note, JP was not arguing for a corporatist state when he was attacking the intermediary bodies for failing the people; he was in fact saying that the nation had no such 'sentimental contract', and the question of the general economy of the society was more important than bonds and effects. The figure of the community that he was raising in the democratic discourse repeatedly was not one of sentiment and bond, but of the way in which counter-power could be and was organized against the dynamics of delegated procedure.[23] JP was thus always operating on two registers – ethical and the political, civic and the programmatic indicating the political. This was in fact indicative of the way in which the anti-colonial manifesto had developed, because in this path the national and the associational were not opposed to each other. By pitting popular associations against representative government and other representative mechanisms, JP would say that he was not at all championing a corporatist nation; he was only drawing the attention of society to the wider reality of democracy.[24] He was not a pluralist therefore in the old functional sense; he was in fact providing a better understanding of 'general will', that is to say understanding of the dynamics of the production of an alternative generality to a politics that had called for the establishment of institutions to represent general will.

And, this is significant. Till date the vagueness of general will (yet the hold of the idea over people that they as nation do constitute a general will) has facilitated the claim of the representative government that it represents the former. But the politics of the anti-colonial world made it imperative for the anti-colonial thinkers to study institutions closely. JP was among those who took this task seriously and in his post-independence speeches and writings he studied the institutions of representative government even more closely to come out with realization that an institution was a *social form*, and therefore there was no mystic in it beyond popular scrutiny. His realization and writings on the institutions of bureaucracy and government particularly in the post-independence period at times echoed the views of Marx, who in *The Critique of Hegel's Philosophy of Right* had said that bureaucracy was the final end of the state, it was a circle from whom nobody could escape, and while it claimed to represent general interest, each bureau went on deceiving the other, thus marking the deadly game of interests. JP's realization akin to this led him to stress the need for parallel institutions to make democracy direct. In as much government and state surveillance needed institutions, immediacy of democracy too called for counter institutional effort, which would be essentially *decentralized* in nature. Thus superintendence over government has to be social, that means widespread, decentralized and village level.[25] It was this parallel history of associations that JP was constantly invoking (and this was the main point in his homage to Gandhi that Gandhi had encouraged the growth of various social associations in the service of the people[26]) in his journey to discover the route to direct democracy. This was of course a tradition beginning in the nineteenth century. The communists had deployed the strategy, before them the militant nationalists. It helped the anti-colonial politics to counter the generality of rule with a parallel generality that was not hegemonic and centralized, but spread over the society and drawing sustenance from the associations that were springing up at every moment of colonized life at all places, anticipated and unanticipated. To the spectre of social and political dissolution of the country raised by Indira Gandhi, JP was saying that if freedom and democracy were to be rescued from the draconian and centralized rule, associational bodies had to be encouraged. As against representative *dejure* bodies, he was thus pitting associations. This was his half-finished blueprint for reorganizing the polity. To be true to him, he was giving us an illiberal conception of democratic politics having deep roots in anti-colonial thinking. It too spoke of general interests, it too created a public, but in this concept the immediacy of people and popular interests as opposed to corporate and group interests was paramount.

We must press this point little more. JP for instance raised the issue of right to work. It meant the freedom of work-based associations that is trade unions. Or, he raised the issue of the right to be heard, which meant not only right to associate but to rebel also, if other avenues of being heard had been shut. Now, as we know thanks to new researches into the history of democracy, these rights had been raised in the nineteenth century. From Tocqueville to Marx all had commented on these rights that went beyond the contemporary theory of liberty.[27] While some said that the state had to take responsibility to provide work or maintain institutions of hearing the people, others thought that this would be over-empowering the state. Still other thought that to gain these rights to the fullest extent, the contemporary social and economic order had to give in to a new order, where these rights would become superfluous. And still others thought that these rights were actually juridical and political measures to create the scope and space to discipline the society and normalize social behaviour so that the polity is never disturbed by deviance. Associations, trade unions, political movements, parties, platforms, solidarities – all these were in the eye of the storm. JP revived the issue of an associational polity in the anti-colonial milieu in an original way, and whoever wants to get an idea of the magnitude of the enterprise he undertook must read the tracts composed in the last twenty years of his life. Association as he formulated the idea contained both hope and revenge: hope for a new democracy, revenge against the mechanisms of deprivation of the liberty of the people. Once again we can hear the echoes of the debate as we see repeated outbursts in government circles in West Bengal against the determination of the opposition in Nandigram to maintain their association against eviction.

To conclude: the anti-colonial culture of generality had both possibilities. One was the corporatist state – a line taken up by Nehru, followed by Indira, emulated by all the all-India political parties, and now evolving further under the impact of the dynamics of the deep marketization of all relations, and the subsequent transformation of the state into a market state. The other was a federal generality produced by the interface of associations, which too drew from the revolutionary culture of generality but refused to relapse into statism that required, as we know, the backing and legitimation by representative mechanisms. The second would revise the theory of democracy in a big way.

The issue of associations thus went far beyond the simple right to congregate or the divide between civil society and political society. In fact the society JP as part of the momentous mass movements of 1964–75 was trying to develop was neither a part of purely civil society, nor purely political society, but civil-political. This civil-political society has nothing to do with the civil society of Locke to Hegel, or the political society enunciated by various writers again through this entire time. It was a society that was acting as the register of collective claim makings, the politics of the collectives such as associations and various contentions involved in this. The difficulty of appreciating associational politics is intimately connected with the archaic views of both civil society and political society.[28]

Notes

1 Karl Marx and Friedrich Engels, *The German Ideology*, Marx Engels Collected Works, Volume 5 (New York: International Publishers, 1973), p. 213.
2 Jayaprakash Narayan, *A Revolutionary's Quest – Selected Writings of Jayaprakash Narayan* (hereafter *SWJN*), ed. Bimal Prasad (New Delhi: Oxford University Press, 1980), p. 18.
3 *SWJN*, pp. 18–19.
4 To avoid any misunderstanding on this point, we should remember that in calling for 'All power to the Soviets', Lenin was aiming at circumventing the obstacles put forward by conventional representative democracy, since he saw the Soviets as direct organs of proletarian rule and emerging directly out of workers' movements. Seen in our context it was like asking for transfer of power to the national political and social institutions emerging directly out of the anti-colonial movements in place of what actually happened, that is transferring power to a party.
5 *SWJN*, p. 233.
6 John Stuart Mill, "On Liberty," in J.S. Mill and A.D. Lindsey (eds.), *Liberty and Representative Government* (London: Dent, 1970), p. 23.
7 Ibid., p. 92.
8 J.S. Mill, "The Subjection of Women", in A.D. Lindsey (ed.), *Liberty and Representative Government* (London: Dent, 1970).
9 J.S. Mill, "Considerations on Representative Government", in A.D. Lindsey (ed.), *Liberty and Representative Government*, Chapter 6, (London: Dent, 1970), p. 229.
10 Ibid., Chapter 18.
11 *SWJN*, pp. 14–15.

12 "The Problems of Socialist Unity", *SWJN*, pp. 72–73.
13 "The Structure of the Socialist Party", *SWJN*, p. 152.
14 All citations in this paragraph from *SWJN*, pp. 181–208.
15 "A Plea for Reconstruction of the Indian Polity", *SWJN*, p. 210.
16 "Putting the Record Straight", *SWJN*, pp. 349–350.
17 R. Samaddar, *The Materiality of Politics*, Volume 2, Chapter 2 (London: Anthem Press, 2007).
18 Samaddar, *The Materiality of Politics*, Volume 1, Chapter 2.
19 *SWJN*, p. 249.
20 "Revolution on the Agenda", *SWJN*, p. 284.
21 "Towards Revolution: Why and How?", *SWJN*, p. 366.
22 Jacques Ranciere, *On the Shores of Politics*, trans. Liz Heron (London: Verso, 2007), p. 43.
23 This point is noted also by one of the most astute analysts of JP's writings. See Bimal Prasad, "Power to People – JP's Approach," in R.M. Pal and Meera Verma (eds.), *Power to People – The Political Thought of M.K. Gandhi, M.N. Ray, and Jayaprakash Narayan*, Volume 2 (New Delhi: Gyan Publishing, 2007), pp. 413–438; for JP's own writings cited here see also, Jayaprakash Narayan, *Communitarian Society and Panchayati Raj*, ed. Brahmanand (Varanasi, 1970); also his "Some Thoughts on the Constitution", *Everyman's*, 26 January 1975.
24 One of the indicators of the degree to which JP disliked the idea of a corporate nation or state is to be found in his attitude to Kashmir and the Northeast. We have to remember that on both of these two issues the traditional Left in India followed the war-like policy of the Indian corporate state and national interest through six decades. JP held remarkably different attitude, congruent with his overall politics, initiated Peace Mission in Nagaland, and of Kashmir, he famously said that since India could not fight on three fronts – poverty, China and Pakistan – would have to decide what they wanted first. His choice was clear – 'Poverty was enemy number one. Let us settle on the other two fronts.' – See Balraj Puri, *J.P. on Jammu and Kashmir* (New Delhi: Gyan Publishing House, 2005), p. 83.
25 It has to be noted that since it was a concrete issue, it called for concrete techniques. I have referred to some of these in the course of this article. For details, see the discussion on 'concrete techniques' in Sebastian Raj S.J., "People's Power through Total Revolution", Paper presented at a discussion on JP co-organized by the JP Centenary Committee, PUCL, and ICSSR, March 2003.
26 See for instance JP's essay on Gandhi, "Gandhi and the Politics of Decentralisation" in Sibnarayan Ray (ed.), *Gandhi, India and the World* (Bombay: Nachiketa Publications, 1970), reprinted in R.M. Pal and Meera Verma (eds.), *Power to People – The Political Thought of M.K. Gandhi, M.N. Ray, and Jayaprakash Narayan*, Volume 1 (New Delhi: Gyan Publishing, 2007), pp. 273–289.
27 For an account of the debate, Pierre Rosanvallon, *The Demands of Liberty – Civil Society in France Since the Revolution*, trans. Arthur Goldhammer (Cambridge, MA: Harvard University Press, 2007), Part III, "Jacobinism Amended", pp. 149–230.
28 For a longer critique of this non-dialectical division, Samaddar, *The Materiality of Politics*, Volume 2, Chapter 5.

5 Citizen as a problem figure for governance

A problem figure

The previous chapters should help us to understand why any thinking on governance has led to ideas of self-government, self-governance and government of the self. Yet the union or the combination of self and government has not been easy. To be truthful, the relation has been always tense and uncertain. To consider the self as an object to be governed has been a dream of moralists and philosophers, but in politics the problem has been like a nightmare. As the preceding account of the ideas of Jayaprakash Narayan showed, the persistent questions have been: How does one define self-government? How does one define self? What is the relation between democracy, governance and the self? In other words, how do we link the issue of autonomy of politics and governance?

In all the possible answers, the citizen is the incipient figure linking these questions, and connecting the three categories: democracy, government and self. The citizen is at the heart of democracy. The citizen represents the political self. The citizen symbolizes the autonomy of politics. Yet the citizen is to be governed. Otherwise the state, and in particular the democratic state, will not run properly. The bourgeois age must ensure that the autonomy of politics be sufficiently predicated upon the sovereignty of the market and the sovereign act of governing. Therefore while bourgeois rule cannot proceed without the autonomous juridical figure of the citizen, governance in bourgeois age must ensure proper running of the market and a guided coordination of the various segments of the society towards producing the sovereign consumer and the labour that will maintain the production of the consumer. Therefore the citizen remains a problem figure. It is the juridical representation of politics and the sovereign consumer individual, yet its autonomy periodically threatens the stability of the government. It threatens to melt into a crowd, and dissolve itself in illegality, insubordination and revolt. How to govern the citizen who should be un-governable, and who must represent the principles of liberty and equality? What about the clash of wills: the will of the government and the will to claim the political society? We shall try to show that these contradictions and its constituting paradoxes did not evaporate in colonial and post-colonial India, but sharpened.

From this angle, the current discussion on citizenship is strangely in an anaemic state. The debate is usually between a liberal-republican model (including the civic community variety) and a multicultural model that allows variegated citizenship. The most an analyst goes in terms of having a certain frame is to set up citizenship as an idea, perhaps also an ideal institution, and then show its various regressions, incompleteness, diminutions and therefore the contests, in one author's evocative term *discontents*.[1] Yet the discussion does not focus on the question: is it in the nature of the political subject that it continuously pushes the frontier of citizenship, or is there a given legal-ethical core of the idea of citizenship to which we are forever trying to approximate through a discourse of rights (and perhaps obligations and therefore right conduct)? The question is crucial because the history of citizenship is extremely contentious, and the mark of the political subject has been more often than not violence. Also, since we have the habit of discussing democracy in normative term, the violent, unruly and the excessive nature of its emblematic institution, citizenship, does not come under scrutiny. It is an embarrassment that is passed over silently. We do not like to discuss citizenship in discussions on governance. The habit now tells us to associate 'people' with politics, 'target population groups' with governance, and 'citizenship' with law and norms reinforcing law. It is not recognized that in the material life of politics, law and governance, the neat categories of people, target population groups and citizen are mixed up.

We are therefore always given a normative idea of citizenship expressed through oft-used phrases 'legal citizenship', 'social citizenship', 'differentiated citizenship', or 'civic community', as if citizenship a pre-set norm and an institution, from which rights flow, and therefore citizens claim certain rights. However, there is also a parallel history less documented in official political accounts of citizenship but archived in various popular registers of protests and rebellions, which shows citizenship as a contested category. The question will be: is citizenship a contested category, what Marx called 'the semblance of reality' – in other words the juridical-ethical veil of a more fundamental process, in this case the process of the emergence of the political subject? What is at work that makes citizenship a contested and contingent notion for governance?

It may of course be argued that if we regard citizenship as having violent foundations then we are conflating politics with war. To this we can reply that politics is indeed declared and often undeclared social war. But more significantly, from the angle of the state the problem of conferring citizenship is how to govern the rights-based subjects in view of how it (the state) came into being. The reason is simple: one cannot govern in the same way as one has inherited power that is by usurping, or conquering, or filling in a void, or contriving a mode of acquiring legitimacy. Therefore the reason of the state which goes by the name *security* is always linked with a world of *government*, which runs on the basis of the principles of legitimacy, utility, ratio and delivery. In speaking of citizenship we are therefore already in a world of government and the reason of the state: a mixture of submission and coercion, regulations and force, legitimacy and extraordinary laws, normalization and strife, high principles and utility and finally, civic life and war.

The citizen in arms

In the besieged city of Delhi during the Great Mutiny of 1857 a Court of Administration (COA) was formed by the mutineer soldiers in early July. It popularly came to be known as the Court of Mutineers. The leading officers of the rebel regiments, which had arrived in Delhi, formed the committee. The committee drew up a Constitution, called itself noticeably not Court of Mutineers, even though people of Delhi treated it as the mutineers' committee, but a Court of Administration (COA). The committee had posts such as *president, vice president,* and had organs known as *committees* – these italicized English words occurring in the documents written mostly in Urdu and some in Persian. The committee had six representatives from the army – two each from the artillery, infantry and the cavalry – and four from civilians. It laid down elaborate rules of procedure of debates, voting and implementation of decisions. The archive tells us the decisions were to be consensual, though in case of persistent difference of opinion majority vote would prevail, and even the protocol of presentation of views inside the committees was well defined. Similar rebel councils were formed by mutineer soldiers at Lucknow, Kanpur and other centres of rebellion. In each of these instances the final source of sovereignty was identified with the emperor or the local king, queen or the prince. In Delhi, however, the profile of the birth of the first generation of citizens was the clearest with its marks of emergence, identity, confusion and the challenge of the time.[2]

The COA functioned as the government till the last day when the British stormed the city on 14 September 1857. As late as on 11 September 1857, it adjudicated a dispute around an abducted woman by the name Khair Roshan and set her free on the basis of her assertion that 'Jabar Sepoy did not abduct me. Pir Baksh Tinman beat me up so I left him and went and stayed with Jabar's wife . . . Jabar did not abduct me'.[3] In its nearly three months' existence, it had devised a mode of governance, appointed and received reports from the police and other law keepers, checked the powers of the emperor, nobles, moneylenders and traders, decided on ways and instruments of raising revenue, and for all these functions gave itself a *constitution*. In this way the Court of Administration became the first form of some consciousness and an organization that would make citizenship possible. The constitution also made it possible to determine duties and responsibilities (with implicit ethical guidelines) of the court members whereby even the issue of the use of an elephant by the commander-in-chief (the head of the rebel forces and the COA) had to be clarified as to whether it was for public purpose (therefore permissible under the public budget) or personal purpose (in that case to be borne by his individual means) notwithstanding the fact that Mirza Mughal, the son of Emperor Bahadur Shah Zafar, was a prince. The small (in print form in English translation three pages) constitution also gave the COA emergency powers, the power to alter its rules, and suggested rules of forming civilian and military secretariats. However, for our purpose even more interesting are the records of letters of instructions and suggestions flowing between the COA and the commander-in-chief, from the COA and its individual office-bearers to police officials, complaints from the citizens of Delhi and orders thereon, instructions on redress of grievances of poor people against misdeeds of the encamped soldiers, rules of buying and consuming opium, on addressing issues of missing or abducted women or women eloping with other men leaving their husbands, or courtesans (thought to be promiscuous) dragging men to the *thanedar* (station house officer) for settlement of disputes and finally communiqués on the vexed question of separation of powers between such as municipal services and police services, or taxation authority and military authority. One of the vexing questions was: who had the duty of removing and disposing of the corpses of dead enemy soldiers or informers or agents of the enemy?

The constitution did not speak of rights and entitlements. Therefore we cannot say that the constitution produced citizens or the citizens had produced the constitution. Still we must remember that Lucknow, another rebel centre, saw during this period the formation of a military cell and a parliament.[4] It was a time of war, rebellion, annihilation of enemies, and the dire challenge of survival along with the task of governing a war-ravaged city overshadowed everything else. Yet, records show traces of a doctrine of freedom from alien power, and hence, responsibility, rule of order and limits even of the power of the emperor, who was now reduced by the colonial authorities to being the king of Delhi and known like that. The constitution was thus a document of defined powers and against arbitrariness. If citizenship had to originate in war, this was one classic example.

In the contemporary account of Charles Ball on the Indian Mutiny, we have a report on the soldiers appealing 'To all Hindoos and Mussulmans, Citizens and Servants of Hindoostan, the Officers of the Army now at Delhi and Meerut' to defend the dignity and integrity of the country.[5] Besides all the steps mentioned earlier, Ball tells us, the COA removed the treasury left by the British inside the fort, did not allow its loot, prevented any distribution of the treasury as booty among the soldiers and issued money from it for the maintenance of the royal household.[6] That this was not an attempt to reinvent royalism or imperial legitimacy was clear from the fact that the titular head of the government of Delhi, Bahadur Shah Zafar, later in his defence at his trial in January 1858, denied any responsibility for the actions of the mutineer soldiers. He said infamously,

> Whatever happened was done by that army, I was powerless. . . . As for the commands and edicts bearing my seals and signature the fact is that since the day this army arrived here and killed the rulers (that is the British) and imprisoned me, I was fully under their control. They would write whatever they wished and get it stamped by my *munshi*, or very often stamped it themselves.[7]

This was incipient republicanism. The mutiny was thus accompanied by a turn to constitution framing, rules and committee formation to pass edicts to govern the land, which must have had mixed origins, in the sense that committee formation was neither wholly modern nor wholly mediaeval and must have come from the lessons the soldiers had learnt in the British army as well as the earlier tradition of village councils. Early citizenship practices were embedded thus in a variety of ways.

The existence of such a committee that would assume the task of governing the city while conducting a war of independence also reflected the age-old moral obligations of the ruler. The principle laid down by the Afghan monarch Sher Shah Suri, possibly one of the best medieval rulers of India, namely 'Justice alone is the mainstay of government and the source of prosperity to the governed; injustice is the most pernicious of things, it saps the foundation of the government and brings ruin upon the rulers'[8] must have been fresh in popular memory. Moral obligations of a ruler implied acknowledgement of certain entitlements of those who were being governed. The white skin conquerors were alien not only because they came from faraway land, but mainly because they were unjust. Anti-colonial notion of citizenship began this way.

We can note some more features of this situation. The records, as the compiler of the records Mahmood Farooqui tells us, show the frequent use of the word *sarkar* (government), which was not strictly the king's government, but government in its own right. The *sarkar* was the recipient of public petitions, issued orders to be obeyed and was legitimate not because it was an imperial government, but a rebel soldiers' council, which was fighting for independence, and had taken it upon itself the task to defend the city and the interests of the city dwellers. Thus, till the last day, prisoners' allowance system was maintained, houses for the lunatics and the destitute were kept running, assistance petitions were discussed, the organization of the sexual life of the city was maintained (therefore the numerous adjudications on complaints around women) and amid all the anarchy, which is the staple stuff of the historians of 1857, a surprisingly active *sarkar* was in place. It maintained order and functioned. Not only the rebel city was waging a war against a preponderant power, but within the rebel city, we must note, a class war was on – between soldiers representing newly constituted politico-military power on one hand and the wealthy merchants and the colonial compradores, spies and agents on the other, also between soldiers and the remnants of the old feudal aristocracy, and then finally between men and women. The class war only emphasized the birth of a new structure of authority. The papers of the Mutiny in Delhi, Farooqui adds, indicate a preexisting system of record keeping and thus the existence of record-keepers, clerks, a rudimentary system of modern governance, some elements of which were perhaps learnt from the colonial superintendence of the city before the rebellion had burst out and driven the colonial rulers out. Also the way in which thousands of labourers were mobilized in those three months was an indication of the presence of a legitimate authority – neither purely colonial, nor simply of the king, nor even purely the legitimacy of a mutineer power, that could simply conscript massive amount of labour and deploy the labourers in defence of Delhi, but this legitimacy may have been a mix of all these three sources plus the legitimacy that owed its existence due to the network of power and structure of linkages that obtained in the relation between Delhi and the vast countryside of Northern India, also between the rebels and the hinterland of rebellion.[9]

Analysis of the intelligence records pertaining to the Wahabi rebellion in India in mid-nineteenth century shows the existence of a surprisingly modern system of information passing from the Wahabi centres in the North (Patna, Delhi, Bareilly, Peshawar) to preachers present in army cantonment towns in deep South, the plebeian nature of their followers there, and once again a combination of republican sentiment, anger against the colonial power and appeals to communal concord between Muslims and Hindus against the 'Christian' race, and a readiness to take to modern forms of politics. Remarkably, even when they considered themselves *ghazis* (holy warriors), they submitted to the administration of the COA.[10]

This history of anti-colonial reason of governance is of course not continuous. Reasons of state and reasons of governance both changed after the suppression of the mutiny and the re-conquest of India by the colonial British power. The full thrust of the liberal way to rule was evident in the post mutiny years with rapid advance of law-making procedure on the basis of successive Law Commissions, Evidence Act, the Penal Code and the Criminal Procedure Code, gradual introduction of limited franchise and representative system of governance, and finally an elaborate way to govern through rule of law as laid down by the Government of India Act of 1935. By these far-reaching measures within a span of about eighty years the possibilities of insurgent constitutionalism had diminished drastically. On one hand mainstream nationalism brought forth a theory of citizenship based on pan-Indian 'republican' identity that would ignore various inequalities and the fault lines of religion, gender, caste and region, and thereby making citizenship the subject of a majoritarian, male dominated polity, on the other hand, nationalism was defined by others outside this majoritarian politics as the space of several nations within India. Thus just like Ambedkar, Muhammad Iqbal was never tired of repeating, namely that the Muslim Indian could become a true citizen, free of social and economic exploitation, only when he or she was free of Hindu domination. Even though efforts like the Lucknow Pact were made from time to time to combine republican citizenship with ascriptive citizenship, these by and large failed till the Indian Constitution could reach an uneasy compromise of the two. But this is a story to which we shall come later.

Before independence could be realized as freedom a citizen as citizen had to be free from other inequalities besides the colonial inequality. Iqbal in fact wrote to Jinnah in 1937,

> Personally I believe that a political organisation which gives no promise of improving the lot of average Muslim cannot attract our masses. Under the new constitution (that is 1935 Act) the higher posts go to the sons of upper classes, the smaller ones go to the friends or relatives of the ministers. In other matters too our political institutions have never thought of improving the lot of Muslims generally. The problem of bread is becoming more and more acute. . . . The question therefore is: how is it possible to solve the problem of Muslim poverty. . . . Happily there is a solution in the enforcement of the Law of Islam and its further development in the light of modern ideas. After a long and careful study of Islamic Law I have come to the conclusion that if this system of law is properly understood and applied, at last the right to subsistence is secured to everybody. But the enforcement and development of the Shariat of Islam is impossible in this country without a free Muslim state or states. This has been my honest conviction for many years and I still believe this to be the only way to solve the problem of bread for Muslims as well as to secure a peaceful India.[11]

When Indians finally became citizens through the religious wars of 1946–48 and a constituent assembly formed on the basis of limited franchise, the figure of the citizen that emerged bore the marks of this heterogeneous history. This fact is however ignored. What we recognize is that the people of India gave themselves a constitution (the opening words of the Preamble being, 'We the People of India Give unto Ourselves a . . . ') and thereby made themselves the citizens, who would henceforth enjoy rights guaranteed by the constitution, and would become at the same time the subjects of rule of law. Yet this double transformation cannot hide a series of important questions: does the dynamics of governance resolve the paradox of citizenship inherent in the duality of autonomy and subjection to rule? Is the post-colonial resolution of the problematic of citizenship, by which I mean the problem of transformation of the subject to the citizen, final? Or does this constitutional mutation actually produce a third figure? Or, is it more worthwhile to find out those traces of insurgent constitutionalism that speaks of other scenes of politics, beyond rule of law, beyond the framework of a liberal polity, governmentality and authority-sanctioned rights?

Security and rights

Production of the citizen through anarchy, revolt and war is a process that irrevocably combines the task of security with that of achieving rights. In order to secure rights, as Michel Foucault was fond of saying, society had to be secured, citizens' security had to be ensured and therefore anarchy had to be banished. The intelligibility of such reasoning was evident in a variety of situations that brought about citizenship. Citizenship was not only a product of the nation or of democracy, but also of a specific form of governance, whereby the citizen would become the simultaneous subject of rights and security.[12] The combination of security and rights, we may say, worked even more forcefully in the colonial context and subsequent de-colonization. The appearance of rights was possible, we can argue along the lines of Charles Tilly, when rights took the nature of claims and entitlements.[13] The citizen was thus entitled to security. Security was the collective name of enforceable claims on delivery of goods, services or protection by specific others. One can also recall Barrington Moore's argument (*Social Origins of Dictatorship and Democracy*, 1966), namely that citizenship rights were historical products and outcomes of extremely acute contentions. These contentions indicated collective claim makings in the origin of rights, and that crucial rights came to fruition by means of rebellions and revolutions.

In the aftermath of 1857 and the next seventy-five years that followed rights spread to larger populations, initially mainly peasant rights, later other kinds of rights (minority rights, labour rights, language rights, voting rights, etc.) as well, and they eventually became citizenship rights. In some cases rights were wrested from local authorities and spread to the larger population from there, as the history of the mutiny showed. In this context we can think of the *praja andolans* (movements for rights of the subjects in native princely states). Rights eventually spread on a national scale, and thus struggles at national scale had to do with the rise and spread of rights.

The entire anti-colonial history of the origin of rights showed one more thing. As the constituent assembly was poised to give formal shape to the institution of citizenship (to be finalized through the Citizenship Act[14]), rights and duties by that time had become enlarged. They implied enforced obligations – the result of bargaining between the two parties – state and peoples, or between several parties and groups. Securitization of life, politics, territory and the emergence of rights as guarantee of existence in a conflict torn society did not come through any evolutionary process; and even if we speak of an evolution, this was marked by contentions. As the Indian constituent assembly deliberations demonstrated, there was hard bargaining over rights. Bargaining was required from both or all sides, and rights and obligations of post-colonial citizenship emerged from this process. It also meant grant of national rights to people as minimally defined as possible. All these mean that citizenship rights have to be seen relationally, and not through any ideological or discursive glass.

We have to pause here to take note of a line of argument, which is sensitive to the uncertain nature of the post-colonial resolution of the problematic of citizenship. It says that the old binary framework of master race and the subject population characteristic of colonial rule survived the process of decolonization, and the colonial rule of difference reproduced itself through the division between citizen and the subject, city and the countryside, reform and repression and between the elite, formal, representative society built around votes, money, property, civility, legality and others and the political society hovering on the margins of formal democracy and negotiating its existence between legality and illegality. For all these reasons, the argument runs, citizenship as an institution does not make any substantive sense to the greater mass of population in post-colonial societies. Surveying what he termed as 'decentralised despotism and the legacy of late decolonisation' in Africa, Mahmood Mamdani in his famous book, *Citizen and Subject*, wrote on the process of the reproduction of colonial rules of polity in details, and concluded that a non-coercive and democratic politics 'require(s) that the nature of power in both spheres, rural and the urban, be transformed simultaneously. Only then the distinction rural-urban – and inter-ethnic – will be more fluid than rigid, more an outcome of social processes than a state enforced artefact'.[15]

This is a compelling vision whose argument is structural in nature. Yet the question will be: what can bring about this transformation? Will the mass movements and resistance struggles he speaks of, or the negotiations on the margins of formal politics that others with similar arguments speak of, be without the citizenship struggles that have a long genealogy in the anti-colonial past, in the history of moral obligations and legitimacies of other kinds? This is where we have to realize the significance of the repeated emergence of the political subject in the anti-colonial and post-colonial time, study the continuities and discontinuities in this history, and the abiding interest of all those who are excluded to become citizens to enjoy rights, liberty and to be considered as equal.

There is no ideal citizen. Even when we recognize citizen as the political subject of a type, we have to still remember that as a phenomenon citizenship can be fruitfully studied only through fiercely contentious events. In Indian history these events were as much the Mutiny of 1857 as the religious wars of 1946–47, or the Royal Indian Naval Mutiny of 1946, or the peasant upsurges of late nineteenth century, or the August Uprising of 1942. We can add several such events: perhaps we can recall the actions of militant nationalists, in as much as the non-cooperation movements led by Gandhi and the Indian National Congress. They are not of uniform nature. They also did not leave uniform consequences. These events are like what Foucault called 'breaches of self-evidence',[16] because each event stops us from constructing a theory of citizenship to be valid across time and space. Each event when interrogated takes us to unanticipated connections, encounters, strategies, clashes, and lends us a different kind of intelligibility on the issue of citizenship. We shall see in that variegated landscape of citizenship the co-existence of British liberal philosophy, anti-colonial rebellions, access to arms by the colonized people thus precipitating the emergence of the *citizen armed* who is the subject on the barricade, the two factors of blood and territory, plus ideas and practices of representative government, and many other features. We shall also see the development of the apparatuses to right size and right shape, respectively, the territory of the country and the people that have influenced the discourse of citizenship in India. We cannot miss the fact, as the events we have referred to on the preceding pages suggest, that citizen as a figure of politics does not sit happily with the discourse of governance. Even though there are innovations in the theory of governance in this neo-liberal age, intending to add flexibility to the apparatus of governance, the figure of citizen exceeds the structural confines of governmental apparatus.

Insurgent constitutionalism

The significant question will be: has insurgent constitutionalism died in face of the relentless march of the governmental machinery? Has the legacy of popular constitutionalism faded away from the memory of the subject?

Part of the answer lies in a new way to write constitutional history in which the history of citizenship is embedded. On one hand there is a Whig view that gives reasons as to why the constitution remains a 'living document', in form of an 'extended borderless body of an unwritten constitution' and thus citizenship will be regarded as a living institution; on the other hand we have the critical view, namely that continuous popular challenges and situations of illegalities and semi-legalities force the judicial-legislative discourse of the polity into keeping the text of citizenship a referral point. Yet to point out the rival Whig and the critical versions is not enough. It is necessary to have a proper historical method to write the constitution's biography. The Whig picture of the constitution in India for instance was largely evoked by the panoramic reports in contemporary newspapers during the drafting of the constitution, and the learned books by Granville Austin and others, which suggested a nationwide public political sphere that was pluralistic, representative and responsive at the same time. Thus grew a mythology further strengthened by reports of jurists, legislators and statesmen deliberating (Nehru's letters to the chief ministers are an instance of evoking this image) on the constitutional future of the country. But precisely at the same time, parallel and distinct from this, in various local meetings, local council deliberations, party assemblies, political rallies and public hearings, groups of populations were experiencing constitutional politics in a different way, which did not take the meaning of the constitution too literally and often mixed illegal and semi-legal behaviour with popular constitutional thinking. Mixing reports and tracts with posters, handbills and manifestos, and using in this way oral, visual and print methods, constitutional thinking spread to wider audiences. Invariably this process evoked and dissolved in turn the distinction between those included and those excluded from the official political nation.

To give one brief example of this: anyone familiar with twentieth-century Indian history knows how much the issue of reservation of jobs, and seats in public educational institutions and legislatures, has been an issue of bloody contention in the post-colonial life of the Indian citizen. We cannot repeat that story here. But we can take up a slice of that – the account of women's reservation, and the ways popular politics has impacted on the constitution's working, given the fact that the constitution has both equality and justice-bearing provisions.

As we know, by the Acts of 1919 and 1935 separate electorates were granted to the Muslims, Sikhs and Christians. Depressed classes also got few nominated seats and later on some elected seats in 1932. The nationalist opinion mobilized under the Indian National Congress opposed special electoral rights, and the nationalist women's organizations like the All India Women's Congress opposed legislative reservations for women, because they thought that reservation went against the demand of the Indian women for absolute equality of political status. However, women associated with the Muslim League argued that reservation was required for women. The Government of India Act (1935) provided forty-one reserved seats for women in provincial legislatures and limited reservations in central legislature. After 1947, independent India's government was called upon to fulfil the promise of ending all forms of discrimination against women and ensuring constitutional equality through non-discrimination and equal protection. But in the following decades women's movement forced the government to realize that non-discrimination was not enough, but affirmative actions were necessary. The struggle for political participation meant presence in the legislatures and all other deliberative assemblies from top to the levels below. The debate on 'quota for women' began in a big manner. Though the Committee on the Status of Women in India appointed by the government in 1971 in its report *Towards Equality* (1974) stopped short of recommending quota of seats for women, it blamed the entire legal-political-administrative set-up for the persistence of gender inequality. The report only accentuated the debate on the quotas as a means for women's political participation and presence in representative organs. It was found out that less than 10 per cent of the tickets were allotted for women in the national elections.

In the 1990s the debate over quota sharpened. A large number of women's organizations approved the idea of quotas as a necessary means to ensure women's representation in legislation-related activity. The National Perspective Plan for Women (1988) recommended 33 per cent of seats in all elected assemblies from village to parliament level. The 73rd and the 74th Constitutional Amendment Acts (1992) provided for reserved quotas for women in local self-government institutions. Thus about one million women got elected in the *panchayat* institutions. Today the demand is to have 33 per cent of seats in national and state legislatures also reserved for women. There are strong differences of opinion on this. There have been numerous attempts to pass the bill since 1996. Some argue that this must include reservation of women belonging to minority communities; some demand that there should be provision for reservation of women belonging to other backward classes, some demand reservation for women belonging to Dalit and indigenous communities. Some say that the beginning should be made with provision for general reservation, because with presence of women in legislative assemblies a big step would be taken towards ensuring representation of women and their political participation.[17]

The dispute over reservation of seats for women is only a part of a much larger story of how to match the constitutional idea of equality and non-discrimination with social demands for justice and compensatory preferences. These preferences have always started as temporary measures, but have proved durable, which only shows the role that popular politics plays in the life of a constitutional institution such as citizenship. Likewise, ideas of justice, secularism, group rights, decentralization, legality, elections and the dynamics of representation – all these have produced unintended results. All these are present in what is called *popular constitutionalism*, and it is this conflictive reality of popular interventions that determines the quality of life of the institution called citizenship. We shall discuss the issue of popular constitutionalism in greater details in the last chapter.

Kalpana Kannabiran in a seminal work has thrown light on the jurisprudence on five non-discrimination rights: disability rights, rights against caste-based discrimination, rights of the indigenous people, rights against discrimination of minorities and finally resistance against sex-based discrimination. Significantly, she does not speak of any liberal right, but elaborates the right to non-discrimination. This is the source of popular constitutionalism, which does not offer any positive definition of justice, but asserts that justice begins with the demand that an injustice that has been committed has to end.[18] In the language of the philosopher '(to imitate a Spinozistic formula) the "just" effort or struggle towards justice or "non-injustice" is already justice itself'.[19]

Likewise, many of the illegalities are to be seen as part of popular politics. Each day we hear one or the other government minister and bureaucrat saying that the illegal movements led by Left extremists known as the Maoists are against the constitution, they do not deserve the protection of law and the constitution and hence there is no scope for dialogue. At the same time we hear other equally numerous voices urging dialogues, which must not flounder on the rock called the law. These experiences should make us sober and help us to realize that the normativity of citizenship is more a political than a legal project. Against a juridical idea of rights and obligations, which is to be invoked under legally defined condition or circumstances we have now the spread of a general desire of justice in the world. Insurgent constitutionalism or popular constitutionalism thrives in such a condition. The intelligibility of the life of post-colonial citizenship resides in such milieu.

We have therefore a fairly revealing picture of this heterogeneous and contingent world of citizenship. We get an idea of the different kinds of power exercising their hold over society and thus influencing citizenship practices of our time. As many histories there are, we can say, as are citizenship cultures and citizenship practices. Yet amid this variegated picture, at least in the post-colonial context we must not lose sight of the insurgent citizen, the key figure behind the legacy of insurgent and popular constitutionalism. In this chapter we have discussed to some extent this legacy. To go beyond the Orientalist framework (which denies any specific genealogy of citizenship in colonial and post-colonial countries), to impact and affect, to move beyond that time and to sketch the trajectory of citizenship *after* orientalism, we have to traverse a different time. We need to seize those moments in our past and present that have symbolized other times, histories and existences. This is what is meant by alterity, to be moved and guided by alterity. That is the way to make sense of the 'immanent other' in studies of citizenship, an elegant phrase whose meanings through Western history have been made accessible to us by Engin Isin in the valuable work, *Being Political*.[20]

To be political, we all have learnt from Machiavelli and his successor appearing nearly four centuries later, Antonio Gramsci, is to achieve 'political clarity',[21] to be alert to moments of contention, to feel always insecure about probable loss of power and therefore devise strategies to make others insecure of their power so that others cannot destroy power of the ruler, to be able to think of the collective only by assuming the profile of a power capable of defending the collective, and thereby preserving and re-creating the commons. If that is so, we must think of a discontinuous way of studying the figure of the citizen – the figure that ended colonialism, brought about an anti-colonial revolution, that compels the apparatus called the constitution to turn the latter against its own self – all these by always invoking other possibilities, telling us of other scenes of politics. One of the discontinuous ways of studying citizenship is to mark out those moments and dynamics when or whereby power and resources are redistributed and a new definition of the community emerges. In fact, the new definition is occasioned by the redistribution, which in turn is occasioned by the interventions of the *people*, who act as *citizens*. This invocation of a specific type of subjectivity, we have to add, cannot be intelligible in terms of governmental logic. The imprints of the philosophical desire for formulating norms for citizenship often find themselves in the register of error; they demonstrates that beyond the norms there is always a 'remainder'. Insurgent citizenship is built on that remainder.

Given the overwhelming presence of politics as governance, we may well ask, are we coming to an end of the classical age of liberal constitution-making, which gave us the myth of the figure of citizen as a rights-bearing and obligation-performing constitutional subject, and therefore of constitutionalism itself? Are we arriving at a more practical age of politics based on a mix of policies as well as practical violence and legalities as well as illegalities? In the background of such a question, the greatest challenge will be how to combine the insights from an insurgent history alluded to in this chapter with a sociological analysis of the particular claims of groups and classes, and therefore of combining a history of popular constitutionalism with a heterogeneous history of citizenship. We shall have to strive relentlessly for that dialectical enterprise. We promise to return to the issue of popular constitutionalism in Chapter 10.

Notes

1 Niraja Gopal Jayal, *Citizenship and Its Discontents: An Indian History* (Ranikhet: Permanent Black, 2013).
2 All facts on COA are taken from Mahmood Farooqui (compiled, translated and edited), *Besieged – Voices from Delhi, 1857* (New Delhi: Penguin, 2010), pp. 53–92.
3 Ibid., pp. 311–312.
4 An English word occurring in Urdu documents; See Rudrangshu Mukheree, *Awadh in Revolt, 1857–58: A Study of Popular Resistance* (New Delhi: Oxford University Press, 1984), pp. 138–140.
5 Charles Ball, *The History of the Indian Mutiny – A Detailed Account of the Sepoy Insurrection in India, and a Concise History of the Great Military Events Which Have Tended to Consolidate British Empire in Hindostan*, 2 volumes, 1858–59 (reprint, Lahore: Sange-Meel Publications, 2007), Volume 1, p. 642.
6 Ibid., Chapter 23, pp. 635–741; on the court and the various measures suggested by the soldiers to the King, pp. 727–728.
7 Farooqui, *Besieged – Voices from Delhi, 1857*, pp. 96–97.
8 Cited in Abraham Eraly, *Emperors of the Peacock Throne* (New Delhi: Penguin, 1997), p. 75; we have to also recall in this context the medieval theory of moral obligations of the rulers during the Mughal Age.
9 On the network of resources (water, grain, men, arms) and linkages that kept the Mutiny alive, see Ball, *The History of the Indian Mutiny*, Chapter 23.
10 Samaddar, *Emergence of the Political Subject*, pp. 39–78.
11 Letter from Lahore, 28 May 1937 – *Letters of Iqbal to Jinnah with Foreword by Quaid-i-Azam* (first published in 1943 by Shaikh Muhammad Ashraf; reprint, Faisalabad: Daira Ma'aref-i-Iqbal, 2002), pp. 23–24.
12 In this context, we can refer to three of his writings, two of them would be the volumes based on his College de France lectures:- Michel Foucault, *Security, Territory, Population – Lectures at the College de France, 1977–1978*, trans. Graham Burchell (New York: Palgrave MacMillan, 2007); Michel Foucault, *The Birth of Biopolitics – Lectures at the College de France, 1978–1979*, trans. Graham Burchell (New York: Palgrave MacMillan, 2008); and Michel Foucault, "Omnes et Singulatim – Towards a Criticism of Political Reason", *The Tanner Lectures on Human Values*, Stanford University, 10 and 16 October 1979, http://foucault.info/documents/foucault.omnesEtSingulatim.en.html (accessed on 17 February 2009).
13 Charles Tilly, "Where Do Rights Come From?" in C. Tilly (ed.), *Stories, Identities, and Social Change* (Lanham, MD: Rowman and Littlefield, 2002).

14 On the history of the Citizneship Act, see Anupama Roy, *Mapping Citizenship in India* (New Delhi: Oxford University Press, 2011).
15 Mahmood Mamdani, *Citizen and Subject – Decentralized Despotism and the Legacy of Late Colonialism* (New Delhi: Oxford University Press, 1997), p. 301.
16 Michel Foucault, "Questions of Method," in James D. Fabion (ed.) and Robert Hurley (trans.) *Power* (New York: The New Press, 2006), pp. 226–229.
17 Zoya Hasan speaks of the 'politics of presence'; see her essay, "The 'Politics of Presence' and Legislative Reservations for Women," in Zoya Hasan, E. Sridharan and R. Sudarshan (eds.), *India's Living Constitution – Ideas, Practices, Controversies* (New Delhi: Permanent Black, 2002), pp. 405–427.
18 Kalpana Kannabiran, *Tools of Justice – Non-Discrimination and the Indian Constitution* (New Delhi: Routledge, 2012).
19 Etienne Balibar, "Justice and Equality? A Political Dilemma: Pascal, Plato, Marx", in Etienne Balibar, Sandro Mezzadra and Ranabir Samaddar (eds.), *The Borders of Justice* (Philadelphia: Temple University Press, 2012), p. 29.
20 Engin F. Isin, *Being Political – Genealogies of Citizenship* (Minneapolis: University of Minnesota Press, 2002), p. 4.
21 Maurice Merlau-Ponty speaks of the virtue of 'political clarity' in his "A Note on Machiavelli", in Richard C. McCleary (trans.) *Signs* (Evanston, IL: Northwestern University Press, 1964), p. 223.

6 The religious nature of our ways of governing

Sanctity, oath, promise

We shall conclude this section with a discussion on how religious beliefs work as ideal of governance. For too much time over the past two and half decades we had discussed secularism and varieties of secularism as the ideal and mode of governance. Let us for once discuss the presence of religion as an ideal for governance. In previous chapters we showed the contentious relation between governance and politics, and discussed how different ideas of autonomous life oriented different ideas of governance. This discussion also brought to light various foundational ideas of self, self-governance, democracy and politics – none of which was left aside or untouched by the all-embracing idea of governing. Is the idea of modern governance then a theological idea? Is the nature of bourgeois rule, priding itself of secular origin and functions, reliant on theological legitimacy? The question is difficult, so is the answer. But to get to the nature of modern governance we must engage in a deep discussion on the issue. We shall have to explore as to why otherwise perfectly secular categories of governance seem to carry marks of religious origins. In this chapter we shall undertake this difficult inquiry.

On 11 September 2012 the Government of India announced a massive rise in the prices of petrol and cooking gas, declared withdrawal of subsidy of cooking gas under a complicated scheme beyond the understanding of most commoners, and withdrew restrictions on foreign direct investment (FDI) in retail business. The ruling party in West Bengal, the Trinamul Congress (TMC), opposed the decision, appealed to the government at the Centre to revoke the decision, and declared that if the central government failed to heed to the appeal of a major UPA (United People's Alliance) ally, it would leave the government and the Alliance. As the central government refused to change its decision, the TMC withdrew from the ruling Alliance and government at the Centre; its ministers resigned from their respective posts; and it accused the ruling Congress Party of trickery and practising falsehood – in its words, breaking a particular promise.

What was the promise? The promise was namely that during the earlier round of rise in the administered prices of petroleum and gas and discussion over the issue of FDI in retail trade, the Congress government at the Centre had made a commitment to the effect that no decision in this regard would be taken without a consensus on the involved issues. Specifically the then finance minister in the Union government had assured the Parliament that the parties and the Parliament would be consulted before a decision was taken on entry of foreign capital in retail trade and insurance. One news agency reported the complaint of breach of promise in this way:

> Kolkata: Opening up a new front against the UPA government, TMC chief Mamata Banerjee on Thursday accused the Manmohan Singh government of going back on its word on involving all stakeholders before opening up multi-brand retail FDI. Referring to the assurance given by then finance minister and current President Pranab Mukherjee in the Parliament, Mamata accused the UPA government of not honouring the commitment made, a news channel reported.
>
> 'The decision to permit 51 % FDI in retail trade is suspended till a consensus is developed "through consultations among various stakeholders. The stakeholders include political parties and states," Pranab Mukherjee had said in both houses of Parliament in December 2011. Mamata's new posturing is expected to make things difficult for the government and also complicates the matter if the Trinamul MPs go ahead and resign from the UPA government. The BJP has also taken a similar line on the issue with LK Advani – in view of the promise made by then finance minister – terming the recent decision by the government as a "breach of trust of Parliament" '.[1]

The theme of breach was reinforced with ethical twist. The same news agency carried further this comment,

> Kolkata: . . . 'I have just come to know through media that Centre has notified FDI in multi-brand retail today. Is it ethical, moral and democratic for a minority government to issue government order forcibly and hurriedly when massive protests against it are taking place across the country?' she (Mamata Banerjee) said on her Facebook page today, terming the move as 'shocking'. She

said, 'These actions by a minority government question its credibility. It also defied democratic traditions in the context of the assurance given in a statement by the former finance minister (Pranab Mukherjee) on December 7, 2011 in Lok Sabha to go in for consensus among all stake holders before taking a decision.'

Banerjee's comments come a day before Trinamul Congress ministers are slated to submit their resignations to the Prime Minister . . .

'It is not understandable as to what has compelled the present minority government to take a hurried decision on such an important issue which touches the livelihood of millions of common people,' Banerjee said.

'Shocking at midnight . . . ,' she said.[2]

The last three words were clearly a reminder of the vow taken by Nehru on the eve of Independence, 'At the stroke of the midnight hour, when the world sleeps, India will awake to life and freedom.' The promise of freedom at midnight had been broken. It was shocking. The West Bengal chief minister Mamata Bandopadhyay was not however alone on the theme of breach of promise. The refrain of breach of promise was elsewhere voiced too. One newspaper carried the news item in a terse manner:

BJP to demand special session to discuss 'breach of promise': The BJP will petition President Pranab Mukherjee demanding a special session of Parliament to discuss the government's decision to allow FDI in multi-brand retail trade, BJP parliamentary party chairman L K Advani said on Wednesday.

'The government had categorically assured that it will not allow FDI in multi-brand retail trade until there is a consensus on this issue. But suddenly it has taken a decision. This is a breach of the promise made to Parliament,' Advani told The Indian Express. 'In fact, this promise was made by the then Finance Minister Pranab Mukherjee. We will petition the President after the September 20 nationwide bandh. We will show his verbatim assurance as the then Finance Minister to the House and demand a special session of Parliament to discuss this breach of promise' . . .

With the entire opposition, and also parties supporting the UPA from outside like SP and BSP along with UPA partner Trinamul Congress, expressing their opposition to the FDI decision, the BJP senses an opportunity to pin down the government to demonstrate UPA's numerical minority in the House.[3]

The president, of course, kept quiet on the matter of promise and the breach. But it was not lost on the readers and listeners of the news that the erstwhile finance minister and now the president Pranab Mukherjee as the main spokesperson of the government in 2011 had repeatedly told the agitators who were demanding the acceptance of a people's bill for the institution of a Lokpal specifically mandated to investigate and arrest the tide of corruption, that the street was not the right place for discussion and decision; and since the government and other political parties may have different views, nothing should be done outside the Parliament.

The invocation of the sanctity of the Parliament is age old, and if we recall William Blackstone, the venerable constitutional commentator of the British Isles with Whig overtones, Parliament is 'coeval with kingdom itself'. And, even though 'the original or first institution of parliaments is one of those matters that lie so far hidden in the dark ages of antiquity, that the tracing of it out is a thing equally difficult and uncertain', yet Blackstone was careful to draw its sketchy genesis from the power of the king to convene the council which would consist of 'all arch-bishops, bishops, abbots, earls, and greater barons, personally; and all other tenants in chief under the crown, by the sheriff and bailiffs; to meet at a certain place, with forty days notice, to assess aids and scutages when necessary'. Parliament's sanctity, he explained, draws,

> first, from the manner and time of its assembling; secondly, its constituent parts; thirdly, the laws and customs relating to parliament, considered as one aggregate body; fourthly and fifthly, the laws and customs relating to each house, separately and distinctly taken; sixthly, the methods of proceeding, and of making statutes, in both houses; and lastly, the manner of the parliament's adjournment, prorogation, and dissolution.

These rules, Blackstone made clear, have evolved, but now that they are in place, they are non-violable. They are rules, and they do not add up to composing a sovereign power; they in fact originate from a sovereign power, which has to convene an assembly of the realm; and but now once in existence they, collectively called the Parliament, are coeval with the realm.[4] In other words, the 'sanctity' of the Parliament which the politicians daily invoke is double faced. They do not replace the executive; they do not also exhaust the executive; yet they are invested with a mystic power without which power over the realm cannot function.[5]

The interesting aspect of this situation is that governmentalization of an institution (through rules, procedures and orders) produces a holy power – doubly holy, because it originates from a holy power, also because the assemblage of certain aspects and procedures makes it sacrosanct, the sacrament of power. Carl Schmitt was therefore wrong when he tried to define the concept of the political as post-philosophical or in this case say post-religious. He famously said,

> A definition of the political can be obtained only by discovering and defining the specifically political categories. In contrast to the various relatively independent endeavours of human thought and action, particularly the moral, aesthetic, and economic, the political has its own criteria, which express themselves in a characteristic way. The political must therefore rest on its own ultimate distinctions, to which all actions with a specifically political meaning can be traced. Let us assume that in the realm of morality the final distinctions are between good and the evil, in aesthetics beautiful and ugly, in economics profitable and unprofitable. The question then is whether there is also a special distinction, which can serve as a simple criterion of the political and of what it consists. The nature of such a political distinction is surely different from that of those others. It is independent of them and as such can speak clearly for itself. The specific political distinction to which political actions and motives can be reduced is that between friend and enemy.[6]

Clearly such post-religious concept of politics is difficult to visualize as there will be always scores of interactions with ethics or morality, aesthetics and economy. Likewise we cannot call it a secular vision of politics, because such a search for a self-evident foundation of the political – as distinct from morality, aesthetics and economy – will be mostly unrewarding. For the same reason it cannot be called a post-secular vision, because while critiquing liberal foundations of politics, it cannot come out of the bind of theology. It is in fact a double bind: theology leading the path to governmental power, governmental power leading to theological glory.

Yet this is not all to the issue of the *sanctity* with which we began. The breach of promise was a breach of sanctity not only because it was a statement given in and to the Parliament and had not been adhered to, but also that Mr. Mukherjee's statement was in the nature of a commitment, an oath, a promise in the nature of an oath, now violated. In politics we witness hundreds of instances, particularly instances of election manifestos, where on the eve of elections promises are given and then violated after the party promising the heaven or what should be the routine has come to power. In fact, as one astute observer of elections in India has commented, with the 'unstoppable rise' of the public or the people, parties hold out promises of all kinds, they are careful not to hurt sentiment of any particular group, on economic matters they can promise both neo-liberal reform and right to food and the election manifesto plays the role of a vital ritual in the exercise of Indian democracy.[7] Election rituals (including promises in elections) are holy. In case of Parliament, such promise, of course, takes an additionally grave character. What is significant here is not that the promises are violated, or that the people draw ethical conclusions from these violations (such as whether x party is trustworthy or not), but that these promises are like un-cashable cheques. You cannot drag the party violating its promises to the court. Law will not take cognizance of the violation.

Why? Because exactly as in the case of constituting a parliament as a sacred body, the democratic public sphere is also constituted by its own specific rules and procedures, which collectively make this sphere democratic, also sacred because it is democratic. In this sphere you can make promise and break it and accept moral consequences, in the long- or even short-run political consequences, but you will not be held for perjury. Therefore oath in cases like this does not express the power of law, but the limit of law, though Agamben chooses to call this as the limit of language arising out of various limits of existing situation. The oath, which 'expresses and guarantees the connection between words and things, defines the truthfulness and force of the *logos*, (and) in blasphemy expresses the breakdown of this connection and the vanity of human language' (italics mine).[8] The violation of oath is equivalent to 'perjury, which separates words from things'.[9] Agamben, however, does not probe further as to why in the modern form a violation of oath in the political sphere is not considered as perjury or blasphemy, and thus punishable by law. Violation of promise in politics evokes moral injunction and castigation. Secularism has ensured that perjury can go unpunished, while creating at the same time an aura of holiness of the sphere where the perjury has been committed. In this sense then we are not in any post-secular situation, for the *secular* contains in it elements of the theological that defines legitimacy and sanctity.

We should attempt if only very broadly an answer to the question, how did this happen? We can see a convergence of conditions at least in India during the modern period, say, roughly from the early part of the seventeenth century, namely, the spreading influence of the idea of a state religion, if not always declared openly, at least followed in practical terms, reinforcing political stability of the ruling class and the oligarchy; this was coupled in less than a century with increasing internal (within India) political fragmentation that inhibited large-scale warfare against other empires and stunted the growth of diplomacy, and finally the growth of an all India educated class that knew how to frame demands of justice and supply the conditions of meeting them in theological-practical/secular terms. The introduction of colonial rule did not basically alter the condition. In some sense it took over the theological-secular mantle of rule, and after less than a century of hesitation it decided to combine the inherited imperial legitimacy with an additional formula of government – the introduction of limited representation marked by the principle of responsibility, again couched in scared language, this time the sacredness of liberal ideas and principles. This very process of law operating in a fixed space called India has now produced impersonal institutions and consensus on the need of a power to make final judgments. But paradoxically it also implies acceptance of the idea that even though the rule will no longer be hereditary that is rule by the principle of blood, yet subjects while being citizens should give loyalty to the authority that precisely because of its impersonal nature can now claim a divine status – again not always declared, but practically accepted.

Such is the genealogy of rule of law in India today, subsuming within it rule by men, rule by custom, rule by orders and regulations and rule by invoking the inexplicable but continuing uniqueness of the country, which the first prime minster of India fondly pointed out by saying,

> Astonishing thought: that any culture or civilisation should have this continuity for five or six thousand years or more; and not in a static or unchanging sense, for India was changing and progressing all the time. She was coming into intimate contact with the Persians, the Egyptians, the Greeks, the Chinese, the Arabs, the Central Asians, and the peoples of the Mediterranean. But though she influenced them and was influenced by them, her cultural basis was strong enough to endure. What was the secret of this strength? Where did it come from?[10]

And, what was his reply? After 'nearly five months . . . writing . . . a thousand hand written pages', he concluded,

> It was presumptuous of me to imagine that I could unveil her. . . . Overwhelmed again and again, her spirit was never conquered, and today when she appears to be the plaything of a proud

conqueror, she remains un-subdued and unconquered. About her there is this elusive quality of a legend of long ago, some enchantment seems to have held her mind. She is a myth and an idea, a dream and a vision, and yet very real and present and pervasive.[11]

This invocation of a mystic past and an inner mystic core of goodness was typical of the India upper-caste Hindu liberal attitude that would tolerate the minorities, allow them also public equality under pressure, but would never concede caste equality (in other words abolition of caste) in social life, and would thus argue for greater governmental power in the form of a centralized apparatus as the best way to protect minorities.

Thus, Nehru in the constituent assembly discussions defended the omission of an entire section on 'Special Provisions Relating to Minorities' in Part XIV in the draft meant to consolidate the democratic arrangements by saying that in democracy such safeguards led to isolation of the minorities, and that unlike in the colonial rule, in republican rule (Nehru termed as 'full-blooded democracy') minorities did not need special provisions, and that these might lead to 'forfeiting that inner sympathy and fellow feeling with the majority'.[12] This was the way, after the most violent religious war in modern Indian history, Indian mainstream politics succeeded to a secular mould. We became post-religious. It was in the same mood that the Union home minister Sardar Vallavbhai Patel remarked in the same assembly on 26 May 1949,

> It is not our intention to commit the minorities to a particular position in a hurry. If they really have come honestly to the conclusion that in the changed conditions of the country that it is in the interest of all to lay down real and genuine foundations of a secular state, then nothing is better for the minorities than to trust the good sense and sense of fairness of the majority, and to place confidence in them.[13]

And then he said,

> What do the minorities desire? Do they want to have any share in the Government of the country and in its administration? I tell you, you cannot have a genuine seat in the Cabinet if you segregate your self from the rest of the community, for the cabinet can only act as a team in a harmonious manner and unless every member of the Cabinet is answerable to a common electorate the

Cabinet cannot function in a fruitful manner. Are you prepared to give up your right of representation in the Government. . . . There cannot be any divided loyalty. All loyalties must be exclusively centred round the State. If in a democracy you create rival loyalties . . . then democracy is doomed.[14]

Jinnah was the evil whose ghost had to be exorcised in order to be secular. The strategic nature of the change was predicated on a select continuity of the past, and its significance can be realized when we see how the principle of secular politics has avoided the other secular principle of autonomy. Just as autonomous faith sects were not tolerated under institutionalized religious regimes (in India as elsewhere), our modern secular republic also does not tolerate autonomous principle in political structure, excepting the meagre provisions of Articles 370–371 of the Indian Constitution. Indeed, to refresh our memory, we must briefly recall the way the Dalit issue was considered in the constituent assembly. The advisory committee in the constituent assembly had identified Muslims, Sikhs, Parsis, Anglo-Indians and Indian Christians as minorities. But Dalits were never considered as minorities, for minority status to the Dalits would touch the very power structure on which rule rested. Long back, Ambedkar had declared that the depressed classes were a minority – a status concealed by their inclusion in the Hindu society. This was during the time of depositions before the Simon Commission. On the political demand of separate electorate for scheduled castes, the nationalist secular leadership had vehemently disagreed. The Poona Pact of 1932 between Ambedkar and Gandhi temporarily resolved the issue with the help of the principle of reservation. But bitterness remained, as remained other economic and political demands of autonomy. The constitution was a contract against the background of the rise of majorities and minorities. A new deal for the religious minorities was ensured through the provisions that recognized religious minorities. And who could forget in such time of bloodshed as of the Partition the Lucknow Pact of 1916 whose ghost still loomed large over the political elders who sat for three years to draw up the basic law? Similarly there was a new deal for the Dalits. But they were not to be recognized as minorities much though Ambedkar had wanted. There were to be reserved seats, along with other affirmative measures (Articles 332–338), but no autonomy for Dalits and indigenous groups. In short in place of minority representation there was to be positive discrimination as the form of affirmative action. If this was a form of inclusion in the political society, clearly those for whom all these were devised were not satisfied. Inclusion through affirmative action left the entire question of excluding the minorities from political society un-addressed.

Given all these, is there a post-secular situation here, by which I mean post-secular situation in politics? We can answer on the state of politics in a double sense: first, secularization makes it possible for politics to accommodate a religious rite like the oath that will now function with ease and an ambivalent status (because its violation is not deemed as perjury); and second, precisely this secularization of politics will now make possible for politics to become constitutively a critique of the rite (in this case the oath given to a forum of sanctity) and to critique the 'sacramental bond' that has linked liturgical rites to practical affairs of governance. A post-secular situation will mean then politics getting over the theology-secularism bind. We may work towards that politics, but our current politics is certainly not towards that.

The legitimacy of the conventional history of secularism rests on a narrative of transition, best theorized by Max Weber. As we all know, he formulated his famous thesis about the secularization of a particular religious tradition in the capitalist economic ethic. However, more interesting is the way he constructed his thesis. In the Weberian account Protestant ethic acts as the *vanishing mediator* in the transition from feudalism to capitalism.[15] The secularization theory has been now critiqued extensively, on the ground of being empirically unsound and narrowly based. But the trope of the vanishing mediator is able to make the idea of secularization look like a real process, while as Agamben points out it functions as a 'signature' of other things.[16] It functions in the conceptual system of modernity as a veiled reference to theology. It allows monotheism to become the presiding theological principle under which secularism works. Thus economic activities may be plural, administrative-governmental practices may be variegated, but legitimacy is drawn from a particular theological attitude of monotheism. It thus cements the unity between being and acting – the sovereign being and the governmental actions and practices. By making this relation transcendental, fractures in political life of the society are cemented. Secularization thesis allows governmental practices look neutral. History thereby becomes always one of governmental practices and never about politics.

From a critical point of view what happens further is even more interesting. Bourgeois rule depends on two orders – the theological and the secular. Yet it pretends as if these two are separate from one another and have nothing to do with each other. The theological order will concentrate on the self, the inner, the domestic, the home and what one jurist has termed as the hostile environment – in other words, such type of environment outside where the excluded (women, for instance) must not think that public liberty prevails, and should expect violence on them. In this way the secular is in fact importing the religious principle by the backdoor, yet the fiction of distinction remains intact. On the other hand the secular will focus on the public, the external, the formal, the legal, where governmental practices will appear as autonomous and self-valid. Order here too functions as a sign of a concept that wants to appear as a real process. Modern governmental reason produces this double structure. The double structure of split and unity allows bourgeois rule to create the fable of liberty and equality (two of the most significant aspects of the fundamental rights included in Part III of the Indian Constitution), to which now the subjects will attach themselves as if this fable is a truth. By taking part in this process of myth creation, governmental reason will now foster attachment to it as truth, and in this process government will continue and survive. This will be the necessary principle of political rationality.

In whatever I have said till now on the religious nature and roots of our political rites, there are certain points that now need to be put together. They act as fault lines in a narrative of secularism that is based on a binary of religion and secularism and a transition from the former to the latter.

- First is the point of violence. Secularism has followed the pattern of large-scale religious violence of which history tells us and has in fact exacerbated the trend and the pattern.
- Second is the point of exclusion of groups from the domain of governing society. In the religious past, women, Dalits, minor sects and minorities, indigenous communities, lepers or the disabled were excluded. In the secular present, and here we have to only take up the issue of women by way of illustration, the inclusion is only in the public sphere, where the constitution guarantees equality, only to deny it in what is considered as domestic, the home, and thus outside the purview of the secular exercise of power and rights. Secularism gives us equality, but not non-discrimination.[17]
- Third, we have this feature of several secular governmental rites, which as in the religious time draw their strength from a mythical narrative of the origins of sovereignty, and secure themselves in divine sphere while exercising power.
- The final point is that this theological-secular exercise of power gives a lie to the story of a post-religious governance (as the

conventional history of secularism would have us believe) or the possibility of a post-secular (in the sense of return to religion) governance.

These four implications of the present situation call for greater investigation. Indeed the mode of power now becomes stronger by drawing on both the religious and the secular governmental operations.

Religious sanctions, killings, secular conscience

On 15 October 2002, five Dalit men were brutally killed on the main road outside the Dulina police post, near Jhajjar town (Jhajjar district), Haryana, in the presence of, and possibly by, a large and violent mob in front of the police and several senior district officials. All five were believed by the mob to have been engaged in cow-slaughter at the time. According to the families of the victims, five men had left Badshahpur village (Gurgaon district) that day at 2.30 p.m. in a hired truck. Kailash was a leather trader who had come to Badshahpur to purchase raw hides from Virender and Dayachand who had the official contract to skin the dead cattle in the area. Totaram was the driver and Raju the helper of the truck which was transporting the hides to Karnal to be sold the next day in the *mandi* (wholesale market for food, grain and so on) held there every Wednesday. According to Narender Singh, the deputy superintendent of police, Jhajjar, the five victims were transporting 238 hides to Karnal and apparently reached the Dulina police post on Gurgaon-Jhajjar road at about 6.00 p.m. They stopped at a deserted spot near the place to skin a dead cow, as they would be able to sell the hide for Rs 1,500 at the *mandi*. About 15–20 people who were returning by jeep along the same road from Dussehra celebrations in Jhajjar town saw the men skinning the cow and assumed that they had killed it first. They started abusing the five men and then took them to the nearby Dulina police post. They put pressure on the police officer in-charge, SHO (Station House Officer) Hoshiar Singh to book them under the act against cow slaughter. An FIR was filed against the victims accusing them of *gaukashi* (cow-slaughter). The victims denied the accusation and claimed to have bought the cow for Rs 200 from one Fakir Chand of Farukhnagar (Gurgaon).

The police sent one of their forces along with four complainants to Farukhnagar; they also took with them Totaram (one of the five deceased) to verify the story. At Farukhnagar they were informed that the cow was already dead when the five men had taken it. Meanwhile, the police claimed, rumours of 'cow slaughter by Muslims' had built up and people returning from Dussehra celebrations in Jhajjar started gathering at the police post in large number. According to the DSP, when the group returned to Dulina from Farukhnagar at about 7.45 p.m., the SHO Hoshiar Singh informed the crowd that the victims were not Muslims and they had not slaughtered a cow. However, as per the police version, the angry crowd refused to believe the police and the victims' claims. The DSP reached the spot at around 8.45 p.m. and according to him by that time the policemen were outnumbered by '1 to 100' and the mob was demanding the handing over of the five men. The city magistrate, the BDO and the tehsildar also reached the Dulina police post. The DSP ordered a lathi-charge to disperse the mob, but it was too large and violent for the handful of policemen present. As per his version given later, the police were rendered helpless as the crowd snatched away the police weapons and then attacked the Dulina police post, surrounding the five men and beating them to death on the main road, even as officials looked on, in DSP's words, 'helplessly'. The mob also set the tempo van loaded with skins on fire.

At about 3.00 a.m. (morning of 16 October) the policemen at Badshahpur contacted the families of the victims and told them to go to see their sons at the Jhajjar Civil Hospital as they had met with an 'accident'. When they reached the hospital, the government officials present there told them to collect the dead bodies and leave soon as people's sentiments were inflamed. The officials warned them that a mob (including those who had lynched the victims) could even attack the corpses of the *gau-hatyaras* ('cow-slaughterers') and kill the family members too. On the same day the Vishwa Hindu Parishad (VHP) and Shiv Sena held a demonstration in Jhajjar submitting a memorandum to the deputy commissioner demanding that no action be taken in the incident. The killers of the five Dalits were glorified as heroes who had avenged the murder of a cow – 'our mother'. The first response of the district administration was to order a post-mortem of the cow on 17 October to verify the accusations of cow slaughter being levelled by the Gurukul, the Gauraksha Samiti, VHP, and the Bajrang Dal. The same day the family members of the victims and other Dalits in and around Badshahpur met at the Ravidas Mandir in Badshahpur to plan future action. They formed the Dulina Nyay Samiti at this *panchayat*. Haryana Mazdoor Kisan Sabha president Ranjit Yadav also attended this meeting. At his suggestion, a *maha panchayat* (a meeting of representatives of all castes and groups) was held at Ambedkar Sabha in Gurgaon on 17 October. People from all castes and sixteen organizations participated.

The divisional commissioner of Rohtak, RR Banswal was directed to conduct the mandatory magisterial inquiry into the lynching. On 19 October the Dulina Nyay Samiti met again at a BAMCEF (Backward and Minorities Communities Employees Federation)-organized gathering of about 4,000 people at Gurgaon and presented a memorandum to the deputy commissioner. This was followed by the holding of an all-caste *maha panchayat* in Badshahpur village on 20 October. People from thirty-six castes and one hundred villages participated. They gave the administration fifteen days to take action against the killers of the Dalit youths, and demanded that the guilty be charged under S. 302 IPC, the FIR of cow-slaughter against the victims be retracted, a compensation of Rs 10 lakh be given to the families of each of the victims together with a government job for one family member.

Pressure mounted on the Haryana government to take action after the National Human Rights Commission on 21 October sent a notice to the state government to file a report on the incident within a week. Though a government job was promised by the government to the next of kin of each of the deceased, the Dulina Nyay Samiti's demand for a judicial inquiry was turned down. On 25 October the IGP Rohtak Resham Singh told the press that the police had identified twenty-eight local residents as having been part of the mob. This identification of suspects coincided with the submission of the post-mortem report of the cow, which revealed that the cow had died the previous day. It was only then that the FIR of cow slaughter against the victims was quashed. The VHP and the Arya Samaj Ashram responded on 26 October by calling for a *maha panchayat* of 180 Gaushala Sabhas in defence of the murderers. A Sangharsh Samiti headed by Pandit Nityanand of the Jhajjar Gurukul was formed on this occasion.

Following the arrests of the accused on 13 November, the VHP and Bajrang Dal activists took to the streets calling for a bandh resulting in the closure of schools, colleges and shops. Agitating villagers blocked all major roads leading to Jhajjar district from Delhi, Rewari and Gurgaon. They resorted to stone pelting and attacked the police. Four policemen including a DSP and SHO Bahadurgarh were injured. The grand council of the upper castes now served an ultimatum to the state government to unconditionally release those arrested or face a statewide agitation and 'chakka jam' (road blockade) beginning on 20 November. *The Sarv Khap Panchayat* also reminded policemen of their shared (Jat) identity with the peasants whose sons were now in jail.

The Haryana police and the state administration emerged as highly culpable in this incident of the lynching of Dalits as well as in its aftermath. Explanations given by the DSP that the police forces were outnumbered, that their weapons were snatched from them and that they feared for their lives begged the question whether it was not the duty of policemen to risk their lives to save the lives of citizens, especially those in their custody. Given that the police had powers to arrest, lathi-charge and fire for the protection of citizens, the concomitant responsibility was to risk their lives for protection of citizens. Subsequent to the killings too, the police came across as heavily compromised. Surprisingly no arrests took place till a month after the incident even though the police had identified the guilty (the eventual arrests too were finally based on the statements of policemen). The collusion of the district administration also with the guilty was apparent in various acts of omission and commission. The presence of the district officials like the City Magistrate Rajpal Singh at the spot and his failure to react or even begin to deal with the situation was damning. The immediate action or ordering a post-mortem of the cow suggested that they held that that the safety of the Dalits was contingent on the supposed criminality of the killings, in other words on whether the cow had been slaughtered or not. The Sessions Court granted anticipatory bail to the accused in January.

What was also most noticeable is the manner in which a seamless common story was woven – the policemen were outnumbered; the lynching was an accident, and the mob was not to blame as they were inspired by religious sentiment for the cow with the victims mistaken for Muslims. In the process the state had lent itself to projecting that Hindu sentiment was above rule of law; that it was acceptable to kill Muslims, if others like the five Dalits suffered, it was a 'collateral' damage. Even the Scheduled Castes and Scheduled Tribes Commission rationalized the lynching as an understandable response to cow slaughter.

Meanwhile politicians, police officers, high bureaucrats all in the wake of the event visited the place of murder and the victims' houses, offered condolences, expressed anger, appeared indignant and issued statements to various effects, and competed with each other in offering compensation.[18]

I have narrated the event at some length because incidents like this tell us the actual ways in which power works, and put to question the neat distinctions we construct in our conceptual exercises. One can ask in this case: what do we make out of this infamous event? Were they massacred because they were thought to be Muslims? Or, was it because they were Dalits who occupied in the eyes of the Hindu caste majority the same position in society as of the Muslims? Were they murdered for cow slaughter? Clearly, notwithstanding the scholarly works on beef eating in ancient India, Dalits found with the skin of a dead cow were a grave offence, and therefore murder was understandable even on the ground of suspicion given the passions of the majority community. Was this then due to religious cause, or caste prejudice, or governmental compromise, or all three? Caste, religion and secular modes of politics had crisscrossed their paths in this case. Each displaced the other in the way power worked. And each contributed in the process to the formation of the theological-secular bind.

The affective subject of politics

However, within the history of this theological-secular combination we can find another history – history of a different model – of governing mode that bypasses the binary of religion/secularism and bases itself on a certain kind of affect, a certain attitude to binding oneself to truth, of affinitive ties characteristic of coalition and a dialogic sprit, whose link with democracy has weakened severely over the centuries. At one level we can say, that while secular politics in India was always the mark of the Left, Left's own political practice was never confined to a dry, statist version of secularism. While it was perfectly secular, this perfectly secular practice evoked something characteristic of political subjectivity, namely its power to produce excess, the excess which pointed to a void in our spirituality and which had the capacity to visit other messages, discourses, styles and forms. If this speaks of large-scale transfer of loyalty and affinity of the subjects from one kind of political force to another, this is true of religious history as well. Richard Eaton in his renowned study on Islam in Bengal investigated the encounter between Islam and Bengal, and showed why in the entire region of South Asia, Bengal became the most receptive to Islam. As we know, the area today (the two Bengals combined) has world's second-largest Muslim population in the world. How did such a large Muslim population emerge in Bengal? What was the dynamics of the transfer of large sections of population from one faith to another? How did a religion suited to town, bazaar and the trader become appropriate for village, land and the peasant? Eaton deployed archaeological evidence, narrative histories, literary material and administrative documents to trace the long historical shift between AD 1204 (the year of conquest by Turks and Persians) to AD 1760, when the British East India Company finally became the dominant power in Bengal.[19] There may be disputes over certain lines of his argument, but the mass of evidence leaves no doubt that a set of governmental factors relating to matter and soul were responsible for the shift. Conversion of believers from one faith to another was neither purely theological nor completely material. The Middle Ages took long to produce such change; today, however, with the protocols of mass democracy in place political conversions take place rapidly. Crucial here again is the nature of governing styles and modes.

Or we can take the instance of the introduction of a syncretic religious fraternity called *Din Ilahi* (Divine Faith) by the Mughal emperor Akbar in 1582. This was not a religion in the conventional sense. It was oriented more towards a rational outlook on governmental necessities than towards faith. It did not have any pantheon, theology or any transcendental understanding. Its aim was to inspire the subjects of empire to lead tolerant, sensible and responsible life. Given the fact that the empire had subjects of various faiths and persuasions, imperial governance required that subjects should realize that anyone could practise any faith one liked while gaining whatever was better in another. In this way, 'peace would be given to the people, security to the empire'.[20]

In post-colonial context we witness at times a revival or a rediscovery of a certain specific historical model of the past, which at some moment had established through certain affective mechanisms the reciprocal bonds of the leaders and the people, between the travelling, itinerant campaigner and the far-flung areas of the land, and which have been now forgotten and violated. We do not know if this type of affective politics forged through an itinerant style, symbolized, for instance, by Maulana Bhasani in erstwhile united India and then Bangladesh (1881–1977) will revive forcefully. But the attempt to recover a past model, even if partially, indicates a process of reconstructing a such a model and reviving a basic but forgotten constituency. This may appear as unusual in secular politics, but this is what happens when politics has taken an affective turn, so much so that we can here speak of the presence of not a *post-secular* politics, but *affective* politics. In other words, this new (to some extent a replica of the old) model of governance tells us something very different. It tells us the possibility of bypassing the religious/secular debate that animated social scientists in India nearly two decades back in the context of the dispute around the Babri Masjid (1990–92) and the consequent riots, attacks on minorities and the large-scale deaths and destruction. We are not for a moment suggesting that that debate had no relevance, or that communalism was not a political issue then. But history today is asking a different question that cannot simply rest with confining itself to certifying a particular government simply on the basis of its self-professed secular credential or certifying the Indian state as secular.

This question is: what is the agent of political spirit? What is the truth of political subjectivity? This is the question asked by present history.

If in India the dispute around the Babri Masjid and the accompanying riots all over the country occasioned rethinking among social scientists and policy makers on the issue of secularism, in the global discourse on governance the need to rethink was signalled in the wake of the US invasion of Iraq and then Afghanistan, the rise of political Islam, the 'war against terrorism' – all these beginning from the early years of this century. The fable of a secular age and the discourse of a secular mode of power both clearly were in need of a new gloss or major revision. Charles Taylor in *A Secular Age* (2007) attempted to redraw the entire story – a major revisionist attempt – of secularism and what came to be known as the secular age. He concluded his exercise with these words, 'We have to understand religious/spiritual life today in all its different thrusts, resistances, and reactions, e.g. discipline, homogenisation'.[21] It was not an analytical approach to the bind, but an attempt to present a different narrative. Trying to be universal and grand in scope, it avoided any analysis of how religion made itself a part of the secular mode of power in the modern age – say in Turkey in the nineteenth century or in East Europe after 1989, or the role of the pope and Christianity in reinforcing the liberal mode of power in the Trans-Atlantic community after the Second World War. Taylor seems to be saying as if had we only cared to be more discerning, we would have discovered our history in a better way. We would have become more multicultural and tolerant.

Around the same time another revisionist attempt was mounted by Jurgen Habermas who asked the question in an article published in 2008 as to whether the European countries were not already in a post-secular stage. The occasion of rethinking, he admitted, was the large-scale entry of immigrants into Europe with faiths other than Christianity, the US war against terror and the conflict of secular societies with fundamentalist beliefs. In a thoroughly Euro-centric view of the world by his own admission, he argued,

> A 'post-secular' society must at some point have been in a 'secular' state. The controversial term can therefore only be applied to the affluent societies of Europe or countries such as Canada, Australia and New Zealand, where people's religious ties have steadily or rather quite dramatically lapsed in the post-War period. These regions have witnessed a spreading awareness that their citizens are living in a secularized society. In terms of sociological indicators, the religious behavior and convictions of the

local populations have by no means changed to such an extent as to justify labeling these societies 'post-secular'. Here, trends towards de-institutionalized and new spiritual forms of religiosity have not offset the tangible losses by the major religious communities.[22]

He then argued that the secularized societies of Europe formed an exceptional phenomenon in the midst of a religiously mobilized world society, and it was erroneous to hold that with modernization the world would witness, in the foreseeable future, the disappearance of religion. The awareness of living in a secular society was no longer bound up with the certainty that cultural and social modernization could advance only with diminishing public influence and personal relevance of religion. Religion was gaining influence not only worldwide but also within national public spheres, and churches and religious organizations were increasingly assuming the role of, in his words 'communities of interpretation' in the public arena of secular societies. In this perspective he felt that the separation of church and state called for a filter between these two spheres – a filter through which only 'translated', that is secular contributions could pass from the confused din of voices in the public sphere into the formal agendas of state institutions. He further argued that the democratic state must not preemptively reduce the polyphonic complexity of the diverse public voices, because it was in no position to know whether thereby it was cutting society off from scarce resources for the generation of meanings and the shaping of identities.[23] The political public sphere must be able to meet their religious fellow citizens as equals. And then he drew the conclusion,

> Were secular citizens to encounter their fellow citizens with the reservation that the latter, because of their religious mindset, are not to be taken seriously as modern contemporaries, they would revert to the level of a mere modus vivendi – and would thus relinquish the very basis of mutual recognition which is constitutive for shared citizenship. Secular citizens are expected not to exclude a fortiori that they may discover, even in religious utterances, semantic contents and covert personal intuitions that can be translated and introduced into a secular discourse. [24]

Post-secular society in short would overcome the limits of secularization by a rescuing process of translation of the traditional contents of religious language in the public-political language.

There are many aspects of this exposition of the idea of a post-secular society – and possibly of a post-secular politics and the state, though Habermas does not make that part clear – that call for discussion. However, this is not the occasion for that discussion, and we shall not gain much also by undertaking that discussion here. Here the interest is around the question, namely, what kind of subject is envisaged here, who is this post-secular subject? What kinds of inter-subjective dialogues are thus being proposed? And therefore, how consistently can we pursue the project of a religious genealogy of reason? Habermas's idea of a post-secular society where religious feelings are translated in secular public-political language of demands, rights, policies, claims, duties, obligations, legitimacy and others through strictly tolerant and rational means based on mutual accommodation of religious and secular subjects is still based on the notion of a theological-secular divide. It ignores the possibility, and perhaps the overwhelming fact, that the subject may be religious-secular, in other words composite; that the secular modes in a society may not have deep foundations and that many aspects of secular power are founded on religious grounds. This is true of the so-called secular/Christian societies of Europe, as of elsewhere.

Yet the fact that the theorist of communicative rationality has to address the issue of religion indicates the presence of the affective subject in politics, with which he has to come to terms. But strictly speaking this is not a new problem. Habermas draws inspiration from Kant, who too wanted to cope with the secular-religious divide and the presence of the affective subject in his distinct way, that is by a priori assumptions. The idea that man can profess or practise faith not for ultimate gain but as the way of a moral being, and only in this way man could be both religious and rational – though as Kant said that there was no inherent need to be so – was succinctly expressed in the title of his essay 'Religion within the Limits of Reason Alone' (1793). Kant wrote,

> Yet an end does arise out of morality; for how the question, what is to result from this right conduct of ours, is to be answered, and towards what, as an end – even granted it may not be wholly subject to our control – we might direct our actions and abstentions so as at least to be in harmony with that end: these cannot possibly be matters of indifference to reason.[25]

Kant could envisage the presence of religion in the formation of a moral subject, but the formation of a rational subject with critical capacity had nothing to do with religion.

It is only in the context of this perpetual dilemma of rational theory of politics that we can make sense of the revolution that Marx brought in our understanding of the affective subject. Marx's famous words were, 'Religious suffering is, at one and the same time, the expression of real suffering and a protest against real suffering. Religion is the sigh of the oppressed creature, the heart of a heartless world, and the soul of soulless conditions. It is the opium of the people.'[26] Marxists and communists have interpreted these words as criticism of religion, and rightly so. But his view also tells us something of the affective subject. Marx argued in the same *Critique*,

> The foundation of irreligious criticism is: Man makes religion, religion does not make man. Religion is, indeed, the self-consciousness and self-esteem of man who has either not yet won through to himself, or has already lost himself again. But man is no abstract being squatting outside the world. Man is the world of man – state, society. This state and this society produce religion, which is an inverted consciousness of the world, because they are an inverted world. Religion is the general theory of this world, its encyclopaedic compendium, its logic in popular form, its spiritual point *d'honneur*, its enthusiasm, its moral sanction, its solemn complement, and its universal basis of consolation and justification. It is the fantastic realization of the human essence since the human essence has not acquired any true reality. The struggle against religion is, therefore, indirectly the struggle against that world whose spiritual aroma is religion.

Thus not only religion remains affecting politics till the world is cleaned of conditions that produce religion and religious wishes and dreams, but that the subject will be marked by affective elements. Marx's critique takes a line different from those of Kant and Habermas on the issue of secularism and secularization of society. In one the presence of society and economy is overwhelming; in the other they give way to ideal constructions. In one the affective elements are part of this world; in the other they are banished from the court of reason.

The insertion of affective elements of life within a new governmental discourse of power has been possible not on the basis of purely secular notions of development, economy and industrialization, but only with the arrival of the notion of *basic masses*. On the other side, confronting this new discourse has been another model of politics, equally old, the right-wing communal version of *affect* advanced with deadly effect and establishing hold over the world of instincts. The history of this double confrontation in India begins ironically from around the same time – the mid-nineties of the past century, co-terminus with the time of the latest round of globalization, when people all over the world started searching for new models of politics. To the extent we can think of a model of politics that bypasses the developmental and in general the economic model of governmentality, we may say that the discourse of basic masses is indeed a way of codifying what both the Right and the Left versions of politics in their conventional or accepted terms have considered as social dangers.

Therefore, the question will be with its natural intelligibility also. This natural intelligibility will be at once both an explanation of the circumstances of the emergence of the new model and a new history of the past, and a desired resolution of the old Left/Right debate. This natural intelligibility would also explain how against dominant patterns of politics people try be autonomous. We can foresee already a new dialectic here, because such reasoning will have already laid out the path of a new round of struggle around issues of governing. The constantly unrealized prospect of politics as life-form keeps on animating popular politics.

Kinship as a problem for modern governance

Let us once more recall the incident at Dulina. We shall see the operation of the principle of kinship besides the others we have referred to in that section. While concluding this chapter we need to revert to the issue kinship as a problem for modern governance in the context of the mixed origin of our modern political practices and the persistence of the affective elements in politics.

Richard Fox published *Kin, Clan, Raja, and Ruler* in 1971 as a commentary on state-hinterland relations in pre-industrial India. The next major work on the ethno-history of kinship was written by Nicholas Dirks, *The Hollow Crown* (1987), in which he argued that comparative sociology had systematically denied the importance of the Indian state by treating caste as essentially a religious phenomenon. Along this line came Margaret Frenz's *From Contact to Conquest* (2003) in which she described the role of kinship in the transition to British rule in Malabar between 1790 and 1805. These ethno-histories because of their method could contest a scripture-centric view of caste and by implication clan, and were able to present before us the phenomenon of kinship as a resource of power. Yet we have to recall that they did not problematize the question of kinship, in short present kinship as a problem for power, by which we mean the modern form – the governmental form of power. They failed to bring out the *borders of kinship*, in other words treating kinship not only as a resource of politics but problem too for governance.

Kinship drawing on religious sanctions is as old as a problem of governance as the business of government itself. Those who govern our societies also have to ensure that affinitive ties are conducted in accordance to the norms and priorities of rule and governance. Recall *Mahabharata*, where kin ties had to be re-negotiated and re-interpreted according to the necessities of rule and administration of kingdom.

In India, we know, colonial rule had intervened with several legislations in the sovereign operations of kinship ties, which brought out the crucial position of women – the woman – in the affinitive arithmetic sometimes known as the grammar of caste ties, tribal ties, village ties, family/marital ties, clan ties and so on. As a result, kinship was perhaps for the first time brought face to face with the reality of modern administration, whose social aim was to bring the modern nuclear family at the centre of a re-organized society. The nuclear family later gave its pride of place to the nuclear individual. But since management of property relations remained the critical factor, as histories of merchant networks in South Asia show,[27] kinship ties readjusted themselves to survive in the changing times. Kinship became not the obstacle to what Marx and Engels had called 'money relation', but a tool to further it. Blood ties and imagined blood ties became crucial in politics from village to capital level. Politics, in these conditions, always meant politics of 'life', reinventing kinship on a perpetual basis. The enactments on personal law, alimony, property management, and measures on common property resource, conversion, inter-faith relations and several other associated issues show that kinship became the object of reinvention for a money-led society. In all these remained less noticed, the role of religions, faith-based institutions, new brotherhoods symbolizing new ties based in these institutions and the way private property was managed through these reorganized ties. In post-independent India for the first three four decades civil legislations starting with the Hindu Marriage Act (1955) were active in bringing old kinship ties in tune with modern governmental rule. Thus, for instance, while explaining how the role of blood was restricted in defining relations, the act said in Article 3 (c), ' "full blood" and "half blood" – two persons are said to be related to each other by full blood when they are descended from a common ancestor by the same wife and by half blood when they are descended from a common ancestor but by different wives'; and then in Article 3 (d), ' "Uterine blood" – two persons are said to be related to each other by uterine blood when they are descended from a common ancestress but by different husbands.' This strategy continued up to the Shah Bano case[28] in course of which the duty of the community to serve modern social needs was emphasized. Yet this governmental strategy did not rule out blood as a factor in secular politics. All kinds of blood ties (including the most fictive) have influenced politics (at times directly as in the case of political parties, at times indirectly when clan leaders became the crucial pillars of political power, vote mobilization, etc. as in the Jat lands of Western Uttar Pradesh or the heartland of the Haryana and Panjab).

In this dynamics of blood/civility, the situation changed in favour of blood ties with injection of money power in the villages, where we now see a resurgence of kinship ties. Also we see all kinds of arguments based on fictive blood ties being aired with defiance, marking an extreme right-wing version of bio-politics. Endogamy is being sought to be strictly enforced. In other cases endogamy is being interpreted in new ways, where a girl cannot be married within the supposed clan, and at times the village being interpreted as the clan and hence within the same village. We can refer to recent *panchayat* rulings in Haryana, strictures on various marital ties crossing fictive divides including religious and caste divides, leading to killings, torture and expulsion of women particularly belonging to Dalit groups. Now we shall have caste enumerations also on a wider scale reinforcing new boundaries. In their trail we shall witness new combinations of caste, clan and geography. Typically thus new social boundaries of exclusion are being drawn. For instance, a cluster of villages peopled by Jats are claimed to be united by caste and geography. The main rule is that all boys and girls within this cluster are considered siblings. The *panchayat* governs the cluster (*khap*) formed by same *gotra* (clan) families from several neighbouring villages. Those living in this cluster are not allowed to marry in the same clan or even in any clan from the same village. Many young boys and girls were killed in the past defying *khap* rules. The *panchayat* imposes its writ through social boycotts and fines and in cases of defiance sometimes end up by either killing or forcing the victims to commit suicide. All this is done on the grounds of honour and brotherhood. The few men constituting the *panchayat* settle disputes and control the lives of the young. Young girls are routinely threatened, abused and killed under the verdicts of these so-called clan councils.

West Bengal, of course, presents a different picture (but only to some extent), mainly due to the factors such as the infamous Bengal Famine, Partition, continuing migration of all kinds and unusual mobility of persons belonging to particular caste groups to towns and outside West Bengal – all of which weakened kinship. We have accounts of famines – starting from the Famine of 1770 and ending with that of 1943 and in between the account of the famine of 1873 – which tell us of scenes of animal existence of humankind and massive migrations in search of security of life. Life in these accounts is the life of the beast, and kinship can provide no security, as Hunter described in *Annals of Rural Bengal*, quoting John Shore,

> Still fresh in memory's eye the scene I view,
> The shrivelled limbs, sunk eyes, and lifeless hue;
> Still hear the mother's shrieks and infant's moans,
> Cries of despair and agonizing groans
> In wild confusion dead and dying lie; –
> Hark to the jackal's yell and vulture's cry,
> The dog's fell howl, as midst the glare of day
> They riot unmolested on their prey!
> Dire scenes of horror, which no pen can trace,
> Nor rolling years from memory's page efface.[29]

Yet here too in Bengal, even after the devastation of famines, power at the village level operates along kinship lines, particularly among the muscle-flexing men of substance in the countryside. Dominant castes and families operate along kin lines. Caste and kinship intermingle. Likewise, jotedars are acutely conscious of kinship factor, and when they give or switch loyalty, they do so massively, as kin groups. Add to these the recent history of the withering or weakening of several traditional institutions in West Bengal under the thirty-three years of party rule, which has instituted new power structures, and has enabled new forms of network and clientele by governmentalizing kinship as an element of social life. The problem of kinship for governance is handled in a new way.

On another note, even in the dry and forest areas of the land, where a new *bahujan samaj* is emerging, we find the conditional relevance of kin ties in politics and governance. Oriya Brahmins are isolated from this *bahujan*, while santhal, munda, sabar, oraon, mahato, mandal, kaibarta, kurmi, dom, kahal, teli, kamar, bauri, hari, mal, sardar, bhumij and several other groups are part of this emerging *bahujan samaj* poised to confront what passes on as developmental governance. Recall the instance of opposing caste assemblages in the wake of the murder of Dalits in Dulina. We have one more illustration of this in North Bengal where the Kamtapuri movement again reminds us of the past – when in Naxalbari peasant revolt the rajbanshis, santhals, oraons, bagdis, Nepali-speaking indigenous groups and others had formed another *bahujan samaj*.

We can therefore note two ways in which kinship re-emerges as a critical factor in politics, and thus as a problem for governance. The first way is through the operation of money, market and modern governmental power which makes kinship relevant today. The second way tells us of a particular kind of resistance to the aforesaid operation of money, market and modern governmental power. It is based on a re-configuration of the kin ties and creates the *bahujan samaj*, which is an alliance on the basis of the principle of 'fold', singularities with a singularity, called the *samaj*. This *samaj* accommodates kin ties on the basis of a reality that no group has monopoly of access to property and resources. While on the basis of all these we can say that kinship constitutes the link between the pre-modern religious regimes and the modern secular state, it is also possible to view the continued existence of kinship under modern conditions of governance at the limit of what Hegel had called the 'ethical order'. Hegel in *The Phenomenology of Spirit* said that the clash between the ethical order and the order of the state is inevitable and tragic. He said that it represents the relationship of self-awareness to other, which constitutes the new relation between them. The ethical law is, in his words, when true is 'unwritten, inerrant, unalterable divine law. It is not anything that an individual can hope either to criticize or justify, and certainly not in terms of mere self-consistency' (paragraph 437). Further, 'ethical spirit is the immediate unity of the substance with self-consciousness' (paragraph 459). Then he says, ethical consciousness is more complete and its guilt in opposing law is more inexcusable, and its act of opposing law shows that the ethical must be actualized, the 'ethical must be actual' for the 'realization of the purpose is the purpose of the action' (paragraph 470).[30]

Is kinship then an enabling linguistic structure, or as Hegel thought, is it a relation of blood, not of norms, but which, by virtue of belonging to nature, now faces the social, or is it a clan tie sanctioned by religion? Whatever be the answer, in post-colonial societies, kinship remains an aberrant transgression for governance, while the money society in the way it has evolved in our part of the world has accommodated this transgression as normal and therefore it is no longer a transgression. Hence we find the government unwilling to come down heavily on the *khap panchayats* and the murders committed by them, and the softness with which it deals the issue of honour killings (including the revival of sati).

This brings us to the most critical of issues relating to the combination of kinship, religion and modern secular regime – that of patriarchy and kinship. These blood ties, invariably located in the figure of the mother, result both in forcing the woman to be constantly on the margin of kinship ties, to be secured, guaranteed, exchanged, gifted and murdered, and in these ways made the tool of maintaining the honour of the clan and purity of blood, and in killings or the least, excommunication of the deviant males. Through all these sacrifices biopower is maintained. In the background of this new form of power and governing, the secular claims of modern governance sound hollow.

Clearly only individual rights cannot be the answer, as the failure of reforms in Pakistan in particular testifies. What is the new ethics we can imagine that will better negotiate the tension between government of society and the government of the self? What are the new ethical ideals that law will actualize? Are there possibilities of legal pluralism here moving away from the model of legal centralism? Perhaps we have some clue to all these urgent queries in the ethical orders implicit in the history of the repeated attempts by lower sects in this subcontinent to create a *bahujan samaj*. But that is not going to be enough, until it addresses the crucial test: where do the women stand in these reconfigured ties of affinity? Likewise, the Dalits, people belonging to indigenous communities, and bands of migrant labour, to whom often the world of kin ties has no meaning apart from that of the imperatives of the labouring world. In this overlapping world of religion-secularism governmental rationality is too happy with ensuring public equality only – for example declaring public discrimination as illegal – while allowing caste and clan-based power buttressed by religious sanctions, and discriminating practices in the 'non-public' sphere, which does not necessarily mean private sphere. It is here where we find the particularities of post-colonial governmentality. These particularities also suggest a new mode of power that subsumes in it both theological and secular forms, because this mode of power aims to cover the entire life. As a result, politics becomes 'politics of life itself' – life that has both theological and secular elements.

If 'kinship is the pre-condition of the human', *bahujan samaj* is one such possible new field of the human. Wherever there has been attempt to create such *samaj*, it has been treated as a crime – for violating caste, clan, property, gender and the existing communication structure. But the fatality and the aberration – both are promising, and they require new ideas of governing the self and the society. Perhaps we can name this new mode of political existence by invoking a phrase of Michel Foucault, namely, *political spirituality*.[31]

Notes

1 "Mamata Drags President Pranab into FDI Muddle", *Zeenews.com*, 19 September 2012 http://zeenewsindia.com/news/nation/mamata-drags-president-pranab-into-fdi-muddle_800726.html (accessed on 27 October 2012).

2 " 'Notification on FDI in Retail Shocking' – Mamata", *Zeenews.com*, 20 September 2012 http://zeenews.india.com/news/nation/notification-on-fdi-in-retail-shocking-mamata_800833.html (accessed on 27 October 2012).

3 *The Indian Express*, 20 September 2012 http://www.indianexpress.com/news/bjp-to-demand-special-session-to-discuss—breach-of-promise-/1005207 (accessed on 27 October 2012).

4 All excerpts are from William Blackstone, *Commentaries on the Laws of England*, Book 1, Chapter 2 "Of the Parliament" http://www.lonang.com/exlibris/blackstone/bla-102.htm (accessed on 28 October 2012); see also http://avalon.law.yale.edu/18th_century/blackstone_bk1ch2.asp (accessed on 29 October 2012); see also in this regard, the path-breaking essays by Joseph R. Strayer, *On the Medieval Origins of the Modern State* (Princeton, NJ: Princeton University Press, 1970).

5 Carl Schmitt wrote of this situation in his typical blunt way, 'For the foundations of the parliamentary legislative state and its system of legality as a whole, it is thoroughly trivial when the substantive principles of the Constitution's principal part are designated all the more emphatically and solemnly as holy, non-infringeable and 'dictator-proof'." – *Legality and Legitimacy*, trans. Jeffrey Seitzer (Durham: Duke University Press, 2004), p. 76.

6 Carl Schmitt, *The Concept of the Political*, trans. George Schwab (Chicago: University of Chicago Press, 2007), pp. 25–26.

7 Asutosh Kumar, "Imaginations and Manifestos of the Political Parties on Ideals of Developmental Governance", in Ranabir Samaddar and Suhit Sen (eds.), *Political Transition and Development Imperatives in India* (London and New Delhi: Routledge, 2012), pp. 121–158.

8 Giorgio Agamben, *The Sacrament of Language – An Archaeology of the Oath*, trans. Adam Kotsko (Stanford, CA: Stanford University Press, 2011), pp. 40–41.

9 Ibid., p. 41.

10 Jawaharlal Nehru, *The Discovery of India* (1946, New Delhi: Penguin Books, 2004), pp. 41–42.

11 Ibid., pp. 627–628.

12 Again, one should relate this with the centralizing trend that Nehru along with others represented in the Constituent Assembly deliberations. Nehru wrote to the president of the Constituent Assembly on 5 July 1947 these words, 'Now that the partition is a settled fact, we are unanimously of the view that it would be injurious to the interests of the country to provide for a weak Central authority which would be incapable of ensuring peace, of coordinating vital matters of common concern and of speaking effectively for the whole country in the international system.' Edited by A.S. Narang, "Regionalism, Alienation and Federalism", in Rashedud-din Khan (ed.), *Rethinking Indian Federalism* (Shimla: Indian Institute of Advanced Studies, 1997), p. 203.

13 *Constituent Assembly Debates* (hereafter *CAD*), Official Report, 1946–1950, Volume 7, p. 272. Patel's remarks brushed aside the weak voices of the Muslim representatives who admitted that time had changed, that they had showed their integrity to the nation and that therefore separate electorate should be maintained. It is clear that the truth games about minority problematic were being played out in the shadow of Partition Kashmir war and the memory of massacres, and continuing migration of thousands

and thousands. Speech of Md. Ismail, Ibid., p. 277; also p. 283; this opinion, however, met with objections from some other Muslim members. For views identical to those of Patel, see the lecture by another Constituent Assembly member, B. Pocker Sahib Bahadur, who had exclaimed in exasperation, 'The majority is a majority, and the minorities are minorities,' and further, 'the idea of getting representation from religious groups is simply ridiculous. . . . The minority must remain a minority. Now before a minority there is only one alternative: It is to be loyal to the majority, and cooperate and gain the confidence of the majority.' – *CAD*, Volume 7, pp. 212 & 218.

14 Ibid., pp. 223–224.

15 The idea of the 'vanishing mediator' has a long lineage. Besides Althusser, Fredric Jameson (1973) analysed the concept, which denotes the function of mediating between two opposing ideas, as a transition occurs between them. At the point where one idea has been replaced by the other, and the concept is no longer required, the mediator vanishes. In terms of the idea of dialectics particularly as propounded by Hegel the conflict between the theoretical abstraction and its empirical negation (through trial and error) is resolved by a concretion of the two ideas, representing a theoretical abstraction taking into account the previous contradiction, whereupon the mediator vanishes. In political history we have seen social movements operating in a particular way to influence politics, until these movements are forgotten or they change their purpose. Jameson (1973, p. 78) wrote,

> Protestantism assumes its function as a 'vanishing mediator.' For what happens here is essentially that once Protestantism has accomplished the task of allowing a rationalization of inner worldly life to take place, it has no further reason for being and disappears from the historical scene. It is thus in the strictest sense of the word a catalytic agent which permits an exchange of energies between two otherwise mutually exclusive terms; and we may say that with the removal of the brackets, the whole institution of religion itself (or in other words what is here designated as 'Protestantism') serves in its turn as a kind of overall bracket or framework within which change takes place and which can be dismantled and removed when its usefulness is over. This is the point at which to observe that such a picture of historical change – however irreconcilable it may be with vulgar Marxism – is in reality perfectly consistent with genuine Marxist thinking and is, indeed, at one with the model proposed by Marx himself for the revolutions of 1789 and 1848. In the former it was Jacobinism which played the role of the vanishing mediator, functioning as the conscious and almost Calvinistic guardian of revolutionary morality, of bourgeois universalistic and democratic ideals, a guardianship which may be done away with in Thermidor, when the practical victory of the bourgeoisie is assured and an explicitly monetary and market system can come into being. And in that parody of 1789, which is the revolution of 1848, it is similarly under the cloak of the traditions and values of the great revolution, and of the empire which followed it, that the new commercial society of the Second Empire emerges

Frederic Jameson, "The Vanishing Mediator – Narrative Structure in Max Weber", *New German Critique*, 1 (winter), 1973, pp. 52–89.

16 Giorgio Agamben, *The Kingdom and Glory- For a Theological Genealogy of Economy and Government*, trans. Lorenzo Chiesa (Stanford, CA: Stanford University Press, 2011), p. 4.
17 Kalpana Kannabiran charts the recent history of jurisprudence dealing with the relation between liberty and non-discrimination. See Kannabiran, *Tools of Justice* (New Delhi: Routledge, 2012).
18 The entire report is summarized and taken from a PUDR (People's Union for Democratic Rights) Report, *Dalit Lynching at Dulina – Cow Protection, Caste, and Communalism*, Delhi, February 2003 and re-published in Ujjwal Kumar Singh (ed.), *Human Rights and Peace – Ideas, Laws, Institutions, and Movements* (New Delhi: Sage, 2009).
19 Richard Eaton, *The Rise of Islam and the Bengal Frontier, 1204–1760* (Berkeley, CA: University of California Press, 1993).
20 Cited from Abul Fazl, *Akbar Nama* by Abraham Eraly, *The Mughal World: Life in India's Last Golden Age* (New Delhi: Penguin Books, 2007), p. xii.
21 Charles Taylor, *A Secular Age* (Cambridge, MA: The Belknap Press of Harvard University Press, 2007), p. 776.
22 Jurgen Habermas, "Notes on a Post-secular Society"; this text was initially written for a lecture which Jürgen Habermas gave on 15 March 2007 at the Nexus Institute of the University of Tilberg, Netherlands, and the English version was published on the web on 18 June 2008 – http://www.signandsight.com/features/1714.html (accessed on 16 December 2012).
23 The similarity of the argument of Habermas with Rawls's idea of 'overlapping consensus' is obvious. Habermas himself notes, 'This is the key issue for John Rawls when he calls for an overlapping consensus between groups with different world views to accept the normative substance of the constitutional order.' This is a reference to *Political Liberalism* by Rawls (1998).
24 Ibid.
25 Immanuel Kant, *Religion within the Limits of Reason Alone*, trans. Theodore M. Greene and Hoyt H. Hudosn, http://www.marxists.org/reference/subject/ethics/kant/religion/religion-within-reason.htm (accessed on 25 December 2012).
26 Karl Marx, *Critique of Hegel's Philosophy of Right* (1843–44), "Introduction", http://www.marxists.org/archive/marx/works/1843/critique-hpr/intro.htm (accessed on 25 December 2013).
27 For instance, Claude Markovits, *Merchants, Traders, Entrepreneurs – Indian Business in the Colonial Period* (London: Palgrave MacMillan, 2008).
28 Shah Bano, a sixty-two-year-old Muslim woman of Indore and mother of five was divorced by her husband in 1978 and was subsequently refused alimony. She had no means to support herself and her children. She approached the court for securing maintenance from her husband. When the case reached the Supreme Court after seven years, the Court invoked Section 125 of Code of Criminal Procedure, which applies to everyone regardless of caste, creed or religion. It ruled that Shah Bano be given maintenance money, similar to alimony. The case created controversy regarding the extent to which the country could have different civil codes for different religions, especially for Muslims in India. The Rajiv Gandhi government passed the Muslim Women (Protection of Rights on Divorce)

Act, 1986, which its opponents argued had diluted the secular judgment of the Supreme Court and, in reality, denied even utterly destitute Muslim divorcées the right to alimony from their former husbands.

29 W.W. Hinter, *Annals of Rural Bengal* (Edinburg: Murray and Gicbb and London: Smith, Elder and Co., 1868, publication of HMSO) http://archive. org/stream/annalsofruralben00huntuoft/annalsofruralben00huntuoft_ djvu.txt (accessed on 5 November 2012).
30 G.W.F. Hegel, "The Phenomenology of Spirit," http://www.marxists.org/ reference/archive/hegel/index.htm (accessed on 6 November 2012).
31 Yet Foucault seems to have missed the challenge of engaging with the most obvious mark of political subjectivity, namely, *autonomy*. What is autonomy? How do we go beyond the Kantian idea on autonomy and make sense of the struggle of politics for autonomy? Is *political spirituality* the other name of autonomy? Readers can notice that the entire first section of this book grapples with the question of autonomy that will define self-governance, self-government or what Foucault preferred to call the government of the self. Since I do not want to repeat what I have already written on this, but which is crucial as reference to the question of autonomy and self-government, readers are advised to consult, R. Samaddar, "Autonomy and the Requirements of Minimal Justice", in R. Samaddar (ed.), *The Politics of Dialogue – Living under the Geopolitical Histories of War and Peace* (Aldershot: Ashgate Publishing, 2004), Chapter 5, pp. 108–158; R. Samaddar (ed.), *The Politics of Autonomy – Indian Experiences* (New Delhi: Sage Publications, 2005), "Introduction", pp. 9–31; R. Samaddar,*The Materiality of Politics*, Volume 2, *Subject Positions in Politics* (London: Anthem, 2007), Chapter 4, "Autonomies of a New Society", pp. 139–166.

Part II

Law and regulations as the framework of governance

7 Rule of law in a society of unrest

The founding reason of rule of law

From ideals and ideas of governance we move on to frameworks of governance. Anyone familiar with decolonized societies is also familiar with the complaint or sigh that there is no rule of law in these societies, people are violent, mad, disrespectful of law, and hence these societies are anarchic. From UN experts busy with mending and fixing social ills to behavioural scientists studying these societies, the refrain is the same. Governance fails because it is not well rooted in law, because crimes are rampant and because rule of law does not exist. In fact most of what is known as restorative exercises in global governance involving restoration of state and structures of government undertakes as the first exercise the task of training police, drafting a constitution, setting up independent courts and introducing criminal and civil law manuals. It seems therefore that an important step in studying the nature of governance in India can begin with an examination of the mourned fate of rule of law in the country. In this exercise it will be not enough to say that the foundations of rule of law are colonial. While that is true, it is necessary also to dig deeper into those foundations, and bring out what exactly rule of law came to signify in a society of unrest. To find that out, instead of conducting a general normative exercise we propose to conduct in this chapter a scrutiny of one of the arch stones in the edifice of rule of law – the Act of Evidence, 1872 (the two others being the Indian Penal Code, 1860 and the Indian Criminal Procedure Code, 1898 subsequently revised in 1973). We shall see how the liberal and colonial practices of law-making were deeply intermeshed, so much so that post-colonial governance today cannot forge its tools without depending on the liberal-colonial heritage of law and law-making.

This colonial-liberal heritage of law-making as part of governance found a profound expression in the Act of Evidence. The following lines were introduced as illustration in the act.

A. A desires a Court to give judgement that B shall be punished for a crime which A says B has committed.
A must prove that B has committed a crime.
B. A desires a Court to give judgement that he is entitled to certain land in the possession of B, by reason of facts which he asserts, and which B denies to be true.
A must prove the existence of those facts.[1]

These seemingly simple and self-evident lines were among the formulations that laid the ground of rational rule by the colonial authorities in India. Appended at the end of Section 101 of the Indian Evidence Act, formulating a principle relating to burden of proof, namely, 'Whoever desires any Court to give judgement as to any legal right or liability dependent on the existence to facts which he asserts, must prove that those facts exist. When a person is bound to prove the existence of any fact, it is said that the burden of proof lies on that person' – these (and similar other) lines in the act on the question of evidence achieved a stupendous feat. They succeeded in setting up the individual as a legal category to be inspected, monitored and judged from now on on the basis of a code by a new form of power, the judicial power. Promulgated in 1872 the Indian Evidence Act demonstrated the way in which the colonial rule in India built up the notion of responsibility, made it one of the pillars of rule, and the discourse of responsibility compelled the people who were being ruled to strive perpetually to become civilized and rational while the same discourse gave the ruler an intrinsic advantage in terms of legitimacy and governance.[2] The ruler assumed the responsibility of providing good rule; the ruled would have to now assume the responsibility of good conduct and growing up. In the lines cited earlier and taken from the Evidence Act we can see how the notion of responsibility was being framed. The state had brought charge against the accused, it was responsible for furnishing the evidence; therefore it had the right to punish. The peasant had robbed the wealthy of land, the wealthy would prove that the land was his and the court would order the land back to the possession of the wealthy. Rule of law signified that one had to be responsible to the law, and law meant due process. Thus, for instance, in the case of expounding the notion of responsibility in the form of 'burden of proof' the Evidence Act explained with whom the burden of proof lay, burden of proof as to a particular fact, the burden of proving the fact, which required to be proved in order to make evidence admissible. In fact the act laid down the burden of proving in different possible situations. Responsibility through the definition of burden thereby made contract, law, individuality, due process and transparency as pillars of new rule against which the individual in the form of the accused as a criminal or a wrecker of property was now situated.

On one hand it seems that governing in this way was a new way of rule, because it involved rationality. In this context the Evidence Act is possibly the best demonstration of how reason was made to work in the process of ruling. On the basis of reason a new form of power grew up, namely judicial power. On the other hand, reason was only another adjunct to the material way in which rule was to be transacted. Not only physical conquest was the basis of the ascendancy of reason, but reason itself also depended on as we shall show in the following pages close physical scrutiny of various kinds. The Evidence Act remains in this way the great instance of the combining reason and physicality in the business of governing. Social technologies indicate different and varying matrix of practical reason, implying certain modes of training and modification of individuals. Drawing on his lifelong work Foucault identified four such technologies – technologies of production, sign systems, power and of the self.[3] While engaging with technologies of power and self, he kept the issue of the technology of production out of a discussion of technology of power. He argued that each had autonomy and specificity, while recognizing at the same time that they ever hardly functioned separately. In a colonial society the interrelations could be only stronger. Freed from any association with democratic restraint, the application of practical reason went to the furthest and demonstrated the overlaps of various social technologies.

In this sense to understand how rule of law functions in a postcolonial democracy it will be instructive to go back to the colonial era, because locating the criminal through categories and technologies was at the heart of the question of the stability of rule, and it was in the colonial era that the expeditionary character of liberal jurisprudence was the clearest, its missionary character at its purest. Who was the criminal? To the colonial rule in the middle of the nineteenth century, the criminal was still a spectral figure, beyond the surveillance of weak administrative machinery, and inhabiting the boundaries of morality and evil, much of which the colonial rule was still labouring hard to understand. The criminal was within the so-called native society that was marked by distinct patterns of caste and domestic violence. In terms of everyday governance this native society was in collision

with a type of civic-mindedness the colonial governance tried to culti-
vate among the people. Colonial rule was not only responsible to the
Crown, but responsible to the subjects also – therefore its mission was
to motivate the people and the society to engage with the crime and the
criminal. Laws therefore had to be public, legislating process similarly
public, trials had to be public, evidence was to be made public and in
this way judging criminality was a public process, which was possible
only if the 'public' was there and present in the process. Therefore
criminal legislation had to operate on two different simultaneous registers: on one hand, it had to argue that criminality was occurring in
the distinct cultural milieus of society and the communities (thus, for
instance, the idea of criminal tribe); on the other hand, the trial and
the punishment process was to be public, non-communitarian, legal
and scientific. Thus, questions like who is a criminal, how criminal elements enmesh with the public or what methods are illegal were issues
that defined the power of the sovereign authority, at the same time
marking the everyday governmentality of rule that needed to cope
with crimes unsettling the society. The problem was acute because the
so-called native society seemed to harbour criminality as simply one
segment of a vast self-governing (in other words god-governing) cosmos. Moulavis and Qazis refuse to pass death sentence on robbers
unless robbery had been accompanied with murder, in some cases they
would be let off with fine and shaming upon being brought back to
their villages, and the Bengal

> robbers (were) not, like robbers in England, individuals driven
> to such desperate courses by sudden want; they are robbers by
> profession, and even by birth, they are formed into regular com-
> munities, and their families subsist by the spoils, which they bring
> home to them; they are all, therefore, alike, criminal wretches,
> who have placed themselves in a state of declared war with our
> Government, and are therefore wholly excluded from every ben-
> efit of its laws.[4]

One has to only read the famous five-volume Bengali non-fiction
narrative of criminals serving jail sentence and in some cases waiting
for execution at the gallows (Jarashandha, *Louhakapat)* to get an idea
of morality of assigning the criminal a place under the sun, not excom-
municating the criminal but appreciating the criminal's place in the
cosmos – a kind of indulgence with which the hard Protestant morality was unfamiliar and therefore the latter could only frown upon the
former.

In the nineteenth-century colonial world of India the alien ruler had to know the subject population closely, a task that the fast-developing print culture and the science of photography made easy, the bodies of the poor, the troublesome and the criminal. While bodies in the early modern period were subject to inspection under many different circumstances such as theft, sexual intercourse, hard labour, punishment, marriage, amusement of the rich or duties in the service of gods and goddesses, these acts of scrutiny now in the age of responsible governance became public because they served a public purpose – that of identifying the criminal, the enemy of the public. The criminal had to be found in reasonable time, investigated, interrogated and sentenced – all in an objective and public way.

The body was to be carefully described if the criminal had to be punished at all. The need for the witness to carefully describe the criminal was partly because people were not what they seemed; in this oriental land the person facing the authorities was not how he appeared at first glance, men passed as women, women as men. Thus, the right body had to be discovered, that is to say the right identity had to be found, and piercing the milieu of concealment the rules of evidence had to discover the *real* person below the surface. All these made bodies, appearances and identities problematic for the nineteenth-century colonial society. As we shall see, this understanding stayed on when the colonial rule was over and the country became independent.

Detecting the crime and the criminal was important because the technology of detection was a miniaturized way of knowing the *true* bodies of individuals or groups, as if that could lead to the unravelling of the mystery of the 'true' mind of the criminal individual and the group – what kinds of bodies harboured what kind of minds and what kind of minds called for what kind of bodily practices – and if such bodies were made visible, described and presented, the process of judgement had become public. The key was the process of inspection, a good inspection led to good evidences, and therefore the act of crime and the body of the criminal had to be watched well, an act that often involved relationships of unequal power. In the court therefore the criminal had to be present – the first step towards making the whole thing public. In the past, bodies of the criminals and the accused were kept away from view for a variety of social and personal reasons. But the imperatives of modern rule required that the people could not always claim the right to keep their bodies private. For solving the riddle of the crime, the body of the victim of the crime or the place or documents associated with crime had to be equally investigated well. Also particular audiences were needed for particular bodily knowledge (thus expert witness had to be summoned). Thus, colour, shape, traits, position, speech pattern, diction, hairstyle, time or moment became crucial. In this way the ground for evidence collection and formulation was laid. Soon the physicality of the task of ruling was to hinge on 'the finger' – a part of the body never thought to be of crucial importance to the identification of a particular soul.[5]

New forms of control and power over unruly bodies also developed around this time parallel to the development of the power of investigation, examination and judgement. Prisons developed. In this process the juridical-political structure of confinement combined two opposite things: public nature of judgement and confining the accused away from the public eye, at times to a penal colony in faraway islands of a sea, creating in the process new 'criminalized' groups whose bodies would be minutely detailed in records only to be brought over to public eye as material of evidence, once another criminal case would come up, – an unending cycle of making public and keeping away from the public criminal matters of society. These places of confinement were within the country and society, yet outside it, with its own specific laws of confinement of dormitories, cells, iron gates and grids of regulation combining with complex interweaving of language, caste and kin. Jails and the penal colony in the Andaman Islands developed by the colonial authorities enabled them to dislocate the criminals while localizing them again in a way where the claims and limits of the 'human' were tested and revealed in lethal form. They were the realization of the fantasy of the colonial reformers to cleanse the society once and for all. In time this technology of mass confinement would help a nation-state to confine the unwanted immigrants and asylum seekers. And in all this the colonial experience was of foundational importance. Jails and detention centres helped democracy and responsible government to come into being. It is in this sense that Giorgio Agamben identifies the emergence of the mass confinement technique in Western modernity as 'the fundamental bio-political paradigm of the West' and 'an event which decisively signals the political space of modernity itself'.[6] Jails and lock ups backing an open court process was indicative of the way in which colonial modernity was reconstituting the society.

The combination of making criminality public and confining the criminal was not a paradox or an anomaly belonging to the past, but the very essence of democracy and democratic rule. Evidence and punishment in the form of jail sentence were the public and the private of the newly emerging political rule called democracy, in the development of which colonial experience was of cardinal importance. In this sense, the history of colonial penal reforms that Radhika Singha describes (up to the 1840s) in exhaustive details gives us only an incremental account of the development of the 'due process' in modern Indian penology. She shows the gradual extension of magisterial authority in matters of curbing vagrancy, fixing responsibility on a specific man for the maintenance of women and children, and thus making the head of the family act appropriately as one. The family head was exhorted to be responsible for rational conduct of the other members of the family.[7] Important will be to consider in this respect the Law Commissions. Backed by utilitarian thinking these commissions were the major instruments from 1830s onwards to turn reason and rationality into strategic instruments for stabilizing colonial rule. Reason from now on dictated new forms and processes of punishment, still closely centring around the body, but making inspection, diagnosis, judgement and punishment all a matter of rational process. Therein lay Evidence Act as Stephen's momentous contribution in the annals of rule of law. There was nothing of humanism or humanitarianism, as Michael Ignatieff suggests, that would underwrite the arguments for a more effective economy of power in a rapidly changing society.[8] Taken together the Indian Penal Code, the Indian Criminal Procedure Act and the Evidence Act were inextricably linked to colonial rule, which was based on selective disciplining, punishment and governance.[9]

But since evidence was a matter of inquiry, logic, proof and cross-examination, merely making it public was not enough. It was necessary to draw conclusions, infinitely sophisticated and minute, from the fact that the process was *public*. Thus, for instance, the word 'confession' was left in the Evidence Act. A confession meant an admission made at any time by a person charged with a crime stating or suggesting the inference that he or she had committed the crime. But an 'admission' meant a statement of fact, which waived or dispensed with the production of evidence by conceding that the fact asserted by the opponent was true. An admission could be oral or contained in documents. Although both the concepts appeared similar, a thin line demarcated the two specifically with regard to their evidentiary value before a court of law. While a confession was a statement made by an accused person, which was sought to be proved against him or her in a criminal proceeding to establish the commission of an offence by him or her, an admission related to a transaction and comprised all statements amounting to admissions. A confession if deliberately and voluntarily made was to be accepted as conclusive of the matters confessed. But it was not a conclusive proof of matters admitted and the person admitting was deprived from taking a contradictory stand thereafter. While a confession went against a person making it, an admission could be used on behalf of the person making it under certain circumstances (as mentioned in Section 21 of the Evidence Act). The act of course declared *vide* Section 24,

> A confession made by an accused person is irrelevant in a criminal proceeding if the MAKING of the confession appears to the Court to have been caused by an inducement, threat, or promise, having reference to the charge against the accused person, proceeding from a person in authority and sufficient, in the opinion of the Court, to give the accused person grounds, which would appear to him reasonable, for supposing that by making it he would gain any advantage or avoid any evil of a temporal nature in reference to the proceeding against him.

We can notice the liminality of the situation as envisaged in Section 24, or the following sections (up to Section 30), as we find that the authors of the act refraining from providing any illustrations, which actually abound the entry titled 'Admissions', under which the sections relating to confession featured. An analysis of the relevant case laws in the past 135 years will tell us why the act in the first place required a fine distinction between admission and confession.

This was an instructive instance of a situation, where the limits of the language were evident in two 'normal' concepts – confession and admission. Yet the requirements of objectivity and logic had helped the justice process overcome such limits. The history of the Evidence Act teases in this way the limits of the meaning of the confession by way of raising a number of issues such as the nature of confession evidence, psychological aspects of confession and interrogation, the nature and character of confessions and the obtaining of confession (interrogation and the regulation of questioning), detailed study of the detention and questioning provisions of the Criminal Procedure and Evidence Acts and the practices in vogue for the detention treatment and questioning of suspects, proving and disproving confession evidence, recording of questioning by different means, corroboration of confession and finally the admissibility of previous police records over discredited confessions and the evidential significance of silence.[10]

Today, of course, the requirements of objectification have led law in many countries to define 'confession'. For instance, the British police and Evidence Act, 1984 (PACE) defines a confession as including: any statement wholly or partly adverse to the person who made it; whether made to a person in authority or not; whether made in words or otherwise. As a result statements made by a suspect which do not contain admissions are not liable to exclusion under Section 76 of PACE (cf. Regina v. Sat-Bhambra 1989 88 Cr App R 55). In terms of unreliable confession the following points have to be noted, as per the wide-ranging scope of Section 76 (2 b) of PACE set out by the Court of Appeal in the case of Regina v. Fulling 1987 2 All E.R 65, namely that it can cover confessions obtained as the result of an inducement – for example a promise of bail or a promise that prosecution would not arise from confession; hostile and aggressive questioning; or failure to record accurately what was said; failure to caution; failure to provide an appropriate adult where one is required; and failure to comply with the Code of Practice in relation to the detention of the accused. The last could include failure to allow sufficient rest prior to an interview; failure of the defence solicitor or appropriate adult to act properly – for example by making interjections during interview which are hostile to the defendant.[11]

We can see here the historical progress in the techniques of rule. We have progressed far from the ancient days when confessing was an act of clarifying the existence and duties of flesh in us, and then when it became the expression of the anxieties of soul, and then confessing became expiation. Here (securing) confession is a technique of proving crime and then punishing the criminal – a process in which an earlier technique is being reshaped in the fire of logic, counter-intuition, argumentation, examination and proof. Yet, it seems that the more law tried to distinguish between confession and admission and went on to detail the economy of confession, something seemed to have been left out beyond these details, these extremely minute differentiations and hair-splitting. Rule of law had to communicate not only promise of rights, in this case rights of the accused, but also ensure subjection to rule. Thus details were important. As we shall see later, confession was to become one of the worst abused parts of the protocol of evidence in trial and punishment. In any case, knowing the nature of confession was important for the new age of reason.[12] In 1773 'on perusing the trials' Warren Hastings was 'struck with surprise to observe, that almost every malefactor confesses himself guilty of the crime for which he is tried, although he thereby subjects himself to the loss of life'. He added,

> As this is a circumstance so extraordinary in itself and so very repugnant to the principle of self-interest by which mankind in general are actuated, I cannot help mentioning it in hopes of obtaining some account of the manner in which this confession

is procured, whether it is not made till after conviction, whether extorted, or whether won by fair promises of forgiveness.[13]

Confession made the elaborate protocols of reason meaningless. Therefore, confession was to be made judicially less significant while information-forming part of the confession was to be of help in finding out other criminals and bust the crime gang. Thus the practice of securing, extorting and fabricating confession remained widespread notwithstanding the Bengal Regulation IX of 1793, though this became less significant in the actual process of trial. One can notice the duality here: due process of law and extraordinary concerns that defy due process. Clearly in what was considered as the pre-age of reason in the colonies, arbitrariness was seen as too much. The governor general in Council therefore instructed the Indian law commissioners on 20 March 1847 to prepare a scheme of pleading and procedure along with forms of indictment adapted to the provisions of the Penal Code. Thus came into operation on 1 January 1862 the Act of XXV of 1861 better known as the Indian Criminal Procedure Act. Reason ordained henceforth equality before the procedure of law, the peasant could now approach the law, the procedure was now detailed, hence time consuming and expensive. The fear of god now gave way to fear of law. The age of rule of law to cope with criminality had begun.

Rule by regulations

Rule of law, however, began with rule by regulations. While the project of establishing the rule of law began first with compiling all old laws and deliberating on them, the colonial government had to issue a series of regulations to survive the foundational years. These regulations were so important for the colonial rule that while the government had by 1860s three law commissions, and gradually formed proper legal authorities so that *rule by regulations* could now be substituted by *rule by laws*, the reliance on regulations remained long afterwards, and the first confident steps of a legal regime in suppressing criminality could be only in the form of a joint rule – by men, regulations and laws. The period of hundred years spanning the time between the last quarter of the eighteenth century and that of the nineteenth century was spent in laying the foundations of an objective science of law and criminal legislation by which an enlightened responsible regime would rule the country. This was not to be a foreign despotic administration, but an enlightened rule to sanitise a country caught in mires of passion, frenzy and unfamiliar ethos. The new enlightened methods would depend on abstraction, classification, typologies and controlling bodies of the unruly elements in a new system of punishment.

Therefore, earlier, for instance, while the *Ain-I-Akbari* instructed the judicial delegates of the emperor 'not (to) be content with oaths and witnesses', hold full investigation, be diligent, and possess 'just insight', it could not tell anything about the actual mode or procedure, and the way in which reason could work in investigation, argumentation and determination. The decisions of the judicial delegates were final. Later on with the arrival of the colonial power the *Nizamat Adalat* was created in 1772 in Bengal Presidency as the highest court of criminal justice whose decisions were to be regarded as precedents. The *Nizamat Adalat* did not try any case, but passed final orders on some cases tried in the district criminal courts. In the early colonial days, ad hoc arrangements were the main method of rule, and were in the form of regulations that controlled police behaviour. For instance, Regulation XX prohibited the *Darogas* from taking cognizance of any charge of adultery, fornication, calumny, abusive language, slight trespass or inconsiderable assault. Persons bringing forward such complaints had to be referred to the magistrate. Or, under the Regulations of 1790, magistrates were required to apprehend the 'disturbers of peace and persons charged with crimes and misdemeanours', but 'confessions were to be received with caution', and they were to 'arrange by public advertisements for the attendance of all parties, witnesses, etc., on the arrival of the court of circuit'. The *Nizamat Adalat* apart from laying down some broad rules of criminal trial had (a) to ascertain if the prisoner had committed any offence and (b) if the prisoner was found guilty, to sentence him, and if not, to acquit him; but again it did not have much to say about the details. The *Mufassil* criminal courts of the Company were unfettered by any definite set of rules of evidence, but they operated on the basis of certain rules drawn from earlier law officers and now forming a sort of vague customary law of evidence. The English law of evidence was not in force. Unless a prisoner declined to put any question to a witness whom he had cited in his defence alleging that he had been tampered with by the prosecutors, it was held to be objectionable for the sessions judge to examine him as a witness against the prisoner. The testimony of one eyewitness corroborated by circumstances was held sufficient to establish charge of homicide. In case of homicide the finding of a skull recognized as being that of a missing boy by a peculiarity of a jawbone was held insufficient as proof of identity. Dying declaration by itself could not be declared as evidence. The evidence of a single witness professing to recognize two individuals as belonging to a gang of robbers was insufficient. Any testimony in case of robbery during first examination before police officers was to be received with utmost circumspection. In case of theft, property found in the drain of the house of the accused was not an evidence of guilt. In case of rape, a compromise filed by the injured party in consequence of the accused person's promise to marry her was inadmissible in a court. In this way, the *Nizamat Adalat* had laid down some rules of evidence for homicide, robbery, theft, rape, forgery, perjury, extortion, oath, jury, deposition and others, and these improved the Regulation IX of 1793, which had laid down certain provisions relating to laws of evidence. There were provisions relating to confessions also – their value depending on time, place and person.

As general principles the *Nizamat Adalat* laid down that if there were gross contradictions in the testimony of the witnesses, the evidence was not to be taken as credible, and prisoners were to be acquitted even against the *fatwa* of the law officers. The evidence of a minor was inadmissible. When there were only three witnesses, one male, and two females, and their evidence was contradictory, the full legal proof was held to be wanting. The evidence of a convict having been taken, with a view to the conviction of a prisoner charged with participation in a *dacoity* for which such convict had already been sentenced, the *Nizamat Adalat* ruled that his evidence was wholly inadmissible. It was not to be taken as sufficient reason for rejecting evidence for the defence that the witnesses named by the prisoner had been accused before the magistrate of participating in the offence charged, but released by that officer. A promise to the prisoner not to prosecute him should not operate in bar of a capital sentence, such promise not affecting the credibility of the evidence generally. In the case of a prisoner standing mute, it was not enough to take the deposition of the civil surgeon as to his sanity or otherwise; the prisoner was to be examined specifically by the court as to the cause of his standing mute. If a case rested on direct oral testimony, unsupported by circumstantial evidence, and the witnesses were under the immediate influence of the prosecutor, it was insufficient for conviction. The evidence of the witnesses for the defence must be heard, however worthless their testimony might prove to be. In the event of the absence of witnesses called by a prisoner in his defence, it was the duty of the sessions judge to satisfy himself in regard to the measures taken for securing their appearance, and to take necessary steps securing their attendance. Unless a prisoner declined to put any question to a witness whom he had cited in his defence, alleging that the prosecutors had tampered with him, it was held that it was objectionable for the sessions judge to examine him as a witness against the prisoner. Slight inconsistencies in the evidence for the prosecution were not to affect its general value. In a case of homicide, a witness appearing to have received property with knowledge that it was not obtained honestly, the *Nizamat Adalat* directed his committal for trial on that charge. His examination on oath was declared inadmissible as evidence against him on his trial. The testimony of one eyewitness, corroborated by circumstances, was held sufficient to establish a charge of homicide. The only evidence against prisoners charged with having beaten and otherwise ill-treated a person so that he (latter) died in consequence, being the declaration of the deceased, it was held insufficient for conviction. It was declared to be highly irregular and objectionable to allude to a paper, termed a dying declaration of a deceased party, as evidence when the authenticity of that declaration had not been proved by witnesses in a trial, and when the declaration was not one made in *articule mortis*, but on the contrary, nearly a month before the date of death of the deceased, at a time when his wounds were not considered to be of a dangerous character. In a trial for murder, the deposition of the deceased, taken before his death, was to be included in the record of the trial, on being duly proved. As regards the admissibility of circumstantial evidence, there were several directions. In a case of murder, evidence that the alleged murderer was thirteen or fourteen *crosh* (one *crosh* is two miles) away from the place in which the outrage occurred, continuously from a time before the murder, until considerable time after its perpetration, was held to be sufficient for the acquittal of the prisoner.[14]

If this was the situation regarding homicide, what was the situation in case of robbery? In a case of robbery, the testimony of witnesses, when contrary to their first examination before the police officers, was to be received with the utmost circumspection, because it was frequent practice to call false witnesses for the conviction of persons of notorious or suspected character. The evidence of a single witness who professed to recognize two individuals as having belonged to a large gang of robbers was held to be insufficient for their conviction. The evidence of an approver, and the admissions of three convicted accomplices, was held to be insufficient legal proof for the conviction of a prisoner charged with having been one of a gang, which committed a desperate robbery by open violence. For theft, the provision was that property found in the drain belonging to the prisoner's house was held not to be evidence of this guilt, as there was nothing to prevent the access of others to the drain. In the case of a forgery, the fact of filing a forged deed in a court of justice by the person interested in establishing its contents was held to afford sufficient presumption that he had filed it knowing it to be forged. But when a prisoner had been found carrying counterfeit rupees for the use of another person, it was held that there was no presumption that he was aware of their nature. When a debtor produced a witness who deposed falsely to having witnessed a payment to his creditor, the court could presume that the debtor had suborned false evidence. In a case of affray a discrepancy in the evidence of the two parties was held to afford no ground for the acquittal of those charged with being concerned in that affray. Credit was to be given to that evidence, which appeared best supported by the circumstances of the case.

Regulation IX of 1793 provided that the religious persuasions of witnesses were not to be considered as a bar to the conviction of a prisoner. If in a case the evidence of a witness was considered inadmissible under the Muslim law on the sole ground that the witness was not a Muslim by religion, the courts were directed to give validity to that evidence presuming that the witness was of Islamic persuasion. Regulation IX of 1796 directed that a prisoner was to be questioned at the time of his being committed or held to bail, and his answer was to be recorded on the magistrate's proceedings, with the specification of any witness named by him. And the courts of circuit were expected to ascertain that all due measures had been taken to cause the attendance of all witnesses both for the prosecution and for the defence. Regulation IV of 1797 prohibited leading questions to witnesses, but allowed cross-examination either by the judge or the opposite party for the purpose of extracting the information they possessed and the discovery of the truth. The court of circuit was directed to take note of any variations in the depositions of the same witnesses before them and the magistrates, but depositions taken before the magistrates were not to be read until the witnesses were re-examined.

Regulation III of 1812 prohibited magistrates from issuing process to witnesses without being satisfied that sufficient grounds existed for the prosecution. In 1837 it was declared that no person could be considered incompetent as a witness by reason of his previous conviction for any offence. However, by the Law of Evidence Act II a witness could be asked whether he had been convicted of any crime, and he might be cross-examined as to previous statements made by him in writing. To improve on previous regulations the Law of Evidence Act II was passed in 1855. The provisions of this act were applicable to all courts in British India. The main provisions were that the only persons declared incompetent to testify were children under seven years of age, and insane persons who appeared incapable of receiving just impressions of the facts in respect of which they were to be examined. No person was to be an incompetent witness due to his interest or relationship. Persons present in a court were to give evidence if so required. A party was allowed with the leave of the court to cross-examine and discredit his own witness. Witnesses were bound to answer incriminating questions, but the answer was not to be used against them unless they wilfully gave false evidence. In cases of pedigree, declarations of bastards and intimate acquaintances were admitted. Finally, the act laid down that the improper admission or rejection of evidence was not to be considered as a ground for a new trial where there was other evidence to justify the decision.

Through all these we can see the emergence of what would soon become of strategic importance in the eyes of the judicial reason, namely the task of situating confession in the right place in the entire protocol of evidence gathering, placing and examining. In the eyes of the government an erroneous idea somehow prevailed in the *mufassil* that a confession was the strongest proof of guilt, and that, all that was required was to obtain one, and, if possible, to get it confirmed before the magistrate. The Company official E. Watson had written in his report of 11 September 1810,

It would be endless entering into a detail of the different modes, in which confessions are fabricated and proved. The usual course appears to be, first, to apprehend as many people as caprice may dictate, and then to select from the number, those individuals who are to confess, and determine on the purport of their confessions. The preliminaries being thus arranged, the victims are made over to the subordinate agents or instruments of police, to be dealt with according to circumstances; and the rest are discharged. It sometimes happens, that they meet with a man whom they are able to deceive, by assurances of immediate pardon, and false promises of future favour and indulgence; in such case, he is usually told, that, by signing a paper prepared by a *buckshee* for that purpose, or repeating before witnesses what he is instructed to say, he will not only escape hanging, or at least perpetual imprisonment, but become one of the chosen of the police, and make his fortune as a *goyendah* (informer, spy); that all he has to do, is to pretend that he was concerned in the *dacoity*, and say, that the gang was composed of particular individuals, who are named to him, and leave the rest to the *darogah*; that there can be no harm in this, because all the world know they are the real *dacoits*. . . . When the prisoner is thus prepared, if there appears no danger of his retracting before morning, he is left in peace, for a few hours; but if any apprehension of that sort is entertained, a *burkundaaz* is sent for three or four people of the village to witness the confession instantly, and they are aroused from their sleep, at all hours of the night for that purpose . . . Sometimes a broken port, an old rag, or some other article of little or no value, belonging to the person robbed, is procured by a *goyendah* or other inferior agent of police, and deposited in a half-dry tank or ditch, to which the prisoner is afterwards taken, for the purpose of bringing it out with great formality, in the presence of witnesses . . . [15]

The trouble was that confession was seldom successfully employed, as a ground for ascertaining truth, but it was considered as authentic in itself and was sent to the magistrate, who committed the accused to be tried by the court of circuit.

And what about the confession of the witness, that is oath taking? There was this assumption behind the rule, which required evidence to be given on oath, namely, that a person with a motive to suppress the truth would tell the truth if put on oath because of three possible sanctions: (a) temporal, which implied penalties of perjury in this world; (b) social, which meant fear of the infamy and loss of honour of a person who swore falsely; and (c) spiritual, which meant punishment in the next world.[16]

But what when the inquiry faced silence from the accused as against confession and admission? Law had to anticipate that condition too. Police questioning of the suspect/accused, its legitimacy and its effectiveness had to be considered, and the right to silence and its consequences had to be deliberated upon. Law had to consider the situation, namely, when the police had questioned a suspect in course of its investigation and failed to disclose a matter that was subsequently relied upon in his or her defence. There was nothing to prevent the police from questioning suspects, and from thereby securing admissions or confessions, which might be admissible in evidence against the accused if the grounds for such admissibility were established. However, a court was not obliged to draw an adverse inference against a suspect, even where it was justified, and it would be open to a court to exclude evidence of what occurred during questioning if it was not satisfied that the accused was fairly treated. A Code of Conduct was subsequently promulgated in terms of the Police Act for situations, where, for instance, upon arrest, a suspect was asked to account for objects, substances or marks found on or in the suspected person's possession, or where upon arrest, the suspect was asked to account for his or her presence at the place where he or she was found. The reflections on silence thus led law to draw a distinction between admissions (whether by words or by conduct) and confessions in determining the 'threshold' requirements for admissibility. Law also obliged the presiding officer of inquiry to inform an accused of the right to silence, of the consequences of remaining silent, that he or she was not obliged to make any confession or admission, and to ask him or her whether he or she wished to make a statement indicating the basis for defence. It also obliged the presiding officer to question an accused where the accused failed to disclose the basis of the defence.[17] Law had to consider both eloquence and silence in terms of the requirements of objectivity that is evidence. The Evidence Act in this way combined the experiences of earlier practices in the form of Regulations.

One can see here the evolving nature of the truth game. Wherever and whenever it was a question of finding out the truth (here truth of the crime and the criminal), the game of reason, examination, analysis and counter-arguments would commence immediately; and it was on the site of evidence that the game would be played. Thus even though the equation of truth and evidence or equating evidence with truth is a more modern thing in terms of morally ruling a society, as the brief account of the relevant Regulations shows, the elements were all there. Rational governance had to only organize the various elements in place in order to bring about the most ruthless yet the most popular form of truth game of our age.

If, as we earlier indicated briefly, ruling a society in this way appeared as laborious, why was such a laborious process needed, invented and improvised? Laborious process meant inventing constraints, and putting these constraints on passions. The working of these constraints also meant that they required time and patience to be put in place; and if these were deep enough they would work as strong buffers to passions. And what better constraint could be in place than the one created by the labour of 'interest', to be precise labour of 'self-interest'? Self-interest if properly encouraged, instituted and made to work strategically could moderate society and reduce crimes or at least made them controllable. Thus, not only submitting to law had its origin in the secret history of self-interest, in the actual legal process of judging a crime the witness could answer truthfully due to enlightened self-interest. Or if the member of a gang turned approver, it was because self-interest motivated him towards being an approver. The guilty confessed on a calculation of gains and loss, In this way the question of motivation appeared again and again in the judgement of evidences produced before the court, because motivation was the sign of self-interest. Self-interest meant calculation, comparison and clarity of outlook. Examination of evidences therefore often involved questions regarding calculation, comparison and opinion. British reformers such as Adam Smith, Bentham, the Mills and others repeatedly stressed the virtue of submitting to order because only through such submission people could be saved from anarchy – the result of unbridled passion. Awareness of self-interest had the capacity to draw people from passions which were listed as: animosity, enmity, attachment, love, the relish of telling others as to what to do and thus getting involved and the relish of being told so, excessive pride, megalomania, dejection, vilification, extreme indignation, primordial inertness or restlessness, delight in conflict, hatred, the obsessive desire to break rules, too much identification with victor or the victims.[18] These lead to crimes. Crimes could be controlled and punished by awakening self-interest in society. Self-interest was reason, practical reason; but as we have seen, it was also procedurally a ruthless and a deadly game.

The significance of procedure in rule of law

To arouse self-interest procedure is important. By the same logic, reason is first of all procedure.

This from day one was clear to the makers of the Indian Evidence Act 2 of 1855. The Select Committee's draft report (1871) took cognizance of the role of procedure in law as distinct from substance. Bentham in England had suggested few years back a division of law between substantive law and adjective law. Adjective law included rules of procedure and rules of practice. It was by this that civil and criminal procedure laws were separately made and developed. Evidence was above all a matter of procedure – procedure of arriving at the truth. Because procedure was important, Maine, later to become Sir Henry Summer Maine, in introducing the first draft bill of the Evidence Act on behalf of the Indian Law Commissioners remarked in 1868,

> No doubt much evidence is received by the mofussil courts, which the English courts would not strictly regard as admissible. But I would appeal to the members of the Council, who have had more experience of the mofussil than myself, whether the judges to those courts do not as a matter of fact believe that it is their duty to administer the English Law of Evidence as modified by the Evidence Act. In particular, I am informed that when a case is argued by a barrister before the mofussil judges and when English rules of evidence are pressed on the attention he does practically accept those rules and admits or rejects evidence according to his

construction of them. I cannot help regarding this state of things as eminently unsatisfactory. I entirely agree with the Commissioners that there are parts of the English Law of Evidence, which are wholly unsuited to this country. We have heard much of the laxity with which evidence is admitted in the mofussil courts, but the truth is that this laxity is to a considerable extent justifiable. The evil, it appears to me, lies in admitting evidence, which under strict rules of admissibility would be rejected than admitting or rejecting evidence without fixed rules to govern admission and rejection. Anything like a capricious administration of law of evidence was an evil, but would be an equal evil, or perhaps even a greater evil, when such strict rules of evidence should be in force as practically to leave the court without materials for a decision. . . . [19]

The dilemma before the Select Committee was clear: it wanted to consolidate the English Law of Evidence, but the question was how to achieve the goal in a situation compounded by the double absence – that of any law of evidence and of standard practice in courts which followed at least three systems – Hindu, Muslim and the English. Modifications were necessary, and these modifications were aimed at gradually introducing a full-scale law of evidence, which would stress on individual depositions freeing them from the supposed threads of kinship, coercion and family linkages. Therefore, we should not be surprised at the fact that just as the Indian Evidence Act came following preparations dating from 1841, it was followed likewise by a series of developments in the form of amendments on fourteen occasions (before the amendments required by the full scale anti-terrorist legislations set in): 1872, 1887, 1891, 1899, 1919, 1926, 1927, 1934, 1949, 1951, 1953, 1983, again in 1983, 1986. Some of the amendments necessitated by the Prevention of Dowry Act and legislations in the nineties such as the TADA or POTA show the continuing necessity of tailoring the laws of evidence according to the political and governmental priorities of the state. One can say this is how reason evolves anywhere and everywhere.

While taking note of the inadequacy of the earlier efforts to draft a suitable legislation, the Select Committee had observed on 15 July 1871,

. . .(The) Commissioners' draft is not sufficiently elementary for the officers for whose use it is designed, and that it assumes an acquaintance on their part with the law of England, which can scarcely be expected from them. Our draft, however, though arranged on a different principle from theirs, embodies most of its provisions. In general, it has been our object to reproduce the English Law of Evidence with certain modifications most of which have been suggested by the Commissioners, though with some this is not the case.

The English Law of Evidence appears to us to be totally destitute of arrangement. This arises partly from the circumstance that its leading terms are continually used in different sense, and partly from the circumstance that the Law of Evidence was formed by degrees out of various elements, and in particular out of the English system of pleading and the habitual practice of the Courts of Common Law. For instance, the rule that evidence must be confined to point in issue is founded on the system of pleading. The rule that hearsay is no evidence is part of the practice to the Courts but the two sets of rules run into each other in such an irregular way as to produce between them a result which no one can possibly understand systematically unless he is both acquainted with the principles of a system of pleading which is being rapidly abolished and with the everyday practice of the Common Laws of Courts, which can be acquired and understood only by those who habitually take part in it. This knowledge, moreover, must be qualified by study of textbooks, which are seldom systematically arranged. . . .

This being the case, we have discarded altogether the phraseology in which the English test-writers usually express themselves and have attempted first to ascertain, and then to arrange in their natural order, the principles which underline the numerous cases and fragmentary rules which they have collected together. The result is as follows:

Every judicial proceeding whatever, has for its purpose the ascertaining of some right or liability. If the proceeding is criminal, the object is to ascertain the liability to punishment of the person accused; if the proceeding is civil, the object is to ascertain some right of property or of status, or the right of one party, and the liability of the other, to some form of relief.

All rights and liabilities are dependent upon and arise out of facts and facts fall into two classes, those, which can, and those, which cannot be perceived by the senses. Of facts, which can be perceived by the senses, it is superfluous to give examples. Of facts which cannot be perceived by the senses, intentions, fraud, good faith, and knowledge may be given as examples. But each class of facts has, in common, one element, which entitles them to the name of facts – they can be directly perceived either with or without the intervention of the senses. A man can testify to the fact that, at a certain time, he had a certain intention, on the same grounds as that on which he can testify that, at a certain time and place, he saw a particular man. He has, in each case, a present recollection of a past direct perception. Moreover, it is equally necessary to ascertain facts of each class in judicial proceedings and they must in most cases be ascertained in precisely the same way.

Facts may be related to rights and liabilities in one of two different ways.

1.   They may be themselves, or in connection with other facts, constitute such a state of things that the existence of the disputed right or liability would be a legal-inference from them. From the fact that A is the eldest son of B, there arises of necessity the inference that A is by the law of England the heir-at-law of B, and that he has such rights as that status involves. From the fact that A caused the death of B under certain circumstances, and with a certain intention or knowledge, there arises of necessity the inference that A murdered B, and is liable to the punishment provided by the law for murder.

     Fact thus related to a proceeding may be called facts in issue unless, indeed, their existence is undisputed.

2.   Facts, which are not themselves in issue in the sense above explained, may affect the probability of the existence of facts in issue, and these may be called collateral facts.

     It appears to us that these two classes comprising all the facts with it can in any event be necessary for Courts of Justice to concern themselves, so that this classification exhausts all facts considered in their relation to the proceeding in which they are to be proved.

If that is how the heirs of Hume and Bentham were defining facts, and reflecting on how law was bringing *facts* into existence, what was happening to the other associated category called 'proof'? In this significant note the Select Committee remarked:

This introduces the question of proof. It is obvious that, whether an alleged fact is a fact in issue, or a collateral fact, the Court can draw no inference from its existence till it believes it to exist; and it is also obvious that the belief of the Court in the existence of a given fact ought to proceed upon grounds altogether independent of the relation of the fact to object and nature of the proceedings in which its existence is to be determined. The question is whether A wrote a letter. The letter may have contained the terms of a contract. It may have been a libel. It may have constituted the motive for the commission of a crime by B. It may supply proof of an alibi in favour of A. It may be an admission or a confession of a crime; but whatever may be the relation of the fact to the proceeding, the Court cannot act upon it unless it believes that A did write the letter, and that belief must obviously be produced, in each of the cases mentioned by the same or similar facts. If for instance, the Court required the production of the original when the writing of the letter is a crime, there can be no reason why it should be satisfied with a copy when the writing of the letter is a motive for a crime. In short, the way in which a fact should be proved depends on the nature of the fact, and not on the relation of the fact to the proceedings.

And then it went on with a remorseless logic that a correct idea of proof could tell us what was *evidence*,

The instrument by which the court is convinced of a fact is evidence. It is often classified as being either direct or circumstantial. We have not adopted this classification.

If the distinction is that direct evidence establishes a fact in issue, whereas circumstantial evidence establishes a collateral fact, evidence is classified, not with reference to its essential qualities but with reference to the use to which it is put; as if paper were to be defined not only by reference to its component elements but as being used for writing or for printing. We have shown that the mode in which a fact must be proved depends on its nature and not on the use to be made of it. Evidence, therefore, should be defined, not with reference to the nature of the fact, which it is to prove but with reference to its own nature.

Sometimes the distinction is stated thus: direct evidence is a statement of what a man has actually seen or heard. Circumstantial evidence is something from which facts in issue are to be inferred. If the phrase is thus used, the word 'evidence' in the two phrases (direct 'evidence' and circumstantial 'evidence' opposed to each other) has two different meanings. In the first, it means testimony; in the second it means a fact, which is to serve as the foundation for an inference. It would indeed be quite correct if this view is taken to say 'circumstantial evidence must be proved by direct evidence'. This would be a most clumsy mode of expression, but it shows the ambiguity of the word 'evidence' which means either:

1   Word spoken or things produced in order to convince the Court of the existence of acts; or
2   Facts of which the Court is so convinced and which suggest some inference as to other facts.
3   We use the word 'evidence' in the first of these senses only, and so used it may be reduced to three heads: (1) oral evidence; (2) documentary evidence; and (3) material evidence.
4   Finally, the evidence by which facts are to be proved must be brought to the notice of the court and submitted to its judgment and the Court must form its judgment respecting them.

These general considerations appear to us to supply the groundwork for a systematic and complete distribution of the subject as follows:

1   Preliminary;
2   The relevancy of facts to the issue;
3   The proof of facts according to their nature by oral, documentary or material evidence;
4   The production of evidence; and procedure. (Italics mine)

One can notice here the strength and dilemma of the entire discourse. On one hand true to the theory of adjective law, the Select Committee tried to erect a truly independent law of procedure. That was its strength. It wanted to define categories or concepts in their own terms. But the Committee was only too aware of the relational nature of these three categories: fact, proof and evidence. With attempts to define the relations between these three categories, also between the process and the substance, and finally between all these on one hand and law and power on the other – clearly the latter half of the nineteenth century was the period of laying down the most objective process of domination possible through settling the objective standards of defining relation between law, facts and decision. This was how judicial power took shape; it was rational; hence it reinforced power and domination. This was procedural knowledge, always a question of right procedure to establish facts, providing proof, and arguing for the relevance. This was judicial power at the behest of a state and its governmental task of maintaining the daily order of the society; and at the heart of this particular form of power was the essence of law, legality and objectivity.

But being objective however requires suitable technologies. We mentioned earlier photography and the development of print culture as two instances. Something more relating to appropriate technology happened later. In fact the Evidence Act stands at the intersection of developments such as the development of the criminal procedure, various anthropometric measurement techniques which soon included fingerprinting, evolution of the colonial systems of classification, machineries of law and order, hardening rules of criminality, the advent of photography and print techniques. These gave form to what Vinay Lal calls the 'epistemological imperatives' of a state, in this case the colonial state.[20] After the conquest of territories, faced with the necessity of settling these territories and endowing them with proper administration, the task was to know the people well. But since every Indian could not be known, and that was scarcely necessary given the fact that the 'Indians lived in communities only', the task was actually to know each and every collective as much as possible. That was how anthropometry and anthropology came into an alliance for producing knowledge of the group, and by virtue of that the criminal group, and by a short route, the criminal mind.

We have to view the codification of the category called the 'criminal tribes' in the Criminal Tribes Act of 187 against this backdrop. The criminal tribes and castes were held to be criminally inclined by birth; India was as a whole a country devoid of law and order, and till the British came the Indians could not be described to have any respect for law. The country was singularly empty of law. All it had was customs and religious observances. This lawlessness nurtured in it crimes and other forms of public disorder, and within this milieu there were groups habituated to crime by birth. Though the operations of the Thuggee and Dacoity Department in British India ceased in 1863, the notion of 'criminal tribes' and 'criminal castes' had taken the place of thugs and dacoits.

The emergence of fingerprint in India is marked by this context. Vinay Lal mentions in this context the crucial role of Edward Henry who in 1891 was appointed the inspector-general of police for the Lower Provinces and Bengal. Edward Henry first experimented with the anthropometric system, but was not satisfied with the accuracy of the measurements. In a report submitted to the government of Bengal in 1896, Henry detailed the experiments he had conducted with fingerprints, which he observed were not only inexpensive to obtain, but also a surer means of detecting and confirming the identity of any given person. At Henry's behest, the Government of India appointed a committee of inquiry to report on the relative merits of the anthropometric and fingerprinting systems. The Committee came to the conclusion that the method of identification of habitual criminals by means of finger-prints could be safely adopted as being superior to the anthropometric method. By a resolution of the Government of India on 12 June 1897, the system of fingerprinting was adopted throughout India. In 1895, a provincial fingerprint bureau was established in Madras (now Chennai), and in 1898 the first national fingerprint bureau in the world was set up at the police headquarters in Kolkata. Act V of 1899 amended the Indian Evidence Act of 1872 to admit fingerprint evidence. Henry remarked in a lecture delivered before the British Association for the Advancement of Science that before the turn of the century fingerprinting had been adopted by virtually all other departments of the Government of India. By 1920s Azizul Haq and Hem Chandra Bose of the Bengal police and once attached to Henry had perfected the system of fingerprinting classification. Shortly before his retirement, Haq petitioned that his services in working out a system of fingerprints be recognized, and the Government of India granted him an honorarium of Rs 5,000. His colleague in the Bengal police, Hem Chandra Bose, was similarly recognized for his services in creating a system of single-digit impression and for creating a telegraphic code for communicating fingerprint classification. This work involved 'arduous labour', and though Scotland Yard itself published a similar telegraphic code in 1921, Bose's work had clearly anticipated that code in virtually every respect.[21] Along with the invention of fingerprint came the development of photography also, which assisted in the development of a system of surveillance through what the colonial rule took to be a more accurate representation of the people. The massive photographic exercise in typology, *The People of India*, initiated at the behest of Governor-General Canning, was transformed by the Rebellion of 1857–58 into an official project of the state, and placed under the control of the Political and Secret Department. These photographs of Indians brought to light not 'individuals' but types,[22] ironically though the Evidence Act as a piece of liberal jurisprudence was based on the individuation of guilt and crime, and therefore on the principle of individual responsibility, crime and punishment.

Simon Cole has noted many similarities between the debate over the impact of the newest identification technology, DNA typing, and the impact of the earlier biometric systems, mainly the fingerprint identification system on criminal justice. Exactly as now, then too questions were raised: how accurate, discriminating and reliable was the fingerprinting system, and how would we measure these attributes? How would the police monitor the application of the new technology of identification to minimize errors? How inclusive should the fingerprinting databases be? What kind of threat did they pose to individual privacy and civil liberties? What was the relationship between the criminal justice application of fingerprinting and other applications in areas like health care, immigration control and scientific research? Did these databases raise the spectre of eugenics?[23] Contrary to the popular image of fingerprinting as tool for forensic investigation, fingerprint identification was developed for purposes of criminal record keeping, rather than forensics. Specifically, fingerprinting was developed in order to facilitate the storage and retrieval of criminal histories by the state. Cole says that the impetus behind the development of biometric criminal identification technologies in the late nineteenth century was complex, including such factors as rapid urbanization; the increasing anonymity of urban life; the dissolving of local networks of familiarity in which individuals were 'known' by their neighbours; growing migration of individuals from city to city, country to country and continent to continent; and the necessity of governing imperial possessions populated by large numbers of people whom it was necessary to monitor, control and identify. Cole also details how in the 1880s two new technologies emerged which promised to solve the problem of aliases by linking criminal records, not to names, but to some representation of the criminal's body. Such a system required that criminal records be filed by some bodily property rather than by name. One of these systems, fingerprinting, is familiar to us today. The other, anthropometry – the measurement of the human body – has largely been forgotten. The two systems battled for dominance until well into the 1920s. Today, of course, anthropometric identification, with its meticulous skull measurements and attention to body size, evokes the pseudo-sciences of phrenology, cranium and their contributions to racist science. Fingerprinting and anthropometry both were closely tied to biologically determinist efforts to find bodily markers of character traits like intelligence and criminality.

Cole further records how latent fingerprints – invisible finger impressions made visible by dusting with powder – had been used to investigate crimes as early as 1892 in Argentina, 1897 in India and 1903 in Britain. But it was only after the First World War that finger-printing triumphed over anthropometry as the standard procedure in law enforcement agencies. Courts allowed law enforcement agencies to retain fingerprint records even when the individual was acquit-ted or not convicted, except in cases of illegal arrests. Optical scan-ning, digital storage and computerized search and retrieval now give fingerprinting the potential to at last live up to its popular image: in which crime-scene technicians can routinely solve crimes lacking suspects by searching latent prints against a large database. Yet there is a decline in the interest in fingerprinting research programme due to several reasons. Cole points out that the biologists had found new biological markers to examine, including, of course, the gene, which was re-discovered around 1900. Second, law enforcement officials, who became an increasingly dominant force within the community of those interested in fingerprints, found it more convenient to treat fingerprint patterns as meaningless information. This kept the iden-tification process focused solely on the individuals and uncluttered with distracting theories about whether race, inheritance or crimi-nal propensity might also be legible in fingerprint patterns. The law enforcement officials dominating the fingerprint community after the First World War had an interest in erasing the history of diag-nostic fingerprint research and muting discussion of the issue. By transforming fingerprint patterns from potentially significant bio-logical markers into merely individualizing information, 'used only for identification', law enforcement officials bestowed a 'purity' or 'neutrality' on fingerprint identification that augmented its credibil-ity as an identification technique among both the general public and the courts. The history of fingerprinting as a tool of identification shows how technological control over ways of observing the body has played an enormously significant role in crime trial, evidence and punishment.

Evidence, truth, punishment, death

Death is the final punishment proper evidence can bring about. Therefore, the exceptions made by the TADA to the Evidence Act and resulting in death sentences are worth noting. These exceptions are further instructive for they do not claim that evidence is not nec-essary; they only make changes in the procedure of what will be considered as in the light of grave offences. They are silent on the question, namely, do these exceptions not change the very category called 'evidence'? If legislating extraordinary laws such as TADA is the technique today to grapple with the objectivity of evidence, in the colonial time it was the technique of building a conspiracy case, whereby members of a 'conspiracy' could be killed judicially on the basis of indirect and circumstantial evidence. Each murder of a colonial official, or assault, or train robbery was an outcome of a conspiracy against the state and the Crown, and therefore the conspirators had to be punished with the extreme sentence. Many were sentenced to death in this way; and in this way each of these cases until today has redefined the relation between death as the final punishment and evidence.

This technique appeared on the basis of two developments – first, the development of treason law in England in the preceding three centuries,[24] and second, by making *association* of the individuals in the colony for any reason, except the most banal, suspect in the eyes of government. Thus the Criminal Code was amended again and again to expand the scope of unlawful association to facilitate charge against the state in face of which the elaborate procedure of the Evidence Act seemed at times meaningless. Thus, Section 16 under Part II of the Indian Criminal Law Amendment Act of 1908 defined 'unlawful association' in the broadest possible way, and Section 17 increased the penalties. The law was amended again in 1932, this time making circulation or publication of literature forfeited by the government unlawful, and brought any possible case of intimidation under punishable offence. In 1938 this was again amended this time aiming to punish acts that seemed to encourage 'mutiny', as Section 2 of the act declared punishable acts with 'intent to affect adversely the recruitment of persons to serve in the Military, Naval, or Air Forces'.[25] We have to see therefore the functioning of the Evidence Act in a relational way, the other elements being the Penal Code, the Criminal Procedure Code, and the Police Act.

To appreciate the extent that relation between death as the final punishment and evidence is redefined by these conspiracy cases, one can study the instance of the Rajiv Gandhi murder case.[26] In the said case in its appellate stage in the Supreme Court, Justice S. Shah Mohammed Quadri had to observe that the conviction of the accused under TADA was unsustainable because: (a) the provisions of sub-sections (2), (3) and (4) of Section 3 of TADA Act would be attracted only when a person accused of the offences under the said provisions has committed 'a terrorist act' within the meaning of Section 3 (1) of the TADA Act;[27] and (b) and the accused must be members of a conspiracy, which means they must be proved to have conspired, and the 'shroud of secrecy' could not be an evidence. He wrote in his opinion,

> Section 120A: Definition of criminal conspiracy – When two or more persons agree to do, or cause to be done-
>
> 1 An illegal act, or
> 2 An act which is not illegal by illegal means, such an agreement is designated a criminal conspiracy:
>
>> Provided that no agreement except an agreement to commit an offence shall amount to a criminal conspiracy unless some act besides the agreement is done by one or more parties to such agreement in pursuance thereof;
>>
>> Explanation – It is immaterial whether the illegal act is the ultimate object of such agreement, or is merely incidental to that object.
>>
>> The ingredients of the offence of criminal conspiracy are: (i) an agreement between two or more persons; (ii) the agreement must relate to doing or causing to be done either (a) an illegal act; or (b) an act which is not illegal in itself but is done by illegal means. The proviso and the explanation are not relevant for the present discussion.
>>
>> Though the meeting of minds of two or more persons for doing/or causing to be done an illegal act or an act by illegal means is a *sine qua non* of the criminal conspiracy, yet in the very nature of the offence which is shrouded with secrecy no direct evidence of the common intention of the conspirators can normally be produced before the Court. Having regard to the nature of the offence, such a meeting of minds of the conspirators has to be inferred from the circumstances proved by the prosecution, if such an inference is possible.[28] (italics in the original)

The government therefore always feels the imperative to re-invent and then manage a legal tradition whereby it can continuously link its evidence theory with the need to punish the accused and the guilty. Thus, like in the colonial time when for punishing the nationalists accused of committing terrorist crimes the evidence theory had to be re-adjusted on several occasions. In 2002 the government set up the Malimath Committee, headed by a former High Court judge, with a broad mandate to 'examine the fundamental principles of criminal jurisprudence, including the constitutional provisions relating to criminal jurisprudence', and suggest amendment. The committee's questionnaire asked: should we dispense with proof of guilt beyond reasonable doubt? Should we not abolish the rights of the accused to silence and against self-incrimination? The committee was vested with the broad mandate 'to examine the fundamental principles of criminal jurisprudence, including the constitutional provisions relating to criminal jurisprudence, and see if any modifications and amendments are required'.

Justice Malimuth Committee posed three major questions:

a   Should we dispense with the basic premise of criminal law, namely, proof of guilt beyond reasonable doubt?
b   Should we not as a consequence do away with the right of the accused to silence?
c   Should we not as a consequence abolish the right of the accused against self-incrimination?

An affirmative answer would have allowed the government to radically revise all criminal laws, and the constitutional law itself. It would have gone against the commonly held basis of criminal justice, namely that the onus of proof was upon the prosecution, not the accused; otherwise the presumption of innocence would be violated and the accused would have been treated as guilty before trial. It was also important to protect the accused against forced confession.[29] Article 359 says that during a state of Emergency, the right to move a court to enforce fundamental rights may be temporarily suspended, but Articles 20 and 21 cannot be suspended. Article 21 concerns the right to life, and Article 20 says, 'No person shall be compelled to be a witness against himself'. The right of an accused to silence, not to incriminate himself or herself, is total.

The right of silence is an intriguing, yet one of the compelling parts of a theory of evidence. We are heirs of the legacy of right to speech, and have heard of the soul's obligation to practise fearless speech. But what are we to say about silence? Like speech, silence too, we can see, is connected with power of a situation or power in a situation.

First, there is this idea that the presumption of innocence of the accused, his silence and the privilege against self-incrimination are responsible for the increase in crime, and since it is assumed that the presumption of innocence is firmly embedded in the Evidence Act, there is almost now a social consensus in favour of a requirement of a change. The act, of course, tells that if A accuses B of a crime, B must establish the same and beyond all reasonable doubt. The provisions of the burden of proof lay down in detail the course of onus of proof available with respect to events and facts during the course of a trial.

Second, there is the idea that there are 'obstacles' to the discovery of truth; indeed obstacles are the evidence that there is truth, and therefore in the administration of jurisprudence these obstacles have to be removed.

Finally, interpretation is the great tool by which the right to silence has been considerably broken down. Thus, a confession outside the court either to a police officer under POTA or the magistrate is admissible. The accused is expected to explain every adverse circumstance to the court at the conclusion of evidence with the court having the power and the jurisdiction to draw adverse inference while formally 'appreciating' the silence of the accused on the evidence against him. Breaking the silence of the accused therefore is accompanied by a strategy of silencing the defence. There is the truth, and if discovery of truth has obstacles that have to be removed. There is also the other side, namely, that truth must have its victims. Therefore, the accused though given the formal right of silence before the executive cannot be allowed to remain silent before the judiciary, and that silence must be broken. This is a system that created legends and legends out of lawyers. The crime and the criminal, the litigant and his cause, recede to the background and the lawyer occupies the centre stage.[30] Truth, fearless speech, inquiry and silence all become subordinate to the *protocol of justice*, which is the other name of the power of procedure, power inherent in a procedure.

That the Evidence Act organizes the relation between truth, evidence and punishment in a particular way, and therefore each time the act changes due to amendment or case laws, the relation is also reorganized, is borne out by some of the recent Law Commission recommendations. The Commission has stated in its report (185th) to the Law Ministry ten years back:

> . . . Law of Evidence is one of the most important laws administered by our civil and criminal courts. Since 1872, when the present Act was enacted, there has been a sea change in human rights jurisprudence all over the world. Seventy years later, basic principles governing human rights were enunciated in the Universal Declaration of Human Rights, 1948. This was followed by the International Covenant on Civil and Political Rights, 1966.

The said Convention has been ratified by India in 1976. Our Constitution came into effect from January 26, 1950. Art. 20 (3) of our Constitution declares the fundamental right against self-incrimination. Art. 21 guarantees liberty and a right to procedure established by law which after Maneka Gandhi, requires the procedure to be just, fair and equitable. Principles of evidence, which are applicable to criminal law, have to necessarily satisfy the basic requirements both of Art. 20 (3) and Art 21. Nor can the procedure be discriminatory or arbitrary; otherwise it may offend Art. 14. Special protection is necessary for women who are victims of crime. Transparency in governmental functioning is an essential feature of democracy. Press freedom has to be protected and its boundaries delineated. . . .

The proposed amendments are intended to conform to these new standards.

We may very briefly highlight a few of the important recommendations made in this Report. Admissibility or otherwise of confessions is covered by sections 24 to 29. We have proposed amendment to sec. 27 to conform to the several judgments of the Courts. Sarkar in his commentary on the Evidence Act, 1872 (15th Ed., 1999, p.534) has stated that while sec. 27 requires to be amended, only a person of the eminence of Sir James Stephen can make an attempt. Such was the magnitude of the task under sec. 27. Sec. 27 is now proposed to be an exception to sections 24 to 26. By the introduction of the word 'or' it applies to facts discovered from statements by those in custody and not in custody. The words 'distinctively' and 'so much of such information' are proposed to be deleted. Under sec. 27, it is further proposed that facts discovered from statements can be admitted in evidence only if the statements have not been made under threats, cruelty, violence or torture. Facts discovered by inducement or promise will still be relevant. We had to differ totally from the recommendation in the 69th Report to incorporation of sec. 26A to make all confessions to senior police officers admissible irrespective of the nature of the offences, a recommendation, which according to us, goes contrary to the views of the Supreme Court and in particular, the views expressed in Kehar Singh's case. What can be sustained under Arts 14 or 21 as an exception in the case of terrorist's confessions or of those involved in organized crime, cannot be made a general rule and applied to the admission in evidence of every confession made to a senior police officer, in the context of every other offence. This would, as per the statement of the law by the

Supreme Court, violate Arts 14 and 21, and all considerations of proportionality. . . .

Regarding 'affairs of State' and production of unpublished government records and 'confidential communications' to a public officer, amendments are proposed to sections 123, 124 and 162, taking into account changes in the law as declared in S.P. Gupta. We have accepted the recommendation in the 69th Report and the 88th reports, which are identical in this behalf. We have, however, proposed one change. Instead of an appeal, as proposed in the 88th Report from orders of subordinate Courts on questions as to affairs of State decided under sec. 123, we have proposed that there should be a 'reference' to the High Court on the said question by the subordinate Court.

With reference to proof of paternity, in sec. 112, apart from the sole exception of 'non-access', other exceptions by way of blood-group tests, DNA have been proposed but subject to very stringent conditions. Further, the benefit of the presumption as to paternity in case of those born during the continuance of a marriage or within two hundred eighty days of dissolution is now extended not only to children of voidable marriages which are avoided but to children of void marriages where a declaration of nullity is obtained, provided such children are, under their respective personal laws, treated as legitimate . . . .

Presumption of genuineness of ancient documents is proposed to apply, in sec. 90, to documents 20 years old rather than 30 years old as done in other countries. It is also proposed to introduce subsection (2) to sec. 90 to include registered documents the originals of which are twenty years old, as done in UP by 1954 Amendment. Sec. 90 raises presumption as to execution, handwriting and attestation. Sec. 90A is proposed, as done in UP in 1954, in respect of registered documents, the originals of which are less than twenty years old, to raise only a presumption of execution.

With reference to persons whose whereabouts are not known, presumption under sec. 108 is modified. As to presumption of death by a particular date, we propose to clarify, while not accepting the view of the Privy Council that, at the end of 7 years, the death must be presumed, unless the person who wants to prove the person was alive after 7 years is able to prove that fact. Of course, if a party contends that the person died by any particular date within 7 years, he has to prove the same. The proposed amendment helps persons to take decisions in respect of remarriage or succession. . . .[31]

Kehar Singh as we know was hanged in the Indira Gandhi murder case, and the punishment was an ironic commentary on the principle of proportionality. Yet more than any other case the trial of Kehar Singh showed how truth constituted its own relation with evidence and punishment. Here not only the 'particular' evidence (of the conspiracy) makes Kehar Singh a criminal – an object of punishment – it also makes the matter of studying the particular mode of the 'objectivation' of the subject an essential task, meaning thereby that we study the methods and techniques used in a particular institutional context to categorize an individual or a group to shape, direct, modify their way of conducting themselves, to impose ends on their inaction or fit it into overall strategies. This is what government is, and it is in this way the Evidence Act aims to control population suspected of committing crimes. The Evidence Act is one of the earliest instances in the country of the phenomenon of what Foucault was to call famously later 'governmentality'.[32]

To remind ourselves: this is exactly what plagued the mind of early legislators and the jurists in colonial India, namely, how to govern the subjects in terms of laws and processes, which would make governable categories out of the subjects. Procedure was therefore important, and the significance of procedure was not lost upon the pragmatic colonial rulers. Truth was nothing if there was a lack of procedure, and procedure had to be marked by evidence, because evidence signalled fairness. The Evidence Act commented,

> These criticisms (of the Act) may be divided into two classes. Some approve of the general principle upon which the Act proceeds (namely, that it is both possible and advisable positively to determine what is evidence), but criticise the actual terms in which such determination is made. Others disapprove, preferring the more practical and historical method of English Law, which confines itself mainly to the negative task of declaring not what is but what is not evidence.[33]

And then, looking back on the amazing range of issues covered in the act (namely, fact, evidence, relevance, strict proof, presumption, inference, conclusive proof, admissibility, explanation, omission, commission, waiver, dissimilar fact, motive, preparation, subsequent conduct, conduct, conspiracy, common design, facts showing state of mind and body, negligence, facts bearing on the question whether the act was accidental or intentional, hearsay and opinion, inducement, threat, promise, confession otherwise relevant not to become irrelevant because of promise of secrecy . . .), the comment continued,

> Possibly no enactment in such few words brought so much assistance to the administration of justice. . . .
>
> The theory of relevancy is concerned with the question: Why is one thing relevant and another thing irrelevant? . . .
>
> The definition that relevancy means the connection of events as cause and effect, leaves us . . . in this difficulty that if we take the words in even the widest comprehensible sense, the definition does not include all facts which we know from our experience to be really relevant; and if we give them a transcendent meaning based upon our knowledge, that all things precedent have gone together to make up the state of things existing at any time, and that no fact could ever have existed without the co-existence of every other fact that did exists at the same time, then the definition includes everything and so ceases to be a definition.[34]

Thus while we need a definition in legal procedure, we must also understand that the definition also requires concrete situation-wise understanding, coupled with a certain transcendental reasoning. Thus the authors of the famous law book, Sir John Woodroffe and Syed Amir Ali, two of the most famous jurists in the second half of nineteenth-century India, followed the even more famous jurist, Sir Stephen the author of the Evident Act, in classifying facts: (a) any part of the fact alleged or any fact implied by the fact alleged, (b) any cause of the fact, (c) any effect of the fact (d) and, any fact having a common cause with the fact in issue.[35] And if this was a fact, then, what was a relevant fact? What are its rules?

Rule 1: No fact is relevant which does not make the existence of a fact in issue more likely or unlikely.

Rule 2: Facts which are a cause of a fact in issue, or are an effect, or which show the absence of what might be expected as an effect of fact in issue, or which are effects of a cause of a fact in issue.

Rule 3: Facts, which affirm or deny the relevancy of facts, alleged to be relevant under Rule 1 are relevant.

Rule 4: Facts relevant to relevant facts are relevant.

We can see that these four rules have strong interconnections, which point to the fact that the entire evidence theory is reducible to certain

definitions, always falling short of real-life events. Ironically an awareness of this makes a strong theory of evidence a compulsory element
in the governance of justice. 'One of the necessary conditions for the
appreciation of evidence is that there must be evidence. This means,
there must be evidence, either documentary or oral. . . . Suggestions
cannot take the place of evidence.'[36] Yet the fact is that evidence production and proof take place in a real world of bloody conflicts and
property wars, and the whole situation is both a result of the social
struggles where law, evidence and in some countries the widening of
the notion and the institution of jury became the primary means by
which the legal enquirers have captured the juridical world.[37]

Yet in the mission to objectify the matter of evidence as part of the
wider strategy to create a rational society, the judges will always have
something final to say beyond the act, words, arguments, depositions
and evidence, because a 'doubt' must pave the way for a 'benefit of
doubt' to be formulated as 'the benefit of doubt'. Thus, even though
the act even in its original form spoke of the burden on the administration to prove the charges it had brought against the accused, the court
had to admit exactly one century later in a rare outburst,

> Credibility of testimony, oral or circumstantial, depends consider-
> ably on a judicial evaluation of the totality, not isolated scrutiny.
> While it is necessary that proof beyond reasonable doubt should
> be adduced in all criminal cases, it is not necessary that it should
> be perfect. If a case is proved too perfectly, it is argued that it
> is artificial; if a case has some flaws, inevitable because human
> beings are prone to err, it is argued that is too imperfect. One won-
> ders whether in the meticulous hypersensitivity to eliminate a rare
> innocent from being punished; many guilty men must be callously
> allowed to escape. Proof beyond reasonable doubt is a guideline,
> not a fetish, and guilty man cannot get away with it because truth
> suffers some infirmity when projected through human processes.
> Judicial quest for perfect truth often accounts for police presenta-
> tion of foolproof concoction. Why fake up – Because the court
> asks for manufacture to make truth look true? No, we must be
> realistic.[38]

This was the law-giver's final failure to reorient a society, because
'truth does not look true enough', or prefect evidence seems 'unreal-
istic', and then the judge has to say, 'Credibility of testimony depends
much on judicial evaluation of the totality', and what is totality, if not
an assessment of the total chain of linkages and relations? Thus, truth

search jumps from issue to issue with each time thinking that the final crystal has been found to test truth, only to recoil at the next moment in order to ask, is the fact and the inquiry relevant, and thus ask further, what is relevance?

The jurists are, however, an incorrigible lot. So the authentic commentary on the Evidence Act commented,

> Knowledge means a state of mind, entertained by a person, with regard to existing facts, which he has himself observed or the existence of which has been communicated to him by another person. . . . Knowledge and actual knowledge have sometimes been held synonymous. . . . Knowledge is nothing more than man's firm belief and is distinguished from belief, in that the latter includes things which do not make a very deep impression on the memory. . . . The difference is merely in degree. . . .
>
> Motive is the longing for the longing for the satisfaction of desire, which includes the mind to wish and then to intend doing something, which would bring about the realisation aimed at. Primal motive is always the outcome of an impulse, which the mind receives from outside, and which owing to the peculiar state in which it happens to be, is susceptible of being affected thereby. . . .
>
> Now the wish for the end is, in turn, succeeded by another phase in the development of the mind. The wish for the end produces certain deliberation of choice of means to achieve the end wished for. . . . There is within the mind, a balance of judgement, which carefully measures the practicability and cautiously weighs the probability of its being carried out. . . .
>
> After the choice of means has been fixed upon, there follows a desire to do the act. The desire to do the act must not be confused with the wish for the end aimed at. The one leads the deliberation, while the other follows in its trail. . . .
>
> Next comes a sterner successor – a determination or the will to do the act. Determination must be distinguished from deliberation. . . .
>
> We have given above a sketch of the operation of the mind and have shown the connection between motive and intention. . . . Intention and knowledge are not necessarily identical.[39]

All these only suggest how death as the final penalty came via a long route with each occasion of such verdict reorganizing the elements, namely truth, evidence and judgement.

Dual realities

From these descriptions one can note that the Evidence Act as a legal measure of governance contained a dual reality. On one hand the act and its discursive surroundings (including the earlier draft bills, Law Commission suggestions, Stephen's notes and later commentaries) gave shape to a reality (about crime, criminology, criminality, trial and punishment) known as rule of law. On the other hand, this reality of rule of law claimed that it was confronted with and was tackling the reality of the passions and crimes in the society. This was, therefore, a classic instance of a correspondence of the history of a discourse to an 'actual past', and illustrative of how a narrative rhetorically functioned within a field of power relations. What did this combination succeed in producing finally? It produced an 'efficient and rational' way of governing society by controlling the extremes; the constitution of a delinquent milieu; strengthening of the legal basis of rule, and by contrast therefore the reinforcement of the opposition between restraint and passion, with the society retaining in its secret depths the spring wells of passion as source of inspiration against law, and defiance against rules of evidence.

In the scheme of rule of law, controlling crime on the basis of evidence therefore was of strategic importance in the sense that evidence helped diagnose the ills of the native society by constantly providing a close analysis of some particular actions and behaviour of men and institutions, and showing how such actions and behaviour stood as microcosms of larger forces. Evidence dissected through logic as a generalized mode of inspection could rationalize the entire society, and help the formation of identities, and manage power for the improvement of the self. Thus, evidence not only produced legal power, but rule of law was also served in a much broader way. The Evidence Act, through hundreds of cases for nearly a century throughout this vast country, created a history of law-abiding and law-defying subjects. This was one major way in which the political subject was being made, in the sense that it taught the emerging political subject what legal power was and what rule of law was in the framework of which politics, henceforth, would have to be carried out. If abiding by law and marshalling evidences against lawlessness for suitably controlling society was a normal activity in a colonial society, disobedient politics had to be abnormal. The Evidence Act addressed and instigated matters related to issues of both power and the self in this way.

The act made crime a banal act – a normal occurrence in a society not used to rule of law, for which the act was to provide 'due process'. In this century, in view of the 'extraordinary crimes' such as the attack on the New York Towers on 11 September 2001 it appears that ordinary criminal legislation and jurisprudence will not suffice, and that extraordinary crimes will need extraordinary legislations. Yet the beginning of criminal legislation under the aegis of liberal jurisprudence surprisingly exuded a remarkable confidence in its mission to cope with crimes, and invested tremendous faith in the capacity of scientific investigation to prove crime, identify the criminal, determine the punishment and judge its due measure. No crime was extraordinary, and no crime was beyond the microscopic power of criminal law. The banality of crime was not because it was happening every day, but because before the power of rational observation it had been reduced to diminished capacity; it had become banal, subject to penal control, and therefore these were dead crimes. Law, the other name of abstraction, perfection, impersonality, objectivity and science, was to apply to all – even if at times differentially to differential circumstances. There was nothing called 'exceptional' and 'beyond' law. If at all criminal legislation had limits, correctional institutions and modes could compensate for them.

Not only therefore discipline had to combine with correction, and new methods of understanding such as sociology, education, statistics, minute observation such as finger-print, forensics, medicine, anatomy or surgery were to be deployed, the relation between society and crime had to be redefined, too. Something more happened. The definition of criminal liability brought, in reality, a new realm of power, namely judicial power. Thus, with the Penal Code, Criminal Procedure Code, and the Evidence Act in place, criminality was the enemy of the public; therefore, the state had to act in public interest. Yet this utilitarian project took time to take full form. Governmental development was possible only after the development of sovereign's less noted functions, such as fuller institutional development of civil authority, or its distributive components such as revenue sharing. This was also possible when as a result of the combination of these two forms of administration – civil administration and property administration – which meant a series of practical developments in managing civil and economic affairs, a relatively independent source and area of power had been opened up, namely judicial power. Till then senators were judges, but now judges had to weigh on the basis of due process whether to invade the private spheres of life, where to locate the source of crime and how to give form on a daily basis to the punitive power of the sovereign. That is why after 1860s we find rapid changes in the institutional sphere in colonial India – changes that had their origins in the 1830s, but initiated in the 1860s. These changes left their deep impact on governance, and the impact continues to this day. Until 1834 the activities of the three presidencies had continued relatively independently, but after the Charter Act of 1833, which vested the governor general in Council with sole legislative authority for British India, events marched rapidly. A law member was added to the Council; in 1837 emerged Macaulay's draft penal code; Law Commission started functioning; and with suppression of Thuggee and then the Mutiny, the truly colonial sovereign emerged with the space to *govern* the society it had just conquered. Evidence Act is the result of that space brought about by conquest, centralization of power and an accompanying reformist strategy that relied on a weapon, peculiarly called 'reason'.

Yet as we know reason has been always aware of its limits. The British did not conquer India with reason only, or even primarily with reason. Force was directly instrumental in making conquest a reality. Subsequent pacification was also possible with the application of direct force. The penal colony that celebrated the commencement of its journey with the assassination of the Governor General Lord Mayo at the hands of Shere Ali, a convict, represented the failure of reason – because the establishment of the penal colony showed that investigation, evidence, trial and punishment meant nothing, if the convict could not be deported far away and resettled in a society that would look increasingly like the hierarchical society they had left.

We are back therefore to the issue raised at the beginning. New mode of crime suppression and control, and new criminal legislation signifies only the partial victory of reason, detachment and objectivity in governing a society. Since at the end of the day all rational methods are aimed at proving the identity of the criminal, the identity question – finally a subjective question, a question of proving subjectivity of the criminal, and thus the subject of crime – sits at the heart of an objective enterprise and marks its final limits. Criminal legislation therefore has produced all through the inquiry: who is the criminal? As if 'who' can lead to 'why'? This is the politics of physicality – knowing the body of the criminal to know his society, mind, moods, habits and soul, and then to control, punish and moderate this body. Facing the political anatomy of body that has committed the crime is the scientific physiology of detection and examination.

While these two registers initially seemed compatible, the romance of science and crime control is now long over. Neither here nor there, the rational space of evidence is one where responsibility no longer makes much sense, day to day expediency rules to the extent that great crimes may pass unpunished or waves of murders produce no 'evidence' before the court, therefore may remain unaccounted for through ages, whereas disorders reappear with food riots, communal riots, excise riots, militia orgies, gang robberies, endemic and often violent smuggling – and that is how the rule of law carries on incrementally, without gloss, without mission, without ethic, the shine on the rule long over. In fact, the next chapter will narrate one such instance of the fate of rule of law in a time of disorder along with the fate of the evidences of disorder.

Yet, in one sense the romantic nature of evidence analysis with a missionary zeal to punish a crime lives on. It is in cinema. This is the second dual reality. We shall end this chapter with a brief discussion of this second dual reality.

Ideology played an important role in projecting the Evidence Act as a narrative and imagery of reason. David Ray Papke has shown how cinema, over the years, has glorified lawyers, courtroom trials and the rule of law in general, thereby depicting a cinematic ideology.[40] But to be effective in that, law and in this case the Evidence Act had to turn itself into an enclave, a self-sufficient domain – physical of course, but more important, a virtual-emotional domain defined by certain boundaries and rules of entrance and exit. This proved to be central to the operation of the law that would normalize the emotional dimensions of the practices of truth-telling.[41] Legal ethics, legal education and other issues of legal culture – indeed the manifold practice of law had to appear as self-sufficient in terms of projecting reason, and making the element of passion as virtual.

The irony in this strategy was and still is that in internalizing all the dualities around truth and untruth the process of justice was emptying itself of any political substance – and going so far as to turn into its opposite, where law would be termed as 'blind' (in Hindi cinema it would be called *andha kanoon*, blind justice). Therefore, in the popular lore on the justice-seeking subject, the subject hereafter will be first going to the court for justice, then will come out of the court in frustration and will take up the flag of instant justice; or as a variant of the theme will produce new evidence by extralegal means to force the court to recognize where justice lay.

The retrospective interrogation of an event as we know is essentially carried out with the help of information submitted as evidence. Just as the discipline of political economy was formed as a machine to produce value, the signs of wealth, but not wealth itself, so the whole system of deposing information was designed as an immense machine to produce the event (to be adjudicated) as a sign of truth and therefore justice, as an exchangeable value to be traded in the universal market of spectacle and catastrophe – in short, to produce a process, a non-event. The abstraction of information here is thus the same as abstraction of the economy. The operation of information around evidence appears as the trans-political stage of truth. We must remember that the non-event is not when nothing happens but an end of contingency, a process of ceaseless updating of claims to truth, of an incessant succession of untruth with truth, the resultant banality marking the zero degree of the event. It is as if a cinema, a succession of shots, where the first shot is of interest, only to the extent that it precedes others, but is removed of any originating status.

In the operation of the Evidence Act, virtuality of the event in question is not thus a metaphor, but a literal passage from reality into fiction, from an event into a virtual process of truth verification – the process in this case being defined in legal terms. What is then the reality principle in this particular operation of law? We may say that reality develops exponentially through evidence, examination and cross-examination. As one looks at the operation of the truth verification procedure in the court and as prescribed by the act, one can almost visualize a script and is able to examine the role of the legal process, the lawyers, judges, jury or a specific doctrine. We can also note how supplementary arguments are made, or the norms on what constitutes a 'fair trial', or a 'legal personality' (for instance, when does a group become a legal personality?) are constructed. The question remains un-answered: what makes a certain behaviour or a certain resolution a norm?

As a general answer to all these questions we can, of course, say that the Evidence Act problematizes these relationships because of its nature as a dual site of rational argumentation and performance of roles assigned by a procedure, that contradictorily also admits passion, emotion, possibilities of ambiguity and contingency. Hence, we have the everyday possibility of the re-surfacing of Draupadi's claims (recall the scene of *bastraharan* in the *Mahabharata*, the claim of the males as to why she should be disrobed in the public and her reply) or what Judith Butler calls as 'Antogone's claims'. But we have to go little deeper here and discuss three problems.

The first problem is with the structural origin of the Evidence Act. The act was based on the divide between white colonial class and the rest of the people brown or black in colour. This racial division of the subjects of law made some people immune from the procedure of rule of law, and made impunity or semi-impunity an integral part of judicial culture, which thrives today in independent India very much. Elizabeth Kolsky in her work *Colonial Justice in British India* documents some of the ordinary incidents of racial violence perpetrated by the white rulers against the Indians and the routine leave they got from the court.[42] Evidence meant unpredictable things in such a milieu. Medical deposition by experts meant similarly unpredictable things. On the other hand, this situation has another structural division in it. This was the division between on one hand rationalists and rational imperial administrators like Bentham, Macaulay, Curzon and on the other hand the powerful white society consisting of sections like army generals, colonels, soldiers, the white planters, ship owners and managers, police officials and mill owners and their assistants. If the former argued that imperial administration could survive only on the basis of equality before law, and therefore the promise of colonial justice must include promise of equality before the eyes of law, the latter argued that any extension of civil jurisdiction over the whites would spell doom for the colonial society, and therefore the practice of colonial power required immunity for whites. Both these divisions provided elements of drama, protest, nationalist outrage. Countless films would be made playing on these divisions, which in turn would become an abiding part of our judicial heritage. Kolsky speaks of 'judicial scandals' that would become perfect material for narratives of various kinds. In some situation one single case would provide an entire dramatic narrative of several sequences of protest, action, violence, rumour and at times open lawlessness. In other cases, these divisions would become the standard material for radical illegalities.

The second problem is around the almost-obligatory presence of rhetoric in the judicial process around evidence. Rhetoric began if we recall not with the task of finding out the truth, but with professing and canvassing what it holds to be true. Rhetoric was therefore alien to a philosophy of truth. This was what the *Mahabharata* had taught us. Yet from Cicero in Rome to Nehru and other leaders in India, persons with legal background have employed rhetoric as argumentative technique in senates, court rooms, legislatures, public assemblies, manifestos and writings of tracts. While reason plays its role, there is a different kind of relation with truth present in the deployment of rhetoric. This is once again one factor why the operation of the Evidence Act appears as a screenplay where truth is not being established straight away (unless it is a crime and suspense story) but being propagated in different ways. The rear windows are always present there – for the director to frame, for the actors in the judicial process to peep in. The truth procedure in the judicial process is not therefore free speech or frank speech, but achieving a position of truth-telling through certain procedures or modes, which at times we can call as rhetoric. The Evidence Act presupposes that with human relations to truth being complex and multifarious, reason will have to work its way to reach truth. Indeed that procedure of working through the procedural activity is the truth. Speech activity around evidence thus always assumes dissociation between belief and truth. The Evidence Act is lodged in this kind of paradoxical epistemic framework.

Countless cinema shots depict vividly the problem of confession as a form of judicial truth-telling. In fact, judicial truth-telling is an activity with a specific nature, which problematizes the issue of evidence (of truth) by agreeing to take into consideration all that can spoil truth, that is the untruths, and is prepared to engage in confrontation with these possible untruths. The problematization of truth thus happens through staging an encounter between possible truths and various impurities and untruths present in the world of truth. Nineteenth century was not the time for a theory of legal pluralism, and it is still not now. So the second problem posed by the Evidence Act is that it requires performance, which complicates the relation between truth-telling and evidence.

Now to the third and last point: the role of special knowledge called 'expertise' in deciphering truth, to the extent that truth discovery becomes less an act of speaking and arguing, but more a process of marshalling expert evidence on the basis of techniques like finger print, DNA analysis, medical knowledge, psychological and behavioural analysis and deployment of other branches of forensic sciences. Partha Chatterjee tells us in his account of the legal dispute over the identity of the person claiming to be the dead Prince of Bhawal[43] how (after the First World War) experts began to be summoned to the court to give opinion on disease, death, disappearance, physical similarities, behaviour and conduct. If this was in the 1920, 30s and 40s, accounts of disputes relating to land entitlements in 1880s and 1890s show how expert advice became essential for survey and settlement operations in order to understand existing rules and protocols of entitlements, the variety of individual and collective entitlements, combination of legal and customary rules and more generally to gain knowledge in order to verify the claims, in this case land claims.[44] The problem was and still is: how was one to understand as to what constituted a legal personality, and how to make use of that knowledge in adjudication of matters in dispute?[45] How will knowledge be construed, measured and verified in the absence of universal literacy and high education, degrees, diplomas and certificates? In this background, expert advice gradually became integral to the process.

We should now understand why a process of legal examination of what is called 'the fact of the matter' has an inbuilt performative element. One may ask: why is there a close similarity between legal truth and what can be called performative truth, let us say, cinematic truth? Chatterjee in his introduction to the account of the case of imposture speaks of the analogy of the legal procedure and the procedure of historical examination of a matter in question, the case being one of the most extraordinary legal cases in Indian history, and says that the narrative method of recounting has much to offer us as distinct from the analytic. This is true, and the *Princely Impostor* is a demonstration of the art of narrative irrespective of the legal resolution of the issue of identity of the supposed impostor, the half-naked and ash-smeared *sannyasi*, the ascetic, as none other than the Prince (the Second Kumar) of Bhawal – a man believed to have died twelve years earlier, at the age of twenty-six, before the ascetic has appeared claiming the identity of the prince. Chatterjee's narrative history gives us the story of a courtroom drama replete with accounts of sexual debauchery, family intrigue and squandered wealth. He presents us the testimonies along with the resultant twists and turns in the account to finally tell us that notwithstanding the final legal decision there is no final proof of identity – particularly in the background of the dynamics of a Western legal system being introduced in an alien social and cultural framework. In fact, he argues convincingly that judicial process had little to do with the notion of fairness, and judicial process in this case was actually a complex negotiation between competing notions of truth. Thus, the procedures of law and historiography can be compared; both need procedures for proof, which are not completely objective, but are not also arbitrary. The point however remains, namely, only with a narrative procedure the similarity can be demonstrated, where law appears like history. The point is: why does a scientific procedure such as examination of evidence require a narrative style? This is where the performative element comes in. Through the court room procedure it becomes a drama, a spectacle – to become a matter of public interest. The fact that a legal dispute can turn out to be a matter of history ensures that it will be amenable to the procedure of a narrative – the final commentary on Bentham's theory of adjective law.

In Vijay Tendukar's play, *Silence! The Court Is in Session* (translated in English by Priya Adarkar, original in Marathi, and first staged in 1967, titled, *Shantata! Court Chalu Aahe*) we find a perfect stage of this double displacement, when in the play another play, a mock court, is to be staged. The play ends with the play (the mock court) within the play also ending, but not before extracting as sacrifice the woman by the name Leela Benare, accused of destroying her womb, produced out of her affair/s with amorous male lovers who would subsequently deny any close relation with her. Evidences of the 'free nature' of the woman are brought out, composed and verified. The aporia in which the judicial system finds itself when faced with a feminist interrogation of power marks the play. But we are not allowed to forget, all this is in the form of play, a mock court and a play within a play, and therefore the chiaroscuro of life and death, evidence and opinion, authority of the judge and the persuasive power of the judicial style and sentiment and logic. In course of her defence Benare says on her earlier attempt to commit suicide, 'I threw myself off a parapet of our house – to embrace death. But I didn't die. My body didn't die. I felt as if feelings were dead. But they had not died either then'.[46] The audience and the spectators listen to her passively as the world listens passively to the power of the verdict of the judge. Evidence is the sword by which this domination is achieved.[47] We can also say that evidence is the script of law's unconscious, hence is its double capacity – to act as the site of reason as well as act as the performative site of the unconscious.

In course of time law and rationality as the framework of governance became the bizarre site of performance. Performance was now a compulsory element in the public administration of justice. Time as well as the in-built structure of what came to be known as rule of law combined to produce the current situation known to all of us as a mixture of too many laws, too many regulations, too many penal provisions, too many exemptions, too many loci of administration of justice. The result is the emergence of a form of power, known as a judicial power, which with the help of reason (as interpreted by it) can make society governable and clean. Without the aspect of public performance this could not have happened.

To conclude: marking the entire scene of crime punishment and criminal governance is a series of dualities in the history of the Indian Evidence Act: the normative and the performative, science of inquiry and the unpredictable script of outcome, procedure and the spectacle built around live deposition, rational considerations and emotion, virtuality and the event and finally, serious business in the court and the element of drama. We may henceforth give the injunction, at the cost of little exaggeration, to see what court is go to the cinema; to see what cinema is go to the court.

Notes

1 Illustration for Section 101, Chapter 6, Part 3 titled 'Production and Effect of Evidence' of the Indian Evidence Act 1872.
2 R. Samaddar, "Colonial Constitutionalism" in R. Samaddar, *The Materiality of Politics, Volume 1* (London: Anthem Press, 2007), pp. 19–38 (earlier published in *Identity, Culture and Politics*, 3 (1), July 2002; also

R. Samaddar, "The Destiny of a Translated Constitutional Culture", Transeuropeennes, 22, Spring–Summer 2002.

3 Michel Foucault, "Technologies of the Self", in Luther H. Martin, Huck Gutman and Patrick H. Hutton (eds.), *Technologies of the Self* (Amherst: University of Massachusetts Press, 1998), p. 18.

4 Committee of Circuit to Council at Fort William, 15 August 1772, cited in Radhika Singha, *A Despotism of Law – Crime and Justice in Early Colonial India* (New Delhi: Oxford University Press), p. 29; *A Despotism of Law* (particularly Chapters 5–6) contains possibly the most exhaustive account of the situation backed by an excellent analysis of the problematic of transition from pre-colonial justice system to the colonial one.

5 For a different account of exhibiting bodily features of the criminals, see Gwenda Morgan and Peter Rushton, "Visible Bodies – Power, Subordination, and Identity in the Eighteenth Century Atlantic World", *Journal of Social History*, 39 (1), Fall, 2005, pp. 39–64.

6 Giorgio Agamben, "The Camp as the Nomos of the Modern", trans. Daniel Heller-Roazen in Hent de Vries and Samuel Weber (eds.), *Violence, Identity and Self-Determination* (Stanford, CA: Stanford University Press, 1997), pp. 106–118; Agamben, *Homo Sacer – Sovereign Power and Bare Life*, trans. Daniel Heller-Roazen (Stanford, CA: Stanford University Press, 1998).

7 Singha, *A Despotism of Law*, p. 125.

8 On such argument relating to penal reform, M. Ignatieff, *A Just Measure of Pain – Penitentiary in the Industrial Revolution* (London: MacMillan, 1978).

9 Anand Yang has argued on the basis of an analysis of the report of the Committee for Prison Discipline in India that labour, discipline, severity of imprisonment and policing the prisoners were the key elements in their suggestions which had nothing to do with humanitarian voices for reform and rehabilitation. See A. Yang, "Disciplining 'natives' ", *South Asia*, New Series, 10 (2), December 1987, pp. 29–45.

10 On the role of confession as evidence, and what it means to confess, see David Wolchover and Anthony Heaton-Armstrong, *Confession Evidence* (London: Sweet and Maxwell Criminal Law Library, 1996).

11 http://www.cps.gov.uk/C:\EvidenceAct\Evidence.UK.htm (accessed on 8 November 2013).

12 Even now this is relevant; for instance Section 76 of the Police and Criminal Evidence Act 1984 (PACE) deals with challenges as to the admissibility of confession evidence in criminal proceedings so as to prevent the confession being adduced against its maker by the prosecution as evidence to show guilt. Section 76(2) PACE directs the court to exclude confession evidence obtained: oppression; and/or in circumstances which were likely to make the confession unreliable. But the prosecutors have to remember that, while the confession itself may be excluded, Section 76 (4) allows facts discovered as a result of the confession or of the way in which defendants speak, write or express themselves, to be adduced where relevant.

13 Cited in Tapas Kumar Banerjee, *Background to Indian Criminal Law* (Calcutta: R. Cambray & Co., 1963), p. 265.

14 This description of the instructions of Nizamat Adalat is drawn from the *Background to Indian Criminal Law*, Chapter V.

15 Cited in Banerjee, *Background to Indian Criminal Law*, pp. 256–257.

16 Ibid., p. 260.
17 It is interesting to see how the Indian Evidence Act was a trendsetter in this respect. As late as in 2002 the South African Law and Justice Ministry was considering proposals almost similar to the lines of an act passed more than a century ago. See for discussions there, http://www.law.wits.ac.za/salc/salc.html (accessed on 21 September 2012).
18 Stephen Holmes lists these on a consideration of words in circulation in the seventeenth and eighteenth centuries – words denoting the antonyms of self-interest as defined by David Hume and Adam Smith. See Stephen Holmes, *Passions and Constraints – On the Theory of Liberal Democracy* (Chicago: University of Chicago Press, 1995), pp. 57–58.
19 Cited in John Woodroffe and Syed Amir Ali, *Law of Evidence*, Volume 1 (1898), 17th Edition, ed. Joga Rao (New Delhi: Butterworths, 2001), p. 24.
20 Vinay Lal, "Criminality and Colonial Anthropology", originally published as introduction to Rai Bahadur Pauparao Naidu, *The History of Railway Thieves, with Illustrations and Hints on Detection*, the reprint edition (Gurgaon, Haryana: Vintage Press, 1995), pp. i–xxvii, of Fourth Edition (Madras: Higgin Bothams Limited, 1915); Yet it is remarkable how the progress of science has not made evidence a matter of less contention. For this see the group of cases narrated in Colin Evans, *A Question of Evidence – The Casebook of Great Forensic Controversies, from Napoleon to O.J.* (Hoboken, NJ: John Wiley and Sons Inc., 2003).
21 Ibid.
22 Ranabir Samaddar, "Terror, Law, and the Colonial State", published text of a public lecture at Omeo Kr. Das Institute of Social Change, Guwahati, 2004; these types were recorded in details with photographs in the Intelligence Bureau records.
23 Simon A. Cole, "Fingerprint Identification and the Criminal Justice System – Historical Lessons for the DNA Debate", in Paul R. Billings (ed.), *DNA on Trial: Genetic Identification and Criminal Justice* (Cold Spring: Harbor Laboratory Press, 1992); see also by Cole for a full history of fingerprint identification, *Suspect Identities: A History of Fingerprinting and Criminal Identification* (New Jersey: Harvard University Press, 2001).
24 Lisa Steffen, *Defining a British State – Treason and National Identity, 1608–1820* (New York: Palgrave, 2001), particularly Chapters 3–4, pp. 69–139.
25 P.C. Sarkar, *Handbook of Criminal Laws in India and Pakistan*, Volume II, "Minor Acts" (Calcutta: S.C. Sarkar and Sons, 1951), pp. 119–130.
26 In the Supreme Court of India Criminal Appellate Jurisdiction Death Reference No.1 Of 1998 (Arising out of D.No.1151/1998) State of Tamil Nadu through Superintendent of Police, CBI/SIT . . . Petitioner/Appellant Versus Nalini and 25 others . . . Respondents with Criminal Appeal No. 321 of 1998 T. Suthenthiraraja @ Santhan & Ors . . . Appellants Versus State by D.S.P., CBI, SIT, Chennai . . . Respondent with Criminal Appeal NO. 322 of 1998 P. Ravichandran & Ors . . . appellants Versus State by D.S.P., CBI, SIT, Chennai . . . Respondent with Criminal Appeal No. 323 of 1998 Robert Payas & Ors . . . Appellants Versus State by D.S.P., CBI, SIT, Chennai . . . Respondent with Criminal Appeal No. 324 of 1998 S. Shanmugadivelu & Ors . . . Appellants Versus State by D.S.P.,

CBI, SIT, Chennai . . . Respondent with Criminal Appeal No. 325 of 1998 S. Nalini & Ors . . . Appellants Versus State by D.S.P., CBI, SIT, Chennai . . . Respondent

27 Section 3(1): Punishment for terrorist acts – Whoever with intent to over-awe the government as by law established or to strike terror in the people or any section of the people or to alienate any section of the people or to adversely affect the harmony amongst different sections of the people does any act or thing by using bombs, dynamite or other explosive sub-stances or inflammable substances or fire-arms or other lethal weapons or poisons or noxious gases or other chemicals or by any other substances (whether biological or otherwise) of a hazardous nature in such a manner as to cause, or as is likely to cause, death of, or injuries to, any person or persons or loss of, or damage to, or destruction of, property or disruption of any supplies or services essential to the life of the community, or detains any person and threatens to kill or injure such person in order to compel the Government or any other person to do or abstain from doing any act, commits a terrorist act.

28 Judgement by Justice Quadri, n 18; the Guwahati High Court in a similar judgement cautioned against loose interpretation of Evidence Act clauses – Criminal Appeal No. 4 (SH) / 2000.

29 These guarantees, one legal commentator reminded us, were required in the context of international human rights laws such as the ICCPR to whch India is a signatory or the Convention against Torture. Praful Bidwai, "Fighting Terror, Upholding Law – The Centrality of Human Rights" http://www.sdnbd.org/sdi/news/general-news/December-2002/21–12–2002/Feature.htm#Fighting (accessed on 30 December 2013).

30 K.G. Kannabiran, "Malimuth Committee – Safeguard the Rights of the Accused", *PUCL Bulletin*, January 2003, http://www.pucl.org/Topics/Law/2003/malimath.htm (accessed on 15 September 2012).

31 Letter from Justice M. Jagannadha Rao to Arun Jaitley, Union Minister for Law and Justice, Government of India – Law Commission of India, 185th Report on the Review of the Indian Evidence Act, 1872, March 2003, DO No.6 (3) (70) / 2001-LC (LS) 13 March 2003.

32 Foucault's exact words were,

> 'We can recall these power relations characterize the manner in which men are 'governed' by one another; and their analysis shows how, through certain forms of 'government', of madmen, sick people, crimi-nals and so on, the mad, the sick, the delinquent subject is objectified. So an analysis of this kind implies not that the abuse of this or that power has created madmen, sick people, or criminals where there was nothing, but that the various and particular forms of 'government' of individuals were determinant in the different modes of objectivation of the subject.'

– This text was first written by Foucault as a retrospective view about his work for the introduction to his book *History of Sexuality*, it was then given by Foucault, under the pseudonym 'Maurice Florence' as the article for the entry 'Foucault' in "Dictionnaire des philosophes" 1984, pp. 942–944.

33 Woodroffe and Ali, *Law of Evidence*, Volume 1, p. 111.

34 Ibid., pp. 112–113.

35 Ibid., p. 117.

36 Ibid., p. 347.

37 Douglas Hay, "Property, Authority and the Criminal Law", in D. Hay, P. Linebaugh and E.P. Thompson (eds.), *Albion's Fatal Tree* (London: Allen Lane, 1975), pp. 38–63.

38 *Inder Singh v. State (Delhi Administration)*, AIR 1978 SC 1091 at 1092 (1978).

39 Woodroffe and Ali, *Law of Evidence*, Volume 1, pp. 761–763.

40 David Ray Papke, " 'Law, Cinema, and Ideology', Hollywood Legal Films of the 1950s", *UCLA Law Review*, 48 (6), 2001, pp. 1473–1493; also at http://tarlton.law.utexas.edu/lpop/etext/ucla/papke48.htm (accessed on 12 October 2010).

41 On the relevance of the idea of enclave to the operation of law, see Shulamit Almog and Amnon Reichman, "Casablanca: Judgment and Dynamic Enclaves in Law and Cinema", *Osgoode Hall Law Journal*, 42 (2), 2004, pp. 202–228.

42 Elizabeth Kolsky, *Colonial Justice in British India – White Violence and the Rule of Law* (Cambridge: Cambridge University Press, 2010).

43 Partha Chatterjee, *A Princely Impostor? The Kumar of Bhawal and the Secret History of Indian Nationalism* (Delhi: Permanent Black, 2002); in this gripping account, see in particular Chapter 14, pp. 237–257.

44 R. Samaddar, *Memory, Identity, Power – Politics in the Jungle Mahals, 1890–1950*, chapter 3; see also for details, *Final Report on the Survey and Settlement Operations in the District of Midnapore, 1911 to 1917* (Calcutta: Book Secretariat Depot, 1918) and *Supplement to the Final Report*, Calcutta 1923.

45 Resumption proceedings were an ample pointer to the problem. Munshis would be crucial in constructing evidence of land titles – to be deposed before the court and settlement adjudication centres. In the early years of Bengal we find one such remarkable figure, Maulavi Ekramuddin, who was the expert in the settlement operations in South West Bengal. The then district magistrate of Bankura Gurusaday Dutt also wrote in details of the Maulavi. On Maulavi Ekramuddin, *Jambani-Jhargram Jungle Survey Report*, filed in the 2nd Sub-Judge Court, Midnapur, 1902; also Babu Bhuvaneswar Sanyal, *Final Report on the Minor Settlement Operations in the District of Midnapore, 1907–13*, Calcutta, 1916; and finally *Bengal Home Political Files*, Calcutta, 1921–23; Government of Bengal, Pol (Conf), 1918, 1921, 1923 (NMML).

46 Vijay Tendulkar, "Silence! The Court Is in Session", in Priya Adarkar (trans.) *Five Plays* (New Delhi: Oxford University Press, 1974), p. 74.

47 In the play a group of teachers plan to stage a play in a village. It turns out that one of the members of the cast does not show up. A local stagehand is asked to replace him and a rehearsal is arranged and a mock trial is staged to make him understand the court procedure. A mock charge of infanticide is lodged against Leela Benare, a female member of the cast. Then the pretended play suddenly turns into a grim game, when one witness says that Benare had killed her illegitimate child by Professor Damle, the missing member of the cast. The charges are leveled in the absence of Damle.

Benare is thrown into the dock and remains there. She tries to extricate herself, but cannot. Witness after witness, charge upon charge is heaped on her. We almost forget that she is a member of an amateur dramatic alliance, whose prime purpose is to educate the public with social and current issues, and who has chosen to educate people with procedures of a court of law. Benare literally tries to escape the court but finds all doors automatically bolted from outside. She is trapped; she cannot escape. She is dragged in the process, and then she dies. The formal charge is of infanticide. The informal charge, as one witness says, 'How could you remain unmarried till the age of thirty-four?' While all these will be staged, we shall not be allowed to forget, in fact from the start, that a judicial court is a seat of justice, and therefore asks of us seriousness and decorum. All protocols have to embody that seriousness.

8 Riot, police and the city

The suddenness of 16 August 1946

Once again let us go back to the colonial time, in fact to the last decade of the colonial rule – the 1940s. To understand the dilemmas, structural peculiarities and contradictions of post-colonial governance it is important to study contentious events which congeal these features and contradictions. This is the method that this book is trying to follow. Governance is a process; yet the process makes sense only when it is held up in the mirror of an event. There is one more reason why we are going to retell in this chapter the story of the riots in Kolkata, known as the Great Calcutta Killings – specifically its first three days 16–18 August, because it is not only one of the foundational images of modern police governance, but also the story of crowds, frenzy, police operations, slums, battle over the urban space, warring blocs and many other things with which urban governance is associated. With Calcutta Riots we can say that the city came to occupy a central place in the history of governance in contemporary India.

Nobody in the city of Kolkata, certainly not the city elders, suspected the day of 16 August 1946 as a day to be particularly watched out. The organ of the Calcutta Municipal Corporation, *the Calcutta Municipal Gazette* in its issue of 10 August 1946 showed no such awareness or inkling of the particular import of the day. The shadow of the infamous famine of 1943 was still over the city. Besides the usual entries *the Gazette* on that day came out with a supplement on 'Grow More Food'. The supplement had short notes on food wastage, food prices, need for balanced diet, the principle and the practices of rationing, role of population growth in causing famine and an overall assessment of the food situation in Bengal. The editor Amal Home in his note was equally innocent. Bengal had come out of famine and war. Rebuilding Bengal, particularly the food situation in the light of another bad year of agricultural production, appeared to be the task.[1]

There are now some accounts on the Great Calcutta Killings, the numbers put by some chroniclers as between 10,000 and 15,000 and by the Bengal government as 4,000 dead and 100,000 injured. Some have placed the number of displaced as 200,000.[2] According to the government, the total loss in the riot was to the tune of one crore rupees.[3] Some of the subsequent discussions on the Great Calcutta Killings or the Week of Long Knives as it was later called have taken note of this lack of awareness of the situation on the ground, a similar lack of any anticipation of the coming bloodbath and bewilderment all around at the sudden appearance of 16 August as the commencement of a week of mass murders in Kolkata.

Various reasons have been put forward as explanations, the most plausible being that the leaders and organizers of the two main parties, the Congress and the Muslim League were still in the old mode of constitutionalist dialogue and had no clue as to the incredible seriousness with which their respective vast armies of followers were taking the claims to independence or *azadi*. It is also said that famine taught various sections of population to treat their claims as life and death stakes. There is also ground to believe as some think that nation building in the subcontinent had to pass through its due process of religious wars, which commenced with the Great Calcutta Killings. These new developments were taking place in subterranean manner.[4] Therefore, the political and educated class leading the city could not anticipate the coming of the Great Calcutta Killings.

The following questions therefore generally emerged in later political and historical enquiries: if the political and the governing class were caught unaware, how did its administrative machinery face the riots? Later inquiries to a great extent revolved around the question, was the administration really unaware? Why did it not call the military? The chief minister had on a number of occasions visited the police headquarters during those calamitous days, therefore what was he doing? What was he briefed with? What measures did he take with the knowledge he gained from his visits? What did the Lt. Governor do? Likewise, the head of the military forces stationed in Calcutta?

This chapter begins from this point, where these questions and their answers leave us. It does not discuss per se the Great Calcutta Killings, but the way the police looked at the riot-torn city, apparently unprepared, overwhelmed by events, and therefore shaping its own conduct in the midst of events, as if in the most *natural* way. After all when we have exhausted various cultural, political and economic explanations the city will still remain a particular configuration of *territory* also. The police attempted to secure the territory inch by inch, by disaggregating it, by policing the parts after bringing them under control, by zoning them, by creating safe havens, corridors and centres. With looters, rioters, murderers, arsonists, provoked and leaders in a state of frenzy, and the political administration either caught unaware or unwilling to act, what did controlling a riot-torn city mean?[5] How shall we understand the dynamics of police conduct in the riot-torn city of Kolkata?

These two questions relating to police conduct and control of territory were interrelated and were complex for Calcutta, as it was the capital of a province where Muslims represented 56 per cent the population and Hindus 42 per cent, and Muslims were mostly concentrated in the eastern part. The province was the only one in which a Muslim League government was in power under the provincial autonomy scheme introduced in 1935 in coalition with the Europeans, and against strong opposition from the Congress and a Hindu nationalist party, the Hindu Mahasabha, which was supported by members of the rich Marwari trading community, dominating the economy of central Calcutta, although European capital was still important. Kolkata population comprised 64 per cent Hindu and 33 per cent Muslim. Violence in Calcutta sparked off further religious riots in the surrounding regions of Noakhali, Bihar and the United Provinces.

At a general level we may ask if riots in multi-community cities have proved to be an abiding feature of post-colonial Indian democracy, how does the governing class bring or fail to bring a riot-torn city under control? How do territory and population mix? In the background of the controversies around the Gujarat riots of 2002 we do not require much to understand the significance of the broad question.

The battle for urban territory

To understand the stake of the two questions raised at the end of the previous section, we should first see even if briefly the way historians have viewed the events preceding the Great Calcutta Killings. Readers will appreciate why in the previous section we used the word 'natural' with regard to the police conduct. Suranjan Das in his study on *Communal Riots in Bengal, 1905–1947* tells the ways in which rioters through the previous two decades had become part of the urban history, congealing in the process rival population groups. Likewise others have shown how strikes, processions, calls for direct actions, street clashes and encounters had all become parts of urban politics by the time the month of August arrived in 1946. These tools of assembly, mobilization and mass demonstration had been refined through application over and over again in the preceding four and half four decades of the century.

One commentator noted,

> From the viewpoint of institutional politics, the Calcutta disturbances possessed a distinguishing feature in that they broke out in a transitional period which was marked by the power vacuum and systemic breakdown. It is also important to note that they constituted part of a political struggle in which the Congress and the Muslim League competed with each other for the initiative in establishing the new nation-state(s), while the British made an all-out attempt to carry out decolonization at the lowest possible political cost for them. The political rivalry among the major nationalist parties in Bengal took a form different from that in New Delhi, mainly because of the broad mass base those organizations enjoyed and the tradition of flexible political dealing in which they excelled. At the initial stage of the riots, the Congress and the Muslim League appeared to be confident that they could draw on this tradition even if a difficult situation arose out of political showdown. Most probably, Direct Action Day in Calcutta was planned to be a large-scale *hartal* and mass rally (which is an accepted part of political culture in Calcutta) which they knew very well how to control. However, the response from the masses far exceeded any expectations. The political leaders seriously miscalculated the strong emotional response that the word 'nation', as interpreted under the new situation, had evoked. In August 1946 the 'nation' was no longer a mere political slogan. It was rapidly turning into 'reality' both in realpolitik and in people's imaginations. The system to which Bengal political leaders had grown accustomed for decades could not cope with this dynamic change. As we have seen, it quickly and easily broke down on the first day of the disturbances.[6]

We are thus faced with a strange paradox. On one hand the evidences suggest that the police was unprepared for what would happen on 16 August that year; yet the more we study the genealogy of the Great Calcutta Killings, the more we are surprised at the lack of awareness of the city administration, elders and the governing class as a whole, given the fact that all trends and incidents were only waiting for one final moment to come together, mix and explode. The riot was in that sense a clarifying exercise.

Let us therefore quickly see what had preceded the Direct Action Day and then what happened. The Muslim League and the Indian National Congress were the two largest political parties in the country at that time. The Cabinet Mission to India (1946) to arrange transfer of power from British rule to Indian leadership proposed an initial plan of composition of the new Dominion of India and its government. However, this could not address the alternative plan to divide the country into a Hindu-majority India and a Muslim-majority Pakistan as proposed by the Muslim League. The Congress rejected outright the alternative proposal. The Muslim League planned general strike (*hartal*) on 16 August terming it as Direct Action Day to protest this rejection, and to assert its demand for a separate Muslim homeland.

Jinnah decided to boycott the constituent assembly and rejected the British plan for transfer of power to an interim government which would combine both the Muslim League and the Indian National Congress. He said that if the Muslims were not granted Pakistan, then he would launch 'Direct Action'. The Muslim League Council Meeting held during the period 27–29 July 1946 passed a resolution declaring that the Direct Action Day was intended to unfold direct action for the achievement of Pakistan.[7]

In any case, from February onwards communal tension had been very strong throughout India. Anti-British feeling was, at the same time, being exacerbated by other political forces who were trying to stage confrontations different from the more dominant ones characterized by communal type and emotion. Violence in Calcutta, between 1945 and 1946, had passed by stages from Indian versus European to Hindu versus Muslim. Indian Christians and Europeans were generally free from attacks as the tempo of Hindu-Muslim violence quickened.[8] During the riots of November 1945, casualty of Europeans and Christians were forty-six; in the riots of the 10–14 February 1946, thirty-five; from 15 February to the 15 August, only three; during the Calcutta riots from 15 August 1946 to 17 September 1946, none.[9] Following Jinnah's declaration of 16 August as the Direct Action Day, the Muslim League chief minister of Bengal, Huseyn Shaheed Suhrawardy, requested governor of Bengal Frederick Burrows to declare 16 August a public holiday with the hope that the risk of conflicts, especially those related to picketing, would be minimized if government offices, commercial houses and shops remained closed throughout Calcutta on that day. Bengal Congress protested against the declaration of public holiday, arguing that a holiday would enable the Leaguers to enforce strike in areas where the Muslim League leadership was uncertain. Also, if a public holiday was observed, its own supporters would have no choice but to close down their offices and shops. Therefore, the Congress Party urged the Hindus to keep their shops open and to continue their business as usual and not to submit to the *hartal*.

The Star of India, an influential Muslim newspaper, published detailed programme for the day, which called for complete strike in all spheres of civic, commercial and industrial life except essential services, and notified that processions would start from several locations in the city and the adjoining areas in Howrah, Hooghly, Metiaburz and 24 Parganas, and would converge at the foot of the Ochterlony Monument (now Shaheed Minar) where a joint mass rally presided over by Huseyn Shaheed Suhrawardy would be held. Against this, Hindu public opinion was mobilized around the *Akhand Hindusthan* (*United India*) slogan. Also we have to remember that following protests against the British after the Indian National Army (INA) trials, the British administration decided to give more importance to protests against the government, rather than management of communal violence.

The reality is that troubles started on the morning of 16 August before the assembly had taken place. Lalbazar (the city police headquarters) had reported that there was excitement throughout the city, that shops were being forced to close and that there were reports of brawls, stabbing and throwing of stones and brickbats. These events were taking place in the north-central parts of the city, such as Rajabazar, Kalabagan, College Street, Harrison Road, Coolootolla, Burrabazar and Entally. The League's rally began at the Ochterlony Monument at 12 o'clock exactly. The gathering was considered as the largest ever Muslim assembly in Bengal at that time. A large number of the participants arrived armed with iron bars and *lathis*. The chief minister apparently had seen to police arrangements that the latter would not interfere. However, there is no record of instructing the police to hold back. But his speech may have meant an open invitation to disorder. In fact, many participants at the rally started attacking Hindus and looting Hindu shops as soon as they left the meeting. There were also reports of lorries coming down the Harrison Road in central Calcutta, carrying Muslim men armed with brickbats and bottles as weapons and attacking Hindu-owned shops. On 16 August in one incident in Bichalighat, seventy-seven Muslims and fifty-nine Hindus were murdered in the first big incident of communal clash. On 17 August more than 400 (according to other reports 500–600) Oriya workers of Kesoram Cotton Mills were massacred in the slums of Lichubagan, Metiaburz.[10] In another incident forty-eight people were butchered on the riverside, and their dead bodies lay there for next few days.[11]

Hindus and Sikhs became as fierce as the Muslims. Parties of one community lay in wait, and as soon as they caught a member of the other community, they would cut him to pieces. Hindus now attacked the Muslims, and if any Muslim was found in house, road or shop, or even educational institution, he was immediately pulled out, and cut into pieces. The figures of Muslim casualties were heavier as Hindu retaliation took pace, and Muslims started leaving the city. Skirmishes and clashes between the communities continued for almost a week. Finally, on 21 August, Bengal was put under viceroy's rule. Battalions of British troops, supported by battalions of Indians and Gorkhas, were deployed in the city. The rioting reduced on 22 August. In these six days thousands died in brutal conditions. Methods of murder varied from stabbing, piercing, torching, bludgeoning, severing limbs, cutting, disembowelling, to gagging, gassing, and throwing half dead bodies in water, and pushing the bodies into waste pipes and drains choking the latter. *Bustees*, already with infamous names such as Nakashipara, Karamtolli, Sahebbagan, became the most gruesome sites of murder. Both economic and commercial interests played their due parts as in Metiaburz killings. Also in these six days, property of un-estimated value was looted with the police at times taking part. Population groups were exchanged from one area to another in a vicious cleansing of the rival religious group. Vast stretches of open space including the *maidan* were turned into shelter camps by the government.[12]

The Chief Minster Suhrawardy claimed that he had put forth a great deal of effort to bring reluctant British officials around to calling the army in from Sealdah Rest Camp. Unfortunately, British officials did not send the army out until 1.45 a.m. on the 17th. There was criticism of Suhrawardy, the chief minister who was also in charge of the Home Portfolio, for his bias and allowing the riots to take place, and of the British governor of Bengal, Frederick Burrows, for not having taken control of the situation. The chief minister spent a great deal of time in the control room in the police headquarters at Lalbazar. We do not know if the city gained from his presence there or its condition aggravated.

Even the military did not have any good word for Suhrawardy. According to one army report,

There is hardly a person in Calcutta who has a good word for Suhrawardy, respectable Muslims included. For years he has been known as 'The king of the goondas' and my own private opinion is that he fully anticipated what was going to happen, and allowed it to work itself up, and probably organized the disturbance with his goonda gangs as this type of individual has to receive compensation every now and again. It is difficult to estimate the number of casualties but I should say it is somewhere in the region of 2 to 3 thousand at least. There were corpses all over North Calcutta, they were in the river, canals, side lanes, in fact, everywhere. The number of shops looted and burnt must be somewhere in the region of 2 to 3 thousand. I personally think that the killings of both sides were fifty, fifty, or if anything, more Muslims than Hindus, but damage financially has been much greater to the Hindus than to the Muslims."[13]

Yet the same report is more significant in terms of the battle for inches of territory in the city ensued. The report continued,

The Hindus started putting up barricades at Tala Bridge and Belgachia Bridge and other places to prevent Muslims processions coming into the town and Muslims goondas went round forcing Hindus to close their shops. As previously mentioned in my D.O. of the 15th the air was electric and this caused crowds to gather, lathis were produced and in no time North Calcutta was a scene of mob riot. By 1100 hours there were brick bat fights all over North Calcutta. . . .

By late in the afternoon the situation changed and the persons involved on both sides were gwallahs, rickshaw pullers, teashop wallahs, pan berri wallahs, cart pullers, cart men, goondas of the worst type. Soon after midnight on the 16/17th these gangs fought out the most desperate battles, murder and butchery of a worst type were carried on in the side lanes and byways of North Calcutta. Round Vivekananda Road/ Central Ave., crossing about 50 Hindu Behari rickshaw pullers were caught in a cul-de-sac and butchered. Further up Central Ave., round the temple which stands in the middle, a party of some 30 Mohamedans was killed. It was during the period midnight 16/17th and 0700 hours on the 17th that most of the casualties occurred. All the roads in the affected areas were red with bricks.

Our patrols were out, but due to the tremendous fights that were going on, it was impossible for us to force our way into the areas in which the main killings were taking place.

The police opened fire in Harrison Road at about 1100 hours on 16 Aug 1946, 2 rounds of buck shot and Barnes and Smith emptied their pistols into the crowd. The crowd dispersed, formed up in Bow Bazaar St and a fight started between the Hindus in Bow Bazaar St. and the Muslims coming up from Lower Circular Rd. I was there at the time and the police finally dispersed the crowd with tear gas. By 1200 hours there were fights in every street and alley from Sealdah to Shambazar. Eastern Command Intelligence Centre jeeps dispersed some of these crowds and stopped the fights without firing, but as soon as we had gone the fights started again. By 1400 hours on the 16th Government were considering calling out troops but the police had only fired the above mentioned number of rounds. . . .

From the time the riots started every little blacksmith was working like mad in his house manufacturing spears, rods and knives. The iron rods used in reinforced concrete building works were all stolen and sharpened at both ends, and the butchery that these crude weapons did has to be seen to be believed. Men, women and children were slaughtered by both sides indiscriminately and when Mullick Bazar was burnt three Hindu children were thrown into the flames.

The result of this riot has been complete mistrust between the two communities. . . . Though the city is quiet now there are still stabbing cases and both sides are very frightened. The trams are running today (22nd). . . . We have cleaned up practically all the corpses, D.D.T. has been sprayed and everything possible has been done. . . . [14]

Almost all reminiscences of the killings conjure up two images: the murders of the innocents with their dead bodies lying around for days, and second, the battle for the territory. And it was by murder that the wresting, possession and control of the territory was to be guaranteed. The connection is important and is brought out vividly in some of the reminiscences.

For example Mother Teresa, then a teacher in a city school remembered,

We were not supposed to go out into the streets, but I went anyway. Then I saw the bodies on the streets, stabbed, beaten, lying there in strange positions in their dried blood. We had been behind our safe walls. We knew that there had been rioting. People had been jumping over our walls, first a Hindu, then a Muslim. You see, our compound was between Moti Jhil, which was mainly Muslim then, and Tangra with the potteries and tanneries. That was Hindu. We took in each one and helped him to escape safely. When I went out in the streets – only then I saw the death that was following them.[15]

One cannot recall murder in a riot without the invocation of territory. Thus, an eye witness account of a travel writer passing through the city at that time had this to say,

Nanda Lal's little 'East Bengal Cabin', at 36 Harrison Road, was located in one of those potential trouble spots where a by-lane of Muslim shops crossed the Hindu-dominated thoroughfare. . . . The Hindu clerks of the Minerva Banking Corporation opposite to the Cabin were frequent customers, as were the boarders in the 'Happy Home Boarding House' near-by. Although Nanda Lal was in the protective shadow of these impressive Hindu establishments, the Muslim quarter began just round the comer in Mirzapore Street, too close for security. On the morning of August 16, Nanda Lal started his oven and set out his tray of sweetmeats as usual. When his little son came out with the jars of mango pickle and chutney, he commented to the child that the streets looked reassuringly quiet. The sacred cows that roam freely through the thoroughfares of Calcutta were sleeping as usual in the middle of the car tracks, and rose to their feet reluctantly, as they always did, when the first tramcar of the day clanged down Harrison Road. Then things began happening so quickly that Nanda Lal could hardly recall them in sequence. But he did remember quite clearly the seven lorries that came thundering down Harrison Road, Men armed with brickbats and bottles began leaping out of the lorries – 'Muslim 'goondas', or gangsters, Nanda Lal decided, since they immediately fell to tearing up Hindu shops. Some rushed into the furniture store next to the 'Happy Home' and began tossing mattresses and furniture into the street. Others ran toward the 'Bengal Cabin', but Nanda Lal was fastening up the blinds by now, shouting to his son to run back into the house, straining to bar the windows and close the door. In the breathing spell offered by this successful move, two of his wife's uncles ran down and helped Nanda Lal build a barricade at the foot of the stairs which would jam shut the door leading to their flat. Whatever benches and tables they could lay their hands on they piled against the door and at the foot of the stairs. Nanda Lal snatched three bicycles from the vestibule and jammed them in amidst the furniture. Then they all ran up to the top floor of the flat, where the women of the house were huddled in the upper floor. Nanda Lal peeped cautiously out of a window. Never had he seen the streets so filled with clawing, surging mobs. In front of the Happy Home, some broken rickshaws had been added to the heap of mattresses, and flames were rising from the pile. When the wind shifted the smoke, Nanda Lal could glimpse figures on the bank steps shaking up pop bottles and hurling them into the crowds – the bottles bursting like hand grenades when they landed. Flames were racing through the dress goods swinging from racks in front of the 'Goddess of Plenty' dress shop and through the crowded living quarters behind the rows of shops. Nanda Lal suspected that much of this was the organized work of goondas. In India 'goondaism' is a profession; goondas abound in a port city such as Calcutta, where they do a brisk trade in smuggling but may also be hired for strike-breaking or religious outbreak.[16]

The imagery is one of full-scale warfare, trenches, barricades, advanced detachment, resistance and others and every inch to be guarded or wrested. The goondas are like the foot soldiers of an army – trained in skirmishes and trench warfare exactly as the foot soldiers are. Probably with this imagery in mind, Claude Markovits commented in his study,

It was actually a fight over who was to be master of Calcutta. By organizing huge demonstrations, occupying the *Maidan*, and using whatever State power it had at its disposal, the Bengal Provincial Muslim League was trying to stake its claim to Calcutta as the capital of a Muslim Bengal, which would be part of Pakistan, whose shape was still hazy at the time. A massacre was probably not the League's goal (although one pamphlet circulating amongst Muslims warned of a 'general massacre' of *Kafirs*, infidels, i.e. Hindus), but the League's supporters did not shrink from using violence on a significant scale to advance their objectives. . . . As for the 'Hindu' political parties, both Congress and the *Mahasabha* were bent on making a counter-demonstration of their superior muscle power. Therefore, they were not adverse to large-scale killings to decisively defeat the Muslim League's attempts to impose its dominance. The massacre was the result of the clash of two wills, between which no compromise was possible.[17]

He further wrote,

Given the tendency of the population in urban areas to congregate in neighbourhoods dominated by one community, most Muslims lived in areas of Northern Calcutta, while Central and Southern Calcutta were almost exclusively Hindu (with a sprinkling of Europeans). Another characteristic of Calcutta's Muslim population was that it was largely composed of poor people, mostly artisans, factory workers, rickshaw pullers and domestic servants. The Muslim middle class in Calcutta was small, in contrast to the much larger Hindu middle class. Big Muslim merchants and capitalists were few, and could not compete with the rich Marwari Hindus. Although Muslims were clearly a minority in Calcutta and occupied a peripheral position in the economic, social and cultural life of the city, the capital was the only large city in the province, and therefore occupied a privileged position in all provincial politics, whether Muslim or Hindu. Suhrawardy had a particularly large following amongst the poor Muslims of the city, and was also rumoured to have close links to the Muslim underworld, which played a significant role in the parallel economy, based on smuggling, gambling, and prostitution, which flourished in the great port-city.[18]

North Indian Hindus (in many cases Dalits) and Punjabis displayed special vengeance on East Bengali Muslim workers in the city, targeting in particular the Shalimar Marine Workshop employing the marines of Noakhali and the East Bengal Muslim *khalasis* in another side of the Ferry Yard, B.N. railway. On the other hand, the Bengal Muslim National Guard wiped off *bustees* in Kidderpore Metaburz area, killing minimum 400 Hindu workers of Orissa working at the Kesoram Mills.[19] Dead bodies lay unattended for days, some bodies clogged pipes and drains, and one account says, 'We had gone about wearing iodine masks for three days and nights and picked up from the street 5869 dead bodies, whole and mutilated, and disposed of them through mass burials and cremations',[20] though others reported of disposals in more unsavoury ways.

Suranjan Das has described the participation of common people in riots as mass communalism distinct from elite communalism and has referred to open street battles between large crowds, also the sporadic acts by small roving bands. The latter often targeted passers-by, and their acts had a random character which contributed to giving the impression that things had gotten completely out of hand, while in fact part of the killings appeared to have taken place in large-scale confrontations between organized crowds. Joya Chatterji's central argument has been that the determined and successful attempt by the Hindu elite, opposed to the rule of the Muslim majority, to take physical control of the city if necessary through violent confrontations led to the 1946 riots. She therefore emphasizes the roles of various Hindu organized groups, linked to the Congress Party and the Hindu *Mahasabha*. Tuker also reports on the intensity of street violence.[21]

This is not the occasion to discuss these different interpretations. What seems in fact lurking behind various analyses and reports is the unmistakable presence of the city as a configuration of territory of a particular type – *territory as the kernel of the city,* and therefore the willingness of both the armies to go to the final extent to change the face of the city forever in their respective favour.

Our chronicle of policing a riot-torn city begins in this background. The chronicle is based mainly on the eleven volumes of proceedings of the *Calcutta Disturbances Commission of Enquiry* (hereafter CDCE) and where necessary, backing it up by other sources.[22]

Political logic, legal logic, police logic

These eleven volumes of course decide nothing as to who caused the riot? Who were responsible for the aggravation of the situation? How should one determine the respective shares of responsibility of the political, administrative, police, military and colonial apparatus of the state? Counsels argued, intelligent questions were raised, lead answers secured, different biases exposed and self-explanations were offered to the Commission by different agencies. Yet the binds and closures on the path of every possible line of enquiry ruthlessly demonstrated themselves. One may ask, why was then the Commission organized? Was it to bring out the truth, and if so what was the truth?

It was not the truth of responsibility or the truth of crime and punishment, but the truth of clarification of the post-riot situation *on the ground*, making clear to all parties after this round of religious war as to who stood where, the respective grounds of possession, conditions of the combatants and armies and the positions the warring forces occupied while the latter were engaged in the race for legitimacy. Even the ways in which the counsels wrangled over the framing of the procedures to guide the functioning of the Commission indicated its nature as a clarifying exercise.[23] Finally when independence was declared and approached, the Commission decided to wind itself up without giving any report, saying that time had changed, and further inquiry would serve no purpose (XI: 244–245),[24] and it was clear that the Commission was an exercise in armistice. It was a mode of declaring truce until the final positions were announced.

Almost from the beginning of the exercise the minutes of evidence recognized that they were dealing with a war situation, not a simple event of communal violence. After all we have to remember that the call for mobilization given in 1946 by Abul Hashim, secretary, Bengal Provincial Muslim League (month not mentioned in the print), was titled 'Let Us Go to War'. In that call he termed the coming electoral battle between the Congress and Muslim League as an impending war in the context of Hindu-Muslim conflict and the denial of the Muslims of India of their right to Pakistan. The Hindu Mahasabha election call spoke of resistance to the last to what it saw the Muslim League designs in the name of self-determination.[25] So questions like what the Intelligence Branch would know or deduce from what kind of evidence or what the word *jihad* meant under what circumstances, how much the military could depend on civilian intelligence inputs and others only formally aimed at securing information on particular relevant points. But in actuality these questions had the function of ascertaining positions occupied by the respective forces. For instance, B. C. Ghose, the principal counsel for the Congress (and the Hindus) asked Brigadier Binny, called as witness and appearing on behalf of the military, 'Supposing on certain days a large number of people were coming to Calcutta, would your Intelligence Branch know it?' And, 'If this large number of people belongs to a certain particular community, would your Intelligence Branch be suspicious?' Brigadier Binny replied, 'I do not understand what you mean by "suspicious" '. Ghose pressed on the point saying that Kolkata had *bustee*s, Hindu areas and Muslim areas, mixed localities, and used phrases like borders, no man's land and 'low wall with barbed wire to prevent homeless people sleeping in the shrubberies'(*CDCE*, II: 2–4). With these phrases Ghose began reconstructing the geopolitics of the city riot – a theme that runs through the entire exercise. Thus we find Kolkata designated by North Calcutta, South Calcutta, *bustee*s, aristocratic Muslim areas, Hindu *bustee*s, Muslim *bustee*s and localities on the edge of clearly designated areas such as Metiaburz, Kalabagan and Rajabazar. Ghose was not content with reconstructing the geopolitics of riot in the city in this way; he also wanted to clarify the slogans of war and the battle cries. Thus he asked Brigadier Binny of the meaning of the word *jihad*, and the question came up, is fasting not also a *jihad* (II: 48)? What sense was the military making of the rising tension in the city in the months preceding the riots?

In his reply the innocent Brigadier reported of 'the INA Hindu volunteers parading different parts of the town just before 16 August with slogans of *Jai Hind* and so on and bravadoing that on the INA day the youth would not be cowed down by police and they would not be cowed down by lathis' (II: 53). On 24 July 1946 students demanded release of prisoners; there were 'communists and socialists' in the crowd. Mr. Yunus, the counsel for the Muslim League, then drew the unflappable Binny into committing himself in evaluating the situation, which Binny was trying to avoid. Yunus asked, 'Was it serious from the point of view of loss of lives?' Binny's reply, 'I am not aware that it was serious'. 'Nor if the next day you found in that particular area or pocket 70 dead bodies, would you consider that serious?' (II: 47, q 731). These were all Muslim dead bodies near Jadu Babur Bazar – roughly from where South Calcutta begins. In his defence of the calm and unconcerned attitude of the army, the Brigadier referred to the INA warmongerings and said that therefore in that perspective they were not particularly worried on the eve of 16 August. Then he painted a picture of the 'natural' warmongering attitude of the Indians with this observation, 'I have often read many statements of acting peacefully in India and they definitely lead to me believe that the interpretation put by Indians was not always the same as the British do' (II: 37; q 59 b).

The same idea was expressed by Lt. General F.P.R. Bucher (Eastern Command), when he said that 'tensions were brewing in the city from the month of February, though essential services were going', and that they could intervene only when the civilian authority requested it, and that it could happen only 'according to well established procedures' (III: 3–7). But in any case, communal conflict was not so much a cause of worry. To the question, 'May I request you to tell me for the purpose of my information, what would require a large number of forces: to quell a communal riot or a riot against law and order?' But the general was not to be trapped. He answered, 'If you have wide scale rioting against law and order as you had in February all over Calcutta, in my opinion that would require a greater force than merely the suppression of communal riots' (III: 7, q 87). In the replies by the senior army officials INA was the big spectre hovering over the city. INA people had arrived in the city (III: 14–15). While many INA prisoners were released, Rashid Ali was not; hence there was tension. Jinnah had denounced this discriminatory treatment, and Suhrawardy led a procession demanding his release. Mr. Yunus then pressed the City Police Commissioner Donald Ross Hardwick to respond to the suggestion that 'only 7 temples were attacked as against 52 mosques' and '17 dead bodies were recovered from a mosque in Baubazar near B.C. Roy's house'. To both inquiries, Hardwick's answer was, 'I do not remember the exact number' and 'I cannot say without looking into the files' (III: q 2355).[26] They even did not know the details of the chief minster's movements on 16–18 August (reply by Walker, III: q 1414). They had only heard cries of *larke lenge Pakistan*.

The colonial government was thus strictly neutral in this war.[27] It would step in after the battle lines had become clear with this round of war over and the results had been clarified. It was the superior power.

At the same time the questions put by the counsels point to a greater underlying reason as to why the superior authority had decided not to intervene. While Suhrawardy had requested the army to help the civilian authority to control the spreading riot and bring back law and order, the army let it play on the supposed weakness of Suhrawardy, namely that his request was not clear and that therefore the army decided not to be proactive in controlling the city. Let the chief minister take the blame. The army's logic was that it did not know if the police force and resources were sufficient in that extremely volatile situation, hence it did not become proactive. The president of the Commission asked Brigadier Mackinley,

> I quite appreciate . . . that the military have always taken up the attitude that they must not be called in unnecessarily and improperly. But when you have got trouble of this size and the police have been operating under the control of either you or Brigadier Sixsmith, I can understand it will be within the power and knowledge of the commanding officer to say when the military ought to come in. But how can a military officer who is not in control of the police operations know whether or not the demand is justified? . . . It seems to me, rightly or wrongly the military had taken on themselves the responsibility of saying, 'Shall we come in, or shall we not? We will come in if only police resources have been used up and we are satisfied that they had been used up.' . . . The only question, we ask you, is, how can you, not having been in charge of the police operations, really know whether or not the resources of the police had been used up, exhausted . . . ? (IV: 35, q. 371–373)

Mackinley's reply was that he was concerned with the safety of the soldier: "Safeguard the soldier who has got only a rifle and no means of using a lesser weapon' (IV: 35, a. 371). To the point then as to what about the protection and safety of the innocent people being killed, the question was, who would responsibly 'make the request of asking the force which can only restore order by taking life' (IV: 35, q. 372). The hesitation of the commanding officers of the army and the chief secretary to explicitly ask the soldiers to become proactive revealed itself under repeated interrogation.

Brigadier Sixsmith confirmed Counsel Mitter's observation about the possibility of 'Hindus and Muslims coming together against the

British', and said: 'Police efforts were exhausted and there were cases of police firing.' Mitter then asked directly, 'Could the riots turn anti-government?' The reply was, 'It might have been.' Mitter pressed, 'Therefore you are suggesting that if the military had been called in earlier, the populace could have turned against the government.' Sixsmith replied, 'We know the situation on the 16th that might have developed into anti-government riots.' P. Norton Zones, the deputy commissioner of police, also deposited that though Hindus and Muslims had not explicitly come together, 'not as such', but (there were) 'looting, burning of vehicles' (IV: 252, q. 210–216, 386).

But asked about specific cases of burning and looting, he said, in Teretta Bazar-Lal Bazar area (where he was on duty), 200–300 yards from scenes of reported trouble, there was 'no sound of riot, gunshot, killing, or cry, *Larke lenge Pakistan*' (IV: q. 573).

There were numerous such statements suggesting the blurred scenario. It was reminiscent of post–First World War Germany when fascist and revolutionary mobilizations in Berlin were taking place simultaneously, and the government never actively intervened lest it should add fuel to the general unrest and help the revolutionary mobilizations. Counsel S. A. Masud had asked P. Norton Zones significantly, 'Do you remember that a political demonstration took place in November 1945 in connection with the INA soldiers. Was any high official injured?' Norton Jones replied, 'An SI (Sub-inspector) and a Deputy Commissioner were injured' (V: 5). It was clear that the memory of the lawlessness of November 1945 was still there when the city again became lawless. Crowds had learnt the technique of confronting the police. Mitter had asked Mackinley, 'Now, when did you first realise that the crowds would disperse at the sight of the police or the military and reassemble as soon as they passed?' Mackinley said, 'It was on the afternoon of the 16th or the evening of the 16th' (IV: 26, q. 254). Police stations such as Bhowanipore were defenceless. The police hesitated to open fire. The attackers were fast and mobile. Goondas were in the crowds. Pakistan was written on the signboards of several shops. Police reinforcements in the form of supply of men, provisions and vehicles, and related logistical arrangements had to face as their adversary the mobility of the crowd. Therefore, for the police the routes of patrol became important. Also the police was aware of a directive introduced in the Kolkata riot of 1926 that it could open fire if it found shops being looted by an aggressive crowd.[28] However, as S. N. Mukherji, the deputy commissioner of the Enforcement Department, said that the chief minister 'did not agree with me and he told me that I could open fire at my own risk' (V: 138, q. 166–170).

The deponents of the police and the military and the counsels who doubled up as investigators together tell us through their interlocution the ways a riot enacts as a war – and thus how the city becomes a battlefield, how respective zones and trenches are marked, how the technique of properly placing barricades is deployed, how armed confrontations take place, how other techniques of urban warfare are improvised and polished, and how like any other war, the urban riot has antecedents. However, what is noticeable is that these antecedents in time become so naturalized that we refuse to take note of them as portents of extraordinary violence. Indeed, as the depositions show, the military, the police, the urban political class, the municipal elders – all were surprised at the extent of the violence in the city. We are all overtaken by the event. The event now guides history. Nobody willed it, yet everyone became a party. Exactly as in a war, it is the nature of war that determines even neutrality, its nature, quality and extent. The police was not determining the course of riot; the riot was determining the course of police conduct. The riot demonstrated the materiality of politics. It showed the police how the crowd was taking a leaf out of history, how the police logic of setting up urban territorial divisions in the form of police stations and zones under the responsibility of respective deputy commissioners ran counter to the logic of territorial divisions in the form of religions-communal configurations and more importantly and more significantly, how in that all round volatile situation no-man's lands were forming and emerging as dangerous killing zones – the most difficult terrain for the police. The geopolitical logic of riot and the administrative logic of policing ran against each other. The logistical difficulties of controlling the city began from this dissonance.

For instance, did the police know, 'What could be the various places, Mohammedan localities, from where Mohammedans wanting to come to Calcutta would come from?' Which were these suburbs? Did it not strike the police 'that these people had come out very early in order to make their *hartal* a success?' 'Can you give the names of these places? Mohammedans coming from these places would be passing through the Shyambazar turnpike?' (V: 143, q. 243–245).

In this continuous remaking of the geopolitical configurations of the city the actors (police, rioters, government and the crowd) were always connected in their emergence and respective roles. Both in Nonapukur tram depot and near the Beliaghata police station the police reported the deadly combination of logistics and space marked by force, congregation, assembly, select application of violence and mobile groups of trucks carrying the attackers. We have to listen to the deposition of P. K. Chatterji, the assistant commissioner of police, North Town, when asked by counsel Bashiruddin, 'Will you kindly look into this Buratolla police station diary – entry 1686? It speaks of two crowds of Hindus and Muslims. (It says) "Hindus are aggressive. Have you got it?" '. The assistant commissioner said, 'Yes', and continued,

> On my arrival with the armed party of the policemen of the police station at the junction of the Beadon Street and Upper Circular Road I found a very big crowd of Hindus of Beadon Street and another crowd of almost similar dimension of Muslims at the east end of the Beadon Street. Both parties were hurling brickbats. We brought the situation under control. Sometime after, trouble started again at the junction of the Karbala Tank Lane and Upper Circular Road between a party of Hindus and another party of Muslims. We brought the Muslim party under control and made them fall back but the Hindu mob came forward along Karbala Tank Lane and started to brickbat the retreating Muslims and the police party. One of the brickbats hurled by the Hindus hit me on the left leg. With difficulty this party was also brought under control. Sometime after a big crowd of Hindus advanced along Circular Road from the North from near the Sahitya Parishad Street and attacked a Muslim crowd near the Karbala Tank Lane. (V: 293, q. 1168–1169)

The police deponents had constant difficulty in marking out for the benefit of the Commission Hindu areas and Muslim areas of the city. What would be the basis of such demarcation? The religion of the inhabitants, the density of the mob, the virulence of the clash, the number of houses, the recording or reporting by the police – how would they make the Commission understand the complexity of the police task at hand? There was no census in 1941; the core riot-affected area of the city (north, central and the northern fringe of the south) that we are discussing could not be more than two hundred square kilometres in size with an unthinkable density of population and closely situated Muslim and Hindus quarters jostling shoulder to shoulder – contiguity and no break, Muslim and Hindu eateries, *khatal*s (cowsheds), temples, mosques, places of congregation, local clubs, small lanes, bazaars, small parks and tanks, schools, colleges, mansions, printing presses, other small manufacturing units, mercantile offices, shops, *bustees* and houses, and in this situation how were the police forces going to zone-mark the city?

Therefore, throughout these eleven volumes we find the police officers in their depositions trying desperately to classify the areas in sections, in this case the North Town, in this way: (Section A) 'Hatibagan, predominantly Hindu area except some pockets of Muslims in little of Bagbazar, a little of Mohanbagan – just pockets'; then (Section B) 'Beniatola – a little of Upper Chitpore Road, Muslim area, I mean Muslim shops, mainly a Hindu area'; then (Section C) 'Duliapara Lane and Ram Chandra Ghosh lane – a Muslim pocket, Muslim traders in cows, some milkmen – otherwise a predominantly Hindu area'; then (Section D) 'Burrabazar Police Station predominantly Hindu area with Muslim pockets, like Amratollah, Lower Chitpore Road'; then finally (Section E), 'from Mechuabazar right upto Coolootolla Street it is predominantly a Muslim area. Machuabazar Street starts from College Street. This is one end; that is on the east. On the west it meets Lower Chitpore Road. From Mechuabazar Street right up to Coolootolla Street it is predominantly a Muslim area. Excepting a few houses in Tara chand Dutta Street and just a few houses in Zakaria Street, it is a predominantly a Muslim area. And if you take the other side of the Central Avenue, from Mechuabazar crossing up to College Street, again the portion south of Mechuabazar Street is predominantly a Muslim area. A little to the north of Marcus Square, there is a big Muslim area', and finally (Section F), 'The area between Keshab Sen Street and Mechuabazar is a purely Muslim area with pockets of Hindus' (V: 318–319, q. 1168–1169). The deponents do not mention *bustee*s. We have to imagine the Commission meeting in a room with learned members trying to understand the huge map of the city hung before them and the police trying to mark out 'sensitive areas', 'delicate situations', 'borders', 'boundaries', 'roads', 'lanes', 'meeting zones' and explaining the 'protocol of receiving a person under attack' in that grave situation, and the need for 'sufficient force to rescue a person or not rescue because otherwise the *thana* would be at risk' (VI: 124–125).

Yet these details were not enough. Was Mechuabazar Street predominantly Muslim? Sir Syed Saleh Lane? 'Prabhat Cinema', which the police deponent thought 'had Hindu houses, but I think there will be Muslim houses there'. Is 'Phulbagan *bustee* a Muslim area'? 'There are Mohammedan houses as well as Hindu houses there.' Then what about the area near Marcus Square? When the deponent again tried to follow the same track, the president of the Commission cried out in exasperation, 'Muslims are everywhere but I want you to apply your mind to the question, when I give you a particular area, please tell whether it is predominantly Hindu or Mohammedan?' So, to a counsel's observation, 'also that part between Mitra Lane and Marcus Square is entirely Mohammedan', the deponent insisted, 'No, there is a lot of Hindu houses also (XII: 117, q. 47–61).

Marking is thus dangerous exercise. You have to do it well; otherwise lives will be at danger; in fact your life will be at stake. The police task of protecting and controlling will depend on how the administration has marked the territory of the city.

Today when we look at the city, same areas but not quite the same, the same quarters of populations but not quite the same any more, we can hardly feel the battle cries, the groans, death calls and cries, the bustle of the 'khatals stored with guns' (VII: 79), the sound of the trucks and lorries hurling down the roads brandishing swords and lathis, besieged places of worship full with mortified people taken shelter there, dead bodies lying around and the whispers of fear coming out of the fortified houses – many now gone under the bulldozers of the developers and many inhabitants of the town leaving the city forever. This is also a city's past. The police depositions bring out under the simplest of pressure the cracks in the city edifice, which still remain today, of course, in other forms, buried tentatively under the bourgeois culture of citizenship, waiting to bare themselves out at suitable opportunities.

Politics can perfectly make sense of these moments of contest, contention, attrition and climactic violence. But has law ever been able to make any sense of crime and responsibility of these what Max-Jean Zins following Foucault calls the 'citizen-massacres'?[29] More importantly, do the differences between the three forms of logic – political logic, police logic and the legal logic – hold any relevance to such situation?

Consider in this respect the following exchange in the Commission between the judicial investigator and a police official: Counsel M. N. Ghose asks Rahimuddin Ahmed, a sub inspector (SI) of the Burrabazar Police Station on 14 February 1947, 'There was a fire at 3 Amratolla Lane. Have you ever been to 3 Amratolla Lane before?' Rahimuddin Ahmed replies, 'I had been to that place; I have gone on many occasions to Amratolla Street.' Ghose, 'Do you know the place the Amratolla Lane?' The SI replies, 'Yes I know the Street.' Ghose, 'Have you ever been to 3 Amratolla Lane?' Rahimuddin Ahmed, 'I had no previous occasion to go there.' 'So, you did not know of any happenings in No 3 Amratolla Lane during the 16th to the 20th?' The SI says, 'No, my Lord.' The Commission did not proceed beyond this simple exchange. We do not know if there was any fire at all, or there was fire but the SI did not know, or if the entry was wrong, and it should have been Amratolla Street, or that there was fire in the Lane, but after bungling the answer the SI did not want to revise his statement. The line in the police station diary is left hanging there (VII: 5). The police deponents time and again confided apprehensions about their own safety and their state of confusion as to whether they should have been proactive in taking the innocent people in the *thana* and saving them from marauding attackers.[30] Perhaps religious affiliations played a part in deciding. Or, take this sequence of questions: Fazl Ali, a member of the Commission seeks confirmation from S. Ahmed, the officer in-charge of the Jorabagan Police Station, 'The enlisted information about attack on this hostel was sent as early as 10.10 am. The information was sent to Amherst Street and from there it was passed on to the Control Room.' The counsel of the Congress Jyoti Mitter butts in, 'The first information to reach any police station was at 10 am. That was Josanko. I am reading from the report, "At 10 am"' (VII: 198, q. 685). Again we can surmise an array of questions here. The volumes are replete with such unsolved questions, on which apparently the cause of justice depended.

The legal logic moving around the issue of responsibility therefore was much of the time built around questions like, was the police prepared for the eventuality? Had it got sufficient information beforehand and exactly when, with how much time to prepare? And then did it act accordingly? Or, did it not get information at all? If this was a dominating concern behind the questions put by the Commission to the police personnel, we do not know if the depositions satisfied them. Consider this phase of exchange of questions to a police functionary D. N. Mullick and his replies:

(Q) Now, in the past when *hartals* were announced or declared by the Congress or by the Communist Party, was there much trouble there? / No, not much. (Q) Perhaps you will agree with me that the Muslims and the Hindus thought of just co-operating with the *hartal*? / Yes. (Q) You belong to a middle class Hindu family. You have friends and relation among Hindus. Now tell me whether the Hindus were very much agitated prior to the 16th – say on the 14th and 15th over Direct Action Day of the Muslims. / I do not know. (Q) Do you read the papers? / Yes . . . (Q) You must have read the speeches in the Assembly and you must have read the speeches of the various speakers in the meetings that took places? / Yes. (Q) And now, perhaps you remember that the Hindus were very much agitated over this Direct Action Day? / I cannot say they were agitated. (Q) Then what was their attitude when the Government announced Direct Action Day as a holiday? / Of course, the Hindus did not like it. (Q) Did any of the local Hindus come to you and express anxiety as to what was going to happen? / No, my Lord. (Q) Are you aware of the fact that the Hindus of your locality were determined to see that the Muslim League Direct Action Day would not prove a success? / I do not know any such thing. (Q) You never heard of it? / No. (Q) Do you know the Lakhi Jute Mills? / Yes. (Q) It is on Belliaghatta Road? / Yes. (Q) Whom is it owned by? / Some Marwari gentleman . . . (Q) Now, on the 15th you got a message from D.C., North's office to this effect that the procession of Tangra and Entally should collect near Entally Market and pass through Circular Road and Dharm-tolla Street, you remember that? / Yes. (Q) Now, this very important information you got on the 15th? / Yes. (Q) Did you take any action on the basis of this information? Did you post any picket in the Entally Market? / No picket was posted. (Q) It is because you had not enough force or you did not consider it necessary? / The order was not like that. (Q) I suppose you thought the Emergency Scheme did not permit that?/According to the Emergency Scheme I had to mobilize the whole force in the *thana* and plain clothes men were sent out. (X: 95)

On this and several similar unresolved questions we have to remember the crucial element was the relation between the police and the mob, the crowd, the mass. Law barely had a role to play here. Therefore, almost voluntarily the police officials were giving information about how crowds formed on the streets, how they mobilized, how they faced the machinery of law and order and how they dispersed. The foot soldiers of politics – the *bustee* dwellers, the denizens of the *khatals*, the volunteers of the parties, the fanatic followers of cults and beliefs – all had learnt through the past two decades how to mobilize and enforce the *hartals* and strikes. Contemporary observers in their writings confirm the police version of the elements present in the composition of the crowds, such as the scavengers, milkmen, potters, *dom*s who work in the burning ghats and the crematoria, artisans in goldsmiths' shops, petty shopkeepers, artisans dealing with scrap metals (called the *kalwars*), dosads, *julaha*s and so on.[31] The police logic was if the city had passed on to the hands of the crowd, which meant that normal governance had failed disastrously, what could the police machinery do? Police task makes sense in normal times, but in cataclysmic time like this, the police could treat the events as facing crowds only. Individual protection, individual action, individual suppression and the like made little or no sense here. Therefore, how could the police help the Commission assign responsibility and direct justice?

The deposition of the Nalini Kanta Chowdhury, the officer in-charge of Shyampukur Police Station, to questions by B. A. Siddiky is significant. Siddiky asked, 'With regard to various entries in the Incidents Diary do you have independent recollection of events with regard to which you had taken personal action?' and 'If news came to you that large crowds had collected at the Five Crossings and people were intimidating the shopkeepers that would not have surprised you, or you would not have been surprised if you got information that large crowds of Muslims had gathered and were intimidating the Hindu shopkeepers. Would that information have surprised you?

N. K. Chowdhury replied, 'Not surprised, because these things happened on many occasions during Congress agitations. This time assaults took place and it was a new thing' (VIII: 5–6, q. 1556–1565). And he followed it up with a description of how large crowds gathered on the road there – specifically on the junction of Barrackpore Trunk Road and Cossipore Road. 'Lorries were sending out hullas (warnings).' The police could only disperse mobs, because many in the mobs were unknown, from different places, 'up country Muslims' (VIII: 13–17, q. 1593). 'Processions clashed against each other.'. 'From Cossipore and Chitpore area hundreds of people, all Muslims, are coming with lathis, swords, etc.' (VIII: 21–24, q. 1848–1849); not satisfied, the Commission persisted and wanted to know, Where were they going? Who were there in the crowd? 'There was Sk. Habu alias Habibur Rahman . . . I thought he was going to attend the meeting at the Maidan.' 'You actually saw Sk. Habu?' 'Yes.' 'Habu is generally known as Habu Goonda?' 'Bully, Badmash (rogue)'. Siddiky asked, 'Because he had not been declared a goonda under the Goonda Act that you call him a bully?' 'Yes'. 'He was known as goonda?' 'He must be declared a goonda under the Goonda Act.' 'But (what did) the people in the locality (think)?' 'They said Habu Badmush' (VIII: 21, q. 1882–1892).

In this strange exchange of information, assertion, definition and confirmation of who could possibly be members of the crowd, we get some idea of the police world, the police planet, in which the crowds feature as actors but half known and half unknown, and therefore a state of uncertainty in the police apparatus of governance. The Commission wanted to know individual acts of arson, murder, perfidy, and so on. These questions must have appeared as inconsequential enquiries, unhelpful also to understand a crisis situation. (See for instance Volume IX for the depositions by A.K.M. Fazlul Sabir Chowdhury, officer in-charge of Manicktolla Police Station and Shamsul Hosain Ali, officer in-charge of Beliaghata Police Station.) These enquiries revolved mostly around when the first report of a trouble reached the police station, whether everything deposed was mentioned in the diary, who remembered what and when and who had seen or heard the first truck carrying agitators or the cry, *Larke Lenge Pakistan* (IX: 153, q. 184–196). In one instance, the police officer N. K. Roy Chowdhury while deposing on the clash between the two communities facing each other on the Ultadanga Road and Fariapukur had to repeatedly answer questions from the counsel Jyoti Mitter, as to exactly which community gathered where and stood on which side of the road – right or left, and the distance between spot A and spot B. 'Where did you see the Hindus and where the Muhammadans?' / I saw the Hindus on the Ultadanga side and also western side opposite to Ultadanga Road, and in front of Fariapukur and Nikasipara I saw Muslims up to that mosque; and opposite to that mosque there is Mohanbagan. Facing east was the Hindu mob and facing west was the Muslim mob. The interlocution went like this:

> The Hindu mob was facing east? / Yes. Therefore the Hindu mob was to the west of Circular Road? / Yes. And the Muhammadan mob was on the east of Circular Road, is that correct? / Yes. (Witness was asked to point out on the map the exact position where the two mobs were. He pointed out Ultadanga Road, Mohanbagan Lane Fariapukur and opposite to that, Nikasipara, and then said.) This Mohanbagan, for instance, is a Muslim *bustee*. Next to that Hindus also live, a few, all respectable Hindus. These people got frightened; they went and joined with these Nikasipara people in front of Fariapukur. Really the Muslims were on the east side facing southwards and the Hindus on Ultadanga Road across Circular Road facing north-east? / Yes. You say Mohanbagan is a mixed *bustee*, predominantly Muhammadan? / Predominantly Muhammadan. Did you see the Muhammadan population of Mohanbagan with the Nikasipara Muhammadans in the crowds? / Yes . . . Did you recognize them? / Subsequently I came to know. So when you saw the crowd, you only saw the Muhammadan crowd. And the Hindu crowd partly on Ultadanga Road and partly to the in front of Nikasipara? / Yes, opposite Fariapukur, west of Circular Road? / Yes. What time did you see this crowd? / From Hatibagan I came straight here about 12–30. About 12–30 you came from the Muslim *biri* shop? / No, from Begum Mosque. . . .

You were driving southwards? / Along Circular Road. . . . What is the distance between the crossing of Ultadanga Road and the mouth of Fariapukur Street? / 50 yards, I think. And you say these two opposing crowds were exchanging brickbats? / Yes. You came from behind the Muhammadan crowd? / In a lorry. . . . You had to charge them? / Yes. Did the *lathi* charge have effect on the crowd? / Yes. I did not assault them. I charged them without hitting them and both parties ran away. Both parties moved subsequently. What did they say? / The Muslim crowd said 'Disperse the Hindus first'. The Hindus said 'Disperse the Muhammadans first.' (VIII: 13, q. 1693–1715)

This was not only a crisis situation, but a border situation (X: 162–163). Violence was always a phenomenon of the borders; it was occurring on the border of two localities, two settlements, on the roads that marked the boundaries of the two, and therefore Entally, Park Circus, Shyampukur, all those borderlands, the murderous zones.[32]

As sporadic clashes and killings continued beyond the murderous week, night curfew had to be extended up to end of December in select areas, such as Beliaghata, Chitpore, Cossipore, Manicktola, Entally and Beniapukur and Watgunj.[33]

More on the limits to legal intelligibility

Before we proceed further, let us pause so that we can think a little on the significance of these depositions in terms of the limits to legal intelligibility on riots. Facets of the Great Calcutta Riot some of which have been discussed earlier were later replicated and found in other riots – though the continuity of these facets of the riot of 1946 remains inadequately recognized.

We can say that the minutes of evidence of the *Calcutta Disturbances Commission of Enquiry* exhibit a sense of innocence to be found already in the nineteenth-century inquiries into riots. The governmental rationality, at least in the colonial conditions of India, had an air of reflecting what we may call *ground conditions*. Commissions became the artefact of modern policymaking. Thus, it was not only Hunter, who refused to condemn the entire community of 'Indian Musalmans',[34] in the inquiry of agrarian riots also, 'peasant distress' was the theme. For instance, in the inquiry report on the Deccan Riots of 1875, historians Vinay Lal and Neil Charlesworth show, agrarian conditions were real causes, and the conspiracy argument found little ground with the Commission for explaining the riots and devising solutions. Vinay Lal has written,

> Quite to the contrary, the commissioners were emphatic in their pronouncement that the riots had not been 'acted upon by persons of higher position and education'. The Deccan Riots Commission's affinity to the commissions of previous years becomes all the more evident when we consider that it was invested with the authority, which it exercised, to recommend legislation that, if accepted and implemented, would affect cultivators not only in the affected areas, but throughout India.[35]

Commissions had to have relevance to the dynamics of policy making.

In that age, which we can say continued in some sense until the 1940s, riots used to take place over places of worship (for instance, 1890, Aligarh, where there was obstruction of places of worship, because apparently a pot of flesh was thrown at night in a mosque, and then beef was hung into two Hindu wells), animal sacrifice (1896, Patna, 1953 Bhopal), playing music and beating drums before the holy places (1941, Kolkata, occasion of Muharram), defiling of sacred texts (1939, Asansol, where the Ramayana was defiled apparently by a Muslim), 'competing religious festivals' on the same day (1871, Bareilly, where Moharram and Ramnavami festivals fell on the same day), and others. In these riots race was the important but suppressed question, and with each round of riots, the project of constructing the 'Hindu race' or the 'Muslim race' would receive one more dose of boost.[36] In some sense the Great Calcutta Killings formed the climactic moment of the racialization of rival communities, though the observation will be incomplete without an additional one that riots not only reflected the making of races, but they were also the apparatus of the process. This continued to some extent for some decades even after independence.[37] In this continuing chronicle of riots no one is a terrorist, and no community is a danger to nation. It is more a case of race, when living together but separately has become impossible because of 'racial' (bio-cultural) difference. The pattern changes with or after the Babri Masjid-related riots, when in place of contested cultural practices deliberate and engineered historical issues become the cause of riots. But this is a different issue into which we cannot go now. Yet from a different angle the Great Calcutta Killings presented discontinuities. In the eyes of the police, as the minutes of evidence suggest, 'direct action' – the idea of *direct action* – had possessed people and transformed the rival communities into mad mobs, intent on changing the destiny of their country, and embarking on frenzied actions.[38] The D Day had arrived. Much preparation through decades, years and months had gone into preparation. Now it must happen.

In this sense not only the August killings were different, but the Commission of Enquiry also proved different in many ways, some of the aspects already indicated. To summarize: identification of individual actions of violence became less important. Likewise enquiries into individual acts of commission and omission of the state functionaries including the police became moments of producing narratives of other kind – for instance of territory, logistics.[39] Moreover, unlike on previous occasions, this time no one had any clue as to how to control the crowd because direct action became the rallying point. And finally, the Commission in this case was not acting on a known phenomenon, and therefore inquiring into the culpability of the event and thinking of policies was to be prescribed. Rather the Commission was opening itself up to an unknown world of knowledge – by which I mean knowledge of police conduct defined in relation to crowd conduct, in relation to economy, society and politics. The Commission had to wind itself up not only because independence was approaching but also because, and this is my argument, the Commission as an apparatus of governing was unequal to the knowledge it had produced; and now it did not know how to use this knowledge for governing. Its two functions as an apparatus of power and an apparatus of knowledge did not sit happily together this time. Its summary closure symbolized a deep internal crisis in the manifold nature of police rationality.[40]

Before closing this chapter I shall try to show with the help of a longish presentation of a police diary – entered as affidavit for the Commission – how the events of 1946 presented police in a new light, a disciplinary institution, but one whose 'secret history' was in its protection and thus security practices. The police as an arm of legality have to operate in the field of illegality. While it knows the rules on the basis of which it will relate to prisons and other legal institutions of punishment, and this is precisely its institutional function of discipline, the Great Calcutta Killings raised the question: can discipline be the basis of its relation with an illegal entity – the crowd? In order to manage legality will it not have to employ modes of security and therefore surveillance on groups of extremely mobile bodies?[41] Also, what will happen if the effectiveness of prison is over, that is criminals mix with the non-criminal population, and form the crowd on the street? Police is trained to deal with the organization of an isolated illegality. Its institutional practices create expert knowledge of delinquent behaviour. But what if the society turns delinquent and what will it do when it finds that its function of discipline cannot automatically ensure security of the population? The police guards against delinquency, but when did it learn to secure territory and thus secure population? Thus the police almost everywhere in the city began its action by trying to protect shop keepers intent on keeping their shops open on 16 August.[42] Then it became busy in saving lives. Security begins with providing security of trade and commerce and then providing security of life. Protection was important, as important or more important, than its counterpart in the form of disciplinary duty.[43] Great Calcutta Killings showed that one function did not naturally lead to the other. The reason of the state found itself only in a fractured form in governmental reason.

More precisely then, the police depositions and the Enquiry show that the police as a legal-administrative calculus of negotiating conduct of population reached its dead end in that time of crisis brought about by a massive spread of illegality. A plethora of divergent police practices collided, whose reports in the form of depositions only served the function of confusing the Commission. As a representative of the internal array of forces the institution of police is intended to modulate the conduct of domestic populations by employing different strategies related to various aspects of life, such as, public health, education, trade, commerce, housing and population management. The city is inconceivable without the police. The police with its manifold functions make sense only in a city. Yet, as the summary of complaints against the conduct of the police and their own defence[44] showed (and on which much of Commission's energy was directed), the police had become as a fragmentary institution at sea swimming aimlessly in the swirling waves of different demands of life – politics, commerce, protection, security, possession and control of urban territory and risk management. Calcutta was no longer a small or medium-size market town requiring a small number of police force in order to function.

The police planet

The diary of a police functionary, Nurul Haq Khundkar, officer in-charge, Burtolla Police Station, records the events and his movements on 16–17 August 1946. Entered as an affidavit to the Commission and presented below it gives us a glimpse of how the police was trying to cope with this extraordinary situation:

16 August 1946: On 16 August 1946 I received a telephone message from Assistant Commissioner, North Town to proceed to the

junction of Beadon Street and Upper Circular Road . . . to stop rioting between Hindus and Muslims . . . in progress there. With S.I. K.C. Mukherji and 6 armed men of this police-station I proceeded to the spot in one of the *thana* lorries. . . . At the junction of Upper Circular Road and Vivekananda Road I met Deputy Commissioner, North Town. Assistant Commissioner, North Town, also arrived there. . . . Under orders of Deputy Commissioner, North, I proceeded to the spot with my men to stop the fight (which was going on) there. By the time I arrived there, the parties swelled to such a dimension that it was impossible for me alone to cope with the situation with a handful of men. I hastened back to Deputy Commissioner North, when Assistant Commissioner, North Town, picked me up in a police lorry with armed and unarmed men in it. We proceeded to Jugipara Lane to approach the crowds both from the south and the north, sending another batch of policemen to the spot to advance from the north. We entered into the lane where fighting was going on. At sight of us closing in from both ends, the fighters made good their escape. . . .

A few minutes after I accompanied Assistant Commissioner, North Town, with my men in lorry patrol along Vivekananda Road towards the west and we went up to the crossing of Central Avenue and returned by the same route. No fighting was observed anywhere, but many shops were found looted, atta, flour and other things were found scattered on the street.

Just after our return to the junction of Beadon street and Upper Circular Road trouble again started at the junction of Kerballa Tank Lane and Upper Circular Road between a party of Muslims and another of Hindus. We brought the Muslim party under control and made them fall back but the Hindu mob began steadily moving forward and all the while hurling brickbats at the retreating Muslims towards Upper Circular Road along Kerballa Tank Lane. When our party tried to persuade them to go back they started pelting us with big pieces of bricks one of which hit me on the left leg. With the greatest difficulty we were able to push back this crowd and the situation was brought under control. But this was not to last long as a few minutes after a big crowd of Hindus armed with offensive weapons advanced along Circular Road from the north hurling brickbats in front of them and soon attacked a Muslim crowd near Kerballa Tank Lane and hurled brickbats right and left. Rai Bahadur S.N. Mukherji and Deputy Commissioner, Security Control, were there with a big force of policemen and tried to disperse both parties but it appeared that it would be impossible to bring the situation under control. However the Muslims were pushed back and they began to retreat but the Hindus advanced further and showered a rain of brickbats on the police. As I was in the thick of this I was again hit by a brickbat on the left knee. Thereafter a tear-gas squad was brought by Deputy Commissioner, Security Control, and tear-gas was thrown which dispersed the crowd of Hindus.

At about 11.30 a.m. while at the junction of Upper Circular Road and Beadon Street with S.Is K.C. Mukherji, K.M. Zaman, Sgt. Lehaney and armed and unarmed men, I received information that an Eating House of a Muslim at the crossing of Cornwallis Street and Beadon Street was being looted. I hastened to the spot with some of the unarmed men in my lorry and found that the said Eating House had already been looted and its furniture and other things were set on fire on the street. . . . I found a big crowd of Hindus at the place. I with my men chased away the crowd. Three or 4 other *biri* shops there owned by Muslims met with the same fate. The owner of the Eating House appeared then and asked for being conveyed to the *thana* with his two servants. I got them in my lorry. At sight of them some men in the crowd came up to my lorry and wanted to drag them down. I chased them away. . . .

At about 3–20 p.m. received information that a mob had attacked the Muslim *bustee* at 76/1, Cornwallis Street, south of Rungmahal Theatre. On this information with S.I. Zaman and a force I went there and found the *bustee* attacked by a large mob which came both from Cornwallis Street and also Sahitya Parishad Street as well. We noticed some of the young men setting fire inside an Eating House and beating men, women and children inside the *bustee*. It was a hard task to disperse the mob which was brick batting us also. We chased them away with determination and were able to arrest one of those who had set fire and beat the people in the *bustee*. . . . On my way back to police-station noticed a crowd on Cornwallis Street opposite Sahitya Parishad Street which was trying to attack the Muslim *bustee* at 76/1, Cornwallis Street, in spite of the presence of the police picket there. I brought armed men from the police-station and posted them there. While I was there information was received by me from . . . the police-station that the house of Mr. Manick Mullick, Honorary Magistrate, was about to be attacked by a Hindu mob to kill the Muslims who had taken shelter in his house. On this information I went to Grey Street and met Mr. Mullick at his door and rescued 6 Muslims from his residence. In front of Mr. Mullick's residence

I found 6 hackney carriages burnt on Grey Street. While returning to the police-station I found 4 Muslims – 3 young men and an old one-lying seriously wounded on B.K. Paul Avenue (in Section A) near its crossing with Grey Street and groaning. I picked them up in my lorry. . . . Thereafter at 112, Grey Street (within Section A) I found a Muslim groaning under a *taktaposh* having had deep stab wounds. I picked him up in the lorry and made arrangement from there to send him to hospital. . . . Continued rescuing who were there trapped in Hindu houses all over the jurisdiction at the request of Hindu gentlemen whom I met in course of lorry patrol in the section. I returned to police-station with force at 9.30 p.m.

At 11–30 p.m. with force went out on lorry patrol in the section. . . . At 12 mid night I came to the police-station.

17 August 1946: At 12.40 a.m. received orders from Assistant Commissioner, North Town, to proceed to College Street where trouble was apprehended. . . . On arrival at College Street Market, found no disturbance there. . . .

While returning to police-station along Central Avenue we found constable Shamsul Huq of Jorabagan police-station lying seriously injured on the head in a semi-conscious state on the east side of Central Avenue in front of Jatin Maitra Park. We picked him up and as we advanced north we found another man, a rickshaw-puller by the name of Tosaddak Mia of 164, Musjid-bari Street, lying unconscious with serious injuries on his person in the centre of the road. We picked him up also and I took both the injured men to Medical College Hospital and when they were being attended to in the Emergency Ward I left. While picking up the second injured man I had noticed dead body of a Muslim lying there. On return from hospital I picked up the dead body and brought it to police-station and then sent it to the morgue.

The Muslim residents of 76/1, Cornwallis Street *bustee* were brought to the *thana* and in the evening as the place was quite unsafe in view of the fact that it was over and over attacked in course of the day.

At 9 a.m. I went out on lorry patrol with force. Found Grey Street, Central Avenue strewn with dead bodies. I arrived at the crossing of B.K. Paul Avenue and Grey Street to the North of which I found heaps of dead bodies of Muslim men, women and children. I started picking up the injured men, women and children in the lorry and sending them to hospital. . . . I patrolled along Central Avenue and Beadon Street both of which were found littered with Muslim dead bodies. In course of patrol received information that murders had been committed in Gulu Ostagar Lane Mosque on the previous night. On this information I went there and found 4 dead bodies lying in the mosque and 1 man was found lying injured in the mosque. Three more dead bodies were lying on Gulu Ostagar Lane in front of the mosque. There were marks and clots of blood in an around the mosque. All these dead and the injured were Muslims. The Muslim population of this place were frightened to such a degree that they were trembling and none had the strength to stand up. I sent the injured men to hospital and started rescuing the Muslims from there in the lorry. It was learnt that in an old building a very large number of rickshaw pullers lived. Out of them only a few were found; there was no trace of the others. . . .

Thereafter I patrolled the jurisdiction in the *thana* lorry. . . . Immediately after, information came of trouble going on around Goabagan Cattle Market which was being surrounded from all sides I went out in a lorry with armed and unarmed men. I found that the Cattle Market was surrounded on the North, Madhab Das Lane and Raja Raj Kissen Street on the East and Mon Mohan Bose Road and Dalimtolla Lane on the South. There were thousands of men in each mob; they were armed with *lathis*, daggers, knives, axes, and spears, the mob advanced from Sahitya Parishad Street along Mon Mohan Bose Road. They had shot guns. This last mentioned mob numbered more than 2,000. All the mobs were hurling brickbats in front of them and advancing towards the Cattle Market. Those who had guns were firing in front of them at random. These men with the mob came towards us on Mon Mohan Bose Road within a distance of hearing. I warned them to disperse but they persisted in advancing further still firing their guns at random, hurling brickbats and brandishing their weapons. I shouted out another warning to them but by now they started brickbatting us and almost surrounded our lorry. I shouted out another warning to them but they did not move back an inch, rather they made a determined move to surround our lorry from all sides. Those who had guns aimed their weapons at us. As a last resort I gave orders to 3 armed men to fire one round each low which they did in consequence of which the crowd began to retreat. . . . The crowd retreated but stopped at a distance of about 50 yards from us and began to shower a rain of bricks at us. Those armed with guns began to fire at us from there. So again as a last resort I gave orders to fire and my men fired five shots more each in quick succession. The crowd began to disperse and I ordered them to cease fire. The casualty was not known as none was found killed or injured at the spot. . . .

At about 4–45 pm, I met Sgt. Lehaney on the Cornwallis Street. He was leading a band of refugees more than 500 consisting of Muslim men, women and children of all ages whom he had rescued from Ram Chand Ghosh Lane. He told me to go there immediately for the protection of the lives of hundreds more left behind. This locality was, he said, raided by a big Hindu mob which carried on looting and slaughter which they would have carried on further had he and S.-I. Zaman with armed and unarmed force not arrived there in time. S.I. Zaman was found bringing up the rear. I went there in the lorry with armed and unarmed men quickly and leaving the lorry on Beadon Street in charge of the driver and an armed man went into Ram Chand Ghosh Lane with rest of the party. The mosque there was badly damaged and about 12 or 13 dead bodies were found lying inside it and 4 dead bodies were found lying on the lane and two very badly injured persons were lying on the lane. We carried them to the lorry and placed them on it. All these were Muslims looking. Thereafter we collected all men, women and children from the locality who numbered more than 100. We came back to the lorry with these Muslim rescues and put some of them on the lorry and as we were about to march to the *thana* a mob of more than 1,000 of low class Hindus armed with daggers, knives and *lathis* rushed upon us. I gave them a warning which went unheeded and was about to catch hold of some women and children when I gave them 2 more warnings but all in vain. Then as a last resort I gave orders to . . . fire . . . I brought two badly injured men to the *thana* and sent them in the *thana* lorry to hospital. At this time there were more than 5,000 refugees at the police-station and there was no sufficient room for their accommodation. The men were given shelter in a cinema house under construction to the east of the *thana* building and the women and children were accommodated in the officer's quarters, on the open roof of the *thana* building and the stairs. During the night there were several attempts by mobs from all sides to attack the refugees and the Goabagan Cattle *hat* but their attempts were every time thwarted by us. Hindus numbering about 12 men also rescued from Nandanbagan *bustee*. They were kept in the *thana* in the constables guard room. During the next day also other officers and I carried on rescue work and by the afternoon the number of refugees came well up to 6,000. Refugees were brought from the border of the neighbouring sections also. . . . (VII: 5–10)

Other affidavits in the same session spoke of similar effort by the police. One such affidavit entered by a Hindu officer says of

> some of the Muslims . . . living near the *thana* premises came back and took shelter and since (we) rescued some of the Muslims, the number gradually increased by the midnight of the 16th and on the 17th too. Most of the Muslims were fasting because it was Ramzan period. They had nothing to eat. However I bought some things for them just to break their fast. They continued to come in. They had no food, or anything of the sort. Then children, babies, and womenfolk were coming for shelter to my quarters. I had a big verandah in my quarters. They consumed everything I had. I did not mind anything for that. There were newcomers to my *thana* and they did not know what was a Muslim kitchen and what was a Hindu kitchen. In the morning naturally they went to the privy, but as there was a great rush, one could expect that there would be some sort of nuisance committed. There is a big latrine in Jorabagan police-station where Muslims, Hindus, and people of every community can ease themselves. I am told that this enraged the feelings of the constables there . . . I explained the matter to them and managed to pacify. (VII: q. 1196)

Police officers like S. N. Routh rose above any communal feelings in discharge of responsibility and demonstrated governmental reason in all its purity. Yet Routh confessed to the Commission, 'Before I took charge of Jorasanko I was very much afraid. I had a peculiar impression of Kalabagan *bustee*. But during the time till the 16th August Kalabagan *bustee* gave me no troubles. Their activities till the 16th August I did not find too much' (XI: p. 122, q. 168). Another police officer, A. K. Mukherjee told a Commission member B. Somayya, to the question,

> What did you do in that mosque?, We waited for a brief period of time and rescued several males, females and children and from their dress it appeared that these were Muslims and we took them in my *thana* lorry and in the weapon-carrier which was with the Assistant Commissioner, North Town, to a mosque in Balmukund Makkar Road adjoining Jorasanko Thana . . . (Q: After coming back to the *thana* did you inform your Officer-in-charge that the mood of the mob, two to three thousand as you saw, was not very good and they were bent on mischief?) . . . When I went there and asked those persons whom I rescued as to what was the attitude of the mob, they told us that about 60 to 70 per cent of them were

friendly to them and they were trying to save them at the cost of their lives and 10 to 15 per cent were violent and tried to do mischief to the *bustee* people. The whole crowd was not hostile to the *bustee* people. About 10 per cent of the crowd were hostile to the *bustee* people and the other 70 to 80 per cent of the crowd were friendly to the *bustee* people and they were trying to save them and it was due to their care that they were able to save them up till that time when we rescued them. (VIII: q. 481, 525)

All these, however, did not convey anything significant to the Commission or counsels engaged by various parties, primarily the Muslim League and the Congress, who either wanted to fix individual responsibility or prove or disprove charges of state abetting of riots and mass murders.[45] All these also will mean very little for historians who are busy in mapping long-term trends in communalism and the eventual breakup of the country. Yet it seems that the Great Calcutta Riots indicated something more and the *Calcutta Disturbances Commission of Enquiry* was grappling with this new phenomenon – unknowingly, ineffectually. The Commission's modality was ineffective because it was based on the banal judicial procedure of evidence (evidence gathering, seeking, testing, examining and concluding on the basis of examination).[46] The new phenomenon I have discussed here related to the mutually constitutive relation between the police and the crowd, which made the connection between reason of the state and reason of governance highly contingent. It is difficult to pass judgment over the quarrel as to what leads to the breakdown of the other. In the case of the Great Calcutta Killings was it that the colonial state was breaking down, it had no strategic reason any more, and hence there was a loss of direction to the police apparatus in those calamitous days, and thus the riots continued in one way or another for almost full one year?[47] For after all, as the police files dating from the first decade of the twentieth century show, the city police was aware of the growing communal configuration of the city territory. Or, was it that with the failure of the reason of governance in the form of police rationality (whose elements I have discussed in the previous section) in those contentious times, the reason of the state made no further sense?

All we can say is that the apparatus of police built by the colonial state was based fundamentally on the obedience of the individuals and individual subjection to the institution of law and order after it no longer required the feudal form of allegiance. It now required a total and exhaustive obedience in their conduct to whatever the imperatives of the colonial state were in relation to protection of economy, commerce, trade, education, health, territory and security of life. The success of the apparatus depended on a smooth interrelation of these imperatives and thus between different functions of the police. The Calcutta Riots showed that there may be moments when the smooth relation will break down, when all bounds of obedience will be broken and populations will imagine their conduct not in juridical terms, but in other possible frames.[48] In other words politics will be conducted no longer in civilian frame, but in the frame of war. In those moments the link between the reason of state and that of government may collapse. The complete failure of police as an apparatus will come out in the open.[49] Therefore four things should not surprise us.

First, borders emerge in situations of violence and hence they are essentially unstable. There is no reason to think that the city is an organic unity unaffected by borders and boundary making exercises. Riots are such an exercise. Indeed through the urban war of August 1946 the internal borders of the city were marked out.

Second, enquiry commissions and judicial deliberations after the infamous riots in post-independence India have often proved inconclusive and have only demonstrated the closure of legal logic.

Third, in view of the past experiences of breakdown of the apparatus of police, which had acquired a kind of social naturalness, the apparatus has evolved further in the form of specialized forces with specific logistical abilities – establishment of special confinement centres,[50] tracking down economic offences, counter-insurgency policing, maintenance of public health intelligence, mobilizing and putting into operation rapid action force to tackle sudden riots, community policing, special ability to undertake relief and rescue operations, airborne supervision and coordinated crowd control, newer techniques such as CCTV and mobile telephony, superior quality and detailed maps of the area of trouble aided by Google and other search engines, newer ways of crowd control to achieve minimum killing and so on. In a more specific way, police reforms ensued in West Bengal to tackle terror, improving methods of selection of police personnel and terms of the top ranking police officers, improving capacity of police stations, intelligence centres and bureaus, state police academies, training colleges and schools, mechanisms of evaluating the performance of police officers, improving special capacities of police in metropolitan areas and finally delineating duties of the civil police, which meant more interaction with the population and more vigorous public relations exercise.[51] Of course, in the final count, for all these reforms the army remained the final model of organization of power, though one may say that while the police acquired more capacity, the general lessons of

1946 were quickly forgotten. Yet riot after riot in post-independence India showed that the police function of providing security to the population depended on the ability to secure territory – a function of essentially military nature.

Fourth and finally, and again a specific development that happened to Kolkata was in the form of a slew of *bustee* improvement programmes in the city over the years culminating in the Bustee Improvement Programme of the Kolkata Metropolitan Development Authority, because no government in West Bengal could forget that the *bustee* was the *other* of the police in those calamitous days – the ghost in hot pursuit of the machinery of law and order. *Bustee* reforms complemented police reforms. But this is another story we cannot go into here.

However, we must not forget that the evolution of the governmental intelligibility involved in these four phenomena owed its presence to bodies, dead bodies in hundreds and thousands, maimed, mutilated, burnt, severed, emaciated, tortured, disfigured and decomposed, which encapsulated various images of the riot. The memory of the bodies displaced the interlocked images of the crowd and the police.[52] The reality of war for territory receded to the background. For a long time to come these dead bodies were to create terror in the minds of the political class governing the land.

Michel Foucault had once commented,

> . . . beneath the lapses of memory, the illusions, and the lies that would have us believe that there is a ternary order, a pyramid of subordinations, beneath the lies that would have us believe that the social body is governed by either natural necessities or functional demands, we must rediscover the war that is still going on, war with all its accidents and incidents. Why do we have to rediscover war? Well, because this ancient war is a . . . permanent war. We really do have to become experts on battles, because the war has not ended, because preparations are still being made for the decisive battles, and because we have to win the decisive battle. In other words, the enemies who face us still pose a threat to us, and it is not some reconciliation or pacification that will allow us to bring the war to an end. It will end only to the extent that we really are the victors.[53]

Notes

1 *The Calcutta Municipal Gazette* (hereafter CMG), Volume XLIV, No. 11, 10 August 1946.

2 We may never know the actual figures. We have various reports of unaccounted bodies being recovered in the following days and months. On deaths – It was difficult to distinguish between deaths occurring between 16 and 20 August and in the following week. Thus, for instance, between 22 and 29 August when sporadic murders were continuing, about twenty dead bodies in various stages of decomposition were recovered from the streets. From the morgue 100 bodies, from the streets 20, and from other places 12 bodies were recovered in this period. – File 398/46, p. 8 (West Bengal State Archives, hereafter WBSA). Decomposed bodies also meant that the figures of Hindu deaths and Muslim deaths may not be correct. One note in the police file spoke of asking the Hindu Satkar Samity of re-checking whether the bodies cremated by it were those of Hindus in view of the high state of decomposition. – Government of Bengal (hereafter GoB), *Home Political*, File 398/46, Appendix A (WBSA). We also do not have any comprehensive account of displacement, relief and rehabilitation. In many cases Hindu and Muslim charity organizations besides the Hindu Mahasabha, Congress and the Muslim League ran their own efforts to help the distressed. On the displaced, we have this particular news item –

> The total number of destitute in Government centres in Calcutta was during the last week of November 13, 800, of whom 5000 were refugees from Bihar. In addition about 1,500 refugees had passed through Government camps to their destinations in Calcutta and elsewhere. This information was given by Sir Walter Garner, Relief Commissioner, Bengal. Sir Walter said that the relief Department was anticipating increased pressure on its organization in Calcutta during the next few weeks, partly as a result of the influx of refugees from Bihar and partly on account of general economic conditions. The Bengal Government had made no representations to the refugees arriving from that province.

CMG, Vol. XLV, No. 1–2, 30 November–7 December 1946 (pp. 5–6). In its issue of Vol. XLV, No. 4 (21 December 1946, p. 78), it reported on the rehabilitation situation and the works by the then Bengal government regarding rehabilitation of the displaced citizens of city due to riots. The government also put 'emphasis on rehabilitation of the displaced citizens from the *bustee*s in their previous homes.' Bihari refugees were accommodated in the Talah Park previously occupied by the military – CMG Vol. XLV, No. 18–21, 26 April 1947, p. 407.

3 CMG, Vol. XLV, No. 13–14, 1–8 May 1947; it also reported expenditure of another one crore of rupees on relief and rehabilitation of the displaced including those from Bihar; one lakh rupees for repair of *dargahs and imambaras*.

4 Some of the accounts are Debjani Sengupta, "A City Feeding on Itself: Testimonies and Histories of 'Direct Action' Day", in *Sarai Reader* (New Delhi, 2006), pp. 288–295, http://archive.sarai.net/files/original/2 ed2f960de6596b5ed75501e6de2c774.pdf (accessed on 2 March 2016); "Calcutta Riot (1946)"; the entry in Banglapedia (Dhaka: Asiatic Society of Bangladesh, 2000); D. Chaim Kaufmann, "When All Else Fails: Ethnic Population Transfers and Partitions in the Twentieth Century",

International Security, 23 (2), Autumn 1998, pp. 120–156; Francis Tuker, *While Memory Serves* (London: Cassell & Co, 1950); Suranjan Das, *Communal Riots in Bengal, 1905–1947* (New Delhi: Oxford University Press, 1991); Jaya Chatterji, *Bengal Divided: Hindu Communalism and Partition, 1932–1947* (Cambridge: Cambridge University Press, 1995); Rakesh Batabyal, *Communalism in Bengal: From Famine to Noakhali, 1943–47* (New Delhi: Sage Publishers, 2005); also for a perspective, Pradip Kumar Dutta, *Carving Blocs – Communal Ideology in Early Twentieth Century Bengal* (New Delhi: Oxford University Press, 1999), Chapter 5, "War over Music: Meaning and Implications of the Riots of the 1920s and 1930s", pp. 238–296; Sandip Bandopadhyay, *Itihaser Dike Phire: Chechalissher Danga* (Kolkata: Utsa Manush, 1992); Janam Mukherjee, *Hungry Bengal: War, Famine, Riots and the End of Empire* (New Delhi: Harper Collins Publishers India, 2015).

5 Only one study by Ghanshyam Shah, "The 1969 Communal Riots in Ahmedabad: A Case Study" of a dozen studies included in the well-known volume by Asghar Ali Engineer (ed.), *Communal Riots in Post-Independence India* (Hyderabad: Sangam Books, 1984), pp. 175–208, takes the question of territory into account. Otherwise in most studies of riots, city as an agglomerate of contested territories is absent. See also, Jayati Chaturvedi and Gyaneswar Chaturvedi, "Communal Violence, Riots, and Public Space in Ayodhya and Agra City: 1990 and 1992", in Paul Brass (ed.), *Riots and Pogroms* (London: MacMillan, 1996), pp. 177–200.

6 Sato Tsugitaka, *Muslim Societies: Historical and Comparative Aspects* (London: Routledge, 2000), p. 112.

7 On this, see H.V. Hodson, *Great Divide: Britain, India, Pakistan* (New Delhi: Oxford University Press, 1997).

8 *Modern Review* noted 'the complete immunity that the Europeans, Anglo-Indians, and excepting a few rare cases, even the Indian Christians enjoyed during the riots' in its report on the killings – September 1946, Volume LXXX, No. 3, p. 172.

9 Donald L. Horowitz, "Direct, Displaced, and Cumulative Ethnic Aggression", *Comparative Politics,* 6 (1), October 1973, pp. 1–16.

10 On the Bichalighat incident, File 398/46, Appendix A (WBSA); on the Metiaburz incident detailed references are in the text.

11 GoB, *Home Political,* File 398/46, Appendix A (WBSA).

12 I have condensed here the findings from newspaper, police and intelligence reports, affidavits, various eye witness accounts, books and submissions to inquiring agencies and commission. For the most gruesome details, see Janam Mukherjee, *Hungry Bengal: War, Famine, Riots and the End of Empire* and Batabyal, *Communalism in Bengal.*

13 "Extracts from a Military Report on the Calcutta Riots", 24 August 1946 (WO 216/662) http://www.nationalarchives.gov.uk/education/topics/calcutta-riots.htm (accessed on 30 April 2014).

14 Ibid.

15 Sister Teresa, "Teacher at Loreto School, Kolkata, August 1946", in Anne Sebba (ed.), *Mother Teresa 1910–1997 Beyond the Image* (London: Orion, 1998).

16 Margaret Bourke-White, "Calcutta 1946", in Bourke-White (ed.), *Interview with India* (London: The Travel Book Club,1951), pp. 27–28.

17 Claude Markovits, "The Calcutta Riots of 1946, Online Encyclopedia of Mass Violence", published on 5 November 2007, http://www.massviolence.org/The-Calcutta-Riots-of-1946 (accessed 29 April 2014).
18 Ibid.
19 Batabyal, *Communalism in Bengal*, p. 239; there is no authenticated data of the number of workers killed there. The numbers range from 400 to 600.
20 P.S. Mathur, "The Great Calcutta Killing", *The Illustrated Weekly of India*, 19 August 1973, pp. 45–47, p. 47.
21 All three accounts are justifiably well known. See Suranjan Das, *Communal Riots in Bengal 1905–1947*; Chatterji, *Bengal Divided*; Tuker, *While Memory Serves*.
22 *Calcutta Disturbances Commission of Enquiry, Records of Proceedings, Minutes of Evidence* (hereafter *CDCE* here and in the text), Volumes I–XIII, Printed by the Superintendent of Printing, Government of Bengal, under the authority of the Calcutta Disturbances Commission of Enquiry, 1946–47 (in-text citations will mention volume, page and where necessary question number); files on reports of violence, police actions and other actions taken by various departments, such as disposal of dead bodies, requisition of forces, internal notes by the Home Department, intelligence inputs and so on, are in West Bengal State Archives, *Home Political*,Confidential File no 351/46, Part B; also in WBSA, "Reports on the Hindu-Muslim Conflict in Calcutta on Direct Action Day", GOB, *Home Political* File 398/46 GOB, and File 390/46 GOB; "Diary of Events of Eastern Command Intelligence Centre from 16th [sic] August to 20th [sic] August" (some of these entered as affidavits for the perusal of the *CDCE*; also some newspaper, magazine and Gazette reports to the extent they throw light on police conduct.
23 *CDCE*, see volume I.
24 Technically, the Commission was adjourned *sine die*. M. N. Ghose on behalf of the government submitted that 'in view of the great changes coming in the country and the constitution thereof and the circumstances under which this application for adjournment is made, I think that your Lordships will be pleased to adjourn it *sine die*'. The president of the Commission said that while the order to close down could come only from the government, 'we make the order now to adjourn the Commission *sine die*'. *CDCE*, volume XI, pp. 244–245.
25 The two manifestos reprinted as Appendix 1 and Appendix 2 to Batabyal, *Communalism in Bengal*, pp. 232–236; see for reference to the manifesto (in pamphlet form issued by Muhammad Usman, a school teacher and secretary, Muslim League, Calcutta District Committee, and mayor of Kolkata in August 1946) and discussion on it, *Modern Review* (printed at Eastern Printers, Kolkata), Volume XXX, No. 3, "Notes", pp. 170–174; for Hindu Mahasabha response, see also "Short Report of Hindu Mahasabha Relief Activities during 'Calcutta Killings' and 'Noakhali Carnage' ", published on behalf of Noakhali Rescue, Relief, and Rehabilitation Committee by K. N. Dalal, Ranjkan Publishing House, Calcutta, n.d. The report speaks in details of the relief camps in the city, p. 2; what is remarkable in these Muslim League and Hindu Mahasabha tracts is the comparatively soft or patient tone. But violence continued in spasms to flare up again and this time severely in Noakhali. Usman, a school

teacher and the Muslim League leader, later met Gandhi in Kolkata next year on 9–10 August to persuade him to stay on in Kolkata to bring peace and save the Muslims from Hindus 'who wanted to even with Muslims', even if for few days. See Pyarelal, *Mahatma Gandhi: The Last Phase*, Volume 2 (Ahmedabad: Navajiban Publishing House, 1965), pp. 363–364; Master Tara Singh, the famous Sikh leader, also invoked the theme of religious war. Penderel Moon, *Divide and Quit* (London: Chatto and Windus, 1961); p. 77; see also Sheikh Muhammad Ikram, *The Indian Muslims and Partition of India* (New Delhi: Atlantic Publishers, 1992), pp. 423–425.

26 In fact the police commissioner was so defensive that he said, 'I presume it is not Government's desire that I should include in my defence response to against every possible allegation in any statement I prepare.' GoB, *Home Political*, File 390/46, p. 1 (WBSA).

27 Rakesh Batabyal's well-researched account of the riots mentions statements of colonial police and high administrative officials in the hour of crisis disclaiming any responsibility to intervene or take any pro-active step to stop riot or help the needy in need of urgent assistance – See *Communalism in Bengal*, p. 253.

28 Besides, by an order a government memo of 1945 (802/28) Bengal district magistrates and the Calcutta police commissioner were empowered to directly call for military assistance in situations of emergency and report the fact to the government immediately. – GoB, Home Political, Calcutta 2 August 1945, West Bengal State Archives, Kolkata.

29 Max-Jean Zins, "The 1947 Vivisection of India: The Political Usage of a Carnage in the Era of Citizen-Massacres", in M. Hasan and N. Nakazato (eds.), The Unfinished Agenda : Nation-Building in South Asia (New Delhi: Manohar Publishers, 2001), Chapter 2, pp. 49–77.

30 See, for instance, *CDCE*, see volume VII, depositions by N. K. Roy Chowdury, officer in-charge, Shyampukur Police Station, and S. Ahmed, officer in-charge, Jorabagan Police Station – p. 217, q. 1142.

31 For instance, Gopal Das Khosla, *Stern Reckoning: A Survey of the Events Leading Up to and Following the Partition of India* (1950, reprint, Delhi: Oxford University Press, 1990), p. 63.

32 Logistics were important precisely to address border situations. Police officer Shakurul Hosain admitted in reply to a question that ideally if he had the forces he 'would have placed a picket at the crossing of the Garpar Road and Bipradas Street' (where on festive occasions there were usually pickets placed) and the 'crossing of Raja Rajnarain Street and Raja Dinendra Street is an important point where two communities meet . . . the Sahebbagan *bustee* verges on the Hindu locality there' *CDCE*, volume IX, p. 150, q. 128–130; additional police forces were requisitioned from the districts (3 inspectors, 2 sub-inspectors, 25 head constables and 212 constables, plus military forces also arrived to guard vital installation) and received on logistical grounds between 18 and 26 August – GoB, *Home Political*, File 398/46, Appendix B (WBSA).

33 *CMG*, Volume XLV, No. 1–2, 30 November–7 December 1946, pp. 5–6; in the same issue it further reported,

> The last day of the Moharrum in Calcutta-Thursday, the 5th December was marked by trouble, resulting in 7 persons being killed and 80 injured. The incidents occurred when the Moharrum processions were proceeding

to their destination and were making their return journey along a scheduled route in East Calcutta. The police and the military opened fire on three or four occasions to bring the situation under control. The police also made lathi charges several times. Among the casualties removed to different city hospitals as a result of the afternoon incidents, there were about 20 gunshot and nearly a dozen stab-injury cases. The rest were lathi and brick bat injury cases and also some acid injury cases.

It again (Vol. XLV, No. 18–21, and 19, 26 April 1947, pp. 408–416) reported fresh flare up of communal troubles in the city on 26 March, 1947. The situation remained unchanged till 1 April, when the military was called out to control the worst-affected areas, such as those under the Manicktalla, Beliaghata, Entally and Chitpore police stations. Since 2 April, the situation gradually improved, the number of incidents steadily decreasing. Again on 10 April, the situation was very tense. Besides the general night curfew, some additional curfew running to even thirty-two hours were imposed in various affected areas. An incident of police excess happened in Central Calcutta on the night of 14th April. The police were alleged to have molested a number of women in a residential house and to have raped a married lady. This incident caused some stir in the city and the situation, which had somewhat improved, again deteriorated. The government of Bengal warned the newspaper editors reminding them that the press laws also governed the publication of court proceedings. Pre-censorship of news and comments regarding police activities were introduced. On 20 April the situation worsened in the Kidderpore area and the spread of riot was marked. The day 23 April was declared a 'hartal' day by the Provincial Hindu Mahasabha president and other prominent citizens. The Hindu Mahasabha and the Bengal Provincial Congress Committee urged disbandment of the Punjabi police and dissolution of the communal ministry. Tension in the city continued to exist and special curfew orders for various lengths of time were imposed on different localities. The hartal on 23 April practically paralysed the city's civic and business life.

34 W.W. Hunter, *The Indian Musalmans* (Reprint, New Delhi: Rupa, 2002); original title, *Our Indian Mussulmans: Are They Bound in Conscience to Rebel against the Queen?*

35 Vinay Lal, "Agrarian Unrest: The Deccan Riots of 1975" http://www.sscnet.ucla.edu/southasia/British/Deccan_riots.html (accessed on 16 April 2014); see on Deccan Riots also, Neil Charlesworth, "The Myth of the Deccan Riots of 1875", *Modern Asian Studies*, 6 (4), 1972, pp. 402–409.

36 On this see, for instance, the study by William Gould on UP, *Hindu Nationalism and the Language of Politics in Late Colonial India* (Cambridge: Cambridge University Press, 2004); on Bengal see besides the works mentioned before Patricia A. Gossman, *Riots and Victims – Construction of Communal Identity among Bengali Muslims, 1905–1947* (Boulder, CO: Westview Press, 1999).

37 On the continuity, see the collection of essays, Ashgar Ali Engineer (ed.), *Communal Riots in Post-Independence India* (Hyderabad: Orient Longman, 1984).

38 The spirit of direct action overwhelmed even long groomed class unity and party loyalty. For some of the details, see Sunanda Sanyal and Soumya Basu, *The Sickle and the Crescent – Communists, Muslim League and India's Partition* (Kolkata: Frontpage, 2011), pp. 115–152; the discussion also includes references to Communist Party union leaders and activists getting involved in communal killings, as in Metiaburz. In a sense *direct action* had a chequered afterlife, for instance, in East Pakistan when Sheikh Mujib gave the call for direct action against the Pakistani military-administrative regime. Decades later in the Shahbag movement in Dhaka the spirit of direct action re-surfaced. One can even say that Gandhi's call for Quit India reflected the same spirit.

39 The argument of logistics cut both ways in those days. While the mob was described as a mobile phenomenon by many police officers, lack of logistical preparation on the part of the police was cited by several other police officers as an important cause of police weakness. For instance, Chief Minster Suhrawardy blamed the new police operation arrangement introduced in the morning of 16 August as the main reason of police weakness. – GOB, *Home Political*, File no 390/46 (WBSA).

40 See note 43, which is important to understand the closure the Commission faced in its inquiry.

41 In the midst of the deposition by S. N. Routh, the officer in-charge of the Jorasanko P.S. on what happened in the area under his jurisdiction, the president of the Commission observed, 'It is an extra-ordinary position that in spite of precautions large crowd were able to gather on the streets during the night of the 17th–18th'. Bashiruddin, one of the counsels, joined in the observation by saying, 'My Lord, it was perhaps due to the fact that the area was so wide and the streets so numerous.' *CDCE*: XI, p. 218, q. 1929.

42 The *CDCE* papers speak in abundant details of how riots began with looting of shops, which had defied the call. Also see on Howrah, GoB, *Home Political*, WBSA, File 398/46; they give light on the role of the outsiders (Howrah Railway Jurisdiction's Report and Measures taken to Meet the Situation – File 398/46, pp. 5–6); they also amply demonstrate the war logic of preparation and counter-preparation, for instance, by relatives and acquaintances of slaughtered boatmen, *WBSA*, ibid. However, we have to keep in mind that protecting European property in the central business district stretching up to Bhawanipore was the first task of the police. There are some reports also of participation by the police in looting.

43 In the first week, ninety-five rounds were fired by the police on twenty-two occasions – GoB, *Home Political*, File 398/46, Appendix C (WBSA). Apart from continuing for four months night curfew over stretches of the city territory, the police also resorted to imposing collective fines.

The Commissioner of Police on the 26th November last imposed further collective fines on inhabitants of certain localities in the city of Calcutta by Notifications no. 176–189 (dated November 19–20). A total sum of Rs 22,000 was imposed on inhabitants of 13 areas of the city. Hindu inhabitants of four areas were to pay Rs. 7000. Muslim inhabitants of 8 areas were to pay Rs.13500 and both the communities of one area were to pay Rs. 1000. The proprietor of a hotel was required to pay Rs. 500. The Commissioner of Police on the 30th November imposed further collective fines of Rs. 12000 on the inhabitants of seven localities of Calcutta by notification Nos. 192 to 196 (dated Nov. 23). On the seven localities mentioned above, Hindu inhabitants of three areas were to pay Rs. 4000 and Muslim inhabitants of four areas were to pay Rs. 8000.

The Calcutta Municipal Gazette, Volume XLV, No. 1–2, 30 November–7 December 1946, pp. 5–6; the Gazette further reported,

> The Government of Bengal have demanded security deposits from the Morning News and Star of India, and banned circulation in the province of International edition of the American magazine, Life, dated the 30th September last for containing prejudicial matters. On the 28th Nov. last, a pedestrian who was ignoring the curfew, was fired upon by a picket and wounded in the left leg. The incident occurred in a south western suburb. In another case, the victim was injured in central Calcutta. . . . The CP announced the imposition of further collective fines, amounting Rs 9000, on the inhabitants of 7 localities in the city.

44 The main seven points were: (a) the police did not interfere actively when the crimes were being committed as proved by the fact that it suffered no casualty; (b) the police took part in arson and killing; (c) the police took no action to secure control over processions; (d) they did not set up any armed pickets in advance; (e) the police showed communal discrimination; (f) they did not respond to calls for help; and (g) they did not commit themselves fully. As we have seen the probing by the counsels was along these lines, and how their inquiries met dead end. Part of the failure of the examination was in the nature of the allegations which the police found ways to defend themselves against. The broad points were – (a) very few police not responding to calls for help could be indentified; (b) opening fire in all cases while facing the crowds would have been risky; (c) in view of the earlier political agitations in the city and allegations of high handedness of the police, it had been asked to exercise restraint; (d) charges of communal partisanship were difficult to investigate as that would have required a special force consisting of non-Hindu and non-Muslim personnel; (e) with limited personnel the police had to authenticate the genuineness of the distress call before rushing to aid; (f) where evidence of police participation in looting and arson were found (four in number), disciplinary action had been taken; and (g) the police suffered few casualties and not no casualty. Note from the Home Department, GOB, *Home Political* File 390/46 (WBSA).

45 Suranjan Das in *Communal Riots in Bengal, 1905–1947* has commented,

> Much of the subsequent (to the Riot) elite political discourse centred round the question: who should bear the initial responsibility for the riots? The Congress and the Hindu Mahasabha put the entire blame on the League: by declaring a public holiday on 16 August the League Ministry gave a "license" to its supporters to commit violence on Hindus. . . . On the other hand the Muslim League argued that the Congress started the trouble in order to create a situation which would force the dismissal of the League government and imposition of Governor's

rule. . . . The fact that Muslims lost more lives than Hindus during the riots was used to counter the charge that the League had deliberately organized the riot. (p. 186)

Das also remarked, 'It is difficult to judge whether the British officials deliberately refrained from doing much to prevent the outbreak' (p. 187).

46 I have given some instances of the way the counsels and the Commission members approached the depositions by the police and military officials; the *Minutes of Evidence* of the Enquiry has several such instances (for instance, questions put by Fazl Ali to police officer D. N. Mullick on the number of houses in a *bustee* in Gope Lane set on fire; by S. A. Masud to Mullick on the fire in Bengal Pottery Factory – CDCE: X, pp. 95 and 107).

47 As various notes given earlier suggest, the riots continued almost right up to 15 August 1947 when Gandhi sat on fast in Kolkata to bring back peace.

48 In the eyes of the administrators and the governing class, it was all a matter of utter lawlessness, 'unbridled savagery with homicidal maniacs let loose' (Tuker, *While Memory Serves*, p. 160), and thus would have to be ruthlessly suppressed because it was essentially a question of law and order. The major English language newspaper in Calcutta at that time *The Statesman* avoided the word 'war', but used 'fury', and commented in its second editorial, 'This is not a riot. It needs a word found in mediaeval history, a fury. Yet "fury" sounds spontaneous, and there must have been some deliberation and organization to set this fury on its way.' 20 August 1946.

49 On this, see Michel Foucault's observations on the history of some of the functions of the police in his College de France lectures (1977–78), *Security, Territory, Population*, trans. Graham Burchell (Kampshire, Basingstoke: Palgrave MacMillan, 2007), pp. 333–358.

50 Actually, immediately after the riots, step was taken to set up emergency jails. – GOB, *Home Political*, File 398/46, p. 7 (WBSA).

51 On a commentary of the West Bengal Police Act, see http://www.human rightsinitiative.org/programs/aj/police/india/acts/critiques/chri's_legislative_analysis_of_west_bengal_police_draft_act.pdf (accessed on 2 June 2014); on the public relations exercise, a plan had been prepared before the riots by the Publicity Department of the Calcutta Police in consultation with Home and Health Departments of the Government to be ready for operation during an emergency, which meant in this case breakdown of the essential services of the Calcutta Corporation for which leaflets relating to public health were kept ready for distribution. So when the communal disturbances broke out on 16 August the Publicity Department was caught unprepared and the publicity material proved irrelevant. – GOB, *Home Political*, File no 451/46, Part B 10 (WBSA).

52 Janam Mukherjee comments at the end of *Hungry Bengal*, 'War masks individuality. The counting of bodies becomes monotonous' (p. 261); numerous commentators also note the spectre of dead bodies in middle-class memory of the infamous famine of 1942–43 and the Calcutta Killings.

53 Michel Foucault, *Society Must Be Defended, Lectures at the College de France, 1975–76*, trans. David Macey (New York: Picador, 2003), p. 51.

9 Two constitutional tasks
Setting up a state and a government

Constitution-making, state-making, government-making

In the wake of the breakdown of the colonial administration and law and order machinery in the forties of the past century, it is not surprising that the Indian governing class used the period of constitution-making (1946–50) to establish a state that could also govern the country firmly. Many factors and trends converged in the making of this dual assignment. These factors and trends came out most clearly in the constituent assembly proceedings. Also the fact that the same body had dual function, as it acted in that period both as an interim law-making body and a constituent assembly (CA) helped to combine the two tasks – setting up the post-colonial state and the government. The interim government cemented these two tasks. Therefore, it will be instructive to view certain sections of the constituent assembly proceedings in that light – as the facilitating site of the two tasks. After all thanks to jurists and commentators we are now used to treating the proceedings primarily as the birth site of glorious developments such as liberty, equality, federalism and independent judiciary.

Though Carl Schmitt had famously remarked that the sovereign is the one who can decide exceptions, modern political societies are born on the basis of two principles, sovereignty and democracy, and these two principles are in general – at the same time and by turn – inseparable and in contradiction with each other. For democracy to be effective, it must create a system of law, which will create the power of the demos, stronger than any other power, and therefore stronger than any other force. Yet, in the constitution of this power, this force, *immunity* must function as the building principle, because the saliency of this power must be recognized in the beginning, in silence, in total conformity and in an unconditional manner. Therefore, there can be endless quarrel in the theory of law and endless political rhetoric around this question, but at the moment of its demonstration sovereignty is not concerned about claim and legitimacy, but it is pure at the moment proper to it, its force showing its character in the decision to take and make exception to any rule that had constituted it in the first place. Dhananjay Chatterji, a prisoner given death penalty thirteen years earlier, was executed in 2004. When there were endless debates, petitions, legal arguments against death penalty and for the right to life guaranteed Article 21, and appeals that the person be given mercy, the state was silent. When the given hour arrived, it simply executed the man. In its moment of demonstration sovereignty is therefore pure. That is why people say that sovereignty cannot be represented in the sense in which in the eighteenth century a king could send some other *body* to represent him (his body) in another court; there could be *agents*, but the sovereign was not representable. In even the most democratic law-making there is thus a silent consensus required to be present at the beginning, that the production of this power must be immune from any exception; if at all there is to be any exception, it is the sovereign who will decide exception. Constitution-making to be successful therefore claims immunity – immunity from democracy and any particular or individual legality – and it is only through this process that the union of democracy and sovereignty is achieved.

In the historical and temporal thickness of democratic law-making in India from 1946 to 1949, the grounds were those of necessity and compulsion on the basis of which claims about immunity of the power being built were made. The member who represented this juridical logic more than any other was Dr Babasaheb Ambedkar. It was a symbolic situation. The man who had opposed any nationalist hegemony during the colonial days, and had used legal arguments to defend group representation in democratic politics, now defended the principles of republicanism, centralism, exceptionality and juridical absoluteness to characterize the power that was there in a *constituent* form, and now being given a constitutional shape that is to say a constituted shape. He was the chair of the Drafting Committee, he piloted the difficult proposals and he decided when to stop deliberations and ruthlessly bring out the support and strength that would carry the controversial proposals through. What is then intrinsic to the process that builds the legal existence of sovereignty? Can democracy ever come to terms with this experience? Or is this the experience with which democracy becomes operational at least at the level of juridical-political reality – the reality of legalities? It will be instructive to study at least some of the occasions when Ambedkar was engaged in building the discourse of a 'sovereign democratic power' that would mark independent India, now free from colonial rule.

In this constituted form, sovereignty would represent democracy. Parliament and other organs would 'represent sovereignty' to the extent that was possible. Sovereignty would decide exceptions, indications of which were to be given in the constitution; and at the end of the whole process the constituted power would accrue more force than the constituent power, because it was now constitutional. None more than Ambedkar, who had at another level been an ardent advocate of rights and dignity of the *Dalits*, understood the centrality of the role of constitution in attaining the union of democracy and sovereignty and giving birth to an awesome power, called the sovereign state of India. Probably there was a connection between the two levels – that of rights and that of sovereignty, because what was at stake was the legal constitution of a democratic sovereign power – a process that must be immune from any temporary consideration in producing legalities of a political society – these legalities including rights, rule of law and legal separation of powers. Again no one other than Ambedkar understood the nature of this double requirement of immunity, of the process (of constituting the sovereign) and the product (the constituted sovereign).

What we are attempting do here is a difficult task for a reader not familiar with the details of constitution-making in India, particularly the intense socio-political strains of quarrel, rivalry, battle and war of words that had beneath them the social wars going on in the country at the time of transition. In some of the exchange of words we reproduce here the reader can see that the Dalit leader is scoffing at the pretensions of the upper-caste representatives in law-making. Law-making, Ambedkar seems to say, is secular and free of all social pretensions. Sometimes he appears to be waging his last battle against feudal remnants through the process of erecting a sovereign secular democratic and republican force pitted against upper-caste, particularistic politics. The mode was one of constructing a universal power, whose other name is sovereignty. This was the dream of the constitutional forces, namely, that the universal power of sovereign would exercise itself in defence of democracy against feudal and casteist obstacles. This is how democracy contributes to the making of sovereign power. The reader has to follow closely the exchange of words in the constituent assembly, extracted here. The extracts are at times lengthy. But it will be good to listen to them to follow the argument of this chapter.

Yet the question will remain whether the logic of sovereign power to acquire strong governmental power can overwhelm the disparate aspirations of dignity, justice and rights – yes, rights that call in the first place for a legally constituted sovereign power as their guarantee.

First stake: erecting juridical authority of the state

Let us follow the exchange of words Ambedkar had with T. T. Krishna-machari on 15 November 1948 in course of a discussion on Article 10 of the constitution.

> A: . . . Observations. . . . I shall make in the course of my speech will be confined to the question of residence about which there has been so much debate and the use of the word 'back-ward' in clause (3) of article 10. My friend Mr. T. T. Krishna-machari has twitted the Drafting Committee that the Drafting Committee, probably in the interests of some members of that Committee, instead of producing a Constitution, have pro-duced a paradise for lawyers. I am not prepared to say that this Constitution will not give rise to questions, which will involve legal interpretation or judicial interpretation. In fact, I would like to ask Mr. Krishnamachari if he can point out to me any instance of any Constitution in the world which has not been a paradise for lawyers. I would particularly ask him to refer to the vast storehouse of law reports with regard to the Constitution of the United States, Canada and other coun-tries. I am therefore not ashamed at all if this Constitution hereafter for purposes of interpretation is required to be taken to the Federal Court. That is the fate of every Constitution and every Drafting Committee. . . .

I shall explain the purpose of this amendment. It is the feeling of many persons in this House that, since we have established a common citizenship throughout India, irrespective of the local jurisdiction of the provinces and the Indian States, it is only a con-comitant thing that residence should not be required for holding a particular post in a particular State because, in so far as you make residence a qualification, you are really subtracting from the value of a common citizenship which we have established by this Con-stitution or which we propose to establish by this Constitution. Therefore in my judgement, the argument that residence should not be a qualification to hold appointments under the State is a perfectly valid and a perfectly sound argument. At the same time, it must be realised that you cannot allow people who are flying from one province to another, from one State to another as mere birds of passage without any roots, without any connection with that particular province, just to come, apply for posts and, so to say, take the plums and walk away. Therefore, some limitation is necessary. It was found, when this matter was investigated, that already today in very many provinces rules have been framed by the provincial governments prescribing a certain period of residence as a qualification for a post in that particular province. Therefore the proposal in the amendment that, although as a general rule residence should not be a qualification, yet some exception might be made, is not quite out of the ordinary. . . . That is the underlying purpose of this amendment putting down residence as a qualification. . . .

Now, Sir, to come to the other question which has been agitating the members of this House, *viz.*, the use of the word 'backward' in clause (3) of article 10. I should like to begin by making some general observations so that members might be in a position to understand the exact import, the significance and the necessity for using the word 'backward' in this particular clause. If members were to try and exchange their views on this subject, they will find that there are three points of view which it is necessary for us to reconcile if we are to produce a workable proposition which will be accepted by all. Of the three points of view, the first is that there shall be equality of opportunity for all citizens. It is the desire of many Members of this House that every individual who is qualified for a particular post should be free to apply for that post, to sit for examinations and to have his qualifications tested so as to determine whether he is fit for the post or not and that there ought to be no limitations, there ought to be no hindrance in the operation of this principle of equality of opportunity. Another view mostly shared by a section of the House is that, if this principle is to be operative . . . there ought to be no reservation of any sort for any class or community at all, that all citizens, if they are qualified, should be placed on the same footing of equality so far as the public services are concerned. That is the second point of view. . . .

Then we have quite a massive opinion, which insists that, although theoretically it is good to have the principle that, there shall be equality of opportunity, there must at the same time be a provision made for the entry of certain communities which have so far been outside the administration. As I said, the Drafting Committee had to produce a formula which would reconcile these three points of view, firstly, that there shall be equality of opportunity, secondly that there shall be reservations in favour of certain communities which have not so far had a 'proper took-in' so to say into the administration. If Honourable members will bear these facts in mind – the three principles we had to reconcile – they will see that no better formula could be produced than the one that is embodied in sub-clause (3) of article 10 of the Constitution; they will find that the view of those who believe and hold that there shall be equality of opportunity, has been embodied in sub-clause (1) of Article 10. It is a generic principle. At the same time, as I said, we had to reconcile this formula with the demand made by certain communities that the administration which has now – for historical reasons – been controlled by one community or a few communities, that situation should disappear and that the others also must have an opportunity of getting into the public services. Supposing, for instance, we were to concede in full the demand of those communities who have not been so far employed in the public services to the fullest extent, what would really happen is, we shall be completely destroying the first proposition upon which we are all agreed, namely, that there shall be an equality of opportunity. Let me give an illustration. Supposing, for instance, reservations were made for a community or a collection of communities, the total of which came to something like 70 per cent of the total posts under the State and only 30 per cent are retained as the unreserved. Could anybody say that the reservation of 30 per cent as open to general competition would be satisfactory from the point of view of giving effect to the first principle, namely, that there shall be equality of opportunity? It cannot be in my judgement. Therefore the seats to be reserved, if the reservation is to be consistent with sub-clause (1) of Article 10, must be confined to a minority of seats. It is then only that the first principle could find its place in the Constitution and effective in operation. If Honourable Members understand this position that we have to safeguard two things, namely, the principle of equality of opportunity and at the same time satisfy the demand of communities which have not had so far representation in the State, then, I am sure they will agree that unless you use some such qualifying phrase as 'backward' the exception made in favour of reservation will ultimately eat up the rule altogether . . . I think this is sufficient to justify why the word 'backward' has been used.

With regard to the minorities, there is a special reference to that in Article 296, where it has been laid down that some provision will be made with regard to the minorities. Of course, we did not lay down any proportion. That is quite clear from the section itself, but we have not altogether omitted the minorities from consideration. Somebody asked me: 'What is a backward community'? Well, I think anyone who reads the language of the draft itself will find that we have left it to be determined by each local Government. A backward community is a community, which is backward in the opinion of the Government. . . . If the local Government included in this category of reservations such a large number of seats; I think one could very well go to the Federal Court and the Supreme Court and say that the reservation is of such a magnitude that the rule regarding equality of opportunity has been destroyed and the court will then come to the conclusion whether the local Government or the State Government has acted in a reasonable and prudent manner. . . . The words 'reasonable persons and prudent persons' have been used in very many laws and if he will refer only *to* the Transfer of Property Act, he will find that in very many cases the words 'a reasonable person and a prudent person' have very well been defined and the court will not find any difficulty in defining it. I hope, therefore that the amendments I have accepted will be accepted by the House.[1]

The jurist here is not playing with words. He is laying down the juridical authority of the state, no matter if in the process lawyers, litigants, courts and legal commentators have a field day in the future of nation's life. Who should have the power to decide as to who belonged to the backward community? How should the principle of equality be enforced? What legal meaning should be obtained from the principle of equality? The matter of reservation or positive discrimination as we know raised a storm in the public, legal and intellectual sphere of the country since the publication of the Mandal Commission Report and the then government's decision at the Centre to implement it (1990). In that context one has to see how one of the most famous principles of governing India was decided while the constitution was being drafted. It had enormous significance for the theme of rights, for standard of rule and for the necessity of a public power to be impartial. And not only that, here the jurist was saying to members, think of the legal tradition (of USA or India), it is on that basis that the juridical authority of the sovereign power would be built. This power would be attentive to inequalities and would take governmental steps to correct them; it would not allow footloose highflying members of the Indian affluent class to seek jobs everywhere; it would combine the contradictory pulls of domicile, nationality and national citizenship in the economic life. Only by satisfying the imperatives of governmentality does the sovereign become the sovereign. Ambedkar was here not only seeing much earlier than Michel Foucault the truth of the relation between sovereign power and the governmental existence of that power; he was probably more realistic.² To legitimize the inherent force of this public power, called sovereignty, this sovereign power must know how to govern, must have the rules and by-rules of governing accepted by the political society and in short must learn how to appear and behave as a public political power not susceptible to any cold weather and knowledgeable enough to act as the guardian of public interest. Sovereign power and governmental power are not at odds with each other; they pre-condition each other's life in the condition of modernity.

Yet, we must not forget that such a combination of sovereign and governmental power can be built only on legal continuities. A new sovereign may appear, old one may die, be replaced, overthrown and so on, but the rules for governing must be there. The sovereign cannot exist in a legal void. Therefore, legal continuities are vital, and none understood the theme of legal continuity better than Ambedkar. In another exchange of words, this time on Article 13, this is what he and Thakur Das Bhargava had to say against each other's position:

> Mahboob Ali Baig Sahib Bahdur: Anyhow I pose this question to the Chairman of the Drafting Committee whether in these circumstances, *viz.,* where there is in existence a provision in the Constitution itself empowering the legislature *or* the executive to pass an order or law abridging the rights mentioned in clause (1), the court can go into the merits or demerits of the order or law and declare a certain law invalid or a certain Act as not justified. In my view the court's jurisdiction is ousted by clearly mentioning in the Constitution itself that the State shall have the power to make laws relating to libel, association or assembly in the interest of public order, restrictions on the exercise of. . . .

> A: Sir, if I might interrupt my Honourable Friend, I have understood his point and I appreciate it and I undertake to reply and satisfy him as to what it means. It is therefore unnecessary for him to dilate further on the point.

> B: Similarly, at present you have the right to assemble peaceably and without arms and you have in 1947 passed a law under which even peaceable assemblage could be bombed without warning from the sky. We have today many provisions, which are against this peaceable assembling. Similarly in regard to ban on association or unions. . . .

A: Is it open to my Honourable friend to speak generally on the clauses?

VICE-PRESIDENT: That is what I am trying to draw his attention to.

A: This is an abuse of the procedure of the House. I cannot help saying that. When a member speaks on an amendment, he must confine himself to that amendment. He cannot avail himself of this opportunity of rambling over the entire field.

B: I am speaking on the amendment; but the manner in which Dr. Ambedkar speaks and expresses himself is extremely objectionable. Why should he get up and speak in a threatening mood or a domineering tone?

VICE-PRESIDENT: Everybody seems to have lost his temper except the Chair *(Laughter)*. I had given a warning to Mr. Bhargava and, just now, was about to repeat it when Dr. Ambedkar stood up. I am perfectly certain that he was carried away by his feeling. I do not see any reason why there should be so much feeling aroused. He has been under a strain for days together. I can well understand his position and I hope that the House will allow the matter to rest there. Now, I hope Mr. Bhargava realises the position.

A: From the speeches which have been made on article 13 and article 8 and the words 'existing law', which occur in some of the provisos to article 13, it seems to me that there is a good deal of misunderstanding about what is exactly intended to be done with regard to existing law. Now the fundamental article is article 8, which specifically, without any kind of reservation, says that any existing law, which is inconsistent with the Fundamental Rights as enacted in this part *of* the Constitution is void. That is a fundamental proposition and I have no doubt about it that any 'trained lawyer', if he was asked to interpret the words 'existing law' occurring in the sub-clauses to article 13, would read 'existing law' in so far as it is not inconsistent with the fundamental rights. There is no doubt that that is the way in which the phrase 'existing law' in the sub-clauses would be interpreted. It is unnecessary to repeat the proposition stated in article 8 every time the phrase 'existing law' occurs, because it is a rule of interpretation that for interpreting any law, all relevant sections shall be taken into account and read in such a way that one section is reconciled with another. Therefore the Drafting Committee felt that they have laid down in article 8 the full and complete proposition that any existing law, in so far as it is inconsistent with the Fundamental Rights, will stand abrogated. The Drafting Committee did not feel it necessary to incorporate some such qualification in using the phrase 'existing law' in the various clauses where these words occur. As I see, many people have not been able to read the clause in that way. In reading 'existing law', they seem to forget what has already been stated in article 8. In order to remove the misunderstanding that is likely to be caused in a layman's mind, I have brought forward this amendment to sub-clauses (3), (4), (5) and (6) I will read for illustration sub-clause (3) with my amendment.

'Nothing in sub-clause (b) of the said clause shall affect the operation of any existing law in so far as it imposes, or prevent the State from making any law, imposing in the interests of public order.'

I am accepting Mr. Bhargava's amendment and so I will add the word 'reasonable' also:

'Imposing in the interests of public order reasonable restrictions on the exercise of the right conferred by the said sub-clause.'

Now, the words 'in so far as it imposes' to my mind make the idea complete and free from any doubt that the existing law is saved only in so far as it imposes reasonable restrictions. I think with that amendment there ought to be no difficulty in understanding that the existing law is saved only to a limited extent, it is saved only if it is not in conflict with the Fundamental Rights. . . .

Now, my friend, Pandit Thakur Dass Bhargava entered into a great tirade against the Drafting Committee, accusing them of having gone out of their way to preserve existing laws. I do not know what he wants the Drafting Committee to do. Does he want us to say straightaway that all existing laws shall stand abrogated on the day on which the Constitution comes into existence?

B: Not exactly.

A: What we have said is that the existing law shall stand abrogated in so far as they are inconsistent with the provisions of this Constitution. Surely the administration of this country is dependent upon the continued existence of the laws, which are in force today. It would bring down the whole administration to pieces if the existing laws were completely and wholly abrogated.

Now, I take article 307. He said that we have made provisions that the existing laws should be continued unless amended. Now, I should have thought that a man who understands law ought to be able to realize this fact that after the Constitution comes into existence, the exclusive power of making law in this country belongs to Parliament or to the several local legislatures in their respective spheres. Obviously, if you enunciate the proposition that hereafter no law shall be in operation or shall have any force or sanction, unless it has been enacted by Parliament, what would be the position? The position would be that all the laws which have been made by the earlier legislature, by the Central Legislative Assembly or the Provincial Legislative Assembly would absolutely fall to pieces, because they would cease to have any sanction, not having been made by the parliament or by the local legislatures, which under this Constitution are the only body which are entitled to make law. It is, therefore, necessary that a provision should exist in the Constitution that any laws, which have been already made, shall not stand abrogated for the mere reason that they have not been made by Parliament. That is the reason why article 307 has been introduced into this Constitution. I, therefore, submit, Sir, that my amendment which particularises the portion of the existing law which shall continue in operation so far as the Fundamental Rights are concerned, meets the difficulty, which several Honourable Members have felt by reason of the fact that they find it difficult to read article 13 in conjunction with article 8. I, therefore, think that this amendment of mine clarifies the position and hope the House will not find it difficult to accept it.

[After this clarification several amendments were not moved.]

A: Sir I move – 'That in clause (4) of article 13, for the words "the general public" the words "public order or morality" be substituted.'

A: Mr. Vice-President, Sir, I move – 'That in clause (5) of article 13, for the word "aboriginal", the word "scheduled" be substituted.' When the Drafting Committee was dealing with the question of Fundamental Rights, the Committee appointed for the Tribal Areas had not made its Report, and consequently we had to use the word 'aboriginal' at the time when the Draft was made. Subsequently, we found that the Committee on Tribal Areas had used the phrase 'Scheduled Tribes' and we have used the words 'scheduled tribes' in the schedules, which accompany this Constitution. In order to keep the language uniform, it is necessary to substitute the word 'Scheduled' for the word 'aboriginal'.

All this happened in the clause-wise discussion on the draft constitution between 15 November 1948 and 8 January 1949. The drafting was by and large over; amendments were being taken care of; and appropriately ideas were now being considered – at times summarily as we shall see soon on the issue of the right to bear arms. Everywhere, or in every case, sovereign power was being defined and given shape to in terms of two principles as indicated in the preceding exchange of words – (a) the power to make exceptions and (b) the benefit of attaining legitimacy by way of deriving continuity from earlier laws.

On the first principle, that is the power to make exceptions, which Schmitt had claimed to be the feature of sovereign power, Ambedkar was categorical. He had this to say on one occasion:

A: . . . Sir, with regard to the argument that clause (4) should be deleted, I am afraid, if I may say so without any offence, that it is a very extravagant demand, a very tall order. There can be no doubt that while there are certain fundamental rights which the State must guarantee to the individual in order that the individual may have some security and freedom to develop his own personality, it is equally clear that in certain cases where, for instance, the State's very life is in jeopardy, those rights must be subject to a certain amount of limitation. Normal peaceful times are quite different from times of emergency. In times of emergency the life of the State itself is in jeopardy and if the State is not able to protect itself in times of emergency, the individual himself will be found to have lost his very existence. Consequently, *the superior right of the State to protect itself in times of emergency*, so that it may survive that emergency and live to discharge its functions in order that the individual under the aegis of the State may develop, must be guaranteed as safely as the right of an individual. I know of no Constitution which gave fundamental rights but which gives them in such a manner as to deprive the State in times of emergency to protect it by curtailing the rights of the individual. You take any Constitution you like, where fundamental rights are guaranteed; you will also find that provision is made for the State to suspend these in times of emergency. So far, therefore, as the amendment to delete clause (4) is concerned, it is a matter of principle and I am afraid I cannot agree with the Mover of that amendment and I must oppose it.

Now, Sir, I will go into details. My Friend Mr. Tajarnul Husain drew a very lurid picture by referring to various articles, which are included in the Chapter dealing with Fundamental Rights. He said, here is a right to take water, there is a right to enter a shop, is freedom to go to a bathing ghat. Now, if clause (4) came into operation, he suggested that all these elementary human rights which the Fundamental part guarantees – of permitting a man to go to a well to drink water, to walk on the road, to go to a cinema or a theatre, without any let or hindrance, will also disappear. I cannot understand from where my friend Mr. Tajarnul Husain got this idea. If he had referred to article 279 which relates to the power of the President to issue a proclamation of emergency, he would have found that clause (4) which permits suspension of these rights refers only to article 13 and to no other article. . . .

Taking up the point of Mr. Karimuddin, what he tries to do is to limit clause (4) to cases of rebellion or invasion. I thought that if he had carefully read article 275, there was really no practical difference between the provisions contained in article 275 and the amendment, which he has proposed. The power to issue a proclamation of emergency vested in the President by article 275 is confined only to cases when there is war or domestic violence.

SYED KARIMUDDIN: Even if war is only threatened?

A: Certainly. An emergency does not merely arise when war has taken place, the situation may very well be regarded as emergency when war is threatened. . . . I will now take up the amendments of my friend Mr. Kamath, No. 787 read with No. 34 in List III, and the amendment of my friend Mr. Sarwate, No. 783 as amended by No. 43. My friend Mr. Kamath suggested that it was not necessary to particularize, if I understood him correctly, the various writs as the article at present does and that the matter should be left quite open for the Supreme Court to evolve such remedies as it may think proper in the circumstances of the case. I do not think Mr. Kamath has read this article very carefully. If he had read the article carefully, he would have observed that what has been done in the draft is to give general power as well as to propose particular remedies. The language of the article is very clear. . . . Sir, there is one other observation which I would like to make. In the course of the debates that have taken place in this House both on the Directive Principles and on the Fundamental Rights I have listened to speeches made by many members complaining that we have not enunciated a certain right or a certain policy in our Fundamental Rights or in our Directive Principles. References have been made to the Constitution of Russia and to the Constitutions of other countries where such declarations, as members have sought to introduce by means of amendments, have found a place. Sir, I think I might say without meaning any offence to anybody who has made himself responsible for these amendments that I prefer the British method of dealing with rights. The British method is a peculiar method a very real and a very sound method. British jurisprudence insists that there can be no right unless the Constitution provides a remedy for it. It is the remedy, which makes a right real. If there is no remedy, there is no right at all, and I am therefore not prepared to burden the Constitution with a number of pious declarations which may sound as glittering generalities but for which the Constitution makes no provision by way of a remedy. It is much better to be limited in the scope of our rights and to make them real by enunciating remedies than to have a tot of piteous wishes embodied in the Constitution. I am very glad that this House has seen that the remedies that we have provided constitute a fundamental part of this Constitution. Sir, with these words I commend this article to the House. . . .

KAMATH: I am equally anxious. Mr. Vice-President, I am here seeking only a little light from Dr. Ambedkar with regard to his amendment No. 820 moved by him. I fail to see clearly why the words in the article as it stands at present should be substituted by the words he proposes to. In case his amendment is accepted, it will mean that Parliament shall have power only for prescribing punishment for the acts referred to in clause (b). Then what about the Parliament's power to make laws with respect to any of the matters which under this power are required to be provided for by legislation in clause (a) Does he intend by his amendment to take away the power which is sought to be conferred by clause (a) of this article? I want to know exactly what the import of his amendment is and why this clause (a) is sought to be amended in this fashion.

A: I am sorry, Mr. Kamath has not been able to understand the scheme which is embodied in article 27. This article embodies three principles. The first principle is that wherever this Constitution prescribes that a law shall be made for giving effect to any Fundamental Right or where a law is to be made for making an action punishable, which interferes with Fundamental Rights, that right shall be exercised only by Parliament, notwithstanding the fact that having regard to the List which deals with the distribution of power, such law may fall within the purview of the State Legislature. The object of this is that Fundamental Rights, both as to their nature and as to the punishments involved in the infringement thereof, shall be uniform throughout India. Therefore, if that object is to be achieved, namely, that Fundamental Rights shall be uniform and the punishments involved in the breach of Fundamental Rights also shall be uniform, then that power must be exercised only by the Parliament, so that there may be uniformity. The second thing is this. If there are already Acts, which provide punishments for breaches of Fundamental Rights, unless and until the Parliament makes another or a better provision, such laws will continue in operation. That is the whole scheme of the thing. I do not see why there should be any difficulty in understanding the provisions contained in article 27 (italics mine)

Thus the power to make exception is a rationally thought-out power invested in a sovereign. It was reasonable and it made sense when read along with the provisions on fundamental rights.

Regarding the second imperative, that is continuity with the preceding legal structure, not only sovereign power was being defined as one who or which could make exceptions on the ground of public order, safety, health and morality – grounds which mostly only the sovereign would define (all exceptional legislations were made on these grounds and were upheld by the court), but legal continuity would also reinforce the sovereign's position. In this operation of the rule of juridical abstraction, low castes or Dalits or the indigenous people would be reminded of the reality again and again on any occasion when they would claim from the state steps for positive discrimination or other rights and advantages, that they were now enabled to do so because they belonged to certain 'scheduled' groups, castes or communities, schedules that again would be decided by the state (including local governments). This is how the public power was being built by rationalizing every conceivable issue of political life; Ambedkar's position was unassailable in the constituent assembly because he represented more than anyone else in that assembly *public reason* – reason based on the imperatives of governing, law and rational rule. That is why he could go instantly into any number of details, at times massive and astonishing, and show how they were appropriate with the task of law-making and rationally governing. Democracy's own sovereign power was being produced in this way.

Thus in another reminder that time had changed and therefore every radical intention of pre-sovereign days could not now be pursued, a reminder that time had changed now that the constitution was being drafted and so on 'our' sovereign power would be ready to defend 'our' interests, and therefore people need not worry so much, not be 'schizophrenic', Ambedkar had this to say in response to an inquiry from Kamath on the right to bear arms in connection to a discussion on Article 13:

A: Now, with regard to the question of bearing arms about which my friend Mr. Kamath was so terribly excited, I think the position that we have taken is very clear. It is quite true and everyone knows that the Congress Party had been agitating that there should be right to bear arms. Nobody can deny that. That is history. At the same time I think the House should not forget the fact that the circumstances when Congress passed such resolutions no longer exist.

K: A very handy argument.

A: It is because the British Government had refused to allow Indians to bear arms, not on the ground of peace and order, but on the ground that a subject people should not have the right to bear arms against an alien government so that they could organise themselves to overthrow the Government, and consequently the basic considerations on which these resolutions were passed in my judgement have vanished. Under the present circumstances, I personally myself cannot conceive how it would be possible for the State to carry on its administration if every individual had the right to go into the market and purchase all sorts of instruments of attack without any let or hindrance from the State.

K: On a point of clarification, Sir, the proviso is there, restricting that right.

A: The proviso does what? What does the proviso say? What the proviso can do is to regulate, and the term 'regulation' has been judicially interpreted as prescribing the conditions, but the conditions can never be such as to completely abrogate the right of the citizen to bear arms. Therefore regulation by itself will not prevent a citizen who wants to exercise the right to bear arms from having them. I question very much the policy of giving all citizens indiscriminately any such fundamental right. For instance, if Mr. Kamath's proposition were accepted, that every citizen should have the fundamental right to bear arms, it would be open for thousands and thousands of citizens who are today described as criminal tribes to bear arms. It would be open to all sorts of people who are habitual criminals to claim the right to possess arms. You cannot say that under the proviso a man shall not be entitled to bear arms because he belongs to a particular class.

K: If Dr. Ambedkar understands the proviso fully and clearly, he will see that such will not be the effect of my amendment.

A: I cannot yield now. I have not got much time left. I am explaining the position that has been taken by the Drafting Committee. The point is that it is not possible to allow this indiscriminate right. On the other hand my submission is that so far as bearing of arms is concerned, what we ought to insist upon is not the right of an individual to bear arms but his duty to bear arms (An Honourable Member: *Hear, hear.*). In fact, what we ought to secure is that when an emergency arises, when there is a war, when there is insurrection, when the stability and security of the State is endangered, the State shall be entitled to call upon every citizen to bear arms in defence of the State. That is the proposition that we ought to initiate and that position we have completely safeguarded by the proviso to article 17.

K: (rose to interrupt).

VICE-PRESIDENT: You do not interrupt, Mr. Kamath. You cannot say that I have not given you sufficient latitude.

So that is how one of the most important questions of rule of law is settled. People have to be disarmed if the rule of law, if necessary, enforceable by arms is to be the basis of democracy. This is so evident to those who are in the business of law-making that on this obvious matter, there cannot be much time to give on this, 'not much time left' (for this), 'sufficient latitude has been given', now be ready to serve the armed forced if the sovereign requires of you, but do not ask the right to bear arms as distinct from the arms of *the armed body* of the sovereign. Because this is the sovereignty of the democratic body, the sovereign could not only ask obedience of the people, but assure the latter also that it is truly public. And, this was significant because it was being held in the context of the discussion on Article 13:

A: Coming to the question of saving personal law, I think this matter was very completely and very sufficiently discussed and debated at the time when we discussed one of the Directive Principles of this Constitution which enjoins the State to seek or to strive to bring about a uniform civil code and I do not think it is necessary to make any further reference to it, but I should like to say this that, if such a saving clause was introduced into the Constitution, it would disable the legislatures in India from enacting any social measure whatsoever. The religious conceptions in this country are so vast that they cover every aspect *of* life, from birth to death. There is nothing, which is not religion and if personal law is to be saved, I am sure about it that in social matters we will come to a standstill. I do not think it is possible to accept a position of that sort. There is nothing extraordinary in saying that we ought to strive hereafter to limit the definition of religion in such a manner that we shall not extend beyond beliefs and such rituals as may be connected with ceremonials which are essentially religious. It is not necessary that the sort of laws, for instance, laws relating to tenancy or laws relating to succession, should be governed by religion. In Europe there is Christianity, but Christianity does not mean that the Christians all over the world or in any part of Europe where they live shall have a uniform system of law of inheritance. No such thing exists. I personally do not understand why religion should be given this vast, expansive jurisdiction so as to cover the whole of life and to prevent the legislature from encroaching upon that field. After all, what are we having this liberty for? We are having this liberty in order to reform our social system, which is so full of inequities, so full of inequalities, discriminations and other things, which conflict with our fundamental rights. It is, therefore, quite impossible for anybody to conceive that the personal law shall be excluded from the jurisdiction of the State. Having said that I should also like to point out that all that the State is claiming in his matter is a power to legislate. There is no obligation upon the State to do away with personal laws. It is only giving a power. Therefore, no one need be apprehensive of the fact that if the State has the power, the State will proceed immediately to execute or enforce that power in a manner that may be found to be objectionable by the Muslims or by the Christians or by any other Community in India.

We must all remember – including Members of the Muslim community who have spoken on this subject, though one can appreciate their feelings very well – that sovereignty is always limited, no matter even if you assert that it is unlimited, because sovereignty in the exercise of that power must reconcile itself to the sentiments of different communities. No Government can exercise its power in such a manner as to provoke the Muslim community to rise in rebellion. I think it would be a mad Government if it did so. But that is a matter, which relates to the exercise of the power and not to the power itself.

These are significant words. Occasioned by social conditions at some point of time there can be limits on sovereign's 'exercise of power', but not on 'sovereign power itself'. 'Sovereignty is always limited' because it must not lose sight of governmental considerations, but these are limits on the exercise of power, and not on the power itself. This is, of course, a classic juridical argument. It is, as the exchanges cited earlier demonstrate repeatedly, monologues in nature, which Kant had thought would be a rational individual's position in a society. 'Monologism' as Jurgen Habermas argued later meant that the individual's participation in public sphere was limited to simple sharing of his or her already-constituted opinions and moral decisions in a hypothetical conversation with oneself.[3] Sovereignty was thus the typical Kantian 'categorical imperative' – humanity must follow this enlightened democratic sovereign power; it was also not an intersubjective process, but a purely subjective process, out of which sovereignty had emerged, and now must practice the process also. Deliberation had its limit – the limit posed by rational choice, decision and imperative. Constitution-making, as if Ambedkar was saying to ill-trained and ill-educated members of the constituent assembly, a curious mixture of ignorant representatives and upper-class dilettantes, was finally a matter of categorical imperative. Certain principles were categorical; they represented reason at its purity. Sovereignty was the foremost of such principles.

In passing then we may ask the question to which we must come back before we conclude: is this deliberation in the constituent assembly a 'promise of a democracy to come'? Or, is it 'the promise of rules, institutions, and a new era of rule' after the popular assembly would be over completing its *raison d'etre*? This question, of course, points to a closure because we must be aware of this in the back of our minds that the process is already on, and while the process today says that only some regulative ideas will be put in place in course of deliberations; *at the end of deliberations*, these regulative principles point to the enormous difficulty of making a transition, which a constitution aims to make – thus the aporia, and the inevitability of a risk – of denouncing the process altogether or accepting it and then exceeding it; and what then remains of the original promise, that of democracy to come? We have to re-think many of the things in the game before we can even suggest an answer.

Second stake: legally constituting a government and a people

In any case, if this was to be the nature of the sovereign power, who were to be the people to constitute the demos and whose acceptance, ownership and obligation make the sovereign exercise fruitful? Who were 'they' who would constitute the public? Would wealth mark them, or education, or the simple fact that they were human beings, or more elementally that they were Indians? Would the demos be homogeneous or would it consist of groups? How would it enforce accountability? In an important essay on the politics of citizenship in a society undergoing transition from colonialism to independence Paula Banerjee has shown how aliens were marked out at the time of transition and constitution-making in India, and thus how indentured Indian labour abroad and other Indians working abroad were left out, and how the emerging discourse of citizenship played itself out at a time when the colonial world was drawing to a close.[4] In giving juridical form to the 'demos' this is how the Drafting Committee chairman explained the legal vision and these were how he saw 'the demos' forming its sovereignty:

> A: . . . Of the other amendments, on a careful examination, I find that there is only one amendment on which I need offer any reply. That is amendment No. 1415 of my friend Mr. Karimuddin. His amendment aims at prescribing that the election to the House of the People in the various States shall be in accordance with the proportional representation by single transferable vote. Now, I do not think it is possible to accept

this amendment, because, so far as I am able to judge the merits of the system of proportional representation, in the light of the circumstances existing in this country, I think, that amendment cannot be accepted. My Friend Mr. Karimuddin will, I think, accept the proposition that proportional representation presupposes literacy on a large scale. In fact, it presupposes that every voter shall he literate, at least to the extent of being in a position to know the numerals, and to be in a position to mark them on a ballot paper. I think, having regard to the extent of literacy in this country, such a presupposition would be utterly extravagant. I have not the least doubt on that point. Our literacy is the smallest, I believe, in the world, and it would be quite impossible to impose upon an illiterate mass of voters a system of election, which involves marking of ballot papers. That by itself would, I think, exclude the system of proportional representation.

The second thing to which I like to draw the attention of the House is that at any rate, in my judgement, proportional representation is not suited to the form of Government which this constitution lays down. The form of Government which this constitution lays down is what is known as the parliamentary system of Government, by which we understand that a government shall continue to be in office not necessarily for the full term prescribed by law, namely, five years, but so long as the Government continues to have the confidence of the majority of the House. Obviously it means that in the House where there is the parliamentary system of government, you must necessarily have a party which is in majority and which is prepared to support the Government. Now, so far as I have been able to study the results of the systems of parliamentary or proportional representation. I think, it might be said that one of the disadvantages of proportional representation is the fragmentation of the legislature into a number of small groups. I think the House will know that although the British Parliament appointed a Royal Commission in the year 1910, for the purpose of considering whether their system of single-member constituency, with one man one vote, was better or whether the proportional representation system was better, it is, I think, a matter to be particularly noted that Parliament was not prepared to accept the recommendations of that Royal Commission. The reason which was given for not accepting it was, in my judgement, a very sound reason, that proportional representation would not permit a stable government to remain in office, because Parliament would be so divided into so many small groups that every time anything happened which displeased certain groups in Parliament, they would, on that occasion, withdraw their support from the government, with the result that the Government losing the support of certain groups and units, would fall to pieces. Now, I have not the least doubt in my mind that whatever else the future government provides for, whether it relieves the people from the wants from which they are suffering now or not, our future government must do one thing, namely, it must maintain a stable Government and maintain law and order. *(Hear, Hear!).* I am therefore very hesitant in accepting any system of election which would damage the stability of Government. I am therefore, on that account, not prepared to accept this arrangement.

There is a third consideration, which I think is necessary to bear in mind. In this country, for a long number of years, the people have been divided into majorities and minorities. I am not going into the question whether this division of the people into majorities and minorities was natural, or whether it was an artificial thing, or something, which was deliberately calculated and brought about by somebody who was not friendly to the progress of this country. Whatever that may be, the fact remains that there have been these majorities and minorities in our country; and also that, at the initial stage when this Constituent Assembly met for the discussion of the principles on which the future constitution of the country should be based, there was an agreement arrived at between the various minority communities and the majority community with regard to the system of representation. That agreement has been a matter of give and take. The minorities who, prior to that meeting of the Constituent Assembly, had been entrenched behind a system of separate electorates were prepared, or became prepared to give up that system and the majority which believed that there ought to be no kind of special reservation to any particular community permitted, or rather agreed that while they could not agree to separate electorates, they would agree to a system of joint electorates with reservation of seats. This agreement provides for two things. It provides for a definite quota of representation to the various minorities, and it also provides that such a quota shall be returned through joint electorates. Now, my submission is this, that while it is still open to this House to revise any part of the clauses contained in this draft constitution and while it is open to this House to revise any agreement that has been arrived at between the majority and the minority, this result ought not to be brought about either by surprise or by what I may call, a side-wind. It had better be done directly and it seems to me that the proper procedure for effecting a change in articles 292 and 293 would be to leave the matter to the wishes of the different minorities themselves. If any particular minority represented in this House said that it did not want any reservation, then it would be open to the House to remove the name of that particular minority from the provisions of article 292. If any particular minority preferred that although it did not get a cent per cent deal, namely, did not get a separate electorate, but that what it has got in the form of reservation of seats is better than having nothing, then I think it would be just and proper that the minority should be permitted to retain what the Constituent Assembly has already given to it.

THAKUR DASS BHARGAVA: But there was no agreement about reservation of seats among the communities and a number of amendments were moved by several Members for separate electorates and so on, but they were all voted down. There was no agreement at all in regard to these matters.

A: I was only saying that it may be taken away, not by force, but by consent. That is my proposition, and therefore, I submit that this proportional representation is really taking away by the back-door what has already been granted to the minorities by this agreement, because proportional representation will not give to the minorities what they wanted, namely, a definite quota. It might give them a voice in the election of their representatives. Whether the minorities will be prepared to give up their quota system and prefer to have a mere voice in the election of their representatives, I submit, in fairness ought to be left to them. For these reasons, Sir, I am not prepared to accept the amendment of Mr. Karimuddin.

As we all know, separate electorate had been a controversial theme in anti-colonial politics on which the nationalists could not come to voluntary agreement during colonial rule. The nationalists could not agree on the dynamics and complexities of representation in a plural society. Year after year minority governments have ruled countries on the basis of first past the vote system, and popular discontent has not been able to find any constitutional way out against a system of representation that falsifies the very ethics of representing the demos. But Ambedkar's vision was clear from the way he was arguing: first (except in cases of scheduled castes and tribes, and reserved non-elected seats for Anglo-Indians) there would be no separate seat for any community, similarly no break-up of the demos according to any communal profile; second, this demos will consist of 'multitude', who may not be literate, but who must perform the first function of the demos, that of electing the sovereign. One can see why the legitimization of sovereignty required a republican demos, towards the creation of which Ambedkar singe-mindedly framed arguments. But was the sovereign to be illiterate? No, here one could ill afford to confuse the demos with the sovereign, as was amply clear from the exchange of words involving Mahavir Tyagi, Kamath and Ambedkar over Article 62:

T: Then there is the amendment of Prof. Shah in which he says that Ministers should know the English language for ten years, and Hindi after the next ten years. I happen to be an anarchist by faith so far as literacy is concerned, I do not believe in the present-day education. I am opposed to the notion of literacy also, even though it has its own value. If I were a boy now, I would refuse to read and write. As it was, I practically refused to read and write and hence I am a semi-literate. The majority in India are illiterate persons. Why should they be denied their share in the administration of the country? I wonder, why should literacy be considered as the supreme achievement of men? Why should it be made as the sole criterion for entrusting the governance of a country to a person, and why Art, Industry, Mechanics, Physique or Beauty be not chosen as a better criterion. Ranjit Singh was not literate. Shivaji was not literate. Akbar was not much of a literate. But all of them were administering their States very well. I submit, Sir, that we should not attach too much importance to literacy. I ask Dr. Ambedkar, does he ever write? Probably he has got writers to write for him and readers to read to him. I do not see why Ministers need read and write. Whenever they want to write anything, they can use typists. Neither reading nor writing is necessary. What are necessary are initiative, honesty, personality, integrity, intelligence and sincerity. These are the qualifications that a man should have to become a Minister. It is not literacy, which is important.

K: Does my redoubtable friend want to keep India as illiterate as she is today?

A: Have you any conscientious objection against literacy?

T: No, Sir.

A: With regard to the educational qualification, notwithstanding what my friend Mr. Mahavir Tyagi has said on the question of literary qualification, when I asked him whether in view of the fact that he expressed himself so vehemently against literary qualification whether he has any conscientious objection to literary education, he was very glad to assure me that he has none. All the same, I wonder whether there would be any Prime Minister or President who would think it desirable to appoint a person who does not know English, assuming that English remains the official language of the business of the Executive or of Parliament. I cannot conceive of such a thing. Supposing the official language was Hindi, Hindustani or Urdu – whatever it is – in that event, I again find it impossible to think that a Prime Minister would be so stupid as to appoint a Minister who did not understand the official language of the country or of the Administration and while therefore it is no doubt a very desirable thing to bear in mind that persons who would hold a portfolio in the Government should have proper educational qualification, I think it is, rather unnecessary to incorporate this principle in the Constitution itself.

And how were the elections to be conducted? Of course, once the sovereign had been instituted, the sovereign could now engage – as the constitutional deliberations envisaged – the administration to conduct and supervise elections in a public and impartial way as against distinct from engaging any private or sectional agency to conduct the elections. Here again, we can see in the light of our experiences how the constitutional world was producing a virtual world of republican democracy by assuming that this *administration* could ensure proper representation. We have thus the real world of sovereignty and the virtual world of republican democracy. Ambedkar was mindful of the administrative needs of the sovereign; hence some suggestions placed by members of the constituent assembly for revision of draft articles were 'unnecessary', some 'superfluous', some 'harmful' and some 'necessary'. Governmental requirements were pre-eminent in this respect, and the demos had to be trained to be aware of that. Thus on technical matters legality defined the core of governmentality, such as on issues involving population figures. Census figures, as all students of post-colonial politics know, have been extremely controversial and the roots of many conflicts. The constituent assembly was deliberating at a time when population groups were up in arms against each other, the country had been partitioned and demography and census were the time bomb ticking all the time. We have seen the grounds on which Ambedkar had rejected the introduction of the principle of proportional representation. His following remarks show that he was aware of the reality of the elites of different community and caste groups trying to increase their domination over the electoral arithmetic, and yet constituent assembly had to move on to give shape to the demos – the popular electorate constituting the nation – ironing out these unhappy realities:

A: Now, Sir, so far as the general debate on the article (Article 149 for holding of elections) is concerned, it seems to me that there are only two points that call for reply. The first point is with regard to the census figures to be adopted for the purpose of the new elections. A great deal of argument was concentrated by many speakers on the fact that the census in certain provinces is not accurate and does not represent the true state of affairs so far as the relative proportions of the different communities are concerned. I think there is a great deal of force in such arguments and, if I may say so, there is enough testimony which one can collect from the Census Commissioners' reports themselves to justify that criticism. I had intended to refer to the statements made by the Census Commissioners on this issue. But, as there is no time, I think I had better not refer to them. Further, the large majority of the members who have spoken on this subject know the facts better than I do. I only want to add one thing and that is that if any people have suffered most in the matter of these manipulations of census calculations by reason of political factors; they are the Scheduled Castes *(Hear, hear)*. In Punjab for instance, the other communities are trying to eat up the Scheduled Castes in order to augment their strength and to acquire larger representation in the legislature for themselves. These poor people who have been living mostly as landless labourers in villages scattered here and there, with no economic independence, with no support from the authorities – the police or the magistracy – have been, by certain powerful communities, either compelled to return themselves as members of that particular community or not to enumerate at the elections at all. The same thing has happened to a large extent, I know, in Bengal. For some reason, which I have not been able to understand, a large majority of the Scheduled Castes there refused to return themselves as Scheduled Castes. That fact has been noted by the Census Commissioners themselves. I therefore completely appreciate the points that have been made by various members who spoke on the subject that it would not be fair to take the figures of that census.

A MEMBER: What about Assam?

A: It may be true of Assam also. I am not very well acquainted with it. As I said I fully appreciate the point that to take those census figures and to delimit constituencies or allocate seats between the different constituencies and between the majority and minority communities would not be fair. Something will have to be done in order to see that the next election is a proper election, related properly to the population figures of the provinces as well as of the communities. All that I can do at this stage is to give an assurance that I shall communicate these sentiments to those who will be in charge of this matter and I have not the least doubt about it that the matter will be properly attended to.

There are other significant instances to show how in the form of constitutionalist exercises and constitutional deliberations, the idea of making governmental tools the principal method to shape the demos became irresistible. We can listen to this extraordinary exchange of deliberations in the constituent assembly in which Ambedkar was once again playing the key role. The matter related to the rights of cultural/religious groups to open their own educational institutions, and get state aid:

A: Now, with regard to the second clause I think it has not been sufficiently well understood. We have tried to reconcile the claim of a community, which has started educational institutions for the advancement of its own children either in education or in cultural matters, to permit to give religious instruction in such institutions, notwithstanding the fact that it receives certain aid from the State. The State, of course, is free to give aid, is free not to give aid; the only limitation we have placed is this, that the State shall not debar the institution from claiming aid under its grant-in-aid code merely on the ground that it is run and maintained by a community and not maintained by a public body. We have there provided also a further qualification, that while it is free to give religious instruction in the institution and the grant made by the State shall not be a bar to the giving of such instruction, it shall not give instruction to, or make it compulsory upon, the children belonging to other communities unless and until they obtain the consent of the parents of those children. That, I think, is a salutary provision. It performs two functions. . . .

KAMATH: On a point of clarification, what about institutions and schools run by a community or a minority for its own pupils – not a school where all communities are mixed but a school run by the community for its own pupils?

A: If my Friend Mr. Kamath will read the other article he will see that once an institution, whether maintained by the community or not, gets a grant, the condition is that it shall keep the school open to all communities. That provision he has not read. Therefore, by sub-clause (2) we are really achieving two purposes. One is that we are permitting a community, which has established its institutions for the advancement of its religious or its cultural life, to give such instruction in the school. We have also provided that children of other communities who attend that school shall not be compelled to attend such religious instructions, which undoubtedly and obviously must be the instruction in the religion of that particular community, unless the parents consent to it. As I say, we have achieved this double purpose and those who want religious instruction to be given are free to establish their institutions and claim aid from the State, give religious instruction, but shall not be in a position to force that religious instruction on other communities. It is therefore not proper to say that by this article we have altogether barred religious instruction. Religious instruction has been left free to be taught and given by each community according to its aims and objects subject to certain conditions. All that is barred is this, that the State in the institutions maintained by it wholly out of public funds shall not be free to give religious instruction.

LAKSHMI KANTA MAITRA: May I put the Honourable Member one question? There is, for instance, an educational institution wholly managed by the Government, like the Sanskrit College, Calcutta. There the *Vedas* are taught, *Smrithis* are taught, the *Gita* is taught, the *Upanishads* are taught. Similarly in several parts of Bengal there are Sanskrit Institutions where instructions in these subjects are given. You provide in article 22 (1) that no religious instruction can be given by an institution wholly maintained out of State funds. These are absolutely maintained by State funds. My point is, would it be interpreted that the teaching of *Vedas,* or *Smrithis,* or *Shastras,* or *Upanishads* comes within the meaning of a religious instruction? In that case all these institutions will have to be closed down.

A: Well, I do not know exactly the character of the institutions to which my Friend Mr. Maitra has made reference and it is therefore quite difficult for me.

MAITRA: Take for instance the teaching of Gita, Upanishads, the Vedas and livings like that in Government Sanskrit Colleges and schools.

A: My own view is this that religious instruction is to be distinguished from research or study. Those are quite different things. Religious instruction means this. For instance, so far as the Islam religion is concerned, it means that you believe in one God, that you believe that *Paigambar* the Prophet is the last Prophet and so on, in other words, what we call 'dogma'. A dogma is quite different from study.

MR. VICE-PRESIDENT: May I interpose for one minute? As Inspector of Colleges for the Calcutta University, I used to inspect the Sanskrit College, where as Pandit Maitra is aware, students have to study not only the University course, but also books outside it in Sanskrit literature and in fact Sanskrit sacred books, but this was never regarded as religious instruction; it was regarded as a course in culture.

MAITRA: My point is this. It is not a question of research. It is a mere instruction in religion or religious branches of study. I ask whether lecturing on Gita and Upanishads would be considered as giving religious instruction? Expounding Upanishads is not a matter of research.

This is how governmentality operates. In this operation, a procedure to standardize 'cases' must be found out with regard to the matter to be administered – in this case the issues of education and public instruction. Thus, while common sense and dialogic wisdom suggested that on the tricky issues of religious instruction, secularism, impartiality of the state and state aid to educational efforts more deliberations were needed – more introspection towards what we call as matters of public instruction involving philosophical and theological education, a matter on which the entire nineteenth-century educationists in India had racked their brains – law needed in their place, *in the first place*, some rational sense to put into operation to straighten the complications in civil education. This is what public voice is, and this is what Ambedkar represented in the constituent assembly, all the more when we see how he was – exactly in the way he dealt with the issue of public instruction – dealing with the matter of personal law, an issue relevant to Part IV of the constitution, the Directive Principles of State Policy. And this is what he had to say among other things on one of the most contentious issues of political modernity. He was counselling reason and moderation, a combination that people do not sufficiently appreciate. Reason tells you to go ahead with your agenda of reform, yet it also counsels moderation, for moderation will give you an insight into the mysteries of the working of a society; and therefore reason always brings in moderation. Has this not been exactly the political essence of constitutionalism – a unique combination of reason and moderation, the other form of sovereignty and democracy? Also, has it not been one of the principal challenges to modernity, particular modernity, to achieve reason with moderation?

Ambedkar thus commented in a unique vein,

> Coming to the question of saving personal law, I think this matter was very completely and very sufficiently discussed and debated at the time when we discussed one of the Directive Principles of this Constitution which enjoins the State to seek or to strive to bring about a uniform civil code and I do not think it is necessary to make any further reference to it, but I should like to say this that, if such a saving clause was introduced into the Constitution, it would disable the legislatures in India from enacting any social measure whatsoever. The religious conceptions in this country are so vast that they cover every aspect *of* life, from birth to death. . . . There is nothing extraordinary in saying that we ought to strive hereafter to limit the definition of religion in such a manner that we shall not extend beyond beliefs and such rituals as may be connected with ceremonials which are essentially religious. It is not necessary that the sort of laws, for instance, laws relating to tenancy or laws relating to succession, should be governed by religion. In Europe there is Christianity, but Christianity does not mean that the Christians all over the world or in any part of Europe where they live shall have a uniform system of law of

inheritance. No such thing exists. I personally do not understand why religion should be given this vast, expansive jurisdiction so as to cover the whole of life and to prevent the legislature from encroaching upon that field. After all, what are we having this liberty for? We are having this liberty in order to reform our social system, which is so full of inequities, so full of inequalities, discriminations and other things, which conflict with our fundamental rights. It is, therefore, quite impossible for anybody to conceive that the personal law shall be excluded from the jurisdiction of the State. Having said that, I should also like to point out that all that the State is claiming in his matter is a power to legislate. There is no obligation upon the State to do away with personal laws. It is only giving a power. Therefore, no one need be apprehensive of the fact that if the State has the power, the State will proceed immediately to execute or enforce that power in a manner that may be found to be objectionable by the Muslims or by the Christians or by any other Community in India.

Thus, modernity brings in power and the scope to change society slowly, gradually, at will, in measure. It does not exhort you to make revolution – revolution belongs to the domain of passion. Foucault was therefore perhaps not right when he placed the political culture of revolt to the annals of modernity. There Burke was more correct when he argued that moderation was the true essence of modernity, and the French were wrong in giving in to passion. This was and still is the political problem of constitutionalism – how to constitute power that will have the virtue of moderation but the characteristic of sovereign? How to constitute a sovereign that will appeal to the democratic spirit yet will rely on the everyday governmentalities characterizing modern political societies? How to create a sovereign that will not act as sovereign while keeping its exceptional power intact?

None knew more than Ambedkar – a political leader, jurist, constitutionalist, mass leader and a moderate all at the same time – to realize that only governmental capability could enable such a unique distinction to achieve. Therefore, even on an issue dearest to his heart, social justice for the Dalits and their emancipation from social bondage, he knew governmental scope and power were the most necessary attributes to bring about any change.

Thus, he commented in one place,

Now, coming to the question of the scheduled tribes and as to why I substituted the word 'scheduled' for the word 'aboriginal', the explanation is this. As I said, the word 'scheduled tribe' has a fixed meaning, because it enumerates the tribes, as you will see in the two Schedules. Well the word 'Adivasi' is really a general term, which has no specific legal *de jure* connotation; something like the Untouchables, it is a general term. Anybody may include anybody in the term 'untouchable'. It has no definite legal connotation. That is why in the Government of India Act of 1935, it was felt necessary to give the word 'untouchable' some legal connotation and the only way it was found feasible to do it was to enumerate the communities which in different parts and in different areas were regarded by the local people as satisfying the test of untouchability. The same question may arise with regard to Adivasis. Who are the Adivasis? And the question will be relevant, because by this Constitution, we are conferring certain privileges, certain rights on these Adivasis in order that, if the matter was taken to a court of law, there should be a precise definition as to who are these Adivasis. It was decided to invent, so to say, another category or another term to be called 'Scheduled tribes' and to enumerate the Adivasis under that head. Now I think my friend, Mr. Jaipal Single, if he were to take the several communities which are now generally described as Adivasis and compare the communities which are listed under the head of scheduled tribes, he will find that there is hardly a case where a community which is generally recognized as Adivasis is not included in the Schedule'

Governance, Ambedkar was arguing, is not only relational, but also contextual. It is a technique aimed to help law and facilitate administration – administration of men and women through administering matters belonging to the affairs of men and women. This was possible only through a combination of standardization and flexibility. Rational knowledge enables standardization. Power enables flexibility.

Constitution-making as an art of governing

Is what we have pointed out while recalling some of Ambedkar's arguments in the long constitution-making exercise unique? Or was his role unique? It is not our case in this chapter to prove them though both of these may have been true, at least true then. Our intention here is to point out how constitution-making skill and perspicacity call for a targeted approach, and that is what is unique as a form of modern political knowledge. As a material practice it is also remorseless in logic. And as a dialogic exercise therefore if it succeeds, it does so only partially.

To understand the point about the constituent assembly and the constitution-making exercise being one of the major tools to bring about a passive revolution in a country marked by unrest, madness, revolts and schizophrenia, we have to recall few known facts here. The demand for a constituent assembly was intrinsically linked to the nation's larger goal of freedom and independence. The resolution for *purna swaraj* (full independence) in 1929 had aroused great nationalist enthusiasm. Reflecting a deep desire among the people to be in control of their own destiny it also represented within itself the idea of a democratic constitution, which would provide a framework for the governance of independent India by the Indian people. Therefore, *purna swaraj* had the idea of a popular assembly consisting of representatives of the people. The Indian National Congress accepted the idea of a constituent assembly in 1934. After that it became a significant part of the nationalist agenda for independent India, the vision of which had its first glimpse in the well-known Nehru Report on the constitution of free India. The Karachi Session of the Indian National Congress held in March 1931 adopted the famous resolution moved by Gandhi, which contained the charter on fundamental rights. It was against this backdrop that the idea of a sovereign, democratic nation born through deliberations in a constituent assembly gradually crystallized. Yet it was precisely in this period that nation's leaders began serious thinking on issues such as personal law reform, educational design and public instruction, planning, construction of big industries, public distribution system and economic revival through the revival of cottage, small-scale and middle-scale industries. War, famine and subsequent unrest only made these governmental imperatives more urgent than ever. By the time limited elections took place in 1946, Partition had been accepted by the nationalist leaders as an evil necessity, territorial considerations had become dominant in all governmental considerations and how to rule had become as important a consideration as to how to become free. Very few constitution-making experiences match the Indian one in depth, in achieving combination of contradictory elements, and giving the constitution a purposeful look, because very few constitutions can match the Indian one in having a targeted approach as its mode. Order, security, integrity, personal freedom, political equality, development, independent judiciary, decentralization, local self-government all these could have appeared in time as disjointed parts of a too cumbersome agenda. But they did not, because they all appeared as implementing tasks of a sovereign state, which would govern the people with its developmental programme through rule of law. The constitution-making exercise was successful in achieving a unique feat of which Immanuel Kant and Edmund Burke would have been equally proud.[5] Our constitutionalists had set in motion a mechanism of power that would be almost self-running except requiring occasional boosts from outside. The details of combining state and the government, sovereignty and governmentality, power and welfare and ruling and development were all laid down in the book with amazing patience – because they knew the precise nature of the job. They knew what they had inherited as the Government of India Act of 1935 was of immense value. It was a given framework with which they could now go forward and add to it.

Only in this perspective we can understand how Ambedkar and others could discipline themselves into not getting reckless and wild with the aroma and the maddening charm of the politics and the act of representing the demos. They never thought that people could be truly represented, as if Carl Schmitt was repeating his lesson to their ears,

> That X steps up in place of an absent Y, or for several thousand such Y's, is thus not in itself a representation. A particularly simple historical example of representation obtains when a king is represented to another king through an emissary (i.e., a personal representative, not through an agent, who carries out tasks for him.) In the eighteenth century this kind of 'representation in an eminent sense' was clearly distinguished from other processes of delegation.[6]

Therefore, having ensured that people's voice was behind it, and that there would be elections, universal adult franchise, local and provincial elections, formation of governments at several levels while the Parliament along the British lines would be the supreme legislating authority in the country, the constituent assembly did not spend much time on working on the theme of representation. Thus many themes were left out such as recall and referendum. Issues of popular will as and when expressed in direct ways were similarly left out; also left out were the complications of group representation at various levels, issues arising out of the many locations of citizenship, relation of representation and participation, ensuring autonomy of people's voices and of distinct areas. Finally, the constitution simply assumed that popular representation and the basic structure provided by the 1935 Act were compatible. With this understanding the constitution now devoted more time and energy on issues of governance, financial and fiscal management, rights and obligations, powers and functions of government and the theory and practice of separation of powers. People became the governed subjects in this dynamics where representatives became the actors, and as if disenchanted with the fury and madness of the people, the representatives had to form a college to (a) decide as to how to introduce the rule of moderation by elaborately laying down to the minutest details the principles and corollaries of everyday governance and (b) invest in the sovereign the power to suspend these everyday rules of governance and life – thus making up the two aspects of sovereign power.

The final immunity of law

From all that we have discussed till now we can say by way of summing up that in this task of framing the basic law, Babasaheb Ambedkar and other law givers concerned with social justice, liberty and other rights were actually concerned with two overwhelming concerns. The first concern related to *conditions of governance*, which means ensuring the right conditions of governing people, conditions of successful government, conditions of stable rule and achieving the right mix of liberty and equality, and freedom and obligations. Therefore, we find in the previous excerpts a dominant tone of moderation, and a concern that the right conditions of rule must be guaranteed through the constitution-making exercise. The second one related to the task of finding a solution of the riddle of the perpetual imbalance between state power, which implied *centralization*, and various forms of governmental power, which implied *decentralization and autonomies*. Caught in these two concerns Ambedkar and his colleagues were unable to work out the full logic of representation, and created what we can call the 'final immunity' of the law.

We should ask: how does this happen in democracy? The situation that Ambedkar faced and in turn reinforced was not unique. It was precisely for the fact that democracy is not an ideal, but a system of government or more aptly speaking a way of governing. Democratic governance means ensuring certain conditions for democratic rule – conditions that may have nothing inherently democratic in it. Therefore, on one hand democratic constitutions often found themselves on what can be called undemocratic features, for instance those carried over from previous constitutions, laws, compacts, policies or violent orgies and carnage; on the other hand the essential fact of governing produces undemocratic results, which we may call the 'deficit of democracy' or the 'democratic deficit'. Thus our specific 'constitutional temper', which seeks to provide solidity of rule as the overwhelming requirement of the polity, was built through the political debates in the nationalist movement preceding the constitution-making exercise – specifically in the thirties and forties of the past century, when people like Tej Bahadur Sapru and C. R. Rajagopalachari repeatedly stressed the importance of constitutional and responsible behaviour particularly in the context of British legal proposals including the Act of 1935. British rule was one of continuous reforms – regardless of the nationalist response, or more correctly speaking, continuously responding to nationalist politics. Therefore, legal reforms became a reality of the politics of the country, as real as other features were, and jurists and lawyers became headmasters and fathers of politicians. It also posed a challenge to the nationalists to continuously defend and legitimate its behaviour in terms of the standards set by the rule. Constitutional behaviour exemplified and framed through the deliberative exercise of 1946–49 thus gained increasing importance in politics in relation to its other imperatives.[7] Thus, people like Ambedkar who throughout the nationalist period had tried to build an alternative idea of the nation distinct from the one developed by Gandhi and Nehru (not that the latter two had the same idea), marked by the ideals of social justice and equality, also became victims of the trope. Rule of law and search for an egalitarian social order was the impossible combination that Ambedkar aimed at achieving.[8] The paradox was demonstrated clearly in the failure of Ambedkar in 1951 to pilot the Hindu Code Bill to enactment after three years of effort. Ambedkar resigned from Law Ministry – the final comment on his efforts to put constitutional behaviour above all and yet help the nation gain social justice. This is the problem of democratic deficit we have referred to in the present context.

To be true, the problem of democratic deficit was encountered in democratic studies long back, and was most acutely described by, among others, Alexis de Tocqueville in his study of American democracy about one hundred years before Ambedkar was piloting the drafting of the Indian constitution. There we find in his study of the tyranny of the majority, the virtues and problems posed by equality, consequences of the presence of religion and race relations in a democracy, centralization, the domination of commerce and several other phenomena that democracy faced and still faces as problems – problems that are not due to insufficiency of democracy, but arise out of its conditions, and therefore produce its deficit. The final supremacy of law emerges in such context.

We may ask: how can democracy and dreams of social justice that suffer at the hands of an impersonal governmental machine escape the aporia that constitutionalism represents? The aporia is symbolized in the immunity of the legal process – the immunity of the constitution, the constitution-making process, and the constitutionalists from the daily vagaries of the politics of the street on issues of rights, justice, claims and enforcement of responsibility. Constitution demanded responsibility; it was responsible to none. It had the final immunity; it was the God because it had combined the power of the sovereign and the tasks of the government. It was not democracy. One cannot say constitution is democracy, but constitution promises democracy – *a democracy to come*, if you follow it.[9] In this promise, we have both an arrival and a postponement. An arrival, because constitutional democracy has arrived, constitutional order has arrived, constitution has arrived; and a postponement because until we follow the laid-down script, democracy will not arrive, therefore we cannot hold constitution responsible for any democratic deficit. To arrive, to come is therefore also to postpone – because to arrive we have taken recourse to some categorical principle. Constitution is the categorical principle, and we have decided to deal later with many of the burning issues of democracy, because we are now interested in setting up the principles mainly.

To give one instance only, the constitution talks only with its citizens and the institutions that govern the citizens. Meanwhile non-citizens grow – aliens, illegal immigrants, refugees, masses of drop outs and a huge army of underclass, not at all addressed by the constitution. Likewise, with ever-emerging hierarchies in the landscape of citizenship, some sections are increasingly out of the constitutional gaze – women of the lower order, starving peasants, an indebted population and the moving migrants forcibly displaced from one work site and life site to another. The constitution promises rights, but does not address the condition of basic rightlessness of those who do not have 'the right to claim rights'. As a consequence, there is now immunity for the constitution. We have issued a promise, and we can now make castles of reason.

Given the significance of the Indian experience, how can the philosophy of constitution envision its path ahead? Let us recall that the eighteenth-century democratic revolutionaries or the mid-twentieth century anti-colonial nationalists had not simply proposed democracy and democratic independence in their given form. They addressed the issue of scale and the emerging modes of control, which are built in the appearance of the nation form in politics, and reinvented as solution the institutional forms and practices of representation. But we demonstrated in this chapter, at both levels of the scale – the global by which we indicate global compulsions which a constitution cannot ignore, and the local by which we mean the micro-compulsions of governing – modern forms of representation will not be able to satisfactorily respond to the demands of the time.

Restorative constitutions are failing, constitutions that aim at restoring the state. The problem of combining democracy with sovereignty has to be thus rigorously studied. In India, the constitution took place amid a civil war, or many civil wars, and sovereign power was proposed as a constituent power to produce and reproduce the people as a peaceful social union in order to end the cataclysmic violence. Yet as we know from the subsequent history of the country, which can legitimately take pride in the success of its constitutional culture, the sovereign could not put an end to violence. The sovereign power reorganized the elements of fear and violence into a coherent and stable political order in which governmentality worked as the main mixer of elements. In this way the sovereign nation state searches for an answer to the problem of civil war. But we are now in a time when problem of scale is acute – sovereignty neither can end civil war nor can it fine-tune the limitless details of governance required to make democratic sovereignty meaningful in the lives of the millions.

We can see two problems here defining the current condition: (a) the constitution produces the citizen as the political subject – subject in a double sense; first, the citizen is the subject by being the main actor in politics, and second by being subject to rules of governance, enmeshed in daily governmentalities, because this citizen is the constitutional product; (b) meanwhile politics has gone ahead, and the emerging political subject today is a product of legality, semi-legality and illegalities, responding to the demands of the scale in novel ways, primarily because this subject is a product not of constitutionalism but of a new politics marked by new sense of justice and dialogue. The production of political subjectivity is a problem for stagnant politics, because stagnant politics does not know how to cope with the issue of excess, which occasions the emergence of the subject.

What political narrative can illustrate this fabulous condition? The condition of reason producing its limits, law leading to its transgression, law chambers and legal assemblies leading to streets and the clamour for rights leading to a still- politics of justice? Surely from within the constitutional discourse we cannot get the answer; situated as we are within the discourse itself. How do we come out? The limits of juridical reason, however, indicate the space, the location of stepping out and where we have to step in – that space, which is defined by three characteristics: (a) a space marked by the co-existence of legality, semi-legality and illegalities; (b) a space marked by dialogues of these three existences; (c) and, a space marked by new and unfamiliar institutional innovations and legal pluralism. To even arrive at this space, not only we must step out of the confines of constitutional discourse, we must also urge a dialogue between the constitution and the new illegalities.

Notes

1 In this chapter I have taken principally from Ambedkar's speeches and replies in the Constituent Assembly, its final stage of deliberations to show his final positions. These excerpts are from 15 November 1948 to 8 January 1949. All citations of his speeches and replies in exchange are from the proceedings of the Constituent Assembly. For details of the extracts see www.ambedkar.org/ambcd/63B1.CA%20Debates%2005 (accessed on 17 October 2008).

2 Though in several of his fragmentary writings and speeches in later years Michel Foucault spoke of governmentality, the reader can principally consult his essay, "Governmentality" presented as part of a course on "Security, Territory, and Population" given in 1977–78 at the College de France, and later published in *Essential Works of Michel Foucault, 1954–1984*, Volume 3, ed. James Faubion, and trans. Robert Hurley (London: Allen Lane, The Penguin Press, 1994), pp. 201–222.

3 Giovanna Borradori, *Philosophy in a Time of Terror – Dialogues with Jurgen Habermas and Jacques Derrida* (Chicago: University of Chicago Press, 2003), pp. 59–60.

4 Paula Banerjee, "Aliens in the Colonial World", in Ranabir Samaddar (ed.), *Refugees and the State – Practices of Asylum and Care in India, 1947–2000* (New Delhi: Sage Publications, 2003), Chapter 1, pp. 69–107.

5 Immanuel Kant, "Third Definitive Article on Perpetual Peace", in Kant (ed.), *Perpetual Peace*, reproduced in P. Barash (ed.), *Approaches to Peace* (New York: Oxford University Press, 2000), pp. 125–126. Burke had said on the necessity of moderation as a constitutional principle,

> I must see with my own eyes, must touch with my own hands, not only the fixed, but the momentary circumstances, before I would venture to suggest any political project whatsoever. I must know the power and disposition to accept, to exercise, to persevere. . . . I must see the means of correcting the plan, where correctives would be wanted. I must see the things I must see. . . . The eastern politicians never do anything without the opinion of the astrologers on the *fortunate moment*. . . . Statesmen of judicious prescience look for the fortunate moment too; but they seek it not in the conjunctions and oppositions of the planets, but in the conjunctions and oppositions of men and things. These form their almanac.' (Burke's Italics)

Cited in Alexander M. Bickel, *The Morality of Consent* (Yale, NH: Yale University Press, 1975), pp. 15–16; *In Reflections on the Revolution in France* (1790; Oxford: Oxford University Press, 2009), Burke analyses the principle of political moderation in the context of French Revolution.

6 Cited in Samuel Weber, *Targets of Opportunity – On the Militarisation of Thinking* (New York: Fordham University Press, 2005), Chapter 2, "The Principle of Representation – Carl Schmitt's *Roman Catholicism and Political Form*", p. 39.

7 On this specific challenge set by the colonial rule for Indian nationalism, see D.A. Low, *Britain and Indian Nationalism: The Imprint of Ambiguity, 1929–1942* (Cambridge: Cambridge University Press, 1997).

8 Gail Omvedt unfortunately misses this point in her otherwise forthright study of Ambedkar in the context of Indian nationalism; see her *Ambedkar: Towards an Enlightened India* (New Delhi: Penguin, 2004).

9 On the idea of 'democracy to come', see the discussion by Jacques Derrida, *Rogues – Two Essays on Reason*, trans. Pascale-Anne Brault and Michael Naas (California: Stanford University Press, 2005).

10 Popular constitutionalism

Constitutionalism a living question

In the light of the previous chapter we may claim that the specific contribution of post-colonial politics to the history of democracy is that it has been able to open up the supposedly closed issue of constitutionalism. It was hitherto thought that constitutionalism was a settled issue; what was called for was right implementation. Constitution as the foundation of democracy was a settled chapter in history. If the post-colonial experience now occasions a divergence of perceptions, then at least two issues are at stake here: first, what is specifically post-colonial in treating the matter of the constitution as a living one? Second, what is specific in the present moment of global history, which makes this question a universal question as well? Living in the post-Foucauldian era where issues of governmentality and governing practices occupy more attention than laws and constitutions, is there anything in popular politics that is making constitution once again a relevant question for states, regimes and polities – with of course transforming the issue of constitutionalism itself in the process?

We can take up the second question first to situate the theme properly, and then proceed towards examination of the first question.

In spite of the narrow basis of constitutionalism in the liberal-democratic part of the world in the aftermath of the Second World War the massive rise of democratic politics and labour movement in the following two decades brought forward several things to be integrated in the respective constitutional structures – equality (US constitution), parliamentary sovereignty as the mark of citizens' supremacy, right to nationalization and social welfare legislations and rights (Great Britain), federalism (Germany) and freedom and national sovereignty (France). In the socialist part of the world too, constitutionalism expanded as social and economic rights were accorded in different countries the most important place in various forms. Likewise in India, which had just got independence in 1947 and where constitutionalism owed its existence primarily to British colonial acts and regulations of the preceding one century – particularly the Act of 1935 – the idea of rights, independence, justice and freedom widened the base of constitutionalism and constitutional politics dramatically. Courts strengthened the juridical discourse. The Indian experience demonstrated the interface of globality and locality since the inception of constitutional order and legally recognized rights, which had been usually considered as domestic developments in respective countries. However, we know that the French Revolution and its declaration of rights swept Europe within sixty years and the anti-colonial revolt in India encouraged similar resistance in defence of national rights in many colonies. The October Revolution (1917) for bread, land and peace – three elementary rights today – encouraged uncounted series of revolts for more than fifty years and new constitution-makings. In the 'rights revolution' therefore we always find the universality of constitutional reason working in the form of a combination of globality and locality.

Present history is marked by an intense discussion of globalization at many levels, in many contexts, and in many forms. In the first place there is contest over universality and its relation with the ongoing conflict between globalization and national sovereignty. Can the constitutional discourse de-link itself from this contentious scene? It cannot. There are several reasons, the primary being the direct impact of globalization on the nation-state. Other reasons are free flow of capital, presidential-style electoral democracy, free trade in the form of the WTO regime, issues of immigration and labour flow and finally the monopoly of nuclear weaponry. These issues have seriously impaired the national constitution as a container of rights and as a form of defence against imperial universality and globalization. Citizenship, for whom rights are meant, has suffered deficit – as concept and institution. Two reasons can be cited – first, the nation-state is incapable today to ensure many of the rights citizens demand and think legitimate and appropriate. Social and economic rights are particularly impaired by the WTO regime. Many of the civil and political rights also have suffered in this way in the new world order. Second is the factor of massive and mixed flows of migration across national boundaries, demanding new responses and new measures of social security. Nations are losing national autonomies. Cultural resistance is not enough. The trans-national corporations override subaltern cultural resistance in many places, because these cultural resistances suffer from the absence of both national and global support and legitimacy.

Existing only as local roots they fail in resisting the vast increase in the flow of finance capital and the ruthless play of monetarist forces. Needless to say, with the increasing deficit of the nation-state, both these consequences have had telling effect on the career of constitutionalism and the rights revolution.

There is no scope to re-enact the path of the Bandung, that is a replay of the politics of conference of Afro-Asian heads of states in the fifties of the past century in Indonesia where those heads of states thought that they had overcome the colour burden. Through consolidating the sovereignty of the nation-states of Africa and Asia, initiating state capitalism within, undertaking massive state expenditures, committing states to large-scale social subsidies and institutionalizing and guaranteeing certain rights mostly political and civil they could initiate a new path against colonialism and neo-colonialism. Bandung failed, as we know. The nation-states were unable to build up independent strong economies. They were unable also to keep free their respective economies from debt-trap. They failed to guarantee basic freedoms to their respective people. Constitutional order collapsed in this way in country after country. Bandung upheld sovereignty as a principle to claim and retain independence, oppose colour divisions and world hegemonies and uphold social commitments to citizens.

Global and local sources of constitutional rights

But then as now global conditions provoked new turn in rights claiming politics and influenced constitutional thinking as in India in unforeseen ways. Today we have several new developments in the light of which sovereignty as a principle has to be reassessed and re-formed (shared forms, diffused forms and autonomies). There is also the feature of rights groups working as networks: rights being anticipated less by law but more by movements, and rights now demanding a redefinition of sovereignty. With this, the three phenomena – nation, rights and cosmopolitanism – have entered a new phase of interrelation. Political struggles even at the grass roots show network pattern, and a kind of functional unity pervades the struggle for rights. In short, in this new phase, legality matters less. A re-conceptualized sovereignty has to accommodate the ongoing rights revolution both in a space defined by the legal form of the state and in face of a 'spaceless, faceless' global enemy of rights – namely empires, MNCs, interventionist armies and flows of finance capital breaking state barriers and attacking domestic economies. The contradiction is at several levels – for instance between global forms of power and local struggles for justice, global form of the state and political democracy and the local nature of rights, economic globalization and the nation-state, the universalizing nature of the rights discourse which explains differential legitimation (that is certain rights are of higher order) of rights and the claims by local struggles for rights and local origins of rights to universality. In this contradictory milieu, elections, parties, press, judiciary and the Parliament are not by themselves the chief markers of constitutional order. On one hand with unparalleled wealth of the commercial class and its control and influence over higher education and the culture industry, old-type representative politics is losing relevance to popular politics. Representatives are less to lead people; they are to teach people to be responsible. Thus like the colonial rulers, independent India's rulers too now have to rebuke the Indians for not being law-abiding, for being irresponsible, for being lax and accommodating to unruly acts and for not living up to promises. The Emergency (1975–77) thus marked in many ways the redefining of the political society in India, which dispensed with utopia along with its rights promises, and hereafter politics would become a serious business of administration, government and ruling.

Yet the roots of a scenario where the constitution is continuously buffeted from all sides by the winds of popular politics and therefore made permanently unstable were, at least partly, in the constitution itself. In the heady atmosphere of national independence in the aftermath of the Second World War the constitution had included certain rights – an act which would have been impossible in today's stifled atmosphere. The document in this way became the inviting flag for popular constitutionalism. The constituent assembly, notwithstanding severe limitations of its basis, signalled the idea that people made the constitution, and that beyond the legislators, judges, jurists, our Blackstones and Kelsens, there stood the people, who had earned freedom and had decided and would decide again and again what should be there in the constitution. This radical republicanism in a way was more unsettling than that of the Western model of republicanism largely derived from the French experience. It led to enormous number and amount of revisions of the text. In terms of constitutionalism at the grass roots, what happened in this period was instructive. Popular politics took its own way in interpreting what the constitution signified. Struggles for autonomy, equality, freedom, participation, representation and what can be termed direct forms of democracy constantly forced re-interpretations in a period of sixty-five years, whose results can be seen in all forms and at all levels. Historian James Vernon gives us a minutely documented account of British constitutional history at the grass roots in the nineteenth century. It shows how at the county level the great reform acts made their own specific sense, not always derived from constitutional functioning at the top.[1] We shall require probably some similar historical distance to write a deep history of the Indian experience of popular constitutionalism.[2]

We can note at least some constitutional features in India that have continuously encouraged popular interventions and interruptions.

In the first place we have to note the factor of the fundamental rights, guaranteed to all Indian citizens. These rights take precedence over any other law of the land (Art. 13). They include individual rights, such as equality before the law (Art. 14), right against discrimination (Arts. 15–18), freedom of speech and expression (Art. 19), right to life and liberty (20–21), freedom of association and peaceful assembly, freedom of religion (Arts. 25–28) and the right to constitutional remedies for the protection of these rights (Art. 32); but more significantly they are viewed in the perspective of the stated goal of abolishing the indignities and inequities of past social practices, prohibiting discrimination on the grounds of religion, race, caste, sex or place of birth; and forbidding trafficking in human beings and forced labour (Arts. 23–24).

Second, these rights also signal the arrival of group rights by way of protecting cultural and educational rights of minorities through ensuring that minorities can preserve their distinctive languages and establish and administer their own education institutions (Arts. 29–30). The combination of political, civil, social and economic (though very few) was unique at that time when the constitution was drafted.[3] These declarations subsequently widened through judicial interventions. Thus, right to life (a negative right) was interpreted positively as indicating the right to means of life. The arrival of group rights was made clearer by Part XVI of the constitution, which on the basis of the constitutional promise of social justice (in the Preamble) declared its promotion by elaborating a series of affirmative-action measures for disadvantaged groups. The 'Special Provisions Relating to Certain Classes' declared reservation of seats in the Lok Sabha and in state legislative assemblies for Dalits and indigenous people. The number of seats set aside for them was to be proportional to their share of the national and respective state populations. Part XVI also stipulated a special officer for scheduled castes and scheduled tribes to be appointed by the president to 'investigate all matters relating to the safeguards provided' for them, as well as periodic commissions to investigate the conditions of the backward classes. In 1969 the Twenty-Third Amendment extended the affirmative-action measures until 1980 beyond the original twenty-year period. The Forty-Fifth Amendment of 1980 extended them again until 1990, and in 1989 the Sixty-Second Amendment extended the provisions until 2000. The Seventy-Seventh Amendment of 1995 further strengthened the states' authority to reserve government-service positions for scheduled caste and scheduled Tribe members. Today affirmative actions are not merely administrative measures. They link rights to justice and help us to situate Part III of the Indian constitution in a refreshing way. Group rights have also led to the right to autonomy, mainly through Article 371 and the Fifth and Sixth Schedules. Rights are not simply to validate a utopia; by linking justice they become the measure by which utopia will be judged.[4]

Finally, we should also mention in this respect the feature known as the Directive Principles of State Policy, which are 'fundamental in the governance of the country', although legally not strictly enforceable. These principles are to assist in creating a social order featured by social, economic and political justice as enunciated in the basic text's preamble.[5] They are guidelines to create a just social order marked by liberty and equality (Art. 31C). Some principles articulate injunctions, for instance, the state 'shall direct its policy' towards securing owner-ship and control of the material resources of the country in a way so that they serve 'the common good'. The state has to 'endeavour to promote international peace and security'. It has to secure work at a living wage for all citizens; encourage worker's participation in industrial management; ensure just and humane conditions of work, including maternity leave; 'promote educational and economic inter-ests of Scheduled Castes, Scheduled Tribes, and other disadvantaged sectors of society'; develop a uniform civil code; offer free legal aid to all citizens; and achieve panchayati raj (democratically elected village councils to function as units of self-government). The Seventy-Third and Seventy-Fourth Amendment Acts (1992) achieved this goal.

Besides these three broad grounds, there are other constitutional fea-tures in the Indian Constitution, such as linguistic and federal rights. These rights not only mark the interface of the global and the local in the emergence of post-colonial democracy and the surge of claim mak-ing politics, but they also can be seen as the continuing counterpoint to the security-centric features of the same text. As we know, in each and every case of declaration of a particular right by the people, the government has been given a free hand by the same basic text and the judiciary to impose curbs in the interests of governing the people, the chosen words or phrases being 'in the interests of the sovereignty and integrity of India', 'the security of the State', 'friendly relations with foreign States', 'public order, decency or morality', 'public health' or in relation to 'contempt of court, defamation or incitement to an offence'. This is the way to manage the utopia, at the same time a strategy to manage the rights by turning these rights into matters of administration, negotiation, rule and control. Part XVIII of the constitution permits the state to suspend various freedoms and certain federal principles during the three forms of states of emergency: an emergency caused by threat or actual 'war or external aggression'; an emergency caused by the 'failure of constitutional machinery' in a state; and an emergency caused by a threat to the financial security or credit of the nation or a part of it. Under the first two forms, the fundamental rights, with the exception of protection of life and personal liberty, and some federal principles, are suspended. There is a considerable amount of literature on the 'securitization' of the Indian constitutional system, its inherent discriminatory nature (with the Muslims facing the brunt of the security system and security legislations, including the extraordinary acts).

In this perspective, the local sources of rights will remain contentious. One instance is the worst and the bloody exchanges of opinion and actual deaths on the streets in India on the reservation issue – particularly on the issue of 50 per cent increase of reserved seats in educational institutions. Also the moneyed classes have refused to accept the Mandal Commission's suggestion of 27 per cent reservation for backward classes in mercantile offices, and in general private sector. The Centre has already directed state governments to increase reservation for backward categories in the state-level institutions. There have been several commissions engaged by both the states and the Centre to put to effect the constitutional provision of reservation for the scheduled castes, tribes and the other backward classes – but discontent has remained among moneyed classes on what constitutes backwardness, and the norms of social justice. Other contentious issues are the right to retain autonomy of cultural institutions of the minorities, state regulations over Articles 19–21 to the extent of taking away life without the due process of law by means of Special Powers Acts. More fundamentally, over the years a conflict has developed over the primacy of commercial interests and the fundamental rights. Add to that the fact that the sovereign today thinks that only 'extraordinary powers' can make state effectively counter the 'global' challenge of terrorism and efforts from outside to undermine the integrity of the country. Globalization therefore is making state soft only in one sense, namely in acknowledging rights of the people, but the same state is hard in coming down on recalcitrant sections of society by assuming special and exceptional powers. This is a global trend, and possibly it has been always so.[6]

In the context of what we have discussed so far, we can note the following four characteristics in this specific discourse on Indian constitutional governance.

The first characteristic of the Indian rights revolution is the salience of group rights, which began with the first moment of constitutionalism in India – the Morley Minto Reforms (1909), and then progressed through various phases to find its shape in the constitution of independent India.[7] This history also includes the story of the issue of affirmative action for the Dalits, which became a contentious issue for the Hindu nationalist leadership in 1929–32 during the two Round Tables convened by the British rulers in London, reaching its climax in the form Gandhi's fast and then ending with an agreement between Gandhi and Ambedkar in the form of Poona Pact. With this was achieved the nationalist consensus for justice for the Dalits, though to be sure the Dalit struggle for justice continued after that. Similarly the issue of autonomy for the indigenous people has a history of negotiation between the globally given constitutional form (in this case, autonomy) and local struggle for land, and forest, rights and political power, particularly by the indigenous people.

The second characteristic is that while rights, especially group rights, make the constitutional discourse permanently subject to popular interpretations and interventions, the particular nature of decolonization and the nature of the transition from colonial subjugation to citizenship marks the constitutional system. Thus, the new government has retained the old security apparatus, added new features to it and turned all rights and justice provisions into governing fields. The governmentalization of rights is a part of the authoritarian structure of rule legitimized by an electoral democracy.

The third characteristic of the Indian discourse of constitutional governance shows how the horizon of rights remains still unmeasured by law – because it is not legality that defines the language of rights but popular ideas of justice. It is this *excess* or the *beyond* that impels law to catch up occasionally with what justice demands. Only in this way we can understand the huge impetus the rights movement has received in the wake of issues of justice due to massive developmental measures in the country.

The fourth feature is the co-existence of two distinct influences – global and the local. A classic instance of such parallel but interacting influences is the right to autonomy, which has deep local roots, but which also represents the globalization of the politics of autonomy.

These four characteristics point to a possible answer to the question we raised in the beginning, namely, what is specific in the present moment of global history that makes this question a universal question as well? We can try to provide a brief answer on the basis of what has been discussed so far.

The present situation known as one of globalization while having some new features bears resemblance with the earlier epochs of globalization also. Just as constitution-making in the mid-nineteenth century (beginning with the last decade of the eighteenth century), or in the aftermath of the Second World War continuing through the next decade or so had global dimensions and roots, likewise we now have the situation where constitutions are being made, re-made, brought back to discussion and being subject to popular interventions in as much as they are being subjected to massive judicial reviews, which reflect of the former. The justice-seeking demands and the calls to activate the justice-bearing provisions in the constitution are competing with the security-centric provisions, dimensions and implications of the same constitution. Securitization of politics in the name of war against terror, growth of oligarchies in democracy, governmentalization of rights and spread of claims to autonomy as the mark of a re-surge of democracy worldwide notwithstanding the domination of neo-liberal ideology – these are all global features.[8]

It is true that in traditional discussion on comparative constitutionalism, we have seldom references to this interplay. Typically the focus is on a comparative study of provisions and the courts, because the attention is on interpretations and the legal task of interpreting constitutions. Yet, how judges resolve the problem of keeping a constitution a living document[9] through 'interpretation' is problematic, because legitimate interpretation can be difficult to distinguish from illegitimate change. There is no inherent criterion of fidelity to the norms of say democracy and federalism. The stakes are high in the matter of how judges interpret a constitution – they may even rule that an army coup is constitutional. Often the greater difficulty of amending a constitution is avoided through the route of judicial interpretation. These comparative studies again often go to extreme length in studying how judges should remedy the failures or limits on the part of the constitution founders in anticipating developments forcing amendments and judicial interpretations. How does one decide if the constitution is somewhere ambiguous? Or, how can we decide the extent to which the meaning of a constitution can and should be determined by 'original' intentions, purposes and understandings of its founders? And, therefore the accompanying question: how much weight to give to 'original' intentions and how much to the 'contemporary' imperatives? Finally, if the court is the guardian of the constitution, and therefore has the duty and authority to interpret the basic text, what exactly is it guarding? Is it a set of reasonably fixed set of rules and principles, laid down at the founding, which must not be changed? Or, does the force of those rules and principles ultimately depend on some abstract principles and values, whose effective protection call for judicial intervention?[10] These questions can hardly be addressed – though they are done in judicial discourses – without reference to the present era of cosmopolitan constitutionalism where lawyers and judges often under the influence and pressure of popular politics look beyond their own borders for ideas from other jurisdictions. All these tell us that comparing legal-constitutional practices must take into account the interplay of the local and the global sources of new constitutional ideas. It is in this way that juridical justice congealed in the form of constitutionalism is permanently subject to change through its recursive confrontation with two facts of life – the fact of a dispute known by the name, litigation when brought to court, and the fact of the production of social norms. Modern experience of constitutionalism is not just marked by the salience of this contradictory experience, but also by another contradiction, which is inherent, namely that between legal norms and popular ideas of justice. At times legislations driven by concerns of social justice undermine juridical justice and vice versa. Likewise, principles of moral justice, developed on the basis of mutual respect in daily interaction and systematized by philosophical ethics, exist in a similar relation of mutual contradiction with claims of the legal just.

It is this contradictory experience – which we can term as the *concrete universality of law* and the constitution – that makes the post-colonial experiences of constitutionalism globally relevant. While constitutions are being made particularly in the post-colonial part of the world (also in countries of Eastern Europe, the scene of 'decolonization by default') to restore the state on the assumed universality of the nature and form of rule of law and democratic legality, the situation is marked with different legalities, illegalities, contested spaces for claims and varying relations between constitution, laws, the law-adjudicating institutions and these contested spaces of claims.

Post-colonial constitutional experience

With the interplay of the universality and specifics of law as the background we can now venture into answering the first question: what is specifically post-colonial in this experience of the constitutional? As a first step towards answering that question, let us first summarize what has been argued till now in this and previous chapters on the Indian constitutional experience. We tried to show how colonial constitutionalism forms a crucial part of the Indian constitutional experience.[11] By the term colonial constitutionalism we indicated the fact that colonial regulation and law-making practices were unique in the sense that while these practices were not covered by mainstream constitutional history and theory, this history of colonial constitutionalism was critical in the evolution of the constitutional experience in both colonies and countries that were the once colonial rulers. We also indicated how in the post-colonial life of a country such as India the story of the emergence of a justice-seeking subject could not be simply reduced to the history of the emergence of a legal category called the citizen, that this story had other elements, which made the 'game of justice' bigger than the story of constitution and laws.[12] We shall now combine these two aspects of the Indian constitutional experience in order to make sense of the specificity of the post-colonial in this.

In India there is a renewed interest in the working of the constitutional functioning due (a) to the current debates over transition, restoration and reform of the state and its legal machinery in the post 1991 period; (b) renewed discussion in legal, security and political circles over the institution of citizenship; (c) fresh inquiries in colonial ways of rule, the continuity of colonial legal structure of law and order and the historical background of the composition of modern sovereignty; (d) and finally, the popular politics of justice posing challenges for constitution and legal machineries to provide spaces for claim makings – a task for which the traditional patriarchal structure of rule of law and democratic legality are ill-equipped. Questions are being raised: how will law deal with a situation of increasing illegality, contentious claims and exceptional situations? Will constitutional legality depend on strategies of differential inclusions to cope with social unrest, increasing illegality, contentious claims and exceptional situations? Why does a democratic constitution produce and tolerate differential citizenship? What will happen then to the outlaws and half-legal entities, such as illegal migrants, refugees and militant oppositionists under constitutional regimes? How will the judiciary as an institution cope with this increasing contentious situation reflecting the pressing claims of various powerless social groups? And thus the most important question, can the constitution produce a dialogic culture in view of various social contentions and claims? Even the government of the day realizes the gravity of the issues. In the past ten years or little more we have witnessed therefore a spate of policies declared by the government on education, right to work, information, right to food, forest rights of the indigenous population groups, social security of the unorganized labour, affirmative measures and several such issues, and action plans (at times enabling legislations) based on these policies. Working through policies is a mode that avoids the obstacle of constitutional immobility, strengthens the executive, gives it more negotiating space to face popular pressures and adds flexibility to the representational system, which would be now hopefully able to re-design the relation between the elected representative, the popular groups and the administrative system. The situation throws new light on the genealogy of rule of law as a plank of governing. It enables us to better understand the relation of rule of law with democracy, popular politics, citizenship and ways of representation.

If the history of constitution-making in most of the world is any guide, we can see that it is violence that makes constitution possible. Violence registers the claims, which the society has to find a way to recognize and settle. Civility is often the mode for that recognition and settlement of claims. Through constitution-making, which is one form of civility, society wants to recognize and settle these contesting claims. Constitution puts down in terms of legal recognition and settlement of these claims what is permissible and not permissible. Law in this way delineates legality and illegality. While in the post-colonial situation contentions continue and violence does not vanish, in fact increases in some cases, in the eyes of law it can only be illegal. One may ask, therefore, how much scope is there of legal pluralism, especially under a constitutional system unable to accommodate contentious claims and boundary transgression by these claims?[13] Issues of immigration, refugee crises and the demands for the constitutional recognition of social and economic rights, increasing pressure on courts to assume executive functions to extricate constitutions from the closure that it faces today – these are only some of the relevant ones that define the borders of constitutionalism today.

Yet as social issues these are not all that new. Anthropologists have a long tradition of studying law mostly as taboo. But it is only recently that violence and illegality – both outside the rule of law – have become concerns of law and governance, so much so that law cannot simply remain content with saying that something is illegal. Owing to the fundamental interface of legality and illegality, the illegal is becoming the main subject of law. Post-colonial experiences of constitutionalism in this way have raised the issue and the possibility of sharing sovereignty. They have by the same token brought back the issue of private property, particularly landed property, in renewed discussion. The post-colonial argument does not discuss the semantics and the legal theories of property. It scrutinizes the issue of property in the context of social justice. This is the death knell of Scottish Enlightenment, because reason has been overwhelmed by passion for justice.

In short, post-colonial constitutionalism tells us of the borders of the constitutional experience. These borders are not new; they are there since the experiences of constitution-making began. Bartolome Clavero in a fascinating essay, 'Why American Constitutional History Is Not Written', tells us of these borders of constitutional experiences in the context of the US constitutional history. Clavero shows how treaties and social compacts prior to 1787 were undermined in the process of constitution-making, and thus different claims earlier recognized were now dismissed through the process. Alternative constitutional possibilities were silenced, and as Clavero says, the American Constitution succeeded in effacing its history while agreeing to become the subject of constitutional biography. The entire set of amendments became the 'extended borderless body of an unwritten constitution'.[14] The constitution became an intergenerational project with a 'deep love' for it shared practically by all US constitutionalists and constitutional historians – 'the real stronghold of Whig history today'.[15]

If that is the case, it calls for a new way to write constitutional history that will tell us the reasons as to why the constitution remains a 'living document'. Either the text is loved and kept alive in the form of an 'extended borderless body of an unwritten constitution', or continuous popular challenges and situations of illegalities and semi-legalities force the judicial-legislative discourse of the polity to keep the text a referral point. Yet to point out the rival Whig and the critical versions is not enough. It is necessary to have a proper historical method to write the constitution's biography. As mentioned in chapter five, the whiggish picture of the constitution in India for instance was largely evoked by the panoramic reports in the newspapers and learned books by Granville Austin and others, which suggested a nationwide public political sphere that was pluralistic, representative and responsive at the same time. But precisely at the same time, parallel and distinct from this, in various local meetings, local council deliberations, party assemblies, political rallies and public hearings, groups of populations were experiencing constitutional politics in a different way, which did not take the meaning of the constitution too literally and often mixed illegal and semi-legal behaviour with popular constitutional thinking. Classic instances of this process are the various judgements on Article 21 (Right to life), the Seventy-Third and the Seventy-Fourth

Amendment Acts, the repeal of the Forty-Second Amendment Act and the amendments leading to linguistic reorganization of states. The press played a central role in spreading popular constitutionalism. Political parties played a similar crucial role. But most remarkable has been the role of the semi-legal and illegal behaviour of sections of society (for instance, armed protest movements) in spreading new ideas on the constitution. These myriad of local articulations have resulted in public political debates, and not the other way round. Constitutional audiences have become in this way remarkably variegated.

One more factor: probably elections, more than all these taken together, impact on popular constitutional conduct. Millions of people, constrained by and freed in turn of various factors, repeatedly went to vote not to select their representatives, but to declare their judgements on rule and the character of governance. In this way in the past sixty years citizenship of the political nation has become a provisional or contingent matter – but provisional or contingent not on the possession of reason, virtue and independence, but on collective political actions including at times collective violence, passionate and emotional public actions and spontaneous and organized political and social movements on the streets. As if, better not to be citizens, but to have the autonomy of collective actions. Each of these outbursts results in modifications of constitutional behaviour of the official nation – through amendments, judgements and enabling legislations. The latter, while recognizing popular dissent, also aims at disciplining and closure of the same. The same institutions (such as parties and newspapers), which in the beginning had been instrumental in spreading the news of dissent, later try to restrict the scope of popular interventions. We have grounds therefore to question the enabling and emancipative tone of Whig historiography that tells that institutions of representative democracy such as political parties, newspapers, free judiciary and Parliament have strengthened constitutional politics in India. This tone hides the fact that their restrictive and masculine ways have sought to discipline popular constitutionalism. In the subterranean world of popular constitutionalism the battle standard for reforms carries the mark of an intense desire for making everything subordinate to the interests of the people. The legal language of citizenship does not matter here much. The tropes of popular constitutionalism put almost a utopian emphasis on the phenomenon of a just people struggling to restore the lost claims for dignity and the lost fruits of past revolutions – in the Indian case the lost fruits of *swaraj*, freedom and independence. The constitutionalist discourse can thus be seen as a narrative of dialogues between power and powerlessness, often being carried on in the sphere of the politically unconscious and disorganized, but alive with the shouts of those excluded from the historical mission of the nation's constitution.

The central conflict in the constitutional sphere is in this way epitomized in the phenomenon of popular constitutionalism. Reforming legislations, policies, court judgements, jurists' arguments – all these often in dramatic way bring out the nature and the fact of contests and challenges put forward by popular constitutionalism. These challenges are at the same time challenges to the limits to our constitutional imagination. The historical method of writing the constitution's biography has to see these as belonging to a 'family of populisms', whose very instability becomes a paramount factor in a constitution's life.

Yet one has to be careful because the entire constitutional story of affirmative politics in India does not present a monolithic and undifferentiated sphere of popular constitutionalism.[16] The story of popular constitutionalism breaks into different narratives of classes and populisms, as diverse and contradictory as the official discourse of constitutionalism. Our historical method must have contention therefore as its principal gradient.

We can now return to the issue of the interface of legality and illegality as one of the features of the contentious scenario. Indeed one can argue that while governmental forms of justice are based on legality and the need to make justice conform to the demands and imperatives of law and legality, popular forms of justice begin on illegal basis because these popular forms have their genesis in confrontation with law. By accentuating different claims globalization forces law and legality to face the demands and imperatives of recognition and the re-distribution of resources. The following narrative will highlight how recognition of claims becomes the starting point of acknowledging the normative base of those claims. Recognition is also a step towards re-distribution, because recognition is essentially one of claims that transgress the boundaries of legality.[17] Recognition, as Nancy Fraser points out, is more than the 'moral psychology of pre-political suffering'.[18] It involves political contentions constantly challenging the bounds of legality and pushes the rulers to redistribute wealth. What will the constitution do in such situation?

To make sense of the contention and the contradiction, we propose to narrate here what happened in Mumbai (Bombay) in 2005 relating to what is known as the bar dancers' case. It is a story of subaltern globalization, the renewed game of the body, the inherent contests in which law plays its role and the ambiguous roles of the state, democracy and the discourse of development.

Bar dancers of Mumbai

The government of Maharashtra, a state in India, banned dance bars from 15 August 2005. The proposal to ban dance bars triggered widespread opposition, and not only from the few lakhs who stood to lose their jobs. Many prominent public figures, including lawyers and activists, took up cudgels for the bargirl. They insisted that work was a fundamental right of those facing the axe. But the deputy chief minister and home minister of Maharashtra, the person behind the ban decision, argued that dance bars were dens of crime and 'anti-national activities' and had to be controlled.[19] Following the ban protests erupted from various sides (social workers, bar dancers, rights activists, lawyers, some political groups, owners of bars where dances were performed and others), while voices in support of the ban came from conservative political sections, vast sections of middle classes, villagers of substance and property and some media groups, and these voices were equally strident. Newspapers reported that the crime rate increased in the city after the ban took place, at least the police was reported to be apprehensive that many dance bar waiters were turning to crime, since their source of livelihood had been affected by the bar ban. Crime syndicates reaped the harvest as gang lords on visiting a dance bar would select the potential recruits, some of whom turn to loot and burgle, and would be later promoted as recruiting agents for more dance bar waiters. One report said,

> Cops admit the spike in Mumbai's crime graph is linked to the thousands of waiters and stewards that have lost their jobs following the dance bar ban. Till last July 30, 189 robberies were registered. In the same period this year, 218 robberies have been registered – a jump of 20 per cent. While there were 21 cases of dacoities last year till July end, in the same period this year, 29 cases have been registered.

'We had arrested one Rajesh Gowda a few days ago who was a waiter earlier but became a robber subsequently', police inspector from Crime Branch said.[20]

The controversy continued nonetheless. A report previously cited also mentioned that the High Court squashed an 'obscenity case' against a Nagpur dance bar. It ruled that the obscenity at the dance bar 'didn't cause any annoyance to anyone'. Another setback to the proposal came with the National Human Rights Commission (NHRC) seeking comments of the Maharashtra government on its reported decision, and star MPs Sunil Dutt (now deceased) and Govinda vociferously protesting against the proposed clampdown. The report asked, 'What is the truth behind the issue? Who are the affected people? Where do "bar girls" come from? What is the economics of dance bars? What are the existing laws?' And then it went on by adding,

> Most bar owners offer security to the girls and provide safe transport to return home after work, which ends at 1 or 2 am. Many bar dancers are married and have children. The clients come from all strata of society. Of late, there have been more college students, young corporate adventurers and even schoolboys who bribe and get in whenever they can. . . . As Madhur Bhandarkar's award-winning film *Chandni Bar* showed, bar dancers are often brought to the city by relatives who exploit their youth to make money. Men sexually abuse some. The condition of such girls is often pitiable. Many are the sole breadwinners of their families if the husbands are alcoholics or absconders. There are also girls who voluntarily work in dance bars for money. It is possible that bars could be meetings places of crime lords, corrupt officials and exploiters of women. . . . Those speaking for this industry say that there are 75,000 dance bar girls, whose jobs are under threat. This will cause a major employment problem for this large section of people whose families depend on the incomes of the girls for their livelihood. The government, however, says that the number is highly exaggerated and actually there are only 11,000 women employed in bars. . . . Even today, on the Foras Road, Grant Road and Opera House there are homes of dancing and singing girls which are crowded with men from very respectable families who are called Sheths in Bambaiya language. Many Bollywood films showcase the lifestyle where landlords, goons, criminals and dacoits have dancing girls perform before them. The states of Bihar, Uttar Pradesh and Madhya Pradesh too are known for this tradition.

And then it concluded by quoting government officials who reportedly said,

> 'The diktat is easier to write than implement. The law, even if passed, will be extremely difficult to implement.' There is confusion as to which bars will have to be closed if discos, pubs and other places can operate. How will the segregation take place?

There is immense opposition to the law and both bar owners, dancers and their supporters will fight the battle. The law has to be drafted carefully.[21]

In any case, the Bombay High Court on Wednesday set aside the law banning dance bars in Mumbai on 13 April 2006. The court gave eight weeks time, during which the cancelled licences of the dance bars could be re-issued. It also gave the state government time to appeal against the order if it wished to. Justice F. I. Rebello and Justice R. S. Dalvi heard petitions filed by the Association of Hotels and Restaurants (AHAR), Bhartiya Bar Girls Union and NGOs like Forum against Oppression of Women and Majlis. The legal distinction between 'prohibited establishments' and 'exempted establishments' drew criticism from the Bench. According to the act, the government prohibited performance of any kind in an 'eating-house, permit room or beer bar'. However, provisions were made to exempt performances in 'theatres, registered sports clubs, three starred hotels and above' or any other establishment which the state government deemed to be significant for tourism promotion. The Bench noted that

> Considering that the object of the legislation is to prevent dances that are obscene and hence derogatory to women's dignity, and to prevent exploitation of women, we find there is no nexus between the classification and the object of the Act. . . . If women, other than as dancers, can work in prohibited establishments and that does not amount to exploitation, we do not see how it becomes exploitation when women dance to earn their livelihood.

Referring to Article 19 (6) of the constitution, the High Court said the amendment to the old Bombay Act was a restriction that 'prevents bar owners from organizing the same or similar dances as in the exempted establishments and bar dancers from performing dances other than those which are restricted'. The Bench held that such a restriction was 'unreasonable, not in public interest and consequently void'. Referring to studies by the Tata Institute of Social Sciences and Research, and the Centre for Women's Studies at SNDT University, Justice Dalvi said only a small percentage of bar dancers were minors, and he directed the two NGOs to hold inquiries and said, 'In case of illegal employment of a minor in a dance bar, the matter must be reported to a police station for action against the bar owner and to rescue and rehabilitate those children'.[22] Presently the case lies with the Supreme Court for a final verdict.

Meanwhile what did the bar dancers feel? Even in alternative jobs as waitresses? Here is a contemporary report:

> The strobe lights have been turned off. But that was a good two years ago. Now, Nikita and Kavita seem comfortable in the dim lights as they make their way around tables at a rundown bar in Ghatkopar, a Mumbai suburb. The bulb sways and you catch the loud make-up as Nikita, a waitress at the bar, pours out another peg for a drunk, leering customer.
>
> 'I don't like this job, but we have to earn our living', says the 16-year-old. It is the job Nikita settled for after the Maharashtra government banned dance bars two years ago. The ban, thought to be tactless and insensitive, left an estimated 75,000 bar girls jobless. Some like Nikita and her aunt, 25-year-old Kavita, found jobs as waitresses and many others turned to prostitution. Activist Varsha Kale, who has been fighting for lifting the ban, says 26 bar dancers killed themselves after the ban. The number is misleading, she says, because some of the suicides weren't recorded. The ban brought their world crashing down. . . . '(Earlier) Money kept coming in and we were well off,' says Kavita. The girls came home to good food and the younger children at home went to schools. But after the ban, everything changed – no films, no good food; just awful, miserable faces at home. 'We used to get lavish tips from customers at the dance bars. But now, we hardly get tips,' says Nikita.
>
> Nikita's mother, Pinky Madiwal, a 32-year-old former bar dancer, fears for her daughter's safety. 'Being a waitress is risky. Our customers at dance bars never misbehaved with us. We usually dance on a special platform or raised dais, at a good distance from the customers.'
>
> The catcalls and wolf whistles sometimes brought the house down, but the girls were safe. But it's difficult being a waitress, says Kavita. 'We have to be wary of unruly customers. It can be tough, waiting at a table and putting up with all the verbal and physical advances.'
>
> At 32, Pinky is already a grandmother. Her eldest daughter Neelu, 19, also a bar dancer, recently gave birth to a daughter. Pinky's youngest daughter Neha, 11, is too young to work. 'She used to go to school when we were dancing. But after the ban, we pulled her out of school,' says Pinky.
>
> 'Those days were different. We earned anything between Rs 500 and Rs 2,000 a day. In dance bars, for the kind of tips we got, the

maximum we had to do was to disclose our cell phone number. But as waitresses, for Rs 100 tip, we have to put up with touchy-feely people. I don't like it,' says Pinky.

Nikita chips in. 'Customers want to get naughty by giving a measly tip of Rs 10.' The lure of quick money has pushed some of the girls into the flesh trade. 'At dance bars, it was entirely up to us if we wanted to go out with a customer. Now girls are forced into it as they don't have an alternative,' says Pinky.

Bar dancers have few alternatives. One of the reasons is that most of them are illiterate and poor. With huge families back home waiting for the girls to bring money, they are desperate enough to take on any job that comes their way.

'It's hard to shake off the stigma. People don't give us jobs,' says Pinky. So distraught was Pinky that she decided to write a book on the pain and suffering she went through. The 400-page book written in Hindi talks about Pinky's life as a bargirl and the bleak days after the ban. Pinky recalls that the ban was so sudden that they thought it would be a temporary phase and that it wouldn't last more than a few days. For now, the case is still pending before the Supreme Court after the Bombay High Court lifted the ban last year.[23]

Yet, it was not pure lament. Some bar dancers decided to fight elections to make their case strong. The British newspaper the *Independent* reported,

The once famous dance-bar girls of Bombay are planning to stage a comeback – by standing as candidates in local elections next month. Their platform is simple: to overturn the citywide ban on their work and reopen the clubs where they used to perform. . . .

It is believed to have put some 75,000 dancers out of work, and now the girls are intent on fighting back. They are to meet tomorrow to decide whether to form their own political party or stand as independent candidates in municipal elections. There was major controversy when the state government decided to close the bars. It accused them of 'corrupting the youth' and being barely disguised brothels, and the bar girls of being prostitutes – accusations the dancers and bar owners deny. They say they were performers and there was no sex involved.

The truth lay in between. Certainly to visit the dance bars you would not think they were brothels. The audience may have been made up entirely of men, but the dancers were fully dressed in

long shimmering length skirts, and beyond the odd exposed mid-
riff there was no flesh on view. The dancers were rarely prostitutes. Some were purely dancers, but their dubious reputation
came from many who worked as a form of courtesan. They would
encourage relationships with regular visitors and agree to meet
them outside. The relationship was financial: they would milk the
men for expensive gifts – a mobile telephone, a television, even a
better flat. But they would rarely sleep with a man until they had
had a relationship for several months.[24]

A BBC report brought out more clearly the dynamics of the politics
of the body entering now official politics. The report said,

Jobless bar dancers in the Indian city of Mumbai (Bombay) say
they will fight forthcoming municipal elections to gain a foothold
in government. . . .
   'We had no voice anywhere so we felt that we needed to have
some sort of representation in the state's municipal corporation
and the legislative assembly'. . . .
   'We plan to fight these elections with all our might and try to get
in as many candidates as possible'.. . .
   The president of the Indian Bar Dancers' Association, Varsha
Kale, says many bar dancers have expressed a desire to enter politics and fight for themselves as well as others.
   She says this was a positive step, but warned that the dancers
may not taste victory in this round.
   'There is very little time (before elections) and many of the former bar girls have been jobless for a very long time. So the kind
of time and power required to win elections is not there,' she says.
   Ms Kale, however, says given more time the dancers will certainly win positions of power.[25]

If this is how the internal dynamics of the politics moved on, were
there other significant dimensions of politics to strike attention? Here
the bar dancers' story becomes linked with more fundamental processes – of subaltern globalization, law, trafficking, protests by human
rights activists, the incorporation of the body in the banal politics of
democracy and the issue of political subjectivity. Flavia Agnes, a feminist jurist, writing on these aspects remarked,

An important feature of a rally organized by bar owners against
police raids in Mumbai on 20 August 2004 was the emergence of

the bar dancer. A large number of girls with their faces covered were at the forefront of the rally holding up placards with blown up pictures of semi clad Bollywood stars. It was a statement questioning the hypocritical morality of the state and civil society. This image became the motif for the media for the following year when the controversy around the bar dancer was raging. . . . During the discussion with the bar dancers, it emerged that while for the bar owners it was a question of business losses, for the bar girls it was an issue of human dignity and right to livelihood. When the bars are raided, it is the girls who are arrested, but the owners are let off. During the raids the police molest them, tear their clothes, and abuse them in filthy language. At times, the girls are retained in the police station for the whole night and subjected to further indignities. But in the litigation, their concerns were not (of course) reflected. . . . As far as the abuse of power by the police was concerned, we were clear. But what about the vulgar and obscene display of the female body for the pleasure of drunken male customers, which was promoted by the bar owners with the sole intention of jacking up their profits? It is here that there was a lack of clarity. . . . An NGO, Prerana, which works on anti-trafficking issues, had filed an intervening application, alleging . . . that bars are in fact brothels and that they are dens of prostitution where minors are trafficked. While the police had raided the bars on the ground of obscenity, the intervention added a new twist to the litigation because they submitted that regular police raids are essential for controlling trafficking and for rescuing minors. The fact that the police had not abided by the strict guidelines in anti-trafficking laws and had molested the women did not seem to matter to them. . . . Suddenly the dancer from the city's sleazy bars and shadowy existence had spilled over into the public domain. Her photographs were splashed across the tabloids and television screens. She had become the topic of conversation at street corners and market places; in ladies compartments of local trains and at dinner tables in middle class homes. Every one had an opinion and a strong one at that. In her favour or more likely, against her; saint or sinner . . . worker or whore . . . spinner of easy money and wrecker of homes or victim of patriarchal structures and market economy? The debate on sexual morality and debasement of metropolitan Mumbai seemed to be revolving around her existence (or non-existence). . . . [26]

The ban and the contest brought out some uncomfortable questions, scarcely discussed in politics of civility. Can the state impose arbitrary and varying standards of vulgarity, indecency and obscenity for different sections of society or classes of people? If an 'item number' of a Hindi film can be screened in public theatres, then how can an imitation of the same be termed as 'vulgar'? Films, television serials, fashion shows and advertisements – all these industries use women's bodies for commercial gain. Then why is the ban on bars, which in any case employ women as waitresses, who will mingle with the customers more than the dancers (confined to the dance floor). If the anti-trafficking laws had not succeeded in preventing trafficking, how could the ban on bar dancing prevent trafficking? 'The "morality" issue had won. The "livelihood" issue had lost . . . in this era of liberalization and globalisation,' Flavia Agnes noted in the same article. During the entire period of controversy, the world of the bar dancer lay beyond controversy, also beyond the gaze of the feminist activists campaigning their cause. The bar dancer carefully guarded her world. Only now and then would it would spill over more as a defiant statement. So while the world was exposed to one aspect of their lives, which had all the problems – of parenting, poverty, pain and police harassment, this was only a partial projection, an incomplete picture. The other part consisted of constant negotiation of their sexuality, the dizzy heights they scaled while they danced draped in gorgeous chiffons studded with sequences, oozing out female erotica and enticing their patrons to part with a generous tip.

But this was not all to it. Jurist Flavia pointed out another angle, more significant than the morality angle but connected to it, namely the issue of women migrants who had flocked to the profession of bar dancing. In the midst of this increasing 'public' vilification of bar girls, on 26 August 2005, around eighty-five bar dancers working as waitresses were arrested. While the arrested bar owners, managers and male staff were released on bail the very next day; the women driven to penury could not pay the amount of Rs15,000 and were languishing in prison cells. They formed yet another layer of bar dancers. They were recent migrants, and extremely poor, and hence still in custody as they lacked even the basic support structure in the city. They did not have any friend or relative in Mumbai, or any identification like ration card or voter card. They were recent migrants. Most girls spoke Bengalis; some admitted to being Bangladeshis while others denied. All of them stated that they hailed from Kolkata and most had Hindu names. In their profession they had, however, taken on names of famous stars from Bollywood or television serials, thus completing the circle of invisibility of their lives. They claimed that they came to the city through some networks, and initially were brought to work as domestic maids but were later introduced to bars where they worked as waitresses or dancers. There was no coercion or force in getting the women to work at the bar. They all stated that while the work was marked by indignity and humiliation, they had no option than going back to the bars to dance, once the ban was lifted and they were released. Migrant workers were common among bar dancers. Police in the midst of the controversy cracked down in many places as 'flushing out operations'. They arrested quite a few, mostly former bar dancers, impoverished, illiterate, mostly Muslim, predominantly Bengali-speaking. Castigated as 'illegal immigrants' they would now languish in prison cells, until they produced papers to prove their claim to Indian citizenship. A lowly placed person in society, the bar dancer living on the edge of life, had challenged the legal mode of governing.

The key to an understanding of such situation is an appreciation of the phenomenon we have termed as popular constitutionalism.

In short, the idea of the basic structure is being subjected to debate again and again in the wake of the subaltern critiques of the working of the constitution, and it is this conflictive reality of popular interventions that determine the quality of life of a constitution.

As the reader will see, by now the original concern of the chapter, namely, 'The Constitution a Living Document?' has become quite complicated. We have already traced factors such as global influences and their interactions with local reasons, the surge of the idea of justice, the interface of legalities and illegalities in the political life of the country and most importantly, the phenomenon of popular constitutionalism. All these factors make contention and not synthesis the principal ingredient of a constitution's life. Contentious politics does not allow a constitution to lead a charmed life of retirement.

Yet precisely because these contentions are unstable in nature, they are not able to set up as a counter to the established constitutional legacy the ideal of another constitution or the parallel idea of a polity constituted by daily dialogues. The police powers reinforced by constitutional legitimacy bring out the limits to popular constitutionalism and make us realize the fact that governmental innovations facilitated by the constitution ultimately reinforce the dynamics of sovereignty, whose one expression is the 'police powers' and the effectiveness of 'rule of law'. There is always an intrinsic tension between the idea of democracy and the idea of a constitution. Constitutions rely on institutional explanations and structures. On the other hand democracies have to allow uncertainties flowing from popular interventions and interrogations. The ideas of freedom, equality and rights are unstable but compelling, and they are seen as plastic in relation to the state's interpretation of the political community in the framework of a constitution. Therefore, in the constitutional discourse politics appears as ugly, at times nefarious, and the political representatives are manipulative. In order to save the citizens from the politicians the constitution provides for judiciary, other institutions and norms as constraints, such as separation of powers.

Through this displacement of politics as activity that contends norms, viewpoints and procedures, the constitution ascribes divinity to its own norms, institutions and procedures, such as law and order machinery, definition of the political community called the country or the nation, judiciary, and what it thinks to be the supreme interest of the nation. The form of the constitution thus faces challenge from the constitutional imagination in popular politics, which continuously throws up a rich plurality of interests and an equally rich range of capabilities.

Illegalities are to be seen as part of popular politics. The bar dancers' case exemplifies that. But this was a rather soft instance. Each day we hear one or the other government minister and bureaucrat saying that the illegal movements led by the Left extremists known as the Maoists are against the constitution, and hence there is no scope for dialogue. At the same time we hear other equally numerous voices urging dialogues that must not flounder on the rock called the constitution. The experiences of South American countries coming out of several decades of dirty wars and embarking on new constitutional journeys stand in sharp contrast with the experiences of failure of the UN and other international managers of peace and stability to restore the state through restorative constitutions in Iraq, Afghanistan and several other places. The latter group of experiences should make us sober and help us to realize that the normative nature of justice is more a political than a legal project. Against a juridical idea of justice to be invoked under specific condition or circumstances a general desire of justice has spread throughout the world. How will constitutionalism fare in such condition?

We may well repeat the question indicated at the end of chapter five, are we coming to an end of the classical liberal age of constitution-making and therefore of constitutionalism itself, and arriving at a more practical age of politics?

Notes

1   James Vernon, *Politics and the People – A Study in English Political Culture, 1815–1867* (Cambridge: Cambridge University Press, 1993).

2   I have benefited greatly on the theme of popular constitutionalism (or as some say, insurgent constitutionalism) from my discussions with Kalpana Kannabiran and the writings of Upendra Baxi. The idea also owes to the life and writings of K. G. Kannabiran. See K. G. Kannabiran, *The Wages of Impunity – Power, Justice, and Human Rights* (Hyderabad: Orient Blackswan, 2004); Kalpana Kannabiran, *Tools of Justice – Non-Discrimination and the Indian Constitution* (New Delhi: Routledge, 2012).

3   Originally, the right to property was also included in the fundamental rights; however, the Forty-Fourth Amendment, passed in 1978, revised the status of property rights by stating, 'No person shall be deprived of his property save by authority of law.'

4   On the role of the discourses of affirmative actions in the history of post-independence popular politics in India, see Bharat Bhusan, "Indexing Social Justice in India – A Story of Commissions, Reports, and Popular Responses", in Ashok Agrwaal and Bharat Bhusan (eds.), *Justice and Law – The Limits of the Deliverable of Law*. Volume 2 of R. Samaddar (ed.) *State of Social Justice in India – Issues of Social Justice* (New Delhi: Sage, 2009), pp. 100–132.

5   The Forty-Second Amendment, which came into force in January 1977, raised the status of the Directive Principles by stating that no law implementing any of the Directive Principles could be declared unconstitutional on the grounds that it violated any of the fundamental rights. The Amendment Act added a new section to the constitution on 'Fundamental Duties' that enjoined citizens 'to promote harmony and the spirit of common brotherhood among all the people of India, transcending religious, linguistic and regional or sectional diversities'. It reflected an emphasis among rulers on the need to impose order and discipline to counteract what was thought to be the unruliness of Indian democracy. After the March 1977 general elections with the defeat of the Congress, the new Janata-dominated Parliament passed the Forty-Third Amendment (1977) and Forty-Fourth Amendment (1978). These amendments revoked the Forty-Second Amendment's provision that Directive Principles would take precedence over fundamental rights. However, the judiciary today agrees that the legitimacy of a state action can be affirmed by the test, namely, if it conforms to a Directive Principle, and if it does, its legitimacy is re-affirmed.

6   The main idea is obviously related to Giorgio Agamben, *State of Exception*, trans. Kevin Attell (Chicago: University of Chicago, 2004).

7   For this complicated history, Ajit Bhattacharjea (ed.), *Social Justice and the Constitution* (Shimla: Indian Institute of Advanced Studies, 1997); particularly the essay by A. S. Narang, "Justice for the Minorities".

8   On this, see the study by Heinz Klug, *Constituting Democracy – Law, Globalism and South Africa's Political Reconstruction* (Cambridge: Cambridge University Press, 2000).

9 On the theme of living constitution in the Indian context, see, E. Sridharan, Zoya Hasan and R. Sudarshan (eds.), *India's Living Constitution – Ideas, Practices, Controversies* (London: Anthem Press, 2005).

10 On this see, Jeffrey Goldsworthy (ed.), *Interpreting Constitutions* (New York: Oxford University Press, 2006), "Introduction".

11 For details, R. Samaddar, *The Materiality of Politics*, Volume 1, *The Technologies of Rule* (London and Delhi: Anthem Press, 2007), Chapter 1, pp. 19–58; also see, Kalpana Kannabiran and Ranbir Singh (eds.), *Challenging the Rule(s) of Law – Colonialism, Criminology, and Human Rights in India* (New Delhi: Sage Publications, 2008).

12 R. Samaddar, *The Materiality of Politics*, Volume 2, *Subject Positions in Politics* (London and Delhi: Anthem Press, 2007), Chapter 2, pp. 63–106; see also, Samaddar, "The Justice Seeking Subject", in Etienne Balibar, Sandro Mezzadra and Ranbir Samaddar (ed.), *The Borders of Justice* (Philadelphia: Temple University Press, 2012), Chapter 7, pp. 145–166.

13 On the issue of boundary transgression by these claims, see Ranabir Samaddar, "Prescribed, Tolerated, and Forbidden Forms of Claim Making", *Policies and Practices*, 10 April 2008, CRG Research paper Series, Kolkata; also http://www.mcrg.ac.in/pp18.pdf ; this text is based on Charles Tilly, *Regimes and Repertoires* (Chicago: University of Chicago Press, 2006), Chapter 4, where Tilly refers to 'prescribed, tolerated, and forbidden forms' of claim making.

14 Bartolome Clavero, *Why American Constitutional History Is Not Written* (Milano: Dott. A. Giuffre Editore, 2007), p. 1522.

15 Ibid., p. 1523; on this see further, James Tully, *Strange Multiplicity – Constitutionalism in an Age of Diversity* (Cambridge: Cambridge University Press, 1995), and Duncan Ivison, *Post-Colonial Liberalism* (Cambridge: Cambridge University Press, 2002).

16 See the essays in Ashok Agrwaal and Bharat Bhusan (eds.), *Justice and Law: The Limits of the Deliverables of Law, State of Justice in India: Issues of Social Justice*, Volume 2 (New Delhi and London: Sage, 2009).

17 On this see, N. Fraser and A. Honneth, *Redistribution or Recognition? A Political-Philosophical Exchange*, trans. Joel Golb, James Ingram, and Christiane Wilke (London: Verso, 2003).

18 Fraser, *Redistribution or Recognition?* p. 203.

19 'The Maharashtra Government's move to ban dance bars has created a furore. At issue is the livelihood of five lakh people, including dancers, owners and bar hands, in this Rs 1500-crore unorganised industry, besides the dangers of moral policing.' A Report by Vimla Patil, *The Tribune*, 30 April 2005.

20 *Mumbai Mirror* cited in, www.dancewithshadows.com/society/dance-bar-crime.asp.

21 "A Report by Vimla Patil", *The Tribune*, 30 April 2005.

22 "High Court Quashes Ban on Dance Bars", *The Hindu*, 13 April 2006.

23 *Indian Express*, 5 August 2007.

24 "Bombay's Bar Girls Fight for Their Jobs on Political Stage", Report by Justine Huggler, *The Independent*, 6 January 2007.

25 "Indian Bar Dancers to Seek Office", A Report by Monica Chadha, *BBC News*, Mumbai, http://news.bbc.co.uk/2/hi/south_asia/6233995.stm.

26 Flavia Agnes, "The Bar Dancer and the Trafficked Migrant – Globalisation and the Subaltern Existence", *Refugee Watch*, 30, December 2007, pp. 18–35, p. 21.

27 Zoya Hasan speaks of the 'politics of presence'; see her essay, "The 'Politics of Presence' and Legislative Reservations for Women", in Zoya Hasan, E. Sridharan and R. Sudarshan (eds.), *India's Living Constitution – Ideas, Practices, Controversies* (New Delhi: Permanent Black, 2002), pp. 405–427.

Bibliography

Agamben, Giorgio, "The Camp as the Nomos of the Modern", trans. Daniel Heller-Roazen in Hent de Vries and Samuel Weber (eds.), *Violence, Identity and Self-Determination* (Stanford, CA: Stanford University Press, 1997), pp. 106–118.

Agamben, Giorgio, *Homo Sacer – Sovereign Power and Bare Life*, trans. Daniel Heller-Roazen (Stanford, CA: Stanford University Press, 1998).

Agamben, Giorgio, *The Kingdom and Glory – For a Theological Genealogy of Economy and Government*, trans. Lorenzo Chiesa (Stanford, CA: Stanford University Press, 2011).

Agamben, Giorgio, *The Sacrament of Language – An Archaeology of the Oath*, trans. Adam Kotsko (Stanford, CA: Stanford University Press, 2011).

Agamben, Giorgio, *State of Exception*, trans. Kevin Attell (Chicago: University of Chicago, 2004).

Agnes, Flavia, "The Bar Dancer and the Trafficked Migrant – Globalisation and the Subaltern Existence", *Refugee Watch*, 30, December 2007, pp. 18–35, p. 21.

Almog, Shulamit and Amnon Reichman, "Casablanca: Judgment and Dynamic Enclaves in Law and Cinema", *Osgoode Hall Law Journal*, 42 (2), 2004, pp. 202–228.

Ambedkar, B.R., Speeches and Replies in the Constituent Assembly, www.ambedkar.org/ambcd/63B1.CA%20Debates%2005

Anderson, Benedict, *Under the Three Flags – Anarchism and Anti-Colonial Imagination* (London: Verso, 2005).

Ashraf, Shaikh Muhammad (ed., and published), *Letters of Iqbal to Jinnah with Foreword by Quaid-i-Azam* (1943; reprint, Faisalabad: Daira Ma'aref-i-Iqbal, 2002).

Backstone, William, *Commentaries on the Laws of England,* http://www.lonang.com/exlibris/blackstone/bla-102.htm and http://avalon.law.yale.edu/18th_century/blackstone_bk1ch2.asp

Balibar, Etienne, Sandro Mezzadra, and Ranabir Samaddar (eds.), *The Borders of Justice* (Philadelphia: Temple University Press, 2012).

Ball, Charles, *The History of the Indian Mutiny – A Detailed Account of the Sepoy Insurrection in India, and a Concise History of the Great Military*

Events Which Have Tended to Consolidate British Empire in Hindostan, 2 volumes, 1858–59 (reprint, Lahore: Sange-Meel Publications, 2007).

Bandopadhyay, Sandip, *Itihaser Dike Phire: Chechalissher Danga* (Kolkata: Utsa Manush, 1992).

Banerjee, Paula, "Aliens in the Colonial World," in Ranabir Samaddar (ed.), *Refugees and the State – Practices of Asylum and Care in India, 1947–2000* (New Delhi: Sage Publications, 2003), pp. 69–105.

Banerjee, Tapas Kumar, *Background to Indian Criminal Law* (Calcutta: R. Cambray & Co., 1963).

Batabyal, Rakesh, *Communalism in Bengal: From Famine to Noakhali, 1943–47* (New Delhi: Sage Publishers, 2005).

Bhattacharjea, Ajit (ed.), *Social Justice and the Constitution* (Shimla: Indian Institute of Advanced Studies, 1997).

Bhusan, Bharat, "Indexing Social Justice in India – A Story of Commissions, Reports, and Popular Responses," in Ashok Agrwaal and Bharat Bhusan (eds.), *Justice and Law – The Limits of the Deliverable of Law*, Volume 2 of R. Samaddar (ed.) *State of Social Justice in India – Issues of Social Justice* (New Delhi: Sage, 2009), pp. 100–132.

Bickel, Alexander M., *The Morality of Consent* (New Haven, CT: Yale University Press, 1975).

Bidwai, Praful, "Fighting Terror, Upholding Law – The Centrality of Human Rights" http://www.sdnbd.org/sdi/news/general-news/December-2002/21-12-2002/Feature.htm#Fighting (accessed on 30 December 2013).

Billings, Paul R. (ed.), *DNA on Trial: Genetic Identification and Criminal Justice* (Cold Spring: Harbor Laboratory Press, 1992).

Borradori, Giovanna, *Philosophy in a Time of Terror – Dialogues with Jurgen Habermas and Jacques Derrida* (Chicago: University of Chicago Press, 2003).

Bourke-White, Margaret, *Interview with India* (London: The Travel Book Club, 1951).

Brass, Paul (ed.), *Riots and Pogroms* (London: MacMillan, 1996).

Brown, Judith, *Gandhi's Rise to Power – Indian Politics 1915–1922* (Cambridge: Cambridge University Press, 1972).

Brown, Judith, *Gandhi and Civil Disobedience – The Mahatma in Indian Politics 1928–34* (Cambridge: Cambridge University Press, 1977).

Burke, Edmund, *Reflections on the Revolution in France* (1790; Oxford: Oxford University Press, 2009).

Calcutta Disturbances Commission of Enquiry, Records of Proceedings, Minutes of Evidence, 13 Volumes (Printed by the Superintendent of Printing, Government of Bengal, 1946–47).

The Calcutta Municipal Gazette, Vol. XLIV, No. 11, 10 August 1946

The Calcutta Municipal Gazette, Vol. XLV, No. 1–2, 30 November–7 December 1946.

The Calcutta Municipal Gazette, Vol. XLV, No. 13–14, 1–8 May, 1947.

"Calcutta Riot, 1946", *Banglapedia* (Dhaka: Asiatic Society of Bangladesh, 2000).

Chakraborty, Rathin (ed.), *Bangabhanga Pratirodh Andolan – Satabarsha Smarak Sangraha* (Kolkata: Natyachinta, 2006).

Charlesworth, Neil, "The Myth of the Deccan Riots of 1875", *Modern Asian Studies* 6 (4), 1972, pp. 401–421.

Chatterjee, Partha, *A Princely Impostor? The Kumar of Bhawal and the Secret History of Indian Nationalism* (New Delhi: Permanent Black, 2002).

Chatterji, Jaya, *Bengal Divided: Hindu Communalism and Partition, 1932–1947* (Cambridge: Cambridge University Press, 1995).

Chaturvedi, Jayati and Gyaneswar Chaturvedi, "Communal Violence, Riots, and Public Space in Ayodhya and Agra City: 1990 and 1992," in Paul Brass (ed.), *Riots and Pogroms* (London: MacMillan, 1996), pp. 177–200.

Clavero, Bartolome, *Why American Constitutional History Is Not Written* (Milano: Dott. A. Giuffre Editore, 2007).

Cole, Simon A, "Fingerprint Identification and the Criminal Justice System – Historical Lessons for the DNA Debate," in Paul R. Billings (ed.), *DNA on Trial: Genetic Identification and Criminal Justice* (Cold Spring: Harbor Laboratory Press, 1992), pp. 63–87.

Cole, Simon A, *Suspect Identities: A History of Fingerprinting and Criminal Identification* (New Jersey: Harvard University Press, 2001).

Constituent Assembly Debates, Official Report, 1946–1950 (New Delhi: Government of India, 1950).

Dalton, Dennis, "The Ideology of Sarvodaya – Concepts of Politics and Power in Indian Political Thought," in Thomas Pantham and Kenneth L. Deutsch (eds.), *Political Thought in Modern India* (New Delhi: Sage Publications, 1986), pp. 275–296.

Das, Suranjan, *Communal Riots in Bengal, 1905–1947* (New Delhi: Oxford University Press, 1991).

Dasgupta, Uma, *The Oxford India Tagore – Selected Writings on Education and Nationalism* (New Delhi: Oxford University Press, 2008).

Derrida, Jacques, *Acts of Literature*, ed. Derek Attridge (New York: Routledge, 1991).

Derrida, Jacques, *Rogues – Two Essays on Reason*, trans. Pascale-Anne Brault and Michael Naas (California: Stanford University Press, 2005).

Dutta, Pradip Kumar, *Carving Blocs – Communal Ideology in Early Twentieth Century Bengal* (New Delhi: Oxford University Press, 1999).

Eaton, Richard, *The Rise of Islam and the Bengal Frontier, 1204–1760* (Berkeley, CA: University of California Press, 1993).

Elkins, Caroline, *Britain's Gulag – The Brutal End of Empire in Kenya* (London: Junathan Cape, 2006).

Engineer, Asghar Ali (ed.), *Communal Riots in Post-Independence India* (Hyderabad: Sangam Books, 1984).

Eraly, Abraham, *Emperors of the Peacock Throne* (New Delhi: Penguin, 1997).

Evan, Colin, *A Question of Evidence – The Casebook of Great Forensic Controversies, from Napoleon to O.J.* (Hoboken, NJ: John Wiley and Sons Inc., 2003).

"Extracts from a Military Report on the Calcutta Riots", 24 August 1946 (WO 216/662) http://www.nationalarchives.gov.uk/education/topics/calcutta-riots.htm

Farooqui, Mahmood (compiled, translated and edited), *Besieged – Voices from Delhi, 1857* (New Delhi: Penguin, 2010).

Final Report on the Minor Settlement Operations in the District of Midnapore, 1907–13, Calcutta, 1916; *Bengal Home Political Files* (Calcutta, 1921–23).

Final Report on the Survey and Settlement Operations in the District of Midnapore, 1911 to 1917 (Calcutta: Book Secretariat Depot, 1918) and *Supplement to the Final Report* (Calcutta: Book Secretariat Depot, 1923).

Foucault, Michel, *The Birth of Biopolitics – Lectures at the College de France, 1978–1979*, trans. Graham Burchell (New York: Palgrave MacMillan, 2008).

Foucault, Michel, *Essential Works of Michel Foucault, 1954–1984*, Volume 3, ed. James Faubion, and trans. Robert Hurley (London: Allen Lane, The Penguin Press, 1994).

Foucault, Michel, "Omnes et Singulatim – Towards a Criticism of Political Reason", *The Tanner Lectures on Human Values*, Stanford University, 10 and 16 October, 1978, http://foucault.info/documents/foucault.omnes EtSingulatim.en.html

Foucault, Michel, *Power*, ed. James D. Fabion and trans. Robert Hurley (New York: The New Press, 2006).

Foucault, Michel, *Security, Territory, Population – Lectures at the College de France, 1977–1978*, trans. Graham Burchell (New York: Palgrave MacMillan, 2007).

Foucault, Michel, *Society Must Be Defended, Lectures at the College de France, 1975–76*, trans. David Macey (New York: Picador, 2003).

Foucault, Michel, *Technologies of the Self*, in Luther H. Martin, Huck Gutman and Patrick H. Hutton (eds.), (Amherst: University of Massachusetts Press, 1998).

Fraser, N. and A. Honneth, *Redistribution or Recognition? A Political-Philosophical Exchange*, trans. Joel Golb, James Ingram and Christiane Wilke (London: Verso, 2003).

Gandhi, M.K., *Non-Violence in Peace and War*, 2 volumes (Ahmedabad: Navajiban Publishing House, 1942 and 1949).

The German Ideology, Marx Engels Collected Works, Volume 5 (New York: International Publishers, 1973).

Ghosh, Anjan, Tapati Guha-Thakurta and Janaki Nair (eds.), *Theorizing the Present – Essays for Partha Chatterjee* (New Delhi: Oxford University Press, 2011).

GOB, *Home Political*, Confidential File no 351/46, Part B.

GOB, *Home Political*, File no 390/46

GOB, *Home Political*, File 398/46.

GOB, *Home Political*, File 398/46, Appendix A

GOB, *Home Political* File 398/46 GOB; File 390/46 GOB.GOB, *Political (Conf)*, 1918, 1921, 1923

Goldsworthy, Jeffrey (ed.), *Interpreting Constitutions* (New York: Oxford University Press, 2006).

Gooptu, Nandini, *The Politics of the Urban Poor in Early Twentieth Century India* (Cambridge: Cambridge University Press, 2005).

Gossman, Patricia A., *Riots and Victims – Construction of Communal Identity among Bengali Muslims, 1905–1947* (Boulder, CO: Westview Press, 1999).

Gould, William, *Hindu Nationalism and the Language of Politics in Late Colonial India* (Cambridge: Cambridge University Press, 2004).

Guha, Ramchandra, "Travelling with Tagore," in Anjan Ghosh, Tapati Guha-Thakurta, and Janaki Nair (eds.), *Theorizing the Present – Essays for Partha Chatterjee* (Delhi: Oxford University Press, 2011), pp. 152–187.

Guha, Ranajit, *History at the Limits of World History* (New York: Columbia University Press, 2002).

Hasan, M. (ed.), *India's Partition – Process, Strategy and Mobilization* (New Delhi: Oxford University Press, 1993).

Hasan, M. and N. Nakazato (eds.), *The Unfinished Agenda: Nation-Building in South Asia* (New Delhi: Manohar Publishers, 2001).

Hasan, Zoya, E. Sridharan and R. Sudarshan (eds.), *India's Living Constitution – Ideas, Practices, Controversies* (New Delhi: Permanent Black, 2002).

Hay, Douglas, "Property, Authority and the Criminal Law," in D. Hay, P. Linebaugh and E. P. Thompson (eds.), *Albion's Fatal Tree* (London: Allen Lane, 1975), pp. 38–63.

Hegel, G.W.F. *The Phenomenology of Spirit*, http://www.marxists.org/reference/archive/hegel/index.htm

Hegel, G.W.F., *Selections from Hegel's Lectures on Aesthetics*, eds. Bernard Bosanquest and W. M. Bryant, *The Journal of Speculative Philosophy* (1886), chapter, "The Idea of Beauty", http://www.marxists.org/reference/archive/hegel/works/ae/ch03.htm#45

Hodson, H.V., *Great Divide: Britain, India, Pakistan* (New Delhi: Oxford University Press, 1997).

Holmes, Stephen, *Passions and Constraints – On the Theory of Liberal Democracy* (Chicago: University of Chicago Press, 1995).

Horowitz, Donald L., "Direct, Displaced, and Cumulative Ethnic Aggression", *Comparative Politics*, 6 (1), October 1973, pp. 1–16.

Hunter, W.W., *Annals of Rural Bengal* (Edinburg: Murray and Gicbb and London: Smith, Elder and Co., 1868, publication of HMSO), http://archive.org/stream/annalsofruralben00huntuoft/annalsofruralben00huntuoft_djvu.txt

Hunter, W.W., *The Indian Musalmans* (Reprint; original title, *Our Indian Mussulmans: Are They Bound in Conscience to Rebel against the Queen?*) (New Delhi: Rupa, 2002).

Ignatieff, M., *A Just Measure of Pain – Penitentiary in the Industrial Revolution* (London: MacMillan, 1978).

Ikram, Sheikh Muhammad, *The Indian Muslims and Partition of India* (New Delhi: Atlantic Publishers, 1992).

Isin, Engin F., *Being Political – Genealogies of Citizenship* (Minneapolis: University of Minnesota Press, 2002).

Ivison, Duncan, *Post-Colonial Liberalism* (Cambridge: Cambridge University Press, 2002).

Jalal, Ayesha, *Self and Sovereignty – Individual and Community in South Asian Islam since 1850* (Lahore: Sang-e-Meel Publications, 2001).

Jameson, Frederic, "The Vanishing Mediator – Narrative Structure in Max Weber", *New German Critique*, 1 (winter), 1973, pp. 52–89.

Jayal, Niraja Gopal, *Citizenship and Its Discontents: An Indian History* (Ranikhet: Permanent Black, 2013).

Kannabiran, K.G., "Malimuth Committee – Safeguard the Rights of the Accused", *PUCL Bulletin*, January 2003, http://www.pucl.org/Topics/Law/2003/malimath.htm

Kannabiran, K.G., *The Wages of Impunity – Power, Justice, and Human Rights* (Hyderabad: Orient Blackswan, 2004).

Kannabiran, Kalpana, *Tools of Justice – Non-Discrimination and the Indian Constitution* (New Delhi: Routledge, 2012).

Kant, Immanuel, *Religion within the Limits of Reason Alone*, trans. Theodore M. Greene and Hoyt H. Hudosn, http://www.marxists.org/reference/subject/ethics/kant/religion/religion-within-reason.htm

Kant, Immanuel, "Third Definitive Article on Perpetual Peace," in Kant (ed.), *Perpetual Peace*, reproduced in P. Barash (ed.), *Approaches to Peace* (New York: Oxford University Press, 2000).

Kaufmann, D. Chaim, "When All Else Fails: Ethnic Population Transfers and Partitions in the Twentieth Century", *International Security*, 23 (2), Autumn 1998, pp. 120–156.

Khan, Rasheduddin (ed.), *Rethinking Indian Federalism* (Shimla: Indian Institute of Advanced Studies, 1997).

Khan, Syed Ghulam Hussain Khan (Tabatabaite), *Sier Mutaqherin Being the History of India from the Year 1118 to the Year 1194 (This Year Answer to the Christian Year of 1781–82) of the Hadjirah Containing in General the Reigns of the Seven Last Emperors of Hindostan and in Particular an Account of Bengal with Circumstantial Detail of the Rise and Fall of the Families of Seradj-ed-Dowlah and Shujah-ed-Dowlah, the Last Sovereigns of Bengal and Oud to Which the Author Has Added a Critical Examination of the English Government and Policy in Those Countries Down to the Year 1783, the Whole Written in Persian by Seid Ghulam Hossain Khan, an Indian Nobleman of High Rank Who Wrote Both as an Actor and as Spectator*, trans. Nota Manas, or Hajee Mustapha, or M. Raymond, 2 Volumes (London and Kolkata: R. Cambray and Co., 1789; reprint, Kolkata: Royal Asiatic Society of Bengal, 1902).

Khosla, Gopal Das, *Stern Reckoning: A Survey of the Events Leading Up to and Following the Partition of India* (1950, reprint, New Delhi: Oxford University Press, 1990).

Klug, Heinz, *Constituting Democracy – Law, Globalism and South Africa's Political Reconstruction* (Cambridge: Cambridge University Press, 2000).

Kolsky, Elizabeth, *Colonial Justice in British India – White Violence and the Rule of Law* (Cambridge: Cambridge University Press, 2010).

Kumar, Asutosh Kumar, "Imaginations and Manifestos of the Political Parties on Ideals of Developmental Governance," in Ranabir Samaddar and Suhit Sen (eds.), *Political Transition and Development Imperatives in India* (London and New Delhi: Routledge, 2012), pp. 121–158.

Lal, Ananda (trans.), *Rabindranath Tagore – Three Plays* (Kolkata: M.P. Birla Foundation, 1987).

Lal, Vinay, "Agrarian Unrest: The Deccan Riots of 1975", http://www.sscnet.ucla.edu/southasia/British/Deccan_riots.html

Lal, Vinay, "Criminality and Criminal Anthropology", Introduction to Rai Bahadur M. Pauparao Naidu, *The History of Railway Thieves: With Illustrations and Hints on Detection* (1915; reprint, Gurgaon, Haryana: Vintage Press, 1995).

Low, D.A., *Britain and Indian Nationalism: The Imprint of Ambiguity, 1929–1942* (Cambridge: Cambridge University Press, 1997).

Majeed, Javed, *Muhammad Iqbal – Islam, Aesthetics and Postcolonialism* (New Delhi: Routledge, 2009).

Mamdani, Mahmood, *Citizen and Subject – Decentralized Despotism and the Legacy of Late Colonialism* (New Delhi: Oxford University Press, 1997), p. 301.

Markovits, Claude, "The Calcutta Riots of 1946", *Online Encyclopedia of Mass Violence*, 2008, http://www.massviolence.org/The-Calcutta-Riots-of-1946

Markovits, Claude, *Merchants, Traders, Entrepreneurs – Indian Business in the Colonial Period* (London: Palgrave MacMillan, 2008).

Martin, Luther H., Huck Gutman and Patrick H. Hutton (eds.), *Technologies of the Self* (Amherst: University of Massachusetts Press, 1998).

Marx, Karl, *Critique of Hegel's Philosophy of Right* (1843–44), http://www.marxists.org/archive/marx/works/1843/critique-hpr/intro.htm

Mathur, P.S., "The Great Calcutta Killing", *The Illustrated Weekly of India*, 19 August 1973.

Merlau-Ponty, Maurice, *Signs*, trans. Richard C. McCleary (Evanston, IL: Northwestern University Press, 1964).

Mill, John Stuart Mill, *Liberty and Representative Government*, ed. A.D. Lindsey (London: Dent, 1970).

Modern Review, Vol. XXX, No. 3.

Modern Review, September 1946, Vol. LXXX, No. 3.

Moon, Penderel, *Divide and Quit* (London: Chatto and Windus, 1961).

Morgan, Gwenda and Peter Rushton, "Visible Bodies – Power, Subordination, and Identity in the Eighteenth Century Atlantic World", *Journal of Social History*, 39 (1), Fall, 2005, pp. 39–64.

Mukherjee, Janam, *Hungry Bengal: War, Famine, Riots and the End of Empire* (New Delhi: Harper Collins Publishers India, 2015).

Mukherjee, Rudrangshu, *Awadh in Revolt, 1857–58: A Study of Popular Resistance* (New Delhi: Oxford University Press, 1984).

Naidu, Rai Bahadur M. Pauparao, *The History of Railway Thieves: With Illustrations and Hints on Detection* (1915; reprint, Gurgaon, Haryana: Vintage Press, 1995).

Nandy, Ashis, *The Intimate Enemy – Loss and Recovery of Self Under Colonialism* (New Delhi: Oxford University Press, 2009).

Narang, A.S., "Justice for the Minorities," in Ajit, Bhattacharjea (ed.), *Social Justice and the Constitution* (Shimla: Indian Institute of Advanced Studies, 1997), pp. 117–132.

Narang, A.S., "Regionalism, Alienation and Federalism," in Rasheduddin Khan (ed.), *Rethinking Indian Federalism* (Shimla: Indian Institute of Advanced Studies, 1997).

Narayan, Jayaprakash, *Communitarian Society and Panchayati Raj*, ed. Brahmanand (Varanasi: Navachetna Prakashan, 1970).

Narayan, Jayaprakash, *A Revolutionary's Quest – Selected Writings of Jayaprakash Narayan*, ed. Bimal Prasad (New Delhi: Oxford University Press, 1980).

Nehru, Jawaharlal, *An Autobiography* (1936, New Delhi: Penguin Books, 2004).

Nehru, Jawaharlal, *The Discovery of India* (1946, New Delhi: Penguin Books, 2004).

Omvedt, Gail, *Ambedkar: Towards an Enlightened India* (New Delhi: Penguin, 2004).

Pal, R.M. and Meera Verma (eds.), *Power to People – The Political Thought of M.K. Gandhi, M.N. Ray, and Jayaprakash Narayan*, Volume 2 (New Delhi: Gyan Publishing, 2007).

Pantham, Thomas and Kenneth L. Deutsch (eds.), *Political Thought in Modern India* (New Delhi: Sage Publications, 1986).

Papke, David Ray, "Law, Cinema, and Ideology", Hollywood Legal Films of the 1950s", *UCLA Law Review*, 48 (6), 2001, pp. 1473–1493.

Parekh, Bhikhu, *Gandhi's Political Philosophy: A Critical Appreciation* (New Delhi: Ajanta, 1995).

Parel, Anthony, *Hind Swaraj and Other Writings* (Cambridge: Cambridge University Press, 1997).

People's Union for Democratic Rights Report, *Dalit Lynching at Dulina – Cow Protection, Caste, and Communalism*, Delhi, February 2003, re-published in Ujjwal Kumar Singh (ed.), *Human Rights and Peace – Ideas, Laws, Institutions, and Movements* (New Delhi: Sage, 2009).

Prasad, Bimal, "Power to People – JP's Approach," in R.M. Pal and Meera Verma (eds.), *Power to People – The Political Thought of M.K. Gandhi, M.N. Ray, and Jayaprakash Narayan*, Volume 2 (New Delhi: Gyan Publishing, 2007).

Puri, Balraj, *J.P. on Jammu and Kashmir* (New Delhi: Gyan Publishing House, 2005).

Pyarelal, *Mahatma Gandhi: The Last Phase,* Volume 2 (Ahmedabad: Nava-jiban Publishing House, 1965).

Radice, C. William, "Lyrical Alchemist – Rabindranath Tagore", http://www.india-today.com/itoday/millennium/100people/tagore.html (accessed on 12 April 2011).

Ranciere, Jacques, *On the Shores of Politics,* trans. Liz Heron (London: Verso, 2007).

Rawls, John, *Political Liberalism* by Rawls (New York: Columbia University Press, 1993/2005).

Ray Sibnarayan (ed.), *Gandhi, India and the World* (Bombay: Nachiketa Publications, 1970).

Rosanvallon, Pierre, *The Demands of Liberty – Civil Society in France Since the Revolution,* trans. Arthur Goldhammer (Cambridge, MA: Harvard University Press, 2007).

Roy, Anupama, *Mapping Citizenship in India* (New Delhi: Oxford University Press, 2011).

Russell, Ralph and Khurshid Islam (eds.), *Ghalib 1797–1869 – Life and Letters* (New Delhi: Oxford University Press, 1994).

Saleem, Ghulam Hussain Saleem, *Riaz us Salatin,* translated in Bengali by Akbaruddin as *Bangler Itihas* from the English version prepared by Abdus Salam Riaz from original Persian in 1904 (Dhaka: Bangla Academy, 1974), p. 205.

Samaddar, R., *Emergence of the Political Subject* (New Delhi: Sage, 2009).

Samaddar, R., *The Emergence of the Political Subject* (New Delhi: Sage, 2010).

Samaddar, R., "Eternal Bengal," in Mridula Nath Chakraborty (ed.), *Being Bengali – At Home and in the World* (London: Routledge, 2014), pp. 181–201.

Samaddar, R., *The Materiality of Politics,* 2 Volumes (London: Anthem Press, 2007).

Samaddar, R., *Memory, Identity, Power – Politics in the Jungle Mahals, 1890–1950* (Hyderabad: Orient Longman, 1998).

Samaddar, R., *The Politics of Dialogue – Living Under the Geopolitical Histories of War and Peace* (Aldershot: Ashgate Publishing, 2004).

Samaddar, R., *Terror, Law, and the Colonial State* (published text of a public lecture at Omeo Kr.) (Guwahati: Das Institute of Social Change, 2004)

Samaddar, R. (ed.), *Refugees and the State – Practices of Asylum and Care in India, 1947–2000* (Delhi: Sage Publications, 2003)

Samaddar, R. and Suhit Sen (eds.), *Political Transition and Development Imperatives in India* (London and New Delhi: Routledge, 2012).

Samanta, Amiya, "Strange Meeting", *The Statesman,* 30–31 January 2009.

Sanyal, Sunanda and Soumya Basu, *The Sickle and the Crescent – Communists, Muslim League and India's Partition* (Kolkata: Frontpage, 2011).

Sarkar, P.C., *Handbook of Criminal Laws in India and Pakistan,* Volume II, "Minor Acts" (Calcutta: S.C. Sarkar and Sons, 1951), pp. 119–130.

Sarkar, Tanikar, "Rabindranath's *Gora* and the Intractable Problem of Indian Patriotism", *Economic and Political Weekly*, xliv (30), 25 July 2009, pp. 37–46.

Schmitt, Carl, *The Concept of the Political*, trans. George Schwab (Chicago: University of Chicago Press, 2007).

Schmitt, Carl, *Legality and Legitimacy*, trans. Jeffrey Seitzer (Durham: Duke University Press, 2004).

Sebba, Anne, *Mother Teresa 1910–1997 beyond the Image* (London: Orion, 1998).

Sen, Amartya, "Is Nationalism a Boon or a Curse?", *Economic and Political Weekly*, 16 February 2008, pp. 39–44.

Sengupta, Debjani, "A City Feeding on Itself: Testimonies and Histories of 'Direct Action' Day", *Sarai Reader*, New Delhi, 2006.

Shah, Ghanshyam, "The 1969 Communal Riots in Ahmedabad: A Case Study," in Asghar Ali Engineer (ed.), *Communal Riots in Post-Independence India* (Hyderabad: Sangam Books, 1984).

Short Report of Hindu Mahasabha Relief Activities during 'Calcutta Killings' and 'Noakhali Carnage (Calcutta: Noakhali Rescue, Relief, and Rehabilitation Committee, Ranjan Publishing House, n.d.).

Singh, Ujjwal Kumar (ed.), *Human Rights and Peace – Ideas, Laws, Institutions, and Movements* (New Delhi: Sage, 2009).

Singha, Radhika, *A Despotism of Law – Crime and Justice in Early Colonial India* (New Delhi: Oxford University Press).

Songs of Kabir, trans. Rabindranath Tagore (New York: MacMillan, 1915), poem 5.

Steffen, Lisa, *Defining a British State – Treason and National Identity, 1608–1820* (New York: Palgrave, 2001).

Strayer, Joseph R., *On the Medieval Origins of the Modern State* (Princeton, NJ: Princeton University Press, 1970).

Tagore, Rabindranath, *Nationalism* (1917, Kolkata: Rupa, 2002).

Tagore, Rabindranath, *Rabindra Rachanabali*, Volume 9 (Centenary Edition, Calcutta: West Bengal Government, 1961).

Tagore, Rabindranath, *Sabhyatar Sankat* (Calcutta: Visva Bharati, 1348 B.S.); also published in English as *Crisis in Civilization* same year (1941).

Tagore, Rabindranath, *Sadhana – The Realisation of Life* (New York: MacMillan, 1916).

Taylor, Charles, *A Secular Age* (Cambridge, MA: The Belknap Press of Harvard University Press, 2007).

Tendulkar, Vijay, "Silence! The Court Is in Session," trans Priya Adarkar (New Delhi: Oxford University Press, 1979).

Tilly, Charles, *Regimes and Repertoires* (Chicago: University of Chicago Press, 2006).

Tilly, Charles, *Stories, Identities, and Social Change* (Lanham, MD: Rowman and Littlefield, 2002)

Tsugitaka, Sato, *Muslim Societies: Historical and Comparative Aspects* (London: Routledge, 2000).

Tuker, Francis, *While Memory Serves* (London: Cassell & Co, 1950).

Tully, James, *Strange Multiplicity – Constitutionalism in an Age of Diversity* (Cambridge: Cambridge University Press, 1995).

Vernon, James, *Politics and the People – A Study in English Political Culture, 1815–1867* (Cambridge: Cambridge University Press, 1993).

Vries, Hent de and Samuel Weber (eds.), *Violence, Identity and Self-Determination* (Stanford, CA: Stanford University Press, 1997).

Wadud, Qazi Abdul, *Saswata Banga*, (1959, Dhaka: BRAC, 1983).

Watson, Alfred, *India's Extremists and the Axis – Would the Indian Congress Party Aid the War? Facts Sweeping Away Much of the Nonsense Talked about India* (London: Great Britain and the East Limited, 1943).

Weber, Samuel, *Targets of Opportunity – On the Militarisation of Thinking* (New York: Fordham University Press, 2005).

West Bengal Police Act, http://www.humanrightsinitiative.org/programs/aj/police/india/acts/critiques/chri's_legislative_analysis_of_west_bengal_police_draft_act.pdf

Wolchover, David and Anthony Heaton-Armstrong, *Confession Evidence* (London: Sweet and Maxwell Criminal Law Library, 1996).

Woodruffe, John and Syed Amir Ali, *Law of Edidence* (1898; 17th Edition, ed. S.V. Joga Rao; New Delhi: Butterworths, 2001).

Yang, Aanad, "Disciplining 'Natives'", *South Asia*, New Series, 10 (2), December 1987, pp. 29–45.

Zins, Max-Jean, "The 1947 Vivisection of India: The Political Usage of a Carnage in the Era of Citizen-Massacres," in M. Hasan and N. Nakazato (eds.), *The Unfinished Agenda: Nation-Building in South Asia* (New Delhi: Manohar Publishers, 2001), pp. 49–77.

Index

For Product Safety Concerns and Information please contact our EU
representative GPSR@taylorandfrancis.com
Taylor & Francis Verlag GmbH, Kaufingerstraße 24, 80331 München, Germany

www.ingramcontent.com/pod-product-compliance
Lightning Source LLC
Chambersburg PA
CBHW060143280326
41932CB00012B/1619